Praise for Y

"*Your Astrological Energy* is especially intriguing and provides a wonderful contribution to astrology in the way it describes the primary symbols, planets, signs, and houses as dynamic energies that can be utilized creatively with endless potential....Speaking from my experience as an astrologer for fifty years, I find each chapter in this book offers motivating energy true to the title. The author weaves an evolutionary energy into the core of each chapter that inspires insights that can lead to building happier relationships, seeking a purpose that fits your soul growth, and finding fulfilling work in the world. Readers will enjoy the positive energy describing the planetary forces at work in each of our lives."

—BERNIE ASHMAN, author of *How to Survive Mercury Retrograde*

"An in-depth self-help resource that helps the reader learn the basics of astrological energy and how to harness it in everyday life. This book offers an intense and deep analysis of the astrological signs, planets in the sign, houses, and how the planetary transits awaken learning and karma in our lives. A rare gem that is easy to read for a beginner but also digs deep into personality, relationships, career, health, and much more for advanced readers."

—SHERIANNA BOYLE, author of *Emotional Detox* and *Just Ask Spirit*

YOUR ASTROLOGICAL ENERGY

About the Author

Carmen Turner-Schott, MSW, LCSW (St. Louis, MO), is a best-selling author of eleven astrology books, a practicing clinical social worker, and an astrologer with national and international clientele. The founder of Deep Soul Divers Astrology, she has worked as an astrologer and with survivors of trauma for over twenty-eight years. Turner-Schott has presented astrology workshops for the Association of Research and Enlightenment, and she is a faculty member and coordinator of the counseling and relationship astrology certificate programs for Kepler College of Astrology.

Visit her at www.CarmenTurnerSchott.com.

YOUR
ASTROLOGICAL
ENERGY

Maximize *the* Power *of* YOUR Birth Chart

CARMEN TURNER-SCHOTT

LLEWELLYN
WOODBURY, MINNESOTA

FIRST EDITION
First Printing, 2025

Book design by Samantha Peterson
Cover design by Shannon McKuhen
The astrology charts in this book were created using the Kepler Superb Astrology Program,
    with kind permission from Cosmic Patterns Software, Inc., the manufacturer of the
    Kepler program (www.astrosoftware.com, kepler@astrosoftware.com).

Llewellyn Publications is a registered trademark of Llewellyn Worldwide Ltd.

Library of Congress Cataloging-in-Publication Data (Pending)
ISBN: 978-0-7387-7941-6

Llewellyn Publications
A Division of Llewellyn Worldwide Ltd.
2143 Wooddale Drive
Woodbury, MN 55125-2989
www.llewellyn.com

Printed in the United States of America

GPSR Representation:
UPI-2M PLUS d.o.o., Medulićeva 20, 10000 Zagreb, Croatia,
matt.parsons@upi2mbooks.hr

Other Books by Carmen Turner-Schott

Sun Signs, Houses & Healing

Moon Signs, Houses & Healing

Astrology's Magical Nodes of the Moon

Phoenixes & Angels

The Mysteries of the Twelfth Astrological House: Fallen Angels

CONTENTS

12: PISCES ✦ 365

INTRODUCTION

Astrology is energy. Everything in our world is made up of energy, and energy is the primary reason why astrology is accurate and resonates with so many people. Even skeptics and people who don't believe in astrology often admit to me that it's accurate and that the personality traits of their birth chart do fit them. When I interpret birth charts and share astrological energies with clients, I tend to get validation from the person immediately. They often ask me, "How did you know that?" I often reply, "It's your energy and the map of your soul."

I used to believe that I could change how people felt about me or I tried to figure out why some people did not like me or treat me well. I would obsess and analyze it because of my sensitive Virgo nature. It took some time, but with getting older, I finally realized that I can't control anyone else or their perceptions. I realized there were only two things you have control over: your thoughts and how you react to the energies that impact your life. Optimistic thinking lifts your energy, making you feel more positive. The mind-body-spirit connection is powerful and there is a lot of research about the power of your thoughts.

When I studied in metaphysical school in the 1990s, they had the students participate in an exercise. We were asked to stand in front of our instructor and hold a heavy book in our outstretched hand. While holding the book we were asked to close our eyes and think of a happy memory. I could feel my arm lift. Then we were asked to remember a sad event, and I felt my arm lower. This was a subtle exercise to show how our thoughts impact our physical body.

Energy is something that is hard to prove but you know it's there because you can feel it. Just like heat coming from a fireplace, you can feel the warmth. Tapping into and understanding astrological energy will help you understand other people. Your relationships will improve and your compassion for other people will increase. Getting comfortable trusting your intuition is the first step in trusting the power of energy. Once you trust what you are sensing, you can use these impressions to help others.

Elements in Astrology

The four elements in astrology play a major role in the energy found in the birth chart. The four elements are fire, air, earth, and water. When I started learning personality temperament assessment tools in my social work career, I received training in administering the Four Lenses personality profile to others. This is when I realized the colors in this personality tool were closely related to the personality traits associated with the elements in astrology. The four primary personality colors were identical to the energy of the four elements. In the Four Lenses assessment, there are four personality colors used to explain an individual's personality: orange, gold, green, and blue. The colors each have personality traits associated with them. Everyone has two main primary colors or personality traits that they show the world. For instance, orange is similar to the traits of the fire signs and in Four Lenses is described as confident, passionate, motivated, and risk-taking. Green personalities are intellectual, aloof, sarcastic, and logical, which is similar to the personality of the air signs. Blue personalities are similar to the water signs, and they are known for being emotional, relationship focused, compassionate, and drawn to the helping professions. Gold personalities are organized, efficient, productive, and like to plan, just like the earth signs. This example shows how astrology is connected to psychology in trying to explain why you act the way you do.

In astrology, fire energy is warm, social, expressive, and passionate. Water energy is emotional, caring, sensitive, and psychic. Air energy is aloof, intelligent, communicative, and rational. Earth energy is stable, solid, grounded, and calm. Everyone has all these energies in their birth chart in varying degrees. For example, some people may have strong earth energies but lack the water element. This lack might affect them by making it difficult for them to express their feelings and emotions.

Tapping into these astrological energies and harnessing the powerful influence they have on your body, mind, and spirit can help you understand yourself and others better. Astrology is a map of your soul, it's your energy blueprint. All of us have all twelve zodiac signs in our birth chart somewhere, so all twelve signs impact our lives. Even if you don't have planets in a certain sign or house, you will experience planetary transits through each zodiac sign and house at some time in your life. It's important to dive deeper and pay attention to the birth chart energies and planetary transits. Tapping into this knowledge can help you harness these transforming energies and use them to heal and overcome challenges in your life. When a planet transits through a specific house, it will intensify the energy and issues of that area of life. The personal planets like the Sun, Venus, and Mercury move quickly through each house, but the outer planets like Saturn, Uranus, Neptune, and Pluto influence each area of life for several years. When you understand planetary energies, you can take control of your life instead of feeling like a victim of circumstance. You can gain awareness of why certain things are happening in your home, career, relationships, and health.

In the upcoming chapters, you can read about each Sun sign, planets in the sign, planets in the house, and the effects of transits through the houses. These tips and insights will help you understand astrological energies and how to harness these energies.

The Birth Chart

The birth chart is calculated based on the month, day, year, and exact time of your birth. Essentially, imagine that you are on earth looking up at the sky when you were born. The planets are all found to be in a certain star constellation, which are the astrological signs. The planets are in a certain area of the sky that astrologers divide into twelve sections like a pie. These twelve sections are what astrologers call the houses. The houses are associated with different areas of life. If you take a picture of the sky at that moment in time and put it on a piece of paper that is the birth chart map.

Astrology is a symbolic language; to read an astrology chart, you have to learn the basic symbols for the signs and planets. With patience and time and understanding energy, you can learn astrology.

The signs and planets are associated with symbols. For instance, Aries is the ram, and in the birth wheel, its symbol looks like ram horns. There are many astrology programs that you can use to calculate a birth chart. For beginners, I recommend visiting the many online astrology sites that offer free chart calculation. One of the most popular is astro.com, or you can contact an astrologer to find out more. In the upcoming chapters, I will explain more about each house, the planets, and signs and the energies associated with them.

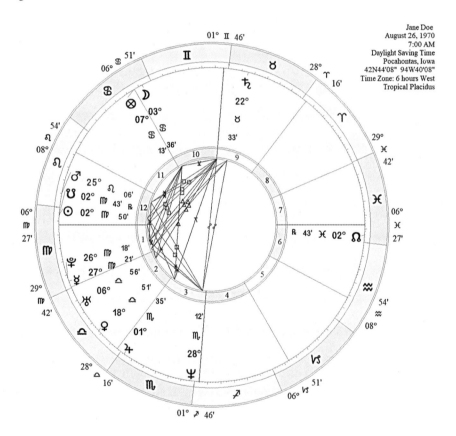

The Transit Chart

Imagine looking up at the sky right now. All the planets are currently in a sign and in a house. Astrologers take a picture of the sky for that exact date, time, and place. We then transpose that transit chart on top of your birth chart wheel. A transit chart can show the energies that are impacting every area of your life in present time. Astrologers look to see what planets are transiting your natal houses and how these transits are interacting with your natal birth placements.

Certain planets transit quickly through the sky, such as the Moon. Every two to three days the Moon moves into a new astrological sign. The inner planets like Venus, Mercury, Mars, and Jupiter don't stay in each house for years, but stay long enough to impact your life for days and months at a time. The outer planets like Saturn can spend two to three years in each house bringing up karmic issues and responsibilities, while Uranus can shake things up and cause change in whatever house it is moving through for a period of seven to eight years. A transit chart is the quickest way for you to see what the current astrological energies are and make sense of the events happening in your life. An example would be if the planet Uranus is transiting your seventh house of marriage and partnership. During this transit you can often experience unexpected changes in your relationships. This energy forces growth, and sometimes separation, divorce, or challenges in your intimate relationships develop.

In each chapter, I will describe the planetary transits through each house. You will be able to understand how these transits can change your life. The inner ring is the birth chart and the outer ring is the transit chart. To calculate your own transit chart, you can go on astro.com and enter your birth information and transit chart option or contact me for a free birth wheel at my website www.carmenturnerschott.com.

The Planets

The energy of the planets influences how you think, feel, and react to life. There are ten major planets that astrologers use to analyze your birth chart. Most people know their Sun sign, because it's based on the day of your birth. The sign Leo is ruled by the Sun and these traits represent your main identity and the personality you show the world. The house the Sun is placed in the birth chart is where you like to express yourself and be noticed. The Sun is often associated with the father figure and how you perceived this relationship. The Moon sign reveals your inner nature, emotions, intuition, and reactions. The sign Cancer is associated with the Moon. The house the Moon is placed will show where you find emotional fulfillment, seek happiness, and find comfort. The Moon is associated with the mother figure, so the way you experienced nurturing and how you perceived the relationship with your mother can be seen by taking a closer look at the Moon's energies.

The Sun and Moon are the two most prominent planet energies in your birth chart. The other eight planets impact your life in different ways and are important to look at as well. Mercury is the planet of communication and intelligence and influences how you think. The signs Virgo and Gemini are associated with Mercury's energy. Wherever Mercury is placed is where you express yourself through writing and speaking. Venus is the planet of love, beauty, and harmony. How you show love, who you attract in relationships, and your relationship style is related to this planet. The signs Libra and Taurus are both ruled by the planet Venus. Wherever Venus is placed is where you seek to express feelings and creativity and maintain harmony.

The planet Mars represents your passion, drive, impulse, anger, and physical stamina. The sign Aries is associated with this planet and this energy shows where you experience conflict and are competitive. Jupiter is a positive planet that represents good luck, wealth, abundance, higher learning, and long-distance travel. Sagittarius is the sign ruled by this planet. Wherever Jupiter is placed in your birth chart is where you seek freedom and adventure, experience blessings, receive protection, and express generosity. Saturn is the planet associated with the responsible sign Capricorn. This planet's energy brings wisdom through experience and discipline. Wherever Saturn is found in the chart is where you will be more cautious, restricted, practical, and focused on being productive.

The rebellious planet Uranus brings a sense of uniqueness, individuality, and change into your life. This energy wants you to question authority and tradition. Sudden changes and growth experiences occur in whatever house Uranus is found. Uranus rules the eccentric sign of Aquarius. The imaginative and idealistic planet Neptune brings a sense of spirituality to your life. Neptune shows where you seek to escape from the world, find solitude, and connect to a spiritual path. The creative, mystical, and compassionate sign Pisces is ruled by this planet.

The Houses

Houses are sections of the sky. There are twelve houses in a birth chart. Each house has energies that impact different areas of our lives. The ascendent or rising sign is the sign on the first house cusp. It influences how we handle stress and respond with courage in all areas of life. The first house impacts our physical appearance and how people perceive us when they first meet us. The second house involves how we make our own money and find security, comfort, self-worth, what we value, and our basic needs. The third house is the house of communication, siblings, short journeys, and basic knowledge. Our parents, early childhood, home environment, future family life, childhood experience, family traditions, and ancestors are all fourth house territory. The fifth house is associated with pleasure, hobbies, children, love affairs, having fun, self-expression, and creativity.

Our health, routine, diet, work ethic, and organizational abilities fall into the sixth house. The seventh house is the descendant opposing the ascendant in the birth chart. The seventh house is the house of marriage, business partners, and partnership in general. Anything taboo and secretive such as death, trauma, rebirth, transformation, healing, and sexuality are all eighth house issues. Travel to foreign lands, religion, philosophy, higher education, exploration, and adventure are associated with the ninth house. Our career, public image, work interests, success, and type of work are tenth house energies. The tenth house is also called the midheaven, which is the highest point in the chart. The sign on the cusp of the tenth house reveals the career energies and types of work we may be drawn to.

The eleventh house is the house of friendship, acquaintances, groups, hopes, wishes, and dreams. The final house is the twelfth house, which is the most mystical, mysterious, and spiritual house in astrology. Twelfth house energy is associated with hidden things, mental institutions, monasteries, temples, higher levels of consciousness, meditation, escapism, service to others, illusion, imagination, secrets, dreams, sleep, and connecting to a higher power. In the upcoming chapters, I will discuss what energies manifest when planets fall in a certain house and what life lessons you might experience. I will also describe how planetary transits through each house will influence your life.

My Personal Experience

When someone walks into the room, they bring with them a certain presence, imprint, or essence. Ever since I was a child, I felt energy. I picked up on other people's thoughts and emotions. I was born emotional and had complex feelings. I could not explain these sensations and feelings through words. I just knew things about people when I was around them. I never understood why or how I knew what someone was feeling. When I was younger, I often doubted myself and was told that it was just my imagination. I decided to withdraw and hide my spiritual abilities. I felt different from everyone in my life and was interested in dreams, angels, ghosts, aliens, and crystals. I was born this way and never taught about metaphysical topics. After several transformative experiences in high school with dreams and intuition, I wanted to seek answers to my unexplained experiences.

At that time, I knew very little about energy, astrology, orbs, or the supernatural. These experiences led me to a small metaphysical bookstore in St. Louis, Missouri, named Mystic Valley. In 1993, I purchased my first astrology book, and the rest is history. As soon as I calculated my birth chart by hand and looked up the meanings, I realized how accurate the energy was. For the first time in my life, I felt validated and realized astrology explained my personality and spiritual experiences.

Astrology became my passion because it validated my personal experiences and feelings. I realized it was a powerful tool I could use to help others heal, transform, and become more resilient. I believe that astrology can help everyone learn more about themselves. I started reading every astrology book I could find. My journey with astrology led to the realization that I was born with clairvoyant abilities. This means I would dream of future events before they happened or pick up on a feeling that later was validated. When I started learning more about having planets in the twelfth and eighth houses, I realized that these energies enhanced spiritual abilities. I became obsessed with these two astrology houses specifically and have spent the last thirty years researching these energy patterns to help others understand their spiritual gifts.

I have always been able to feel people's energy. When I first meet someone, I can feel the different astrological energies surrounding their physical body. I can feel if someone has a lot of the earth element in their birth chart, because I instantly feel a grounded, stable, calming energy. I feel a deep, sensitive, emotional energy when someone has a lot of water in their birth chart. When someone has fire in their chart, I feel warmth, confidence, and passion. If I can't quite feel or sense someone's energy, then I know that person has a lot of the air element in their personality. This is one example of how astrology and energy impact life on earth.

Astrology can be studied as a science. Regardless of if you believe in it or not, the energies affect your life. Just like gravity impacts everyone on earth, astrological energies are constantly influencing our thoughts, emotions, behaviors, and actions. When we pay attention to these energies, we can tap into them to help us overcome obstacles and challenges and recognize our strengths and weaknesses. We can use this energy to achieve our goals, heal, and find greater balance.

As a counselor, I like to tap into astrological energy because it helps me understand people. I observe personality traits and can narrow down what someone's rising sign is often by their appearance. My first impression of people is usually right. The rising sign or sign on the ascendent is known as your mask. It is the first thing people judge you by. The rising sign is also the energy you can tap into to deal with stress in your life. It takes a while to get to know others deeply because you are witnessing the rising sign traits first. Later on, when you start to learn more about people, you begin to sense their Sun sign personality traits.

The energy of the Sun sign shines through when I spend more time with someone. Once someone begins to trust me and open up more, that is when I witness the energy of their Moon sign. The Moon sign represents your deeper emotional nature, intuition, and instincts. The Moon sign and house it's located in the birth chart is also where you find emotional fulfillment, happiness, security, and comfort. It takes time to connect to others emotionally and build trust. When you become more vulnerable and express your inner feelings this encourages deeper connections. You readily show your Moon sign traits to people you care about. I believe the Moon sign is even more powerful than the Sun sign. Emotions are powerful, and tapping into your Moon sign energy can help you overcome loss, grief, and challenges and build greater resilience. I hope you enjoy learning more about different astrological energies and can utilize this energy in your own life.

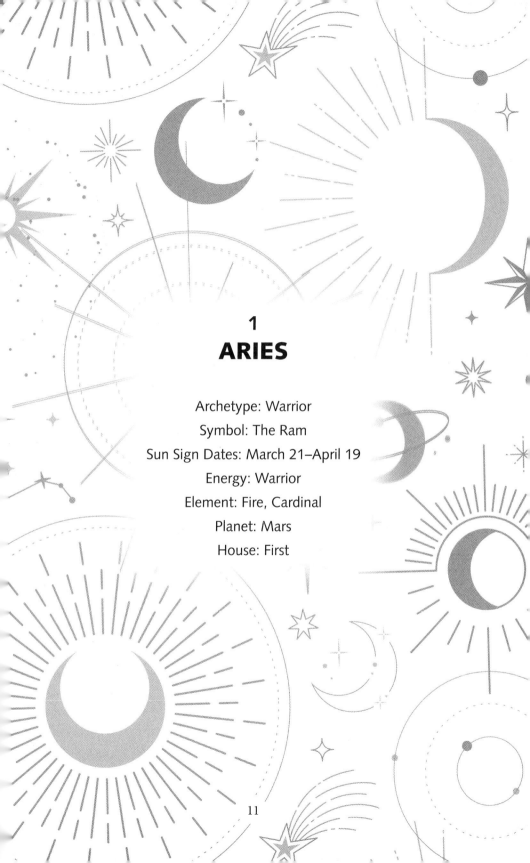

1
ARIES

Archetype: Warrior

Symbol: The Ram

Sun Sign Dates: March 21–April 19

Energy: Warrior

Element: Fire, Cardinal

Planet: Mars

House: First

I f you have Aries in your birth chart, planets in the first house, or are experiencing planetary transits through the first house, this chapter will cover information regarding these energies. If you don't, you can still learn about Aries energy and incorporate it into your life. The placement of Mars in the sign and house will show where you express Aries energy. It is important to look at what house the sign Aries falls on in your birth wheel because this is where you will feel passionate, confident, assertive, motivated, and in the moment. Harnessing Aries energy gives you the courage to pursue your goals, resilience to overcome obstacles, and a competitive spirit.

Aries Energy Words

Independent, resilient, competitive, temperamental, passionate, confident, daring, straightforward, adventurous, bold, athletic, action oriented, motivated, impulsive, restless, impatient, self-centered, aggressive, self-focused.

Aries Motto

As an Aries, I never give up. I'm passionate, impulsive, and impatient about getting what I want. I am confident and trust my gut. I strive to succeed, and I am very competitive. I want to act and hate waiting around for others. I motivate others and enjoy leading teams. I dislike authority or having to follow other people's rules. I can't be controlled and crave independence. I thrive when I have autonomy and can make my own decisions.

Harnessing Aries Energy

Aries energy is exciting and fresh. This energy feels new, innocent, friendly, and is like the Sun rising each day. Life is an adventure and there is motivation to focus on positive things. Aries energy is confident, bold, daring, and assertive. There is always something to look forward to. Embracing change and taking risks can help us connect with Aries energy. Harnessing Aries energy gives us courage, self-confidence, bravery, and a desire to speak the truth!

Harness Bravery

Aries is the embodiment of warrior energy. Brave, courageous, and passionate, there is an aggressive spirit within them that doesn't give up easily. Warrior energy is aggressive, fierce, bold, action oriented, and does not take no for an answer. It's courageous and runs into battle impulsively, not caring if it's dangerous. It's also competitive, athletic, and self-focused with a desire to win. Warrior energy pushes us forward with a focus on the future. It helps us move forward easily and let go of the past. Because this energy is fast, quick, and impulsive, it can help us overcome challenges and emotional setbacks. It enhances our ability to become more resilient. It helps us embrace change with courage and focus on making hard decisions. You will want to look at your birth chart to see where you have Aries to harness this warrior energy.

Action Oriented

Aries is ruled by the element of fire. Fire burns, sizzles, and can take over a situation quickly. Fire energy is what helps Arians accomplish their goals. In fact, this energy is intense and never gives up. It's competitive and fierce, because waiting is not an option and action is the key. It's important to be physically active—it's impulsive, impatient, and restless and likes to be moving.

Fire signs are self-starters and enjoy the adventure of starting something new. Anything that brings a challenge is often something they want to pursue. Fighting hard for what it wants and doing something about it are Arian strengths. This energy is charismatic, charming, driven, and full of confidence. Fire energy is soothing and brings warmth and inspiration.

Starting New Things

Cardinal energy is associated with the seasons of the year in tropical astrology. Aries energy is during the spring season and it's a time when flowers are blooming. Everything comes to life during Aries season. Cardinal energy likes to be the first to do things and motivate people to do something new. Arians like for others to do the practical planning and implement their ideas. Quickly sharing creative ideas with a group then moving boldly to the next idea is classic of Aries energy. It's hard for them to sit still because they have an inner drive to succeed. Motivated and comfortable with change, they crave newness because it makes them feel alive.

Stagnation can lead to boredom and increase impatience. Irritability can creep in when they have trouble coming up with something new to do. Action is important to them, so they don't give up easily. In fact, actions speak louder than words, and they want people to do what they say they will do. Born with a high stamina and energy level, Aries is fiercely driven and smoldering hot. This energy is intense and encourages us to always be looking toward the future, taking risks, and overcoming challenges.

Harness Passion

Aries is ruled by the planet Mars. Their energy is passionate, hot, and fiery, so you can feel its flames of desire. Honest, truthful, blunt, and straightforward Mars energy speaks up about what most people are afraid to say. Mars in Roman mythology is the god of war and, not unlike Aries, likes to rush into battle to fight for what he believes in. This energy makes us feel alive and intensifies our need for adventure. Go by gut instinct and listen to intuition.

The planet Mars is associated with anger, aggression, competition, violence, rage, and bravery. When angry, frustrated, or feeling betrayed, Mars energy lashes out aggressively. Because it likes quick, fast, straightforward action, this energy is felt strongly and it's hard to contain.

Everyone can harness Mars energy by following their gut instinct and trusting their inner voice. This energy can't be withheld or stopped; if it is, it will seep out in other ways, causing tension. In fact, Mars brings an enormous amount of physical energy that needs to be expressed. A need for independence, autonomy, and a sense of healthy competition are crucial for Aries. Exercise, and physical activity help burn off the irritable side of Mars. Passionate, impulsive, and impatient, this energy makes us courageous!

Harness Self-Reliance

The first house in astrology is the house of the self. It's where we express our personality out in the world. The first house forces us to use our voice, speak up, and go after what we want. It's the area of life where we react in the moment and can be a little impatient. Planets placed here can make us blunt and have a desire to speak the truth.

Things like bravery, self-reliance, and courage come by focusing on our own needs. It's a place in the birth chart where we stop focusing on others and begin to question what our goals are. There is a strong sense of independence and a need for autonomy. Life experience teaches them that they can't always depend on others. In fact, people with planets placed here are often resilient and can heal quickly. They have an ability to overcome challenges by doing something to move forward and let things go.

Having planets in the first house can create an assertive, aggressive, motivated, fun-loving, expressive, and impulsive energy. This area of life can reveal how we pursue our goals. This is the area of life where we ask ourselves, "What about me?" The first house's energy encourages us to rely on ourselves and become self-reliant.

Aries Rising

When people first meet Aries rising people, they see them as confident, brave, and assertive. Because this is a powerful and strong ascendant, others might perceive them as arrogant and aggressive. There is a boldness about their personality that makes others take notice, and they can sometimes steamroll over others. They are strong, resilient, and action-oriented people.

Aries risings have larger-than-life personalities that can be charming, magnetic, and confident. Sometimes their energy can come across like a bulldozer plowing its way through the environment. Nothing stops them from moving forward and pursuing what they want. In fact, they can expect other people to get on board or get out of their way. Winning is important to them and they like to be the first at everything and prefer competition and challenge. If something is easy to attain, they might lose interest quickly.

Aries risings can be impatient and restless souls. They are always on the go and need physical activity. They can get a lot done because of their high energy and positive attitude. They want things done quickly and don't enjoy waiting for others. Many are natural leaders, who pioneer new ideas and become entrepreneurs. Working for themselves and having a sense of autonomy is where they thrive. Because they are assertive, standing up for other people and fighting for the underdog help them feel like they are making a difference.

Their confidence helps them overcome challenges and live out the intense energy they feel within. Passionate, romantic, optimistic, and energetic, they need to learn to rest. They are always planning the next big adventure, and sometimes this can take away from living in the moment and feeling their emotions fully. Connecting with people and developing partnerships can increase their chances of happiness and bring greater success.

They appreciate honesty and people who aren't afraid of telling them the truth. It's hard for them to stay quiet when they care about something. Fiercely loyal and passionate, they can have an impulsive need to speak up. In fact, being truthful, blunt, and straightforward are their strengths. Their cutting honesty and their words can sting because they are very direct. Their emotions quickly rise and it's difficult for them to hide their anger or frustration.

Sometimes they act before they think things through. The impulsive side of their personality can lead to disappointment and conflict. It's important for them to learn how to control their temper, because it can help them overcome many challenges in their relationships. When they harness patience, they can achieve their goals and dreams faster than if they only act with self-interest.

How to Harness Planets in Aries

When planets are in Aries, you can be passionate, motivated, straightforward, confident, impatient, and impulsive.

Sun in Aries

Sun in Aries individuals are warriors who have a competitive spirit and want to win. Driven to succeed, they overcome challenges quickly and they grow when there is adversity. There is nothing they won't do to achieve their goals. Confident and brave, these individuals fight for what they desire. When they set their mind on something, no one can prevent them from working hard to get it. They can tap into their inner motivation to overcome challenges and obstacles. Because they are energetic, motivated, and driven, they never give up. They crave movement and can feel quite impulsive and impatient. In fact, they thrive when they can pursue excitement, adventure, and competition. If something is too easy, they will become bored and lose interest.

Rash, assertive, truthful, and straightforward, they are not afraid of telling others how they feel. Just like a knight on a white horse, they often find themselves rushing into battle to save others. They like a challenge in their love lives and like the thrill of the chase. Fighting for the underdog and advocating for others comes naturally for them. There is a confidence and warmth that others feel instantly. They shine when they are able to express their high energy levels. If they learn to harness passion, they can be successful in many areas of life.

Moon in Aries

Moon in Aries individuals are one of the most resilient Moon signs. Because they can emotionally adapt to crises, they overcome challenges quickly. In fact, they can find change invigorating. When they experience challenges, it can trigger their survival instinct. Because of their fierce emotional nature, they work hard to let go of the past and focus on the future.

They feel more alive and inspired when they are able to express how they feel. It's important to them to share their feelings with people they trust. Sometimes they get impatient if they can't act in the moment. In fact, they like immediate responses and don't like to be held back. Bold and courageous, they want to face obstacles head-on. Because they are quick to anger, what they feel comes out in unexpected ways. But they should be careful about being too impulsive and reacting too quickly. Learning to be more patient can help them avoid power struggles in their relationships. Sometimes they need to slow down, wait, and take a break before they respond.

Freedom and independence are important to them and they value self-expression. They can find comfort through pursuing their goals and motivating other people.

In relationships, they are romantic, sexual, and flirtatious. No one has to guess about whether they like them or not. Assertive and blunt, they will let you know how they feel. They have a desire to express their feelings in the moment and it's hard to hide them. Restless at heart, they ooze passion. Experiencing newness in relationships brings emotional fulfillment. It's important for them to feel a sense of adventure and excitement in their relationships. When they care about someone, they are affectionate, generous, and protective. In fact, they enjoy the feeling of being in love and can be ardent lovers. Their happiness comes through feeling free to express their intense passion. If they can harness courage, they can grow stronger as a person and use their passionate emotions to overcome adversity.

Mercury in Aries

Mercury in Aries individuals are impulsive thinkers who have a desire to speak their minds. Their communication is often blunt, direct, and honest. They enjoy expressing themselves through words. But sometimes their words can be used as weapons, especially if they feel irritated. Being more patient and learning to control their impulsive reactions can help prevent unnecessary conflict in communication.

They value learning new things and are passionate about projects that bring excitement. In fact, coming up with new ideas is what motivates them. They tend to think about their own needs and wants and can be a bit self-focused about what they believe in. It's important that they slow down to really listen to what other people have to say. Because of their quick approach in communication, it's hard for them to be patient enough to wait for others to finish their sentences. Sometimes they interrupt others, but they do this because their thoughts come up intensely in the moment.

Learning new things can inspire them, but they want to act on what they know. It's important that they take classes they find interesting and useful. If not, they can zone out and have a hard time sitting still. Mental restlessness and boredom can become unbearable for them.

Direct communication helps them gain allies because people appreciate their honesty. Also, they like people who get straight to the point. Once they express what they think, they are often finished talking and move on to something new. In fact, social expectations and small talk seem useless to them. If they can harness assertiveness and be direct in communication, it will help them build stronger relationships.

Venus in Aries

Venus in Aries individuals are seeking passion, romance, and love. They are always ready for a challenge and like to feel the rush of adrenaline when they meet someone they are attracted to. Many times, they can be attracted to partners who are hard to get. If love comes too easy for them, they often grow bored and quickly move on. In relationships, they need excitement, affection, and a little bit of conflict. But one of the most important things is that they have some type of sexual chemistry with their partner. Because they show love through physical touch, it's important they find a partner who is compatible. If not, there can be impulsive endings because they can break ties and move on quickly.

Bold, confident, and self-assured, they need a partner who is as strong as they are. They like to take charge in love and many enjoy the thrill of the chase. They can have a complex love nature but are passionate and charming lovers.

They can struggle with commitment because at heart they are self-reliant and independent. In fact, they don't want to rely on others to fulfill their needs. They are known to move on quickly once the romance, passion, and excitement of a relationship wears off. Sometimes they leave a trail of brokenhearted exes behind them. For someone to catch them, it's usually a person who is as fiercely independent and confident as they are. Relationships can work well if their partner helps them grow and keeps the excitement flowing in the relationship. Harnessing commitment can bring more long-term relationships into their lives.

Mars in Aries

Mars in Aries individuals are powerful and action focused. They will fight for what they want with a fierceness that others can't match. Aggressive and rash, they act first without thinking things through. They need to be cautious about conflict and irritation overwhelming their lives. In fact, a big lesson for them is to learn how to compromise with others. One of their biggest lessons is learning to be less selfish and learning to focus more on the needs of others. They are learning the art of balance in relationships.

Passionate and driven souls, when they set their intentions on a goal, there is nothing and no one that can stop their enthusiasm. Because they boldly pursue what they want, they can often inspire other people. Because of their personality, they are great in a crisis. They step in quickly and take charge in stressful situations.

They enjoy high-stakes situations and adrenaline-pumping experiences because they help them feel alive. Because of their impulsive nature and tendency to take risks, they are also prone to accidents. In fact, they can be risk-takers and should slow down and be more cautious when driving or operating machinery.

Fierce competitors, they are athletic and physically active, which can help them excel in sports. Moving around is a good way for them to express their pent-up energy. In fact, because of their high stamina, most people can't keep up with their constant motivation to be doing something. Pursuing hobbies can help them find emotional fulfillment and an outlet for their competitive spirit. Sometimes their quick temper and impulsiveness can be hard to control. But their anger can also be a transformative force that helps them overcome heartbreak and move on quickly from challenges. If they can learn patience, they can feel more balanced.

Jupiter in Aries

Jupiter in Aries individuals can grow through expansion and learning. They are generous and like nice things, but there are times they can be overindulgent with spending money or giving money to others freely. They try to see the good in people and are naturally optimistic. Many have a can-do attitude that helps attract people and situations that can help them obtain their goals.

Life struggles and challenges are seen as small bumps along their path.

Because they are headstrong and confident, they believe they can do anything they set their minds to. Their confidence and courage are strong, which helps them accumulate what they need. No one can convince them that things won't work out.

They enjoy pursuing hobbies, taking classes, and learning new things. Positive and motivated, they have an internal drive to avoid negativity and focus on the future. Making the world a better place is important to them, and they can be loving, affectionate, and supportive to people who ask them for help. If they learn to harness a down-to-earth approach, it can help them see things in more practical ways.

Saturn in Aries

Saturn in Aries individuals might repress or restrict their passionate desires. Self-expression doesn't always come easily for them. Even though they feel powerful emotions, they might not feel comfortable with them. They can be serious, disciplined, and hardworking. Achieving their goals and being successful are things that help them build self-confidence. They might need to put extra effort into overcoming pessimism and a negative attitude. Because negative thought patterns can impact their mood, they can experience irritability and frustration. There are times they might repress their anger, and this can cause physical issues such as headaches. Many feelings can bubble up when they don't have a healthy outlet to express their emotions. Sometimes they feel trapped if they can't move freely and have autonomy. In fact, they might like to control their impulses and desires.

Responsibilities can sometimes feel like burdens. They need to focus less on others' actions and build more confidence in their own abilities. Sometimes they can doubt themselves too much and struggle to make decisions. The good news is that they have patience and discernment to think things through before they act. There are times when they might have to sacrifice something and need to focus on the needs of their family, friends, or a partner. Harnessing a strong work ethic and a disciplined approach will help them achieve their goals.

Uranus in Aries

Uranus in Aries individuals are born with an unconventional and non-traditional style. They like to shock people by what they wear, how they act, and what they say. Independent and freedom loving, they are rebels at heart. Thrill-seeking behavior is common with this placement, because of their desire to rebel against rules. In fact, rebelling against authority figures often happens, especially if this individual doesn't respect the person. It's hard for them to follow other people's rules because they like to do their own thing.

Autonomy is crucial because they need to feel free to be their own unique self. It's important for them to be able to act on their eccentric and creative ideas. Innovative, forward thinking, and full of unique ideas, they don't conform easily to what others want. In fact, they are not afraid of conflict and are good at debating others about their beliefs. Other people are not sure if they can depend on them because of their unstable energy and behaviors. There are times they can be impulsive and reckless just to see the look on someone's face. In fact, they might even like to incite arguments to overcome boredom.

Computers and technology might interest them, and this is a way they can network with other people from all over the world. Being part of a group or organization that shares the same goals and passion can help them expand their minds. Sometimes they like to stand out and get attention through technology and social media.

They can have a surprising temper that sporadically comes out when people are not expecting it. In fact, this can catch people off guard and shock them. Because of their impatience and restless nature, it can be hard for them to maintain balance. Outdoor activities, spending time exploring new places or ideas, can help calm their nerves. Harnessing patience and learning to ground their wired energy can help them relax.

Neptune in Aries

Neptune in Aries individuals have an idealistic and mysterious nature. Artistic, creative, and social, they are concerned about helping others. They can hide their aggression and passionate side. Expressing themselves might be difficult because they might be more self-conscious about how people perceive them. Sometimes their anger can be something they successfully repress because they feel it's wrong to feel it. But it's important for them to allow intense emotions to be expressed. It might be easier for them to write about how they feel and journal their emotions.

Sensitive to their environment, they may have empathic abilities. They need to be careful about absorbing negativity from the environment. Feeling overwhelmed by emotions can happen because of their sensitive nature.

Deep down they like to compete and win, but they might be in denial about their competitive emotions. Sometimes they don't see things clearly, because their feelings can cloud their judgment when they react purely on emotion. Idealistic at times, they can see people and the world with rose-colored glasses. Deception can sometimes leave them feeling hurt and distrustful of others.

These individuals have an uncanny ability of making their ideas come true. Manifesting their desires can happen easily when they are connected to a spiritual path or higher purpose. If they can harness a spiritual outlook, they will become a stronger leader. In fact, the powerful emotions they feel can be used to overcome heartache and life crises.

It's important for them to spend time alone. They truly need a quiet and serene environment where they can recover from everyday life. In fact, solitude can help balance their energy. Building stronger boundaries can also help them protect themselves and prevent burnout. Self-care and having time to withdraw from the world can help them find a greater sense of purpose.

Pluto in Aries

Pluto in Aries individuals can be intense, determined, and impulsive. They drive forcefully toward what they want regardless of who or what is in front of them. Strong-willed and sometimes known as thrill seekers, these individuals can struggle in relationships. In fact, they dislike feeling dependent on others, which can bring challenges. Because they don't trust others easily, they focus on self-protection. Sometimes they seem guarded and skeptical about other people's motives. Opening up and letting other people into their inner world can help them feel supported.

Driven to succeed at all costs, they can be loners. Sometimes secretive, they don't readily trust others or share. It's important that they find time to relax even though they are good at taking charge during a challenge or crisis. They need to take breaks and learn to let go. If they are struggling, they will often isolate themselves and focus on healing.

Magnetic and charming, they can attract others to them easily. They are intense and passionate about what they feel and they can have issues with expressing anger. Their strong personality can overwhelm others. If they can learn patience, then they can avoid unnecessary conflict with others.

Planets in the First House

When planets are in the first house, you will want to focus on your own needs, express yourself, and achieve your personal goals.

Sun in the First House

These individuals have an instinctive nature and need to express themselves. They take charge and react in the moment. Although they can be a bit self-focused, they are also very giving. Typically, they have a sunny and optimistic disposition. People take notice of them immediately and can feel their confident energy. They have a powerful and recuperative energy that can be used to overcome crises and speak their mind. Physically strong, their body reacts to stress and the environment they find themselves in. Strong and resilient, they can overcome obstacles and illness faster than other people. Once they make up their mind to do something, they can have an overconfident, arrogant, and selfish approach. If they can harness their passionate optimism, they can overcome criticism and challenges effortlessly.

Moon in the First House

These individuals have a passionate, emotional nature. They are boisterous, assertive, and fight for the underdog. A fast-paced, competitive, and emotionally intense environment suits them best. They are natural at reacting in the moment and have a powerful intuition and gut instinct that is rarely wrong.

Restless at heart, they need movement and change in their lives. Emotionally, they can find comfort through expressing themselves and speaking up. In fact, they might be natural advocates and courageous in fighting for what they believe in. Sometimes they are seen as aggressive, straightforward, and direct. The reason they speak up is because they have a desire to tell the truth and share their feelings with others.

They want to be liked by others and can be sensitive to criticism. But then on the other hand, they can cut ties and move on quickly toward goals regardless of if they have support from others or not. Obstacles can ignite a fire in their hearts. They might have a survival instinct that kicks in during times of stress that helps them tap into emotional resilience. While they have the strength to push through hardships, they can also be very sensitive and loving. They can wear their heart on their sleeve but also be assertive and straightforward if a situation calls for it.

Powerful emotions often bubble to the surface quickly and this can make them impatient and impulsive. In fact, they might struggle with anger and uncomfortable feelings. A hidden temper might boil underneath the surface. So, they can benefit through physical activity and doing something to express those intense feelings. A benefit is for them to use their anger to overcome challenging situations. If they learn to harness emotional strength, they can snap out of depression quickly and move on with their lives.

Mercury in the First House

Blessed with a strong intellectual approach to life, these individuals are intelligent, communicative, and assertive. They make an impact on those in their environment and will share their opinions openly and honestly. Sometimes they can interrupt others because of a strong desire to talk and an inner restlessness. Often in the moment, they want to share intensely and passionately what they think with the world. It's important that they make time to write and journal to release their thoughts and find balance.

They crave constant movement, communication, and change. Although they love to learn and network with others, they can grow bored easily. Sometimes they can experience anxiety due to their overly active mind. In fact, they can struggle with sleeping and experience insomnia.

Focused on their own ideas and beliefs, it can be difficult for them to listen to others. What they think can affect how they feel more than most people so it's important to implement positive thinking. Their worrisome thoughts can influence them both physically and mentally. Learning mindfulness and ways to quiet their mind can bring greater peace. Finding time to relax and taming their anxiety can help them develop stronger mental resilience.

Venus in the First House

These individuals are charming and charismatic. Their natural magnetism draws people to them. Experiencing love, pleasure, and creativity are priorities for first house Venuses. Romantic and passionate about love, they desire intimate relationships. In fact, they like the thrill of the chase. If someone doesn't seem interested, then they might try even harder to get their attention. New relationships inspire them to express their ardent feelings and make them feel alive.

Independent and adventurous, they need to feel a sense of freedom in relationships. They are often interested in fulfilling their intense desires. In fact, sometimes their self-centered behavior can cause difficulties in their relationships. Because they expect a high level of emotion and passion in love, they can feel disappointed. If someone doesn't live up to what they expect, then they can end things abruptly. In fact, they are known to quickly fall in and out of love. On a positive note, they can also compromise in relationships and they have a good way of supporting others.

Creativity in their self-expression can manifest through their appearance and how they portray themselves to the world. Sometimes they can have artistic abilities and a strong urge to show others their talents. It's important that they show their unique style through clothing, jewelry, and how they socialize with others.

Flirtatious, fun loving, and friendly, it's important for them to connect with other people. Being alone can be difficult because having a partner is often a priority. A lot of their time is spent seeking love or finding a deeper connection in relationships. They need to focus on increasing their sense of identity free from others. Learning to love themselves free from other people's opinion is their key to happiness.

Mars in the First House

Strong-willed and dominant in all areas of life, these individuals are fiery and aggressive. It is hard for them to hold back when their gut instinct is to act. Their impulsivity can lead to conflict with others. One common problem is they tend to only be aware of their own needs. Extremely self-focused at times, they are driven to work hard for their personal goals. It is important for them to take other people into account as well.

Sometimes they get irritated and angry if they don't get what they want. Passion is important to them, and they like to feel alive. Risk-taking behavior can lead to accidents, but feeling the pulse of adrenaline and overcoming challenges inspires them. They have a fire inside that motivates them to keep going. Sometimes restless, they have a hard time relaxing and sitting still. In their mind, there is always something they need to do.

Relationships can end abruptly and painfully if they don't cultivate patience. Slowing down and thinking things through helps them make better decisions. Their impatience can scare people away or make it hard for others to understand them. But once they make their mind up to do something, there is no one who can stop them from achieving their dreams. If they can learn to harness their anger, it will help them heal from loss, heartbreak, and disappointment.

Jupiter in the First House

These individuals have a positive and generous presence. They can have a larger-than-life presence. People notice when they walk into the room. They are very confident in themselves and their abilities. Positivity attracts people and they have a way of uplifting others with their friendly and cheerful energy. In fact, because of their optimistic attitude, they believe they can achieve any goal they decide to pursue.

Outgoing, social, and a natural motivator, people tend to trust them instantly. These individuals see the best in every situation. Physically, they bounce back fast from sickness and can heal quickly. The positive energy of Jupiter helps their physical bodies overcome stress.

These individuals enjoy helping others and have a generous nature in relationships. This placement decreases self-focused energy and increases a desire to help others. Even though they want to succeed, they have an interest is seeing other people reach their goals. It is important to harness a can-do attitude.

Saturn in the First House

These individuals have a shy, private, and serious personality. Rigid and cautious, they are very set in their ways and might find it difficult to compromise. Being so cautious, their realistic approach to life can make it hard to have fun. In fact, their seriousness can lead to self-esteem issues and self-doubt. Extremely self-disciplined, they can easily restrict themselves from things that are bad for them. In fact, they might have a strict diet, exercise routine, or regime that they follow.

When people first meet them, they think they are older than they are. Super responsible, they are productive and dedicated to achieving their goals. People with this placement are wise souls who may have felt pressure to grow up fast. Some might have found themselves taking care of their younger siblings or a parent while they were growing up. Committed relationships can seem fated and karmic. Oftentimes, they have a lot of lessons to learn about expressing themselves and trusting others. Harnessing persistence and organizational strategies can help them achieve success.

Uranus in the First House

Born with unusual interests, beliefs, and hobbies, these individuals walk to the beat of their own drum. Unconventional at heart, they want to stand out and often get attention. In fact, they like to shock people by how they dress and what they say. There is something about them that makes people take notice. A kind of electric energy that is unsettling and creative attracts other people who are nontraditional.

It's important for them to feel free to explore their unique self-expression. Following others or conforming to what society wants them to be is difficult. Because of their strong need for autonomy, they often rebel against authority. In fact, disrupting the status quo can bring unexpected changes and excitement to their lives. Being spontaneous and impulsive can sometimes lead to reckless behavior. So, it's important for them to learn patience and to think things through before they act.

Sometimes they find themselves in controversial situations. Because they like to push the limits, they can experience unusual relationships with others. At times they are unpredictable and people perceive them as unstable. It's difficult for others to know their next move because they don't always know themselves what they will do.

An unsettling energy can follow them, creating unexpected change. In fact, change can help them grow and release stagnant energy. They may have a fiery temper that can shock others when they feel ignored, judged, or when someone tries to make them conform. Being impatient and impulsive can make it difficult for them to maintain balance. Their radical ideas and eccentric desires can sometimes make other people feel uncomfortable. These individuals need to learn to harness patience and work on calming their electric energy.

Neptune in the First House

This placement can create a mysterious and illusive personality. Spiritual, idealistic, and creative, this individual has hidden talents. In fact, other people might perceive these individuals as secretive and dreamy. Because they are imaginative and idealistic, they like to escape from responsibilities.

Extremely empathic and psychic, they take on the energies, thoughts, and emotions of people in their environment. They might lack boundaries and they can get overwhelmed emotionally. It is important that they learn to protect themselves from being hurt.

Mystical experiences and dreams can help guide their life, giving them glimpses of the future. Sometimes it's hard for them to focus or complete tasks, and they can feel scattered and disorganized.

Daydreaming and zoning out are common with this placement. It's like they detach and mentally travel to another world. Sensitive and compassionate, they can sometimes feel like a victim. Because of their idealism, they can expect other people to be kind and open like they are. When they realize that is not the case, they can feel sad, depressed, and disillusioned. It's important that that learn to be more practical and realistic about people and the world.

The world can seem too heavy, causing them to try to escape into a fairy-tale dream. Having solitude and time alone is critical to their mental health. Spending time doing solitary activities like meditation, reading, writing, and journaling can help them heal, balance, and ground themselves. If they can implement stronger boundaries, they can prevent heartache and disappointment.

Pluto in the First House

This individual has an intense and grounded energy. They have a powerful energy that others notice immediately. There is an air of secrecy that surrounds them, which makes others feel like they are hiding things. Because they are loners, they are very private about what they think and feel. In fact, they may think they don't need anyone but themselves to survive. Trusting others can be difficult and they expect people to prove themselves. Resilient and self-reliant, they know what it's like to be betrayed, so they have learned the art of self-protection.

Trusting others is never easy with this placement. Because they expect loyalty and total devotion, they have high standards in relationships. Relationships can be a constant source of growth and filled with transformation. Intimacy can be challenging because they can have a deep desire for it, but then on the other hand, they fear it. People seem to either love or hate them, and sometimes there is no in-between. They have an intense emotional nature and their energy is filled with passion, desire, and competition.

Natural leaders, they like to take charge and be in control of situations. They have a natural sense of urgency that makes them want to plot and be strategic. A magnetic energy surrounds them and attracts passionate partners who help them reach their goals. They sometimes attract people who want to share deep, dark, and taboo secrets with them. In fact, they might feel like there is a sign on their back that says, "Come to me for help."

Figuring out what makes other people tick comes naturally to them. Deep soul divers at heart, they prefer to live deep beneath the surface, overwhelmed with strong emotions. Lukewarm feelings won't do the trick for them, because they want to totally merge and bond with others. Sometimes they are interested in psychology, astrology, and alternative healing methods. They might be interested in finding new ways to help people heal trauma and overcome difficult experiences. If they can embrace change and allow themselves to transform, they can grow stronger and more resilient.

Planetary Transits through the First House

When planets transit the first house, you will feel an urge to speak up, stand up for your own needs, and be motivated to achieve your goals.

Transit Sun

The shining Sun moving through this house will give you extra energy and stamina. This is an excellent time to focus on your own needs and desires. The warmth of the Sun will increase your energy for the next thirty days. You can accomplish more this next month due to an increase in optimism and confidence.

If you can harness this powerful energy of self-reliance and courage, you can achieve many things. This is a great time to accomplish your goals and start a new project you have been putting off. You can feel more inspired and motivated to act on your impulses and gut instinct. If you are normally cautious, you might feel a lot more outgoing and friendly.

You can be more focused on your health, physical appearance, and how you feel. It's a good time to tap into your intuition and take some risks. Because you have more energy, you might want to make needed changes in your life. Right now, you might want to speak up and share what you really think with others. In fact, you might find it easier to express your true desires, beliefs, and thoughts. If you're typically shy, you might be surprised how you want to get attention or are forced into the spotlight. You might feel a need to be independent, self-focused, and ready to get what you want instead of always focusing on others. Harness self-expression and share with others what you feel, think, and want in a direct way.

Transit Moon

As the Moon moves through this house for two and a half days, emotions come to the surface and bubble with intensity. This is an excellent time to accomplish tasks that you have been putting off. You might feel more motivated to get things done and act on your intuition. It will be harder

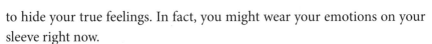

to hide your true feelings. In fact, you might wear your emotions on your sleeve right now.

Trust your gut instinct and listen to your inner voice. You can be more impulsive, impatient, and focused on your own emotional needs. Don't take things too personally, because your emotions are right on the surface. Any little thing can trigger a reaction and outburst. It's a good time to think before you make decisions.

Emotional and physical changes are common during this time. There may be a desire to change your physical appearance. You can be more focused on meeting new people and having intimate connections. If you are normally independent and self-reliant, you might prefer relying on others for emotional support during this cycle.

This transit pushes you to get in touch with your inner feelings and accept your vulnerability. Emotions can ebb and flow, because they are going through many ups and downs. You might feel unsettled, restless, and impatient. Harness stability so you can feel comfortable expressing your feelings and being more vulnerable with others.

Transit Mercury

This energy can help you focus more on your thoughts and beliefs. Overthinking can lead to indecision or overanalyzing what you really want. Be careful about needless gossip and don't believe everything you hear. Communication is intensified during this time, forcing you to express what you feel and think. In fact, you might be mentally restless and overshare with others. You might later regret being honest and open with others, but the energy forces you to be more truthful.

This is a good time to tap into new, creative, and fresh ideas. Restless energy can make it difficult for you to relax. You might benefit by writing down your thoughts to get them out of your body. Being honest with others will help you avoid relationship conflict. Because arguments are more common right now, make sure you utilize direct communication. Start speaking up for yourself, your needs, and use your voice to address any fears you have with communication.

Transit Venus

This is a pleasant time when you might feel much more outgoing and social. For five weeks you may feel a desire to splurge on things you enjoy. You might want to buy new clothes, eat at your favorite restaurant, or go to a concert. If you are typically shy, you might feel more outgoing and flirtatious. Socializing and networking with others helps you connect. You might tell people how you really feel during this transit.

This is a time you might want to focus on your appearance. You can be interested in getting your hair styled, buying new clothes, or pampering yourself. An increased desire to get along with others can create more peaceful and harmonious relationships.

You might be attracted to someone new. It is not uncommon to start a new relationship or decide to commit. In fact, romance and pleasure can bring greater happiness. People seem to be drawn to you and there is an increase in compliments from others. Everything seems to flow right now, and you might feel like telling people how you really feel.

Expressing your creativity and visiting an art museum can bring fulfillment. If there are relationships in your life that need mending, this is a great time to heal them. You are feeling more cooperative, understanding, and concerned about other people's needs right now. The efforts you make to connect with others and socialize will benefit your creative and artistic endeavors.

Transit Mars

This transit can ignite your passionate side. The next eight weeks can awaken your temper, passion, and competitive drive. There is a noticeable increase in your energy level and you can feel motivated to move, act, and do new things. You might be motivated to get in shape and build an exercise plan.

Stress and tension can cause headaches and happen more frequently during this cycle. It might also be difficult to sleep and you can struggle with insomnia. Because you have a lot on your mind and are feeling restless, it's good to get things done.

You might feel irritable and a bit impulsive. It's important to be cautious and patient. You can be prone to accidents during this time, so pay attention to your surroundings when you're driving, cooking, or doing anything with machinery.

If you have been stagnant, this transit will help you make decisions you have refused to make. In fact, you can grow a lot and make needed changes in your life. New beginnings and a sense of excitement help you connect to your passion. There seems to be an uprising within that helps you realize what you really want.

It's hard to sit still right now and you might want to explore. Just be careful and don't do something impulsive you might regret. It can be hard to follow through with new projects, so be cautious about taking on too much. Suppressed anger can erupt from within, which can be surprising and shocking to others. Embrace this new energy by speaking up for yourself and being more direct.

Transit Jupiter

This is a good time to be positive and tap into your optimistic side. There is a feeling of good luck and fortune surrounding your life. You can feel motivated to meet new people and feel more open-minded. There is a positive energy surrounding you right now.

For the next year you can be interested in learning new things, being more adventurous, taking risks, exploring new things. It's a great time to celebrate your wins and overcome your losses. It's important to step back and be thankful for what you have. It's a good time to count your blessings and tell people you appreciate them.

There is not much that can bring you down right now because you can see the bright side in negative situations. In fact, this is a great time to let go of the past and forgive others. Generosity abounds and you can feel inspired to help others.

Expansion is possible regarding your goals, ideas, and projects. If you are typically a cautious person, this energy will give you the confidence to speak up and be more assertive. Being able to move around and feel independent helps you fully enjoy this transit. You might want to travel and go on a trip. The urge to enjoy the good things in life is intensified, but just be cautious of overindulgence. Do things in moderation and you will be fine.

Embrace positive feelings and express gratitude for the things happening in your life.

Transit Saturn

This transit can make you feel heavy, rigid, and cautious. This transit makes it difficult to feel light, free, or have fun. For the next two to three years it's a time when you can be forced to take on more responsibilities. It can feel like you are being tested in areas that impact your sense of autonomy and ability to take care of your own needs. In fact, you are more focused on the practical side of life.

You can feel burdened by others right now, which makes relationships challenging during this time. There can be a desire to break free and find freedom from duties. But no matter what you do, it's hard to enjoy the things you usually enjoy doing. In fact, it's challenging because of your increased cautiousness and inability to fully express your emotions. Because you feel restricted and blocked, it's a struggle to communicate.

There can be a serious energy affecting you, so it's important to take care of your health and physical body. Try to make time for exercise, movement, and focus on making changes to your diet.

Dwelling on negative things will only make you feel more anxious and depressed. It's important to work on seeing things clearly and realistically. Don't be afraid to make decisions during this time. If you are normally outgoing, or optimistic, then you might find yourself feeling more pessimistic and sarcastic.

There is no way to avoid the realities and karma influencing your life. It's a time when you can grow stronger as a person. There is a slow, patient energy of change stripping away your outdated beliefs. Your long-term goals can take time to manifest because of delays. In the end, the hard work you have done will pay off. Be patient and don't give up.

Harness realism while acknowledging small positive things in your life. Remember that you are not alone and you don't have to do everything yourself. Open up and trust others more with your inner feelings and talk with someone you trust who can ease the burdens of this transit.

Transit Uranus

This transit can bring unexpected and shocking changes into your life. For the next seven years, your personality and identity can be forever changed. This energy is electric, unstable, and swoops into your life unexpectedly. Feeling secure and stable is challenging with this transit. It might feel like something powerful is influencing your beliefs and emotions. In fact, you can feel more rebellious and need more freedom to make your own decisions. If you are not typically independent, then you might feel uncomfortable with the change in your personality.

You can feel unsettled and feel like you don't know what is going to happen next. Because of an increased desire to take risks, you might rebel against authority. You might feel more unconventional and seek new ways of expressing yourself. In fact, you can alter and change your appearance drastically. If you dressed traditionally, you might shock others with a new style, ear piercing, haircut, or tattoo.

Expressing yourself fully and embracing your eccentric side comes naturally right now. There are major changes and past-life energies playing out during this time. There can be a destined feeling with the unexpected events that continue to transpire in your life. Just when you think things have settled down, something shakes up your world.

If you feel trapped in unhealthy situations or relationships, this energy often forces you to change. There are many awakenings occurring to help you snap out of the stagnant energy of the past. Because relationships can be tested at this time, separation and conflict can arise. It might be a good time to discuss deep-seated issues, but it might require professional counseling and support. Sometimes divorce happens during this transit. For instance, it can be triggered if you have been stuck in an unhappy situation where you were not growing as a person.

Also, if you are single, there is often an exciting relationship that can start a new cycle. You might get married and move across the world. You can attract partners who are eccentric, creative, and freedom loving. You are not being punished even though there are times it might feel like the universe is constantly forcing you to let go of your comfort and security. Harness change and accept that life is shaken up right now to help you grow. Once you embrace the energy of change and stop resisting it, every-thing will shift and you will wake up and feel like a brand-new person.

Transit Neptune

This transit can last for up to fourteen years and it opens your spiritual ideals and psychic abilities. Your intuition is awakened during this transit, but you need to learn to have confidence and trust your abilities. Height-ened sensitivity can happen in relationships and with the environment. In fact, you are much more sensitive and compassionate during this transit.

It's not uncommon to become interested in mysticism, New Age top-ics, and spirituality during this cycle. You might try to eat a plant-based diet, meditate more often, and enjoy solitude. If you are typically social, then you might feel an increased desire to be alone.

There can be more people sharing their pain and personal problems with you. You are more sensitive to your environment and there is a myste-rious energy surrounding your aura. This attracts all sorts of mystical and creative people and those who need help. Because your boundaries seem lessened during this time, it makes you more vulnerable to being hurt. There is a lot of healing that can take place, especially by being of service to others and supporting them.

Idealism and seeing things with rose-colored glasses can cause diffi-culties. It's important for you to have stronger boundaries and be more cautious about trusting others. In fact, it's crucial to ensure you truly get to know others before you fully trust them. You might develop relationships with partners who struggle with addiction or who have escapist tenden-cies. There is also a danger for you to start drinking more to cope with your heightened emotions. Be aware of any unhealthy behaviors that start to develop so you can make changes as needed.

You can be easily deceived and even lied to during this transit. Try to see people clearly and trust your gut instinct. Don't ignore your intuition, because it's intensified at this time to help you connect more deeply with the world. You can be feeling a bit lost and even like a victim in some cir-cumstances. Because your emotions are so raw, you might want to escape from the hustle of the real world. Finding time to withdraw and spend more time in solitude can be beneficial.

It's a good time to connect with your soul and your inner self. Journal and write down your dreams and insights. Dreams can be more vivid and even psychic, giving you future warnings. Having boundaries so you can protect your sensitive energy and avoiding negative situations can help prevent your energy being depleted. Trusting your intuition can help you survive this powerful transit!

Transit Pluto

This is a transformational transit that can impact your life for decades. This is a healing transit that can slowly shake up the inner depths of your soul. This energy opens all your hidden wounds and this can be painful. Physically, emotionally, and mentally, you experience death and rebirth. Your life is forever changed, and this can be an uncomfortable transition. Sometimes you can feel this energy slowly creeping into your life and it can be unsettling.

If you are normally calm and unemotional, it can take some time to get used to your new feelings. In fact, intense emotions such as jealousy and revenge can bubble to the surface. Change seems to be all around you and continues to influence every area of your life. Who you are as a person and your main identity are transformed. When this transit is over, you will look back and may not even recognize yourself.

What is important about your sense of self, passion, and needs will go through major changes, and there can be an identity crisis. You might want to make changes to your appearance, health, identity, and relationships. There is no hiding during this transit, and it often reveals the truth about life and your relationships. You are trying to figure out who you are, what you want, and your long-lasting goals.

It can sometimes feel like the old you disappeared and the new you is unrecognizable. Allow yourself to change and don't resist it! Harness transformation and allow yourself to heal. When you come out of this energy, you will realize how strong you have become.

Ways to Harness Aries Energy

- Act in the moment.
- Think about your own needs.
- Speak up and tell the truth.
- Be confident and brave.
- Become self-reliant and independent.
- Take more risks.
- Stay physically active.

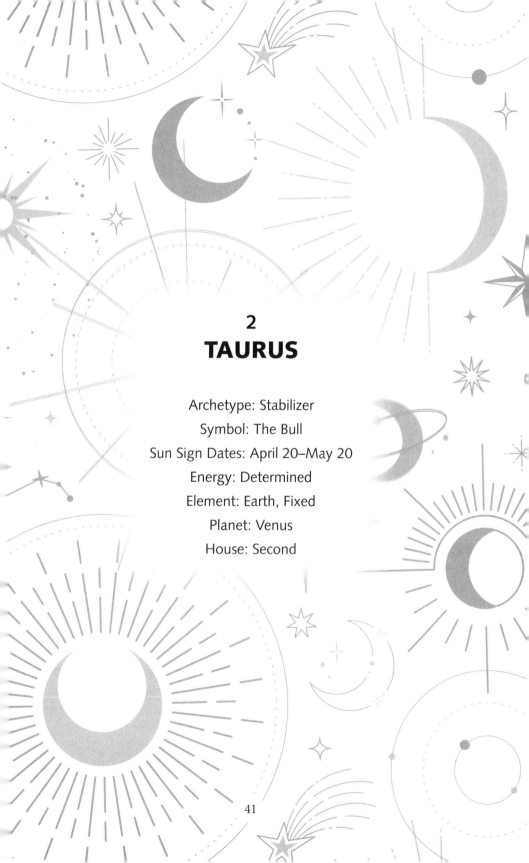

2
TAURUS

Archetype: Stabilizer
Symbol: The Bull
Sun Sign Dates: April 20–May 20
Energy: Determined
Element: Earth, Fixed
Planet: Venus
House: Second

I f you have Taurus in your birth chart, planets in the second house, or are experiencing planetary transits through the second house, this chapter will cover information regarding these energies. If you don't, you can still learn about Taurus energy and incorporate it into your life. The placement of Venus in the sign and house will show where you express Taurus energy. It is important to look at what house the sign Taurus falls on in your birth wheel because this is where you will want to find comfort and stability, plan for the future, and feel secure. Harnessing Taurus energy gives you greater patience, determination, stability, and an ability to achieve your goals through concentrated effort.

Taurus Energy Words

Determined, patient, stubborn, stable, structured, strong-willed, grounded, earthy, calm, slow, methodological, quiet, rigid, committed, organized, focused, resistant, artistic, musical, attractive, charming, sensual, affectionate, persistent.

Taurus Motto

As a Taurus I need to have a thought-out plan. I can be quietly competitive. I am strong-willed, and once I make up my mind, there is no one who can change it. I do everything slowly and don't like to feel rushed. Change can be difficult for me. I am connected to the past and it's hard to let things go. Loud noises and chaos make me anxious. I take my time doing things the right way, because I don't want to waste my energy. I am stubborn and like things done my way. I need a calm and peaceful environment to feel safe. I enjoy owning nice things and crave financial security. I am a dependable and reliable person. I am patient and value financial success.

Harnessing Taurus Energy

Taurus energy is calm, stable, and earthy. This energy is comforting, sensual, and can feel like a big warm hug. Taurus energy is mature, trustworthy, and patient, which can make other people feel safe, supported, and listened to. If you are feeling uneasy, anxious, or stressed out, tapping into Taurus energy is a way to find greater peace. Enjoying fine dining, delicious food, affection, art, and beauty is the embodiment of this energy. Taureans are determined, patient, steady, loyal, and like to plan. Taking risks does not suit them, because they prefer to plan each move slowly before they make it. In fact, waiting is their forte, as well as their patience. Other people might perceive them as lazy or slow to get things done. The truth is they are not capable of rushing; their energy is too practical. Developing patience, connecting to the earth, acknowledging what is valuable in our lives, and setting practical goals are all ways we can harness Taurus energy. Tapping into Taurus energy brings us greater stability, comfort, security, patience, and determination to realize what we truly value.

Never Give Up

Taurus energy is a determined, strong-willed, and stubborn force of nature. Adapting to change and new information can be difficult. Taureans can be practical, deliberate, and stable, which gives them a relaxed approach to life. Also, because this energy is earthy, it can help us get centered and calm. This energy is good at waiting, slowly plowing through the field, taking time to plant the seeds. Patience is what helps Taureans achieve their lofty goals.

Taureans tend to be stubborn and often set in their ways. Once their mind is made up, their determined energy pushes them forward. Sometimes narrow-minded, they don't always see the bigger picture. This energy helps us listen to ourselves and not give in to others' negativity. It helps us focus on what is real, practical, and valuable. Fiercely strong-willed and determined, it's important to stay adaptable and open-minded to other people's views. You will want to look at your birth chart to see where you have Taurus to harness this determined energy.

Grounded

Taurus is an earth sign. Earth can be heavy, solid, and rooted because it supports water, trees, plants, and animals. Earth energy helps Taureans accomplish their goals by giving them a strong sense of purpose and patience. Planning what action to take is the key to their success. It can take time for flowers and vegetables to grow in the soil. We have to use water, pull weeds, and wait for nature to run its course. We can't force things to happen before it's time. Because of this, earth signs are known to be steady, reliable, and organized. Earth signs are the workers of the zodiac. They get stuff done! They like being efficient, making plans, and setting practical goals for the future. Being productive and working hard are what earth signs do best. Earth energy can bring comfort and a feeling of unwavering support in times of crisis. If they can harness perseverance, they can accumulate knowledge, wealth, and success.

Stable

Taurus is a fixed sign. This energy is known to be efficient, determined, strategic, and grounded. Fixed energy is good at planning, calculating, and waiting for things to bloom at the right time. It's slower and needs more time to manifest itself. Because of this, it doesn't like to feel rushed. Waiting is important, so being forced to make decisions prematurely is stressful. Fixed energy likes to know what is going to happen and what is expected of them. They typically believe they are right about things, and they can be inflexible, argumentative, and resistant to change.

If a fixed sign changes, it's often in small baby steps that other people might not even notice as change at all. Fixed signs take orders from cardinal signs and then work hard to manifest the results. Everything they do has a purpose, and if it's not going to help them achieve their goals, then they won't bother to waste their energy on it.

Stuck in the mud with their feet firmly planted, change can be painful for them. Listening to others and truly hearing what they have to say can take time. This energy believes it's right and resists feeling uncomfortable. Due to their stubbornness, their stagnant energy can make it difficult for them to act. It can also force them to stay trapped in the past and struggle to embrace growth or change. Born with strong values and a practical mind, fixed energy is dependable. Fixed energy helps us have structure and a steady path to follow. Tapping into fixed energy can help us feel firm in our place in this world.

Harness Peace

Taurus is ruled by the planet Venus. Venus is the Roman goddess of love, relationships, luxury, beauty, and harmony. This is similar to how Taureans live life; they seek pleasure and like the nice things. Venus is associated with partnership, compromise, creativity, affection, and romance. Just like Taureans, Venus likes pretty things and a peaceful environment. In fact, peace, harmony, creativity, and artistic abilities are strengths of this energy.

This energy makes us charming, attractive, and sensual. There is often the ability to help soothe others and make them feel at ease. This planet can reveal the type of person we are attracted to in relationships and how we express love. It also represents beauty, aesthetics, and how to establish peace. Harmony is critical for Taureans to feel safe and secure.

Wherever Venus is in our birth chart can show where we need to compromise and focus on collaborative partnerships. Writing, making art, singing, dressing up, wearing makeup, and fixing our hair are all ways we connect with this energy. Because of a deeper need for affection, hugging others, holding hands, and cuddling with our pets can bring greater comfort. It's sensual, romantic, and flirtatious energy.

Security and Safety

The second house in astrology is the area of life that shows where we make our own money, plan for the future, seek self-worth, and realize what we truly value. Taurus is the ruler of the second house and this energy is all about patience, dedication, loyalty, and commitment. There can be a greater need for peace, harmony, and material comfort when planets are in this house.

The second house is where we find stability and where our needs are met. The key purpose of this house is to have basic needs met. There can be a focus on having food and money to survive. In fact, how we overcome hardship, accumulate possessions, pay our bills, and provide for our family's security are key issues.

This house influences what kind of material possessions we accumulate. There might be a love of collecting things and buying antiques. But how we find financial security and how we make money for our basic needs is the focus. We all know that money brings greater security and makes things easier. Although, we also need to realize that money doesn't always bring happiness.

When planets are here, there can be a fear of lack, not having enough money to live comfortably, and the feeling that financial stability can bring emotional security. Sometimes the second house encourages us to hold on tightly to our possessions and even outdated things that are weighing us down. Letting go and releasing old things can help eliminate hoarder behaviors. But because of a reluctance to change, it can make it difficult to release old energy as well. It's important to purge possessions, memories, and emotions that no longer serve a purpose. In fact, this can help manifest a more positive energy and create greater abundance.

This area of life represents where we can plan, conserve our energy, and establish emotional comfort. It can be hard to take risks when planets are here. Being practical, thrifty, and conversative with finances is highlighted. There are times people with planets here can be seen as thrifty, stingy, and rigid. Because of a fear of not having their needs met, there can be challenges with spending and being generous.

Second house energy can be patient, reliable, sensual, and strong-willed. It's not just the house of money, but it's a place where we can find what is important in our lives.

We might build an empire of wealth, but later in life realize that we squandered our health or ignored important relationships. We can't take money or possessions with us when we die, and value can come through more than just material gain. In fact, planets here can help us connect with what we truly value, whether that is wealth, happiness, good health, peace, or comfort.

Second house energy encourages us to work hard to accumulate security, but more importantly it helps us build a legacy. We might also build greater self-esteem and gain an increased sense of self-worth without having to own material possessions.

Taurus Rising

When people first meet someone with Taurus rising, they perceive them as grounded, calm, and pleasant. Appearing clean and professional is important to them as well. Their grounded energy can bring a calming influence into other people's lives. There is a friendliness about them, but also a quiet shyness. It takes some time for them to feel comfortable, and they will open up only once they really get to know others. They are reliable and dependable, which is why people are drawn to their soothing presence. They have a gift for making other people feel at ease. There is an earthiness about their personality that makes others feel safe to open up. On the other hand, people might see them as opinionated, but also stable within themselves. Their gift is patience and an ability to listen to others before they speak.

Taurus risings tend to be fixed in their ways, and once they make their mind up, it's difficult to change it. The stubborn streak they possess can cause conflict in relationships and with professional colleagues. At times they can be seen as a know-it-all because of their strong will and their thought-out words.

Slow and methodological, they strategize each potential outcome and weigh the cost and benefits. Their lack of quick decision-making can frustrate others who prefer a fast decision-making approach. They typically dislike being rushed, preferring to observe all options and think it through before making decisions. Their patience won't allow them to make rash decisions.

They need to feel a connection with the environment they are in and with the people around them. The five senses are associated with Taurus energy. Many have a heightened sense of smell and taste. In fact, they can be sensitive to loud noises and sounds, preferring a quiet environment. They often dislike anyone who is loud, brash, or disruptive.

In relationships they can be sensual and affectionate, and physical touch is critical for them to feel loved. Holding hands, hugging, cuddling, or a pat on the back are all ways they show affection. They can prefer to show affection in private and only when they feel comfortable. Because trust is important to them, they won't commit fully to someone until they prove themselves reliable.

Practical in everything they do, they don't give in to a false sense of urgency. They move toward goals at a snail's pace because it makes them feel in control. If they say they will do something, then they will do it eventually. But some people might believe they are lazy, prone to procrastinating, or simply don't care enough. In fact, the opposite is often true; they just need more time than others and don't want to burn out. They don't want to waste unnecessary energy on things they deem unimportant.

They value security more than anything else, but are often labeled rigid, cautious, and obstinate. Because they know exactly what they want in life, it helps them stand firm to stubbornly defend their position. In fact, it might take time for them to get motivated to start working toward their goals. But once they decide on a course of action, Taurus risings pursue their goals with a single-minded approach and implement practical steps to attain them.

They prefer to do things the way they always have done them, which can cause stagnation and a failure to grow as an individual. Taurus risings like nice things and are comfort loving. Because they can be nostalgic, they can be pack rats who save everything they have ever purchased or keep a scrapbook of all the memories of their first true love.

Taurus risings need to learn the importance of change and moderation. They can overindulge in things that stimulate their senses. Some may have problems with food or addictions like smoking, alcohol, sex, or spending. They enjoy repetitive action, which can be useful or detrimental to them. For instance, smoking is common simply because of the tendency of habit formation, but many also like to exercise and become passionate about their health.

They enjoy harmony in relationships but can be a bit possessive. Once they are in a relationship, they are committed, affectionate, and enjoy physical intimacy. It's hard for them to let go of people and relationships.

Comfort can come in many different ways and it's important they find out what works best for them. In fact, they might benefit by having a pet to cuddle with, or by making pottery, or gardening. Finding hobbies that help them feel grounded can encourage them to seek out those positive habits.

How to Harness Planets in Taurus

When planets are in Taurus, there is a focus on stability, finances, building security, finding comfort, and accumulating wealth.

Sun in Taurus

Sun in Taurus individuals have a calm and soothing presence. There is often a sense of beauty, elegance, and artistic style that attracts others. On the other hand, they can have a tenacious strong will, stubborn streak, and determined way of pursuing what they want. Taureans have an ability to patiently plot, plan, and envision what they want to do in the future. Because their symbol is the bull, they are slow to anger and like to take their time enjoying nature and their surroundings. They crave security, sameness, and comfort. There can be a strong drive to accumulate money, finances, and material possessions.

A strong will and inability to take other people's advice can lead to conflict. But they are also patient, calm, and peaceful, so they can benefit by listening more to others. Because they are easygoing, they don't allow others to disturb their inner peace. They are good at developing and keeping boundaries.

Taureans need financial security before they are willing to take unnecessary risks. Many enjoy pursuing a more artistic and creative career but can put that on hold due to their fears of not being able to support themselves financially. If something is too impractical, they might doubt its accuracy or ability to benefit their goals.

They shine when they are working and accomplishing tasks. Just like oxen plowing the field, they work hard to achieve what they want. Firm, steady, and well balanced, these individuals are averse to taking risks.

In relationships, they can have a soothing energy that helps others feel supported. They can help ground people who are anxious, worried, or highstrung. In fact, they shine when they express their affectionate, loving, and passionate side.

When they believe in something wholeheartedly, there is no one who can change their mind. If they do change, it will take consistent effort and a practical approach to reason with them. Resistant and headstrong, these individuals rely on themselves to get the job done. Because they don't want to be rushed or told what to do, they can appear inflexible. By being more open-minded to the opinions, advice, and beliefs of others, Taureans can find greater peace in their lives.

Moon in Taurus

Moon in Taurus individuals crave financial security to feel emotionally secure. As one of the most affectionate Moon signs, Taurus Moons make great friends and partners. They can make you feel supported and cared for with their calming presence. Committed and devoted partners, they can sometimes stay in relationships longer than they should. It's because change is difficult for them and they don't like to give up.

When they have an emotional connection with someone, they can be possessive, jealous, and struggle with self-esteem issues that can impact their ability to trust others in relationships. They expect the same amount of loyalty they give to others and have specific expectations. Affectionate lovers, they need physical touch and intimacy in their relationships.

Slow to anger, they are practical and try not to react to things they can't control. Change and growth can be challenging, but they need to step out of their conservative ways. Calm, loyal, and possessive, they like to show others how they feel and can be very giving. Buying loved ones gifts and doing little things to prove their love help them express their deeper emotions.

Their emotional fulfillment can come through building security, wealth, and emotional comfort. Also, they need a sense of peace and harmony in their lives. They are known for their perseverance, reliability, and practical approach to situations. Often, they choose to get involved with people who can benefit them in some way. They do better in a serene environment or when they can get outside in nature.

Uncomfortable with surprises, they lack spontaneity and crave routine. Crisis and change can be hard for them because they need structure, routine, and physical activity. Music, food, scented candles, and perfumes bring a sense of comfort. Being cozy and relaxed can help them balance their emotions. Because their senses are heightened, they can be impacted by strong scents, certain clothing, and loud noises. Happiness can come when they feel free to express their intense passion and pursue their many goals. When they can have a solid routine, it can help them balance their uncomfortable feelings.

Mercury in Taurus

Mercury in Taurus individuals don't speak until they have planned out each word they will say. Slow and deliberate, they like to get their point across and often repeat themselves to hammer in their points. Always prepared before they take on anything new, they need to feel completely ready before they talk. In fact, if they feel caught off guard, or emotionally overwhelmed, it can cause them to withdraw from others.

Practical communicators, they value a logical and stable approach to communication. At times, talking can seem trivial to them unless there is a purpose for it. Because they are shy, they need time to gather their thoughts before they share them verbally. If they have to present information, then they need to prepare and get organized.

Deeply resistant to the ideas of others, they believe they are right. Communication can be challenging at times because of their strong-willed approach. In fact, it's almost impossible for them to take advice from other people, unless they can prove them wrong. These individuals are opinionated and tend to believe they are always right. Other people need to convince them that their ideas have value. Their stubbornness can sometimes create conflict at work and in professional relationships. They hold on tightly to what they believe in and find it difficult to change direction. They have excellent memories but lack listening skills at times, because their mind is often made up before others start talking. It's important for them to trust others' opinions and become more adaptable.

They prefer cuddling up with their favorite pet and reading a book versus going out and partying. Loud noises and sounds can disturb them; they do best in a peaceful, quiet, and harmonious environment. In fact, they can become overwhelmed with too much noise and chatter. Too much social activity can drain them quickly because they need time alone to ponder their thoughts.

They can be excellent at planning for the future because they are focused on saving money, accumulating finances, and strategically plotting their goals. On the other hand, they can also value creativity, art, and beauty. If they can harness open-mindedness in communication, it can help them adapt to other people's views.

Venus in Taurus

Venus in Taurus individuals enjoy pleasure and participating in harmonious relationships. Slow to fall in love, they can be cautious about giving their heart away to just anyone. In fact, they have high standards, and they will not commit if there are challenges. To them, it's not worth the risk of being hurt or wasting their time and energy.

Once they trust someone enough to be in a relationship with them, they need physical touch. They are very sensual and romantic at heart, which is why physical touch is crucial for their happiness. But they also need affection, which is why love and sex often go hand in hand. They can be possessive and jealous, which is why they aren't the type to date around.

They want someone who is as devoted and committed as they are. It takes them time to commit in partnership or with friends, but once they overcome their cautiousness, they can fall in love. They prefer relationships with people they feel are successful, practical, hardworking, loyal, and reliable.

Lucky with money, they often benefit through their partner in some way. There can be a love of comfort, and many enjoy eating and drinking. Although, food can also be used to cope with their unpleasant emotions. Sometimes they find it difficult to be healthy because of a need to overindulge in the things they enjoy. Harnessing affection can help them develop more long-term relationships with people who can support them.

Mars in Taurus

Mars in Taurus individuals have a passionate and sensual nature. Like a boiling pot that is slowly simmering, they can take a long time to show emotions. If they become irritated or angry, it's slow to rise to the surface. Once their patience has run out, watch out, because they can react like a bull who sees red in the competition ring. In fact, they start out slowly showing signs of frustration and then quickly explode in aggression. Although this is often a rare sight, because they are extremely patient and understanding most of the time. If they are pushed to this point, it's often because something made them feel disrespected or ignored.

Once they choose a course of action, there are very few people who can stand in their way. They slowly plod along, taking baby steps, and thinking through each move they make. Determination and a strong will to achieve results push them toward their goals. Success is important to them, and so is accumulating financial wealth. In fact, their patience is a virtue, and they can strategize each goal in detail while visualizing the results. Practical at heart, they work persistently to move forward toward their desires.

In relationships, conflict is not easy for them because they prefer being able to compromise. They need physical touch and intimacy to feel alive. Sensual, possessive, and sometimes domineering, they like to be in control. Their tendency to be possessive and sometimes jealous of what other people have can push people away. Also, they sometimes struggle to listen to other people's points of view. They can believe they are right regardless of what other people say.

Their temper can cause depression or unhappiness if they don't learn how to control it. Because they are introverted, they might choose to repress their passionate emotions. They like to control the outcome of situations but have to learn to let go and be more trusting. Harnessing trust and releasing possessive behaviors will help them in all areas of their lives.

Jupiter in Taurus

Jupiter in Taurus individuals are big spenders and like nice things. Anything they do that involves finances, banking, and investments can be successful. Good luck and fortune can come easily because of their generous nature.

Having a sense of security is very important and they value their ability to accumulate possessions, especially money. Although they might worry about security, they don't typically have to worry about finances. Most marry someone who is financially stable and can support their practical goals. In fact, they might inherit money or benefit from the finances of their partner.

Sometimes Jupiter creates a need for overindulgence in the things they love. Things like overspending and a desire for luxury can cause financial stress or arguments in relationships. Highly optimistic and positive, they don't always worry about money like other people do.

Learning new things and taking classes to enhance their artistic abilities can bring happiness. They can have a passion for art, painting, and listening to music. They might have a beautiful singing voice and enjoy performing onstage.

Collecting art, making jewelry, and participating in special hobbies can inspire them. Because they value peace, harmony, and comfort, they might enjoy collecting material things that help make the environment aesthetically pleasing. If they learn to harness optimism, they can find happiness through self-expression, creating something beautiful, and being more giving to others.

Saturn in Taurus

Saturn in Taurus individuals often fear not having enough financially. They can be overly responsible, serious, and restrict their own needs. Their anxiety and controlling nature can impact their ability to accumulate money and possessions. Their self-doubt and pessimistic nature impact their ability to create abundance. It's important for them to find something they truly value, like companionship, love, or career success.

Their feeling of lack can start in early childhood and be created by the way they were raised. They might have had to grow up fast and help work to support their family. Financial burdens might have impacted their parent's ability to nurture their needs. Because of this, they often believe that money makes life easier. Frugal at heart, they would like to put money away in savings for their retirement and for unexpected future events. People might perceive them as thrifty and not giving. In fact, their financial success often comes later in life. Once they get older and wiser, they can release their fear of losing their comfort.

There are karmic lessons surrounding issues of giving to others, which can come full circle when they mature. They know what it's like not to have what they need, so they want to plan for future crises. It's common for them to become more giving as they grow older. It's important for them to harness harmony in their lives. Finding what they truly value can help them find the everlasting stability they seek.

Uranus in Taurus

Uranus in Taurus individuals have enhanced eccentric, unconventional, and creative tastes. The traditional side of Taurus is blended with a unique outlook. They could shock people with how they dress by picking bright colors to wear and unique outfits. Beauty and self-expression are extremely important for their sense of self-worth.

Freedom loving and adventurous, they can take more risks because of a desire to force change. If things feel stagnant, they might want to shake things up. In fact, they might need to influence others through pursuing their artistic and creative talents. They are eccentric and have strong opinions, but the good news is they are often more open-minded than other people.

Collecting unusual possessions or accumulating money in unique ways is common. They might have eclectic tastes and enjoy buying unusual items. Finances often fluctuate with this placement because of their impulsive spending habits, but they usually have what they need. Saving money might be more difficult for them. In fact, their views about financial security often go through unexpected changes.

Because they are intelligent, innovation or scientific discoveries can bring extra income. Socializing and networking with others can help them feel calmer and more grounded. Marriage and commitment are more challenging because of their need for freedom and independence. Harnessing autonomy and a sense of freedom in their life helps them grow.

Neptune in Taurus

Neptune in Taurus individuals have a need for a deeper awareness of what is valuable in life. There is a gentleness to their personality and a sensitivity to the feelings of others. Because of this, they attract people who have problems and those who seek a comforting presence. Their calm, peaceful, and understanding personality helps them connect to the environment. Psychic, intuitive, and emotionally sensitive, they can connect to the spiritual realms easily. In fact, writing, listening to music, meditating, and practicing yoga are all things that can help them feel more grounded.

They can be artistic and enjoy exploring ways to express their creative talents. The work they do and the goals they set for themselves often involve spirituality, helping professions, or an artistic career. In many cases they are natural bodyworkers, energy healers, psychologists, counselors, and astrologers.

Unusual ways of making money come naturally to them. They use their idealism, imagination, and mystical wisdom to create financial stability. Money can be challenging for them to understand, and financial stability might be harder for them to obtain. They are more concerned with ideals and values than they are with material possessions.

They need to be cautious about getting taken advantage of and listen to their intuition. Sometimes they can feel deceived by those closest to them. Learning to listen to their intuition and connecting with their practical side can help them balance these energies. Connecting to something bigger than themselves and making time for solitary activities helps them feel safe and comfortable. If they can harness faith and focus on their soul's purpose in life, they can find peace.

Pluto in Taurus

Pluto in Taurus individuals have a passionate determination and a strong desire to achieve financial independence. They understand how other people can help them and like to connect with successful contacts to achieve their goals. Shrewd and calculating, they don't do anything without a plan. In fact, they can work hard, long, and methodologically to achieve their goals. Once they make up their mind, they are determined, driven, and competitive in reaching their personal goals.

In relationships, they can be intense and possessive. There can be a powerful sex drive and need for physical affection. Jealousy, secret keeping, and obsession are things they might battle with. In fact, they are stubborn, and there is nothing they won't pursue if they feel it can make them money. They realize the power of financial security and how having wealth can open doors and enable them to pursue their expensive hobbies. Patience and smoldering intensity help them overcome obstacles. Powerful changes can impact their security and comfort, but they actually have a strong healing capacity and can be resilient. Once they feel financially secure, they can relax and enjoy the fruits of their labor. If they can harness their natural endurance and tap into their power, they can successfully build their empire.

Planets in the Second House

When planets are in the second house, you can be focused on finding comfort, making money, building security, having stability, and accumulating wealth.

Sun in the Second House

These individuals have a grounded, calming presence that makes others feel at ease. They attract money easily and enjoy collecting things. Being comfortable allows them to relax and focus on feeling secure. Practical, hard-working, and realistic, they focus on what is lasting and true. It does not matter how much money is in the bank; they often worry about not having enough. There can be a fear of lack, and they don't want to suffer to survive. They want things to come easily and want to avoid crisis and change.

Focused on the past, they are deeply connected to their memories, and some are pack rats, saving small items that remind them of good times in their lives. They are nostalgic, struggling with forgiving and releasing outdated energy. Holding on to material things and emotions are a way for them to keep things the same.

They shine when they can make their own money. Persistent, strong, financially calculating, they don't give up easily. In fact, being stubborn and strong-willed can help them be patient. Even if they are struggling, it can be hard for them to accept help from others. It's important that they learn to listen to other people's ideas and opinions.

Accumulating possessions and living in luxury can help them connect to the earth. In fact, having money and financial security is one of the most important things to them. Having stability and comfort is important for them to be happy. Releasing their grip on material possessions can lighten the heaviness of accumulation. If they can harness letting go, they will be able to connect with what is most valuable to them.

Moon in the Second House

These individuals will find emotional fulfillment through feeling financially secure. They want to make sure their basic needs are met. So having material things, saving money in the bank, owning a home, and having a stable job are important for them. Sometimes they worry about losing people or struggling financially. Oftentimes, their worries are irrational and based on fear. No matter how much money they save, they can feel a sense of lack. Once they have financial security, later in life they can focus more on what brings them joy.

They are calm and need a peaceful environment to live and work in. Stress can impact their emotions and cause anxiety. It's important they experience comfort and stability or they can worry needlessly. Emotional fulfillment can come through figuring out what they truly value. Their sense of self-esteem can increase when they learn to believe in themselves. If they can trust the universe more to provide for their basic needs, then they will thrive. Money doesn't always bring happiness. Because they want to succeed, they can struggle with realizing what they value the most. Later in life they often realize that good health, happiness, love, and harmonious relationships are more important than wealth.

Fluctuations in income can impact their thoughts, feelings, and happiness. In fact, this is one of the thriftiest placements of the Moon. It can make it difficult for them to spend money or splurge on themselves. Saving money for a rainy day helps them feel in control of their life and finances. Life happens and there are always unexpected things that change. It's not uncommon for their finances to go through many ups and downs. Trying to control how other people spend money can cause serious issues with romantic partners, friends, and children.

They can often dig their heels in because they are stubborn, rigid, and resistant to change. Because they often feel they are right, it's difficult to change their mind or traditional beliefs. Their relationships improve when they can truly listen to others and are able to learn the art of compromise.

Emotionally possessive, jealous, and affectionate, they need intimate relationships and physical intimacy in their lives. Because they are reliable and dependable, they can make committed and loyal partners. They need friends and people in their life whom they can trust and rely on.

Any kind of change is difficult for them. They avoid crisis and drama because they prefer experiencing harmony and peace. Any kind of unexpected event or upheaval makes them nervous. They prefer to stay balanced emotionally. For them to do that, they often move slowly, planning each step they make, and this helps them feel balanced.

Creative, imaginative, and artistic, they can make money pursuing their artistic hobbies. Laid-back, easygoing, and comfort loving, they like to relax and enjoy good food. Pets can bring joy and support their need for affection. If they learn to harness financial security, they can open up their hearts and take more risks.

Mercury in the Second House

These individuals reach their goals through communicating. They spend a lot of time thinking about how to make money and accumulate possessions. They might enjoy writing, teaching, journalism, podcasting, or anything that allows them to share their creative ideas with others. They can turn their hobbies into a business or make money in creative ways. Building financial security comes easily for them because they have a gift of connecting with the right people who can benefit them.

Slow to open up, they are patient and try to get to know others before they share too much. Excellent listeners, many people enjoy sharing their problems with them. Because of their stable and practical approach, they can give excellent advice.

Communicating with other talented people can open doors and opportunities. Deeply connected to their beliefs, they can be rigid and believe their way of doing things is the best.

Learning to value their mind and what other people think can help them reach their goals. Naturally charming, they might have a way of convincing people to do something, which makes them a good salesperson. They need to learn to harness connections and show generosity to those who support them.

Venus in the Second House

These individuals are creative, affectionate, and easygoing. They have a magnetism and allure that attracts others. In fact, there can be something soothing about them that makes other people feel calm and relaxed. Pursuing pleasure, artistic pursuits, and interacting with others socially bring greater harmony into their lives. Because they are friendly, magnetic, and attractive, many people want to be around them. It is hard not to like them, because they have a way of making people feel loved, supported, and cherished.

In relationships, they need stability in love. Love interests usually have money and are financially successful. But the most important thing to them is loyalty and commitment. Sometimes possessive in relationships, they like to know where they stand with partners. They often prefer dating someone who is more successful than they are. Because they are hardworking and achievement focused, they expect their partner to be also. They can be attracted to a partner who is wealthy and can support them financially. Although, they also care about affection and being in love, which makes them have high expectations in relationships. They are reliable partners other people can depend on. In fact, they expect others to be just as dedicated and invested in the relationship as they are. If they feel someone isn't, they are able to move on and look for someone who fits their needs.

Many have artistic abilities, singing abilities, or a desire to express their sensitive side through creativity. Because they like nice things, they can overindulge in sensual pleasures such as food, sex, or sleep. They like to own beautiful possessions, purchase art, and decorate their home and office.

Financial security brings peace and enables them to pursue their hobbies. They like to spend money on themselves and others and can have extravagant tastes. After all, they enjoy the good things in life. If they can learn to harness their sensuality, they can connect to pleasure, happiness, and joy.

Mars in the Second House

These individuals are determined and assertive, so they go after what they want. There is a competitive streak when it comes to obtaining material resources. They dedicate their energy to passionately pursuing their goals. Courageous and intense, they are driven to accumulate possessions and obtain financial independence.

Passionate and driven to accumulate money, they are aggressive in their approach to success. Fierce and energetic, they worry about not having enough money, so they strive to obtain it no matter the cost. They can sacrifice long hours working and depriving themselves of luxury to obtain stability.

Difficulties often come from impulsiveness, overspending, and taking unnecessary financial risks. But they are lucky and can quickly recover from losses and debts. They are strong-willed, determined, and impatient when it comes to getting what they want. Waiting can be difficult, and they lack patience when emotions are involved.

Savvy, calculating, and enterprising when it comes to earning money, they always find a way to attract people who can benefit them. Many are natural entrepreneurs and might own their own business.

Financial security and material stability are tied to their sense of self-worth. Money doesn't always bring happiness. They feel they must have all their needs met before they can give to others. In many ways, they need to connect with what is truly valuable to them. Their self-centered approach to earning and spending money can cause arguments with others.

Experiencing peace, love, and harmony is crucial for their overall well-being. They often find it easier to do these things later in life. Learning to balance between what they want and what they actually need can help them find a deeper value in life. If they can harness a strong sense of self-worth, they will realize that money does not always bring happiness, it can just make life easier.

Jupiter in the Second House

These individuals are lucky with money and accumulate material things easily. They enjoy nice things and can have expensive tastes in food, clothing, antiques, and travel. Money can be made through travel and connecting to people they meet through social events. Helping others can bring positivity, comfort, and happiness into their lives.

Abundance comes when they harness the energy of manifestation. Thinking positively and believing they can have what they want helps them attract good fortune. This is a lucky placement, which can bless them with a generous, optimistic, and expressive way of sharing their resources.

Although, it's good to be cautious about overindulgence, extravagance, and overspending because those behaviors can create problems if they aren't careful. Having balance is the key for continued security and stability. Spending money on outdoor activities, education, and travel can help them connect to their self-worth. Because they value learning, creative ideas, and open-mindedness from others, having friends and groups to be part of can be supportive. If they can harness the natural energy of abundance and believe that they can attract what they want and need, life can provide what they need.

Saturn in the Second House

These individuals worry about not having enough money. Cautious, they don't like taking risks with their finances. Deep down they crave stability but often find themselves anxious about the future.

Karmically, they may have not had enough money, food, or creature comforts as a child. These past experiences can impact the way they view money. They may fear having to struggle to provide basic needs for themselves and their family. Because of these fears, they can seem frugal and cautious with spending. In fact, they prefer not spending money and saving it for a rainy day. They often feel like they have to work harder than others to accumulate finances or reach their goals.

Wealth comes slowly because of their patient personality. But they have to put a lot of effort into having what they need. Their hard work pays off and eventually they can reap what they sow. Control issues surrounding money can cause conflict with their family and partner. Practical, disciplined, and patient, they slowly save and plan for the future. Owning their home and having a retirement plan will help them feel secure.

They need to learn to enjoy life and accept gifts from others. It's difficult for them to accept help from others because they are super responsible. They need to remember that other people can assist them in attaining their goals, but they have to open up and trust.

As they get older, they grow wiser about what is most valuable to them. Love, companionship, good health, and happiness are things they often neglect until later in life. Gaining a sense of self-worth can be difficult because they are hard on themselves. They need to learn to loosen up and enjoy what material success can bring. If they harness wisdom, they can share with others what they have learned along their path.

Uranus in the Second House

These individuals can make money in creative, unique, and inventive ways. They like to own unusual items. Spending more than they make is common due to their need for autonomy and self-expression. Owning exotic items, antiques, or art or spending money on creative hobbies can bring fulfillment.

Financial freedom is what they dream of, but their financial stability can ebb and flow. One problem they often face is erratic changes in their income from unforeseen and shocking changes. Although there can be losses financially, there are also unexpected ways money can come to them. In fact, they might inherit money, property, and possessions at some time in their lives.

If they become too rigid or stuck in their ways, they are forced to grow. Digging deeper and recognizing what is truly valuable to them is the key. Their unique view of themselves and the world can help them find comfort. They don't have to make money in traditional ways; in fact, that would be difficult because they get bored easily. They prefer making money in inventive or nontraditional ways. They can harness change to awaken and realize what they truly value.

Neptune in the Second House

These individuals are intuitive and have a different view about making money. Deeply spiritual, they value stability and peace more than positions. They can be creative about how to obtain material possessions. In fact, they might like to collect spiritual items such as religious artwork, paintings, statues, and crystals. Surrounding themselves with spiritual images and possessions can bring a sense of security.

Financial stability can help them connect to their spiritual needs. Self-worth and self-love are important, and they value kindness. Feeling connected to their possessions can bring happiness, but they often are unfulfilled with the material things that surround them. They might prefer finding a soul mate and experiencing a mystical connection to the divine instead of making money.

Idealistic at times, they need to be cautious about being too trusting with their money. In fact, it's not uncommon to be deceived by someone they trust. It can be a difficult lesson that people are not always how they appear. If they learn to have stronger boundaries and be more realistic about finances, they can feel more secure. Sometimes they attract money easily and don't have to worry about having enough to survive. It can seem like the universe always provides when they need it most. If they can harness realism, it will help them balance financial and emotional needs.

Pluto in the Second House

These individuals understand that money equals power. Financial wealth and stability are something they strive for. They have a desire to accumulate funds to create change in their environment. Making money, finding success, and accumulating material possessions can temporarily fulfill their needs. But, in the long run, they have to transform and heal deep-seated issues of self-worth.

Driven and calculated in the pursuit of their goals, they have a stamina most people don't have. They are at their best when they are taking risks and pushing the limits. Happiness comes through more than just having power and wealth. It's important that they be cautious about obsessing and focusing too much on material things. It can be all or nothing for them with matters of security. They will stir things up, take rash action, and seek profound change to feel alive. It's like something inside them makes feeling safe, secure, and comfortable feel wrong. They have to get comfortable having stability and comfort in their lives.

They can make money through healing endeavors. Career fields such as energy healing, counseling, astrology, criminal profiler, and business owner can be attractive. They can make their money through diving deep into the hidden, secret, and taboo issues of society. They don't like to rely on other people to make money; they dislike owing anyone anything. Owning their own business and having complete control of their earning potential can bring peace. If they can harness self-worth and be more trusting, they can overcome challenges.

Planetary Transits through the Second House

When planets transit the second house, it awakens a desire to find comfort, security, and material success and brings a clearer focus on what you value.

Transit Sun

The Sun moving through this house can cause you to focus more on finances. For the next month, this can be a good time to invest your money or focus on purchasing something new. You need to focus more on what you are spending. You can tap into a powerful energy of self-reliance and courage. This makes it easier to overcome obstacles with an optimistic and positive attitude. This is a great time to accomplish goals and start new projects you have been putting off.

It's important to focus on what makes you happy and comfortable. Think about the future and your savings account. Don't miss tapping into this positive energy to create financial happiness. Pay off your debts, save some money, and create a list of future financial goals. If you want to own a home or pay off debt, put some money in a savings account.

You might have to pay more attention to what you value. Questioning what is really important in your life can help you realize that money doesn't always buy happiness. This can be a good time to think about how you can express yourself and build greater security and comfort. Harness this energy of lightheartedness and happiness and appreciate the little things that bring you joy.

Transit Moon

The Moon moves quickly through this house but can shift your focus to security needs for the next few days. As the Moon moves through this house, issues with practical matters and money usually pop up. You could experience fluctuations in finances and might have to spend money on something you didn't expect. For example, you might have a flat tire, or an automobile needing maintenance. In fact, you might have to pay more attention to issues regarding self-worth and spending habits.

Fluctuations in your mood can impact your money. This is a good time to figure out what you really need versus what you want. If there are money issues, this transit can make you face reality. You might need to get practical, determined, and work on developing a solid financial plan.

Your emotional fulfillment is tied to the state of your financial stability. This transit pushes you to get in touch with where you need to get organized and be more patient about security needs. You want to feel comfortable and reduce stress concerning the future. Harness determination and develop greater confidence in your ability to earn your own money. Trust yourself and your ability to have financial security. Believe in yourself and that you deserve financial success.

Transit Mercury

This energy forces you to think about financial matters. For the next thirty days, you will be focused on second house issues such as security, paying bills, finances, and debts. Conversations about money will come up and you might seek financial advice. Meet with someone you trust who can offer practical advice about making a financial plan. Listen to others and get advice from a professional if needed.

Network and join a group to chat about investment opportunities. You might want to spend money on learning about financial planning or take a class. It's time to get organized with your finances. Address outdated or problematic beliefs about money. There can be a greater need to communicate with your partner and others about your security needs. Fix issues before they cause anxiety and worry.

Harness communication and sharing your fears during this time to help you find a greater sense of security. Develop a routine and spending journal to get organized. Knowing what you are spending, how much, when, and addressing problem areas will give you a sense of control.

Transit Venus

This is about a five-week transit, but it can shake up things in the love department. There is an increase in harmonious energy. In fact, you can be more focused on showing someone how you truly feel. It's a good time to commit if you are in a lasting relationship and make it official. If you are dating, you might meet someone who is successful and can support you in some way.

You may feel a need to buy something you have always wanted. If you always wanted to purchase that special item, you might do it during this transit. Go after what you want and what makes you happy.

There is also a need to feel peace, comfort, and harmony in relationships. Spending money on loved ones is a way to show love. Surprise someone with a gift or night out at their favorite restaurant. You might be interested in purchasing beautiful possessions such as art, crystals, perfume, or jewelry. This energy can help you tap into your artistic and creative side.

There can be a tendency to overindulge during this transit. Make your environment prettier by rearranging things, hanging new artwork, lighting candles, or playing soothing music. Harness a sense of harmony and express your creative needs.

Transit Mars

This transit lasts about forty-five days. This energy can ignite your sense of passion regarding finances. You would like to have money so you can spend it. Impulsive purchases can happen during this time. In fact, conflict regarding security and the future can happen because of differences in values. If you are in a relationship, you and your partner might disagree on how you are spending money. You and your partner might argue about your spending habits. On the other hand, you might be more interested in saving money as well.

You might get promoted, or get a raise, or find a new job that pays more money. Because of increased determination and drive, there is a chance of jealousy, tension, and arguments with others.

You can feel energized right now and might have more energy to work toward your financial goals. This is a good time to think about what you want and need. If you feel like you have not been able to purchase certain items, this is the time you might demand to have them. In fact, you can feel a bit more self-centered right now and stubborn about what you desire. You might even purchase an expensive item during this time, like a house, car, or other luxury item.

Changes regarding your finances, security, and plans can inspire growth. Patience is thrown out the window right now because you want to act on your gut instinct. Because you can feel more confident, there is a chance you can invest in something risky or be drawn to gambling.

If you want something now, you will do whatever you can to get it. You are more courageous and confident at this time in your life and a bit rebellious. Because you are motivated to make changes, this is a good time to focus on what you value and what can support your goals. Rash decisions and impatience can make you regret your actions. It's important to slow down, take a deep breath, and think things through before you do something you might regret with your finances. Harness a sense of self-reliance and tap into the confident energy of Mars to reestablish what makes you feel supported, safe, and secure.

Transit Jupiter

This is a time when you can tap into expansive energy. This is a yearlong transit that can help you open any blockages with finances, money, self-worth, and security. Good luck and increased fortune often occur during this transit, bringing greater abundance.

You might get a new job or a raise. There is a chance you might start a new business partnership that can bring in some extra cash. There could be a hobby that you decide to pursue and get unexpected financial income from it.

It's hard not to feel positive during this time. Everything seems to be working out for you in the money area of life. You might feel more self-confident because you are now seeing the benefits of all your hard work. It's about time you experience increased success, fortune, and stability because it helps you feel more comfortable.

All this positive energy can help you feel better about yourself, increasing self-esteem and confidence in your abilities to earn your own income. Anything you plan and patiently work for during this time can be successful. All this feel-good energy can lead to overindulgence in spending and taking risks. Be careful not to overdo it, or you could take on extra debt.

It's important to make smart decisions and be more realistic. It's a good time to balance giving and receiving during this time. You feel more generous and want to give to others. In fact, you could donate money to a shelter for dogs or donate clothing or material possessions you no longer need. Releasing old possessions, ideas, and beliefs can attract a new positive energy into your life. Be careful of hedonism, because so much positive energy makes it easy to go overboard on sensual pleasures. Harness the energy of expansion to increase abundant energy and the ability to manifest your goals.

Transit Saturn

This transit can last for two to three years and increase responsibilities. You can feel more cautious about financial matters. There can be a fated feeling to all your material endeavors. You are being forced to get practical, organized, and grounded in what you really want.

Planning for the future can be your primary focus. Making money will be important, but you will struggle with spending money. Because of your fears surrounding lack and not having what you need, you can be more cautious. Issues from your childhood involving self-esteem may reemerge. It's a good time to heal these issues once and for all.

If you were raised in a home where money was scarce or you saw your parents struggling to pay bills, these insecurities can resurface during this time. Discipline, structure, rigidity, and realism can help you accomplish your material goals during this transit.

This is a heavier transit and brings a restrictive energy, and at times, you could experience depression. There is a seriousness and sense of burden influencing everything you do right now. Because the planet Saturn is the teacher, it can bring awareness to all the issues you have not been recognizing in regard to finances, self-worth, and values.

If there is something you have always wanted to do, like a hobby, job, or business idea, then this is a good time to start making plans for it. It's time to work hard and dedicate time and energy for what you want with patience, determination, and calculated steps. You deserve to manifest the future you want. It is time to harness wisdom and implement the lessons you have learned along the way.

Transit Uranus

This transit can last for about seven to eight years and it's signaling transformative changes to your financial situation. The energy is unsettling because it is affecting the area of life where you seek security and comfort. Increased income or wealth can come through inheritances, your partner, or through a job promotion. But there can also be losses affecting your money and earning potential. For instance, maybe you get injured and you aren't able to work as much or you get laid off. You could take on a second job to bring in more money or get a new job where you have to travel, which might cause you to spend more. Fluctuations in income are normal during this transit.

You might want to buy unique possessions and express your creative talents to make an additional income. Pursuing hobbies can bring comfort and build your self-esteem, but you can also grow through doing something creative and innovative.

Unexpected changes can come and might change what you value and need. There can often be an awakening that impacts your self-esteem and forces you to grow. For example, you might wake up one day and realize you're not happy; this will cause you to seek answers and rebel against the status quo. If you feel trapped and unhappy with yourself, this transit can force you to rebel and seek your own answers.

Planning for the future is not easy when Uranus is here because it likes to test you as soon as you feel comfortable. It electrifies, shakes up, and blindsides you when you least expect it. It's a good time to harness change and adapt to the new experiences that come your way. Release the past and embrace the future. What you value at the end of this transit will be uniquely different from what you valued before.

Transit Neptune

This transit can impact your finances for up to fourteen years and can inspire you to find meaning in your life. Financial matters can seem overwhelming and confusing during this time. Money in general can be something that seems illusive and there can be misconceptions surrounding financial obligations. In fact, money can seem trivial to you right now.

It can be a good time to focus on what is meaningful, comforting, and supportive to your spiritual goals and aspirations. Happiness can be found in deeper connections and by exploring what you truly value in life. All kinds of mystical questions will be influencing you now. Because you are seeking answers to the purpose of life and your own destiny, you might want to withdraw from the tedious routines you have done in the past.

Disappointment and loss can create suffering and financial struggles. Beware of falling prey to scams that convince you to invest your money. A desire to escape from financial responsibilities can cause problems. Try to see your money situation clearly and take off the rose-colored glasses.

This is a time when you can focus on meaning and increasing self-esteem. There needs to be a higher purpose in what you save money for. Whatever it is, you need to be clear about what you want and avoid escaping from responsibilities. You could be able to make money doing something spiritual, such as astrology, energy healing, psychic readings, or hypnosis. Harness meaning and connect to what your soul truly desires.

Transit Pluto

This transformational transit can affect your life for decades. It makes you feel like the universe is pulling the rug out from underneath your entire life. Pluto often forces change and transformation in areas related to security, self-esteem, and finances. Powerful feelings are at play and can impact your ability to feel in control. There is an unsettling energy that can make you feel insecure.

You might be tested right now. In fact, you can feel like what you value is completely changing. Losing something that was important to you can cause suffering, but also awaken a desire for reflection. It's not uncommon for deep wounds and emotions to come up to the surface. This transit can ignite major upheavals that impact your ability to feel comfortable. Hang in there and harness strength, because once this cycle is over, you can feel much more resilient.

The unsettling energy forces you to dig deeper and spend time in introspection. You have to let go of things that are no longer useful. Release, forgive, and cut the ties with old energy. Eliminating excess and things that are weighing you down can help you feel lighter. Donate items you don't use anymore, downsize, and clean out your closets. If you can harness the strength of letting go of the past, it will be easier to shift into the changes this transit brings.

Ways to Harness Taurus Energy

- Slow down and learn patience.
- Think through and plan for the future.
- Be determined but control stubbornness.
- Get outdoors and spend time in nature.
- Focus on stability and self-worth.

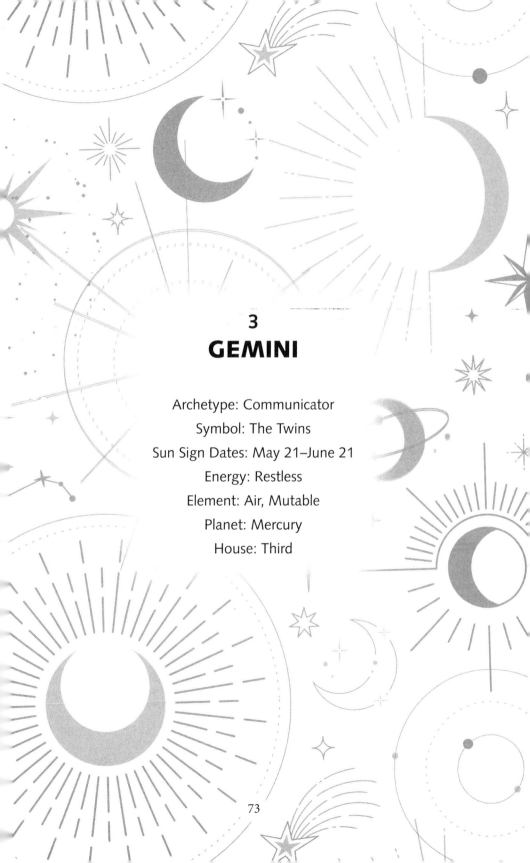

3
GEMINI

Archetype: Communicator
Symbol: The Twins
Sun Sign Dates: May 21–June 21
Energy: Restless
Element: Air, Mutable
Planet: Mercury
House: Third

I f you have Gemini in your birth chart, planets in the third house, or are experiencing planetary transits through the third house, this chapter will cover information regarding these energies. If you don't, you can still learn about Gemini energy and incorporate it into your life. The placement of Mercury in the sign and house will show where you express Gemini energy. It is important to look at what house Gemini falls on in your birth wheel, because this is where you will want to explore, learn, communicate, and socialize with others. Harnessing Gemini energy gives you an ability to express yourself through movement, words, writing, and networking with other people.

Gemini Energy Words

Restless, energetic, independent, talkative, intelligent, indecisive, friendly, scientific, studious, witty, social, communicative, hyperactive, superficial, observant, curious, agile, clever, gossipy, humorous, adaptable, knowledgeable, unreliable, scattered.

Gemini Motto

As a Gemini, I can be indecisive and need to be allowed to change my mind. I am a free spirit and I don't like to be tied down. I am adaptable and go with the flow. I am easily bored and need a lot of mental stimulation. A good conversation means more to me than physical affection or sappy emotional displays. I enjoy socializing and spending time with friends. Talking and sharing ideas makes me happy. I am restless and enjoy travel. Learning new things and pursuing hobbies makes me happy.

Harnessing Gemini Energy

Gemini energy is restless, quick, and changeable. This energy is unstable, friendly, and quick. Constantly changing, this energy adapts to new things. Geminis are intelligent, witty, sarcastic, and communicative. They enjoy reading, taking classes, traveling, networking, and communicating with friends. In fact, they hate being bored and need mental stimulation. Geminis are great at sharing information, discussing their interests, and making people laugh.

If they know someone, they can't help but talk about them in social settings. Sometimes they struggle to keep other people's secrets because they tend to repeat what they are told. They tend to gossip about people when they don't feel connected to others. Typically, it is out of innocence if they repeat secrets or reveal private information. They don't do it to hurt others purposely; it's usually because of their strong desire to talk. Geminis have difficulty being alone and need to keep busy. Developing social connections, allowing change, traveling, and learning new things are ways to harness Gemini energy.

Always on the Go!

Gemini energy is restless and always in motion. Their energy is fast and quick and always on the move. There is an uneasiness that pushes them to explore new things. Constant boredom can cause discontent, causing them to change direction or shake things up. Gemini energy is communicative, social, friendly, and adaptable. Mentally acute and intelligent, sharing knowledge is important to them. Their desire to learn helps them broaden their social circle.

Restless energy is content with being free and independent. Frequent travelers, they connect through conversation and flirting with others. They need to connect to people on a mental level. Speaking and writing are also ways they calm their inner restlessness.

Feelings of anxiety can make them overanalyze people's behavior. Observant, this energy is always aware of what is going on around it. Geminis sense other people's thoughts and analyze body language.

Born with the gift of gab, gossip intrigues them, and they like to be in the know. Because this energy is unstable and unreliable, it is hard to tie down. Committing to one thing can be hard and they always like to have two options. This energy is quick to move on and leave everyone else behind. In fact, commitment can be challenging for them because they like change. They won't wait for approval from others and are adventurous explorers.

Their restless energy pushes forward, always exploring. It is important for Gemini energy to stay grounded and take time to settle down.

Adaptability

Gemini is an intellectual air sign. Air is light, sharp, and clever. It gives them a quick, sharp, and fast mind that can solve problems easily. Air energy helps Gemini connect to their intelligence and blesses them with a brilliant mind. Like a computer, their mind is always on a high frequency.

Tapping into this energy involves adaptability and being open to new ideas. It takes time to analyze and figure things out, but this energy gives inspirational ideas. But we can't always find the answers through thinking. Sometimes we need to communicate with others, connect socially, read, and study to find out what we need to know. Knowledge is power for air signs.

Air energy is always changing and is sometimes hard to grasp. We breathe air, but we can't see it. So, to connect to air energy, it's important to connect to the mind. This is why the air signs are known as the communicators of the zodiac. Being gifted with a special way of thinking, they can accomplish a lot in academics, publishing, and can make excellent teachers. Adventurous and active, physical movement helps them think clearly. If they think outside the box and tap into new ideas, they can accomplish any task.

Easygoing Energy

Gemini is a mutable sign. Mutable energy is characterized by flexibility, understanding, and adaptability. Always changing to adapt to the environment, mutable energy never gets stuck doing things one way. Geminis are easy to get along with because they remain open to other people's ideas. Going with the flow in a relaxed way helps them adapt to change.

Mutable signs like to please others and strive for harmony. Flexible at heart, their ability to shift direction helps reduce stress. They believe it's important to be open-minded, so sometimes they can be indecisive and struggle making choices. In fact, they can see the good in many different things.

This energy needs to communicate their own needs and make sure there is a good balance in their relationships. Change is easy for them, but settling down, committing to something, or picking a course of action can be a struggle. Mutable energy can see all the possibilities and the positive side about every choice. If a mutable sign resists change, it's often because they have grown tired of giving in to other people's needs.

Geminis are sometimes erratic and can be unreliable. Everything they do is to keep a sense of freedom in their choices. Feeling trapped, micromanaged, or controlled scares them. Listening to other people's wants and needs is their forte.

Mutable signs believe peace is better than conflict. Due to an openness in all areas of life, they can seem flighty, when in reality, they are intelligent and mercurial. They love to hear all the variables of a situation because the more variety the better. Mutable energy helps us use our intuition, perception, and talents to get along with others. Tapping into mutable energy can help us have more fun and enjoy new opportunities.

Harness Thinking

Gemini is ruled by the planet Mercury. This energy is intelligent, witty, open-minded, and changeable. Mercury is the planet of communication, intellect, and curiosity. Quick, restless, and fast, Mercury energy rules writing, speaking, publishing, television, and radio. Anything that can spread knowledge and uplift the minds of others is mercurial. Mercury blesses Geminis with an analytical mind and sarcasm.

Because it's easily bored, this energy needs mental stimulation to keep invested in things. Sharing ideas with others and connecting socially are ways this energy works. Everyone can harness Mercury's energy by learning how to communicate better. Regarding relationships, if Mercury can't communicate with someone easily, it grows restless and quickly moves on.

Mercury blesses us with the ability to express ourselves through writing and speaking. It also enhances how we learn and remember information. Writing, reading, taking a class, doing a podcast, and teaching others something are all ways to harness Mercury energy. Connecting to new people, being adaptable, and opening up verbally helps this energy seep into the world. Wherever Mercury is in our birth chart, it will show where we need more communication.

Connect with Others

The third house in astrology is the house of communication, learning, and basic knowledge. Gemini and Mercury energy are associated with the third house. Our childhood experience with teachers and early schooling are influenced by what planets are in this house. Sometimes planets here can make it hard to sit still and learn in a traditional way. This area of life can also reveal how we learn and experience difficulties in retaining information or excelling in school.

This is the area of life where we socialize and connect to other people. Writing, publishing, radio, television, and early childhood schooling are third house territory. The third house represents our need to communicate, form social bonds, and express our thoughts. With the birth of technology, there are now many ways to connect. All forms of communication belong in the third house.

This area of life reveals how we interact with our environment. The third house represents our relationships with our siblings, cousins, classmates, and neighbors.

When planets fall into this house, there is a focus on communication and travel. Sometimes the third house encourages us to move around, get outdoors, and take short journeys in our neighborhood. This energy can make us desire a sense of freedom, exploration, and can push us to talk with others in our immediate environment.

This area of life represents where we find mental stimulation and often blesses us with natural teaching abilities. The positive traits of Gemini are found here and make us friendly, witty, intelligent, talkative, and restless. The third house forces us to study and to use what we learn to teach others. It's the area of life where we ask ourselves how we can communicate, network, and connect with other people. After we know what is important to us, we can share with others through all forms of communication. We can build communication skills and gain a sense of acceptance through teaching, writing, journaling, and researching topics we are interested in.

Gemini Rising

When people first meet Gemini rising people, they are perceived as high-strung, restless, talkative, and friendly. They can be risk-takers who enjoy meeting new people. In fact, the newness of getting to know someone is the most exciting time for them. They have a powerful impact on their environment and people feel them coming a mile away. Gemini rising energy is flamboyant, larger than life, and magnetic.

They can be seen as restless and unreliable at times, because others can feel an unsettled energy emanating from their aura. The energy they give off can make other people feel like they can change their mind at any minute, which is often the case. It might be hard to understand their dual nature. Gemini risings are adaptable and open to change direction when something new catches their eye.

Born with a high energy level and mental stamina, their presence makes others feel inspired to explore and accept change. People might perceive them as ever adaptable, funny, friendly, communicative, but also fickle. There is an airiness about their personality that makes others communicate and share things with them easily.

Gemini risings have two sides to their personality, as they are the twins. The energy of duality rules them. Change and variety drive them to seek knowledge and expand their minds. Highly intelligent, they have good comprehension skills when the subject is something they find interesting. If not, boredom drives them crazy and can lead to irritability and agitation.

Gemini risings thrive on change and find monotony excruciatingly hard to live with. It's hard for them to commit to one course of action. They are adaptable, and once they make their mind up, it can easily change with new information that comes their way. Because they can think fast on their feet, not many people can keep up with them mentally.

Their flexibility and unstable energy can cause conflict in relationships and with professional colleagues. Sometimes they say they will do something, but they forget about it or move on to something new. They don't ask permission from others; they just move on. If they start a project, they have trouble finishing it because a new project may fall into their lap. Or something more interesting catches their eye. It's important that they work on dependability and responsibility, because if not, other people won't trust them.

Because they like variety, they get bored easily in relationships, especially traditional relationships. Sometimes they do better when they can date more than one person. They are attracted to many different types of people, but a mental connection is needed for them to be physically attracted to someone. Often friends become lovers for Gemini risings. They need partners who allow them the autonomy and flexibility to be themselves and to come and go as they please.

These individuals have a heightened intelligent awareness in social situations and are flirtatious. Social chameleons, they can morph and become like those they socialize with. If people are happy, they can be fun and happy; if people are witty, they can quickly tap into their dark humor. Cracking jokes and making people laugh comes naturally for them.

Gemini risings can experience anxiety and worry. Overthinking can make them indecisive. Adaptable in everything they do, they thrive in a high-stress environment where things are always changing, and they tend to dislike rigid, controlling, or jealous people. Friendly at heart, they show they love you through talking to you about how they feel. Sometimes they overanalyze their feelings and overthink things until they don't know what they feel anymore.

Having mental stimulation is important to them, so playing games and discussing world events are some ways they connect with loved ones. Others might believe they are not able to commit to ideas, projects, or people. They rebel against authority, confinement, or people who try to make them conform. In fact, they might challenge others and purposely do the opposite of what people want them to do. Rebellious free spirits, they want to travel and explore the world.

Gemini risings need to harness adaptability as this helps them overcome stressful situations. They are sensitive to their environment and are prone to allergies. Physically, Gemini risings can look tall and thin, typically with long legs and arms. They feel grounded when they allow themselves to slow down, remain calm, and think through things before they act.

How to Harness Planets in Gemini

When planets are in Gemini, it enhances your ability to communicate, socialize, adapt, and connect with people.

Sun in Gemini

Sun in Gemini individuals have an active, restless, and changeable personality. Friendly, social, and sensitive, they can connect to others easily. Their wit and intelligence attract others. They have a secret twin who surfaces when they feel stressed or overwhelmed. In fact, the twins struggle to balance their thoughts and emotions. But they can be receptive, impressionable, and friendly.

They can find it hard to stay grounded and committed to things. They have a sense of wonder that pushes them to explore the world. They love to read and broaden their minds. Excellent communicators, sharing ideas is how they connect with the world. They have a great memory and ability to remember information that is interesting to them. Sometimes they appear anxious, nervous, and agitated, like they are always in search of something they struggle to find.

They might struggle with sleep problems because their energy and mind are always on high alert. Meditation might be difficult for them because they find it challenging to stop their active thoughts. Breathing exercises and active meditations where they can calm their mind are beneficial.

Feeling free and having a sense of independence is important for their overall happiness. Rebellious and freedom loving, if they feel tied down or controlled, they can shock others with their sharp tongue. Their words can cut like knives when they are angry. If they learn to harness calmness, they can feel peaceful and less stressed.

They love to travel. Wanderers at heart, they are nomads who enjoy movement, exploration, and adventure. They can be unpredictable and can find it hard to commit and complete things that they said they would. Change is a major part of their personality, and having variety helps them avoid boredom. If they don't feel like they are having fun, connecting with others, and mentally challenged, they can cut ties and change direction quickly. Sometimes other people feel hurt and take this behavior personally.

They find it hard to listen to others and often take over conversations, abruptly interrupting others because their energy forcefully expresses itself. It's important that they practice listening to others and giving people a chance to share their ideas. Sometimes argumentative, they have a strong drive to get their point across. Using their words is how they get what they want.

Geminis need to connect mentally with others first before they can be physically attracted and form relationships. Friendships, acquaintances, and social networks are where they shine. People love them because they are friendly and verbally expressive. Talking, gossip, and sharing every-thing they know in a trusting and kind way make others open up to them. It's hard not to like Geminis because they can make you feel like they really care about you.

On the go, fast, restless, and quick to change, they don't like to sit still. They are persuasive and can sell anything with their smooth talking. When they talk, people listen. Debating ideas and beliefs inspires them. Geminis like a good mental duel. If they can harness mindfulness, then they can still their active minds, which helps them find greater balance.

Moon in Gemini

Moon in Gemini individuals are friendly, open, and charming. They are restless and always thinking about what to say and need to communicate. Talking about their feelings can help them feel better emotionally. Indeci-sive, they make decisions based on how they feel in each moment. React-ing to fleeting feelings can throw others off. Because of this impulsivity, some may see them as unreliable and flighty. Emotional fulfillment often comes through connecting, socializing, and making friends.

They need to feel free and independent in their work lives and in per-sonal relationships. Commitment can be challenging for this Moon sign, because they often end relationships abruptly because they feel tied down. In fact, they often prefer dating and just being friends. If a project, relation-ship, or idea becomes boring or mundane, they can get agitated and move on fast. They need mental stimulation, excitement, and variety. Because they are often high-strung, it's hard for them to relax and be calm.

Learning is important to them and they like to accumulate knowledge. They can be avid readers and playing mental games can help them unwind.

These individuals can find their emotional fulfillment through intellectual pursuits. Born with the gift of multitasking, they can have several projects going on at once. Open-minded and accepting of other people's differences, they make supportive friends and coworkers.

Irritable and moody at times, they lash out at others when they get overwhelmed. They overanalyze their own feelings, which makes it hard for them to fully feel their emotions. They often prefer to intellectualize emotions and focus on facts. It's important for them to connect with their own feelings. Change and growth can be challenging, but they need to step out of their avoidance tendencies.

Comfort often comes through spending time with people they care about. In fact, they dislike being alone. There is a desire to have people around all the time for conversation and companionship. They like to be part of a mission, so being part of a group with like-minded people can be fulfilling.

It's difficult for others to keep up with their high-level energy and constant on-the-go mentality. Sitting still is difficult unless it involves reading, games, or intellectual challenges. Learning patience and developing listening skills will help them in relationships. They are good at talking to others but are not always the best listeners. Their mind is so quick and agile, they are always thinking of what to say next. Their thoughts are restless, so they tend to cut people off when they are sharing things.

Comfortable with surprises, they thrive with spontaneity and the unexpected. They are witty, humorous, sarcastic, and receptive and often like to show others how they feel through talking. They want people to like them and can adapt easily to what others want, sometimes neglecting their wants and needs. Contentment comes through variety even in stability. Harnessing friendliness helps them connect to others, which brings greater emotional fulfillment.

Mercury in Gemini

Mercury in Gemini individuals are witty and quick to react. Excellent communicators, they thrive when they are sharing information. Knowledge intrigues them and inspires them to explore the world. In fact, they like to know a little bit about everything. Overstimulation is where they thrive. Because they like to change their mind, they can appear unstable at times. They grow bored easily if they are not passionate about the subject. Daydreaming, fidgeting, and getting lost in their thoughts is common.

Fast learners, they do well in school as long as the subject catches their interest. Duality of thought helps them see both sides of issues. Communication is critical and expressing their ideas helps them organize their mind.

Impressionable and receptive, they pick up on what others are thinking in social situations. Talking can be a means of survival for them and they are known to find it hard to keep a secret. Sometimes they get sucked into gossip because they love to socialize with others.

They value logic and reason. Highly intelligent, sometimes they get so immersed in their thoughts that they seem detached. Their open-mindedness is a strength that helps them connect with many different types of people. Witty, they pick up on social cues that many other people miss. In fact, they often catch people off guard with a comment or dark joke that makes everyone laugh. They are entertaining, but others may think they are too logical at times.

Natural debaters, they like to argue their point of view and challenge other people's ideas. Charming and social, they can convince others to join their cause. They don't hold on to ideas and can shift what they believe quickly.

These individuals can communicate with anyone and make people feel at ease. Other people open up to them because of their ability to inspire others. They are excellent teachers and speakers who can motivate others to learn new things. If they can harness listening skills, they can find more fulfillment in relationships.

Venus in Gemini

Venus in Gemini individuals are attractive because of their sense of humor. While they are quick to fall in love, they can change their mind just as fast. Fickle, indecisive, and bored, they often rebel when they feel tied down. Monotony and restriction cause unhappiness. In fact, commitment can be challenging for them as they are attracted to several people at once.

Playful and friendly, they can charm others easily. They seem flirtatious and easygoing. Talking comes easily and communicating with others is how they fall in love. The friendships they make are important to them and they often fall in love with friends. They don't need sex or physical touch as much as most people do. It's just as important to them to have good conversation and share similar hobbies.

They can talk about anything but tend to feel uncomfortable expressing how they feel. These individuals have trouble connecting to deeper emotions and like to stay on the flexible surface of topics. They need a partner who is easygoing, adaptable, and understanding. They may feel comfortable in open or polyamorous relationships. Being allowed to be free and independent means a lot to them. Because they are curious and fascinated with anyone new, if they feel someone is stagnant, they become uninterested. They are attracted to intelligent, interesting, and unique people.

They are exciting in love and can make loved ones feel invigorated and cherished. Lighthearted energy flows from them and their amazing ability to connect with others in social situations is alluring. Harnessing commitment helps them solidify their relationships.

Mars in Gemini

Mars in Gemini individuals have an insatiable desire for variety. Restless, easily bored, and driven to explore new things, they can have an overwhelming amount of energy. Once things grow boring, they can feel drained. Passionate and talkative, they can talk for hours. In fact, they like telling stories and making people laugh with witty comments.

Many of them are great with their hands and can be natural athletes, writers, musicians, and artists. Born with quick reflexes, they might have excellent hand-eye coordination. It's important for them to have a sense of autonomy, freedom, and independence and an ability to express themselves.

They can rebel against authority or people who try to restrain their interests. Verbally combative at times, especially when they are upset, they have a strong drive to speak up. Their words can become targeted missiles when they are angry and cause harm. Intense emotions can quickly come up, and they can feel like they have to communicate them in that moment. Friends and family might spend hours on the phone listening to them analyze and explain every single detail that happened that day to upset them.

They are strongly committed to what they believe in. It can be difficult for anyone to influence their choices. They quickly react and sometimes talk too much, leading them to regret oversharing. Their energy is explosive at times, because they are impulsive and may feel like they have to verbalize it.

Nervous and restless, they find it hard to sit still and focus. They need variety in their schedule to avoid boredom. Irritated easily, stress can affect their physical body. They can feel drained from their constant critiquing. Intrusive thoughts can cloud their mind and make it difficult to sleep. Freedom-loving tendencies can make it difficult to commit in relationships. Also, their difficulty listening to other people's ideas can cause conflict and confusion. They are attracted to someone's mind and a good conversation is better than sexual intimacy.

They have a strong, confident mind, but they also can adapt to new information. Sustained interest in things is not common with this placement. In fact, they tend to take on too many projects, which can result in burnout. Their love of variety can become a burden if they don't learn to balance their goals. Darting around like a rabbit, they are quick and always keeping themselves distracted. They grow impatient with others, who are not as quick as they are. Harnessing patience in all areas of their lives will help them calm their restless energy.

Jupiter in Gemini

Jupiter in Gemini individuals attract good luck because of their friendliness and social skills. Adaptable and intelligent, they can attract opportunities through friends and colleagues. Good fortune can come through teaching, writing, communicating, publishing, and any work that involves using their hands. Sometimes Jupiter creates abundance, and they can become scattered in communication with others.

Because they value exploration, newness, fresh ideas, and intellectual pursuits, they grow when they can learn. They can have talents using their hands, such as playing an instrument, painting, building furniture, and fixing things. Highly intelligent, they are forever students who are always seeking to learn more about the world. There is often a desire to travel to faraway lands. They might even work overseas and live in a foreign country at some time in their lives. Expansion of ideas and knowledge inspire them to grow. They value friendliness, openness, variety, and social connections. If they learn to harness curiosity, they won't grow bored and restless.

Saturn in Gemini

Saturn in Gemini individuals have a fear of criticism. These fears can restrict their self-expression and ability to communicate with others. Uncomfortable with superficial conversations, they often avoid small talk. They are serious about communication and prefer practical and real conversations.

Feeling vulnerable in social situations can scare them, so they prefer being guarded to protect themselves. It's important for them to use logic to solve problems. Precise, accurate, and intellectual, they make excellent teachers and coaches. Heavy burdens and insecurities might weigh them down. They need movement and being outdoors can be beneficial to their health.

People might see them as introverted or socially awkward. Once they trust someone, they are more prone to open up and share information about themselves. There are karmic lessons surrounding communication, trusting others, and developing social connections. Letting down their walls can help them feel more comfortable with communication and making friends. It's important for them to harness logic, so they can use their mind to solve problems.

Uranus in Gemini

Uranus in Gemini individuals enjoy interesting communication and social networking. They seek freedom and they don't want to have to conform. Freedom loving and independent, they need to keep moving. Growing and broadening their mind with unusual ideas can bring inspiration. Change is important to them and they don't like to feel stagnant. Their aura draws people into their circle. Because they have an ability to charm others with their words, they can sway many people to their side.

They are drawn to unique, eccentric, and innovative ideas, so they might be interested in New Age philosophies. Things that are unexplained fascinate them and inspire them to grow. Imaginative and creative, they can experience flashes of insight or visions of the future.

Born with writing and speaking abilities, they often stand out from the crowd. Original thinkers and communicators, they can inspire others and make them laugh. Explorers, travelers, and seekers of knowledge, they thrive on original ideas. If they learn to harness originality in life, they will never be bored.

Neptune in Gemini

Neptune in Gemini individuals are imaginative and creative. They have a mystical energy that attracts others. Highly idealistic, they struggle to interpret what other people are really saying. Talking about deep, spiritual truths is intriguing to them. Boring, mundane, and logical topics make them restless. They enjoy exploring the depths of their mind and talking about unexplained experiences. Psychic experiences often come through talking and writing. In fact, many of them have creative gifts and enjoy working with their hands in some way. They may excel in creative pursuits such as writing poetry, painting, sculpting, or building things.

Empathic and highly sensitive to their environment, they are sensitive to their people's energy and especially to what people say. They pick up on the subtle energies and body language of others. They are very perceptive and compassionate conversationalists.

Meditation might help them use visualization techniques to focus their thoughts. Hypnosis, automatic writing, or channeling information through speaking and writing might be a dormant gift they can tap into. If they can harness their imagination, they can be known publicly for creating new ideas, products, or scientific research.

Pluto in Gemini

Pluto in Gemini individuals are intelligent, alert, and intense communicators. Their communication skills tend to get them what they want. Powerfully persuasive, they can get people to listen to their ideas. They are commanding teachers who inspire others to grow and change. Transformation and healing come by expressing themselves through talking or writing. Their minds are always diving deep, so it is hard for them to quiet their restless thoughts. Deep thinkers, they enjoy research to find hidden truths and knowledge. Transformation can come through changing their beliefs and ways they communicate with others. For instance, they might be raised with dogmatic beliefs, but as they mature, they may cut ties with traditional ways of thinking. Their use of logic to solve crimes or unveil hidden information can become an obsessive hobby. Some might be interested in being a therapist, journalist, or crime novelist. If they harness deep thinking, they can solve many problems.

Planets in the Third House

When planets are in the third house, you express yourself by communicating, writing, teaching, learning, and traveling.

Sun in the Third House

These individuals are seekers of knowledge and love to communicate. They need freedom of movement and enjoy networking with neighbors, siblings, and driving. Adaptable, flexible, and intelligent, they make friends easily. Restless and impatient, they need mental stimulation. When they are traveling and seeing new things, they feel their best.

Connecting people is one of their talents. Forever students, they love to learn things on their own. They can be talented with their hands and succeed at carpentry work, mechanical abilities, drawing, and writing. Natural teachers, they like to share information and knowledge. Cheerful, social, and friendly, they connect easily with others. If they have siblings, they can play a huge role in their lives. They need to harness learning and accumulate information to spread it around in their day-to-day lives with those around them.

Moon in the Third House

These individuals will find emotional fulfillment through communication. Connecting with others and sharing similar ideas brings them happiness. Expressing themselves through writing and teaching people makes them feel useful. They possess a gift for teaching complex concepts in an easy-to-understand way. Breaking things down easily and talking about how to do things comes easily for them. People appreciate their down-to-earth teaching approach. Emotionally connected, they can adapt to their environment.

Charming, witty, and friendly, many people are drawn to them. They need to communicate to feel loved. Unstable, imaginative, and adaptable, their moods go through ups and downs. Sometimes high-strung, when they are emotionally upset, they use their words to fight. They need friends and family to understand their need for movement. Freedom loving, they like to be able to roam and explore. Being outdoors can bring healing and creative ideas. If they can find relationships with people who have similar interests, it encourages them to share their ideas.

Mercury in the Third House

These individuals have an alert and inquisitive mind. Communicating with people and handling multiple projects helps them stay engaged. They grow bored easily and can find it difficult to stay rooted in one place. Their mind is restless and always on high alert. Intelligent, logical, and articulate, this individual loves a good debate. At times they can enjoy arguments because they challenge their minds. They use knowledge and information to gain people's trust. Witty, humorous, flirtatious, and social, they attract many acquaintances. Gossipy and fickle, they can struggle with keeping secrets. If they know information they want to share it freely. They want the freedom to believe whatever they want and learn about topics that interest them. Networking and making social connections help them share thoughts in an open way. They need to learn to harness decisiveness to make lasting plans and projects work. Worry and indecision impact all areas of communication. If they learn to connect their beliefs to their emotions, they can find a sense of purpose. Mental stimulation is needed in all relationships for them to stay interested.

Venus in the Third House

These individuals are charming, artistic, and socially adept. They have an ability to use their words to sway others to their side. They like to talk about art, love, and beautiful things. Some might have singing abilities or a beautiful, soft tone of voice. Their social life is active with many trips and excursions. Natural writers, they can write about their feelings and love life. Love connections could come through travel or short journeys. They dislike conflict and can bring peace to difficult social situations. Natural mediators, they understand what people really need. Diplomatic and sensible, they can help others find common ground. They understand that peace and harmony are needed when working on projects, sharing ideas, and communicating with others. If they can learn to harness their magnetism, they can find that they attract everything they want easily.

Mars in the Third House

These individuals are blunt and direct. Impulsive communicators, they find it difficult to hold back or not share their opinions. Forceful, confident, and courageous, they aren't afraid to stand up for what is right. They have a strong desire to learn and speak the truth. Fakeness frustrates them and can make them lash out in anger. Clear and straightforward communicators, they enjoy sparring with their words. Friends, family, and love interests need to be able to keep up with them mentally. Emotional communicators, they aggressively seek knowledge, so they tend to know a lot about many different things. Forceful at times, they can scare other people away. Enthusiastic about learning new things, they often have a gift of working with their hands. Words can cut like knives and hurt others in their environment. They have to harness tact and learn to be more patient when socializing.

Jupiter in the Third House

These individuals are positive and communicate easily with others. Restless at times, they need to feel free. They may want to travel or enjoy being outside. Growth comes from pursuing and learning many new things. Siblings can bring support and blessings. If they can harness their natural optimism, it will help them overcome challenging times. The mind and thoughts impact their health and outlook. They can expand abundance when they focus on what is going right in their lives. Pursuing a variety of hobbies helps them quench their thirst for knowledge. Curiosity and openness to new people, ideas, and relationships will help them attract good luck.

Saturn in the Third House

These individuals have a serious and responsible way of communicating. Cautious and distrusting of new information, they need time to process ideas. They tend to wait and think things through. Slow to believe new things, they can be a bit pessimistic. Reliable, grounded, and disciplined, they can put a lot of effort into learning new things. They are studious and serious about their pursuits. They don't readily share information or how they feel. It takes time for them to open up and verbalize their thoughts. Karmically, they might feel uncomfortable in social situations or when publicly speaking. Many will connect with friends and family who talk to them first. Those who are more talkative can bring them out of their shell. Communication can be more challenging for them until they trust the environment, people, and social situations they find themselves in. These individuals need to control their thoughts to ensure they don't fall into depressive paths. If they harness flexibility, it helps them overcome pessimism, restriction, and shyness.

Uranus in the Third House

These individuals are original and inventive communicators. Independent, rebellious, freedom loving, and eccentric, they need to be able to express their ideas. Teaching, writing, publishing, and lecturing are natural avenues for them to share out-of-the-box ideas. Innovation is important to them because they may question traditional ways of expressing knowledge. They like to learn new things and avoid mundane topics. Boredom can force them to break free and roam in search of answers. Traveling and connecting with other people who share similar interests can be fulfilling. Fixed, strong-willed, and mentally confident, it's hard for them to open up to other people's ideas. Creative, imaginative, and nontraditional, they tend to look at things from a different perspective than most people. Sometimes they don't feel people understand what they say or listen to them. If they can harness originality, they can become excellent creative writers or journalists.

Neptune in the Third House

These individuals are imaginative and sensitive to the environment. Insightful and creative, they have intuitive feelings about people. They can sometimes read other people's minds or have heightened senses. Finishing people's sentences and knowing people's true intentions can cause them suffering. They see through what people try to hide. Secretive themselves, they don't always communicate easily with others. Deep, spiritual, and psychic, they are attracted to metaphysical knowledge. They seek deep communication with other people. Mysterious, other people don't know what they truly think or feel. Sometimes they overshare with the wrong people and can get hurt. Other people might hide things from them and there is a sense of illusion regarding communication, travel, and siblings. Idealistic daydreamers, they express themselves better through writing than through talking. Artistic, creative, and compassionate, they need to develop strong boundaries. If they can implement boundaries with others, they will be able to refrain from oversharing with people they can't trust. They flourish when they make connections with people who share similar mystical interests.

Pluto in the Third House

These individuals are intense, secretive, and deep communicators. Born with a penetrative mind, everything they express is intense. Deep, honest, truthful, and powerful in communication, these individuals have an ability to make other people feel uncomfortable. Their magnetic presence inspires others to share their secrets with them. Sometimes they dominate conversations and take control of what is said. Secretive, private, loyal, and a bit manipulative, they like for others to listen to them. They want to get to the truth and don't like small talk. Traveling and networking can bring out powerful changes in their lives. They reshape their ideas by connecting to the emotions of situations. Evolution, growth, and transformation come through allowing old views to die and embracing new ideas that foster growth. If they can harness transformation and allow themselves to trust others, they will develop deeper connections with those around them.

Planetary Transits through the Third House

When planets transit the third house, you want to socialize, communicate, learn new things, travel, and connect with others.

Transit Sun

The Sun moving through this house will influence communication with neighbors, friends, and family. This positive energy will impact you for the next thirty days. It's a good time to connect with people in your immediate environment. The Sun lights up a desire to share information. Focus on sharing and listening to stories. Everything gets busy, and you could feel more motivated to travel. Short trips and social events can bring new people into your life. This is a great time to tell others what you really feel about something. Clear the air and verbalize yourself clearly. You might feel more talkative than usual so make plans with friends and family.

Focus on what makes you feel energized and what topics you want to learn. The energy increases your interest in study, exploration, reading, and writing. It's all about self-expression right now, so if you are typically quiet, you will be more vocal. You can feel more restless and indecisive. If you have not taken a vacation, this will be brought up for discussion. Allow interactions with others and allow these people to inspire your mind. Other people in your immediate environment whom you typically don't notice will stand out to you right now. Change your routine and everyday patterns.

Transit Moon

The Moon moves quickly through the third house. Tap into this emotional energy for the next few days and communicate your needs. As the Moon moves through this area of life, you will feel more outgoing and assertive. You might have to communicate your ideas and feelings with others. Fluctuations in your mood can cause miscommunication and faulty perceptions. You might interpret what someone says incorrectly and take it personally. This is a great time to express yourself through talking and writing. Harness extroversion during this time to bolster social connections. Network with your neighbors, friends, and family. Casual conversations take on an emotional tone, stirring up inner feelings. Trust your gut instincts now and listen to what other people have to say.

Transit Mercury

Energy levels are heightened in relation to socializing and group involvement. There is an increased desire to communicate for the next month or so. Meeting new people is common during this transit, as is visiting with neighbors, relatives, and friends. Conversation flourishes and you feel like connecting with others. An urge to speak up and talk more than usual is common. You can't seem to settle down or relax. Mental stimulation makes you more curious and you tend to overthink things. Talking on the phone, driving around town, and shopping will connect you with people you have not seen in a while. There is a desire to settle down, but it's hard to settle down the electric energy impacting your mind. It can be mentally exhausting and you can feel restless.

Difficulties sleeping and sitting still can hinder your ability to relax. Reading, talking, writing, and solving puzzles can help you adapt to this energy. Make sure to be honest in all areas of life. Don't promise more than you can deliver. Harness mental energy to express yourself fully. Adapt to your environment and go with the flow. Implement a routine if you feel anxious.

Transit Venus

There is a desire to be more social and pleasant during this time. Passionate feelings are ignited and last for about twenty-three days. The energy of love flourishes. There is a desire to seek companionship and talk with others. You might feel more cheerful and able to mediate conflicts. You will feel like a peacemaker and want all social interactions to remain positive. This is a time to focus on fun, happy, and pleasurable activities. There is beauty surrounding you. You may have an impulse to decorate, enhancing your environment with art and attractive objects. Stop and take in the fine things in your environment and appreciate what you have. This is a good time to tell people you appreciate or love them. Venus brings peace and understanding in all areas of life. If you can harness the energy of peace, you can transform relationships.

Transit Mars

This energy will increase your passion for reaching out to others. You may feel overconfident, which can cause conflict with others. You will have more energy than usual for travel and exploring. Be cautious when driving or doing anything with your hands as you are prone to accidents during this time. Impulsive communication can lead to arguments with those around you. You will feel more assertive and argumentative. Share your ideas with others and take a deep breath before speaking. Try not to take things personally. Keep busy running errands and communicate your ideas. Harness patience and think things through before reacting. If people don't agree with your ideas, there is an urge to fight for what you believe in.

Transit Jupiter

This is a great time to communicate with those around you. The next year you will feel more friendly and social. There will be an expansion of knowledge and a desire to accumulate information. Communication with others flows easily and people will understand what you have to say. Beliefs that you previously held can be expanded and broadened. There are new ideas and attitudes that will change how you perceive the world. You will want to explore the immediate environment and travel. A sense of adventure and wonder inspires you to seek faraway lands. Movement is important right now, as you feel more restless. Learning new subjects and taking classes can bring positive ideas. Writing and teaching can bring in extra income. You feel more generous and hopeful than usual. Just make sure not to overindulge or share too much information with people you don't know well. Sociable, friendly, and open-minded, you will meet new people who could offer you opportunities. If you harness generosity, more opportunities will manifest in your life. When you give freely to others, the energy comes back tenfold. Enjoy this positive energy and tap into it. See the good in people and benefit from open communication.

Transit Saturn

This transit can last for two to three years and how you communicate can be challenged. You will feel more cautious about sharing ideas with others. Communication can feel like work and take a lot of extra effort right now; things don't flow easily. You can feel anxious conversing with others. You might feel hesitant to share information with others and cautious about meeting new people. Mental activity slows and strains communication. You will want to communicate about practical life issues and find solutions. Pessimism can interrupt open sharing of ideas. It is challenging to express yourself during this time. Small talk seems petty and you aren't interested in gossip. Karmic issues involving siblings, relatives, and friends can expose themselves. Serious topics are important to think about, although you might keep them to yourself. Dedication to knowledge will help you reach your goals in the long run. It is a good time to harness practicality and network with people who can support your future endeavors.

Transit Uranus

This transit can inspire you to change and communicate differently. New opportunities come into your life. It can last seven to eight years and cause a lot of unexpected changes. The energy is innovative, radical, and unique. Routines change and are unstable. Write, talk, and share your ideas with others. Connect and form new social connections. It is important to find people who are seeking similar answers. It might be time to join a group. You want to communicate in new ways and can shock people with what you say.

Dramatic changes to your belief system shift who you are on a deeper level. Allow change and adapt to new experiences that come your way. Instability in communication with others can feel exciting. You want to snap out of the boring social rules. You might be attracted to unusual ideas and spend time studying a new religion or philosophy. Flashes of insight and imagination can bring solutions to problems. You may feel inspired to write and feel more imaginative and creative. Unexpected changes can affect those around you. You might feel a bit rebellious and want to lash out. You will challenge rules and traditions. Harness independent thought and look at things from an entirely new point of view. What you were taught to believe will be transformed. When this transit ends, you will have an entirely new way of looking at the world.

Transit Neptune

This transit can impact how you communicate for up to fourteen years. You might feel more inspired to learn spiritual topics and communicate with others who share similar interests. There will be a shift with communicating with others in a more spiritual way. This is a time you will need to make emotional connections with people in your environment. Sharing stories, memories, and dreams of the future are highlighted.

Secrets and illusions can influence how you perceive information. Try to see things more clearly and don't idealize your beliefs. Deception can occur if you are not completely honest with others. Your thoughts might feel hazy, illusive, or difficult to express. You might feel more comfortable writing down your feelings. If you like to write, this would be a great time to use your imagination. Miscommunication happens because people don't understand what you are really trying to say. You may feel disappointed with those in your immediate environment. You might seek to withdraw and prefer being alone with your own thoughts. Escaping from everyday social activities and spending time in solitude helps you get in touch with what you truly believe. It's important to find people like you or connect with people who believe in the things you are passionate about. You might change your spiritual beliefs and want to travel to sacred lands. Harness connections and communicate about spiritual topics. Take a class to learn more about astrology, crystals, or healing.

Transit Pluto

This transformational transit can transform your belief system. This energy can affect how you think and communicate for a decade. If you used to be shy, this transit can make you more outgoing. If you had dogmatic beliefs, this transit will encourage you to grow. You might experience lessons that make you more open-minded. Pluto forces change in the way you communicate with people who are close to you. Powerful feelings and fears can arise. You can feel as if everything you have believed is being tested. Cutting ties with people in your circle and meeting new people is common during this time. New feelings and desires force self-reflection. You want to understand other people's perspectives. Any old and outdated belief systems will be destroyed and reborn. You will be forced to think differently.

Diving deep and researching spiritual topics such as the afterlife, astrology, and healing might help bring answers. You will seek knowledge regarding taboo subjects. Intense conversations and arguments can spur conflict. You might choose to walk away from certain people who are not supportive of the new you.

There is an urge to speak up and tell the truth. You can heal by expressing yourself or writing down your feelings. Your day-to-day plans can change unexpectedly. It is important to let go of beliefs, ideas, and plans that are not helping you grow. Eliminate negative thoughts and tap into your power. If you can harness telling the truth and communicating openly with others, there will be real change in your life.

Ways to Harness Gemini Energy

- Socialize and be friendly.
- Write and journal your thoughts.
- Travel and explore a new place.
- Take a class and learn something new.
- Communicate with others.
- Get outdoors and breathe some fresh air.

4
CANCER

Archetype: Mother

Symbol: The Crab

Sun Sign Dates: June 22–July 22

Energy: Nurturing

Element: Water, Cardinal

Planet: Moon

House: Fourth

I f you have Cancer energy in your birth chart, planet placements in the fourth house, or are experiencing planetary transits through the fourth house, this chapter will cover information regarding these energies. If you don't have Cancer planets, you can still learn about Cancer energy and incorporate it into your life. The placement of the Moon in the sign and house will show where you express Cancer energy. It is important to look at what house the sign Cancer falls on in your birth chart, because this is where you will feel emotional, protective, and desire comfort. Harnessing Cancer energy brings you greater emotional connections, heightened intuition, psychic impressions, imaginative ideas, and deeper feelings.

Cancer Energy Words

Emotional, moody, caring, nurturing, protective, intuitive, sensitive, romantic, imaginative, artistic, affectionate, loyal, private, shy, smothering, tender, gentle, loving, devoted, receptive, psychic, reflective, homebodies, passive-aggressive.

Cancer Motto

As a Cancer, I care about my friends and family. I am intuitive, sensitive, and feel other people's emotions. Expressing my feelings and doing things for people I care about are my priorities. I am affectionate and enjoy nurturing others. My emotions fluctuate and I need time alone in my home to reflect on my emotions. The cycles of the Moon impact how I feel and sleep. I fluctuate between emotional highs and lows. Using my imagination to express myself through music, art, and writing helps me balance my emotions. Being near water helps me heal.

Harnessing Cancer Energy

Cancer energy is caring, kind, and emotional. This energy is warm, cozy, and comforting, as well as slow and protective. Intuitive, perceptive, and psychic, this energy brings out deep insights through emotional connections. They often enjoy cooking, cleaning, protecting loved ones, and listening to other's problems. Cancers are shy and prefer to be home alone or spend time with family. They don't like being forced into large social situations and prefer small groups. Helping those in need can make them feel happy, and they like to listen to others' problems and give advice. If they know someone is suffering, they might do whatever they can to offer help and support. Sometimes they find it difficult to have boundaries with family and friends. They can let other's feelings and experiences affect their mood. People are drawn to their warm and caring energy. Cancers often hide their true feelings deep inside and only share with those they trust. Nurturing others and ourselves is how we can harness Cancer energy.

Harness Kindness

Cancer embodies nurturing energy. Their energy is warm, calm, and caring. There is an understanding nature that surrounds them and draws people into their lives. Moody at times, their feelings can ebb and flow. Emotionally perceptive, their nurturing energy is open, inviting, and absorbs things in the environment. They long to feel wanted and needed. Nurturing energy is needed to connect to the emotions of others.

Quietly, they listen and observe their environment. They pick up on subtle cues that most people miss. Withdrawing comes naturally as they are introverts who need time alone to recharge. They seek kinship especially on the emotional level. Worriers, they fuss over feelings of discomfort and the fear of the unknown. Impressionable, emotionally responsive, and gentle, this energy is aware of the needs of others.

Born with a natural motherly instinct, this energy wants to protect and show affection to those in their lives. Supportive, secure, and devoted, this energy needs to help people. They are connected to their childhood and can hold on to people, places, and things. This energy focuses on what can help other people feel better. It is important to have boundaries and find balance. We will want to look at the birth chart to see where we have Cancer to harness this nurturing energy.

Calmness

Cancer is ruled by the water element. Water flows, reacts, and is soothing. Always fluctuating, sometimes it's calm and other times it can feel like a tidal wave. We bathe in it, run our hands through it, soak in its warmth and coolness. Water energy helps Cancers connect to their feelings and intuition. Water gives them a perceptive, psychic, and impressionable energy. Like the tides of the ocean, water energy is changeable and has highs and lows. It can be calm and suddenly turn into a tsunami.

Tapping into this energy requires being more sensitive and vulnerable. Answers to problems come in flashes of emotional insights and gut reactions. It's important to learn to trust water energy, because it is rarely wrong. The best answers are found through the senses and connecting to our inner voice. Sometimes we need to be still and connect within. To connect to water energy, we have to focus within and connect with our feelings. Water signs are the feelers of the zodiac; they react and are instinctual. If we need someone to share deep emotions with, those with water energy will likely understand.

Take the Lead

Cardinal energy is associated with Cancer. This energy pushes for action and inspires others. Always planning ahead, they are rooted in leadership. This energy takes charge and motivates people to keep going. We have to be bold and brave when dealing with cardinal energy because it wants to usher in new ideas. Cardinal signs like to start new things and allow others to go forth and finish them correctly.

They are not known to be a flexible energy because they expect others to listen to their guidance. They believe it's important to take charge. In fact, sometimes they can push their ideas on others. They need other people to make their ideas become a reality.

Honoring relationships and being more open-minded can help them get what they want. Cardinal energy always sees what is possible with dedication, hard work, and planning. They can become bored easily, feel unstable, impulsive, and become risk-takers.

Listening to other people is not their greatest strength, because they prefer to run forward with a sword in hand and expect others to get in line behind them. True leaders, they take on the stress and the challenges of starting something new. They can feel their best when they can experience a sense of newness every day. In fact, monotony disturbs their ability to be creative.

Cardinal signs believe change is better than stagnation. Being forced to stay on one path can irritate them. Its confidence and innovative nature help them usher in what they want. Tapping into cardinal energy can help us think about the future, come up with new ideas, and overcome challenges.

Harness Intuition

Cancer is ruled by the Moon, connecting the sign to the tides of the ocean. Reflective, calm, and intuitive, Moon energy helps us find answers and harness emotions, feelings, gut reactions, and inner voice. The Moon governs desires, deep-seated feelings, and connections to loved ones. This energy relates to how Cancers feel; they want to help others who are suffering. The Moon affects our inner lives and stirs up feelings. Anything that makes us feel sensitive and vulnerable is related to the Moon's energy. Connecting to the energy of the Moon helps us dive deep within the soul and bring forth hidden emotions. Reactive, sometimes Moon energy can cause drama, conflict, aggression, irritability, and sadness. Sharing what we feel with those we trust helps us balance Moon energy. Always shifting and changing like the tides of the ocean, Moon energy brings heightened intuition. An inner knowing and ability to be empathetic comes from the Moon. Everyone can harness the Moon's intuitive energy by going within and reflecting. Expressing emotions through writing, listening to music, meditation, mindfulness exercises, or solitude helps us tap into the Moon's energy. Connecting to the past, our childhood, parents, siblings, and home brings comfort and an appreciation of the Moon's energy.

Get Cozy

The fourth house in astrology is known as the home and family house. Home is where the heart is, so having a stable energy in this area of life helps us feel comfortable. Cancer and Moon energies are associated with the fourth house. It's where we build a safe, secure, stable, and comfortable homelife. What type of childhood we had, our relationship with our parents, grandparents, and childhood friends, falls under this area of life. The fourth house reveals a lot about our instinctive patterns and behaviors. Traditionally associated with the mother, this area of life shows life situations that were happening when we were born. Were we a planned birth or a surprise? What relationship do we have with our mother, and what connection do we feel with her?

This area of life also reveals how we want our own home to be. Our roots and the family we identify with reveal themselves. Do we want a cozy home or a large expansive home? What we value in our home and family lives is something we need to think about. The energy of the fourth house gives us a sense of rootedness and belonging. The relationship we have with our parents is important to our emotional strength and resiliency.

The fourth house makes us focus on deep emotions and family ties. Cooking, cleaning, decorating, cuddling with pets, sleeping, and spending time with those closest to us is fourth house territory. Sometimes the fourth house encourages us to escape from the stresses of the world. It makes us want to stay safe at home and reconnect to the values that are most important to us.

Feeling our emotions and allowing nostalgia into our lives helps us remember that we came from somewhere. Grandparents can also be a strong influence in our lives. Caring, comforting, nurturing, motherly, protective, safe, warm, and secure. The fourth house encourages us to connect and reminisce about the past and our upbringing. Sharing memories and childhood photos connects us to the past. The fourth house is where we seek a home. It's the area of life where we want to seek refuge and safety. The fourth house energy encourages us to nurture, take care of, and love our families. We can build a strong, solid foundation at home even if we didn't have that growing up. Our current home and future home are just as important as our childhood home. We can start today and in the present moment to make our home our castle, a haven away from the ugliness of the world. The home should be a place where we can retreat, root ourselves, and find solace.

Cancer Rising

When people first meet Cancer rising people, they perceive them as warm, quiet, shy, and sensitive. The energy they express makes others feel comforted and taken care of. Cancer rising people are attractive, intuitive, and attract others who have pain. Naturally compassionate, their presence makes other people gravitate to them like moths to a flame. However, people also perceive them as private, moody, cold, or standoffish. Like a crab with a hard shell, it takes time for them to trust and be vulnerable. They are very protective of themselves, and they tend to trust their first instincts about people. Absorbing all the energies in their environment, they sometimes become overwhelmed with emotion and lose touch with what they are truly feeling. They are intuitive and need to trust their gut instincts. Withdrawing into their home to reflect helps them.

Cancer risings have a deeply sensitive personality; they have a shell that goes up to block out negativity. They enjoy taking care of friends and family. Safety, comfort, stability, and affection are critical for them to feel grounded. They have instincts, reactions, and feelings swell up from within that serve as messages to help guide their lives. Moody and irritable at times, their moods can fluctuate with the cycles of the Moon. Depression can impact them when they are in a stressful or toxic environment. They need a peaceful and harmonious homelife.

Cancer risings are focused on creating a comfortable home environment. They take things personally and can get their feelings hurt easily. They need time to think, as their emotions often take control. They need a few close friends to spend time with and they are happy. Because they are shy, they prefer a small group of friends or a quiet night at home. Sometimes controlling, they withhold information. Taking things personally is instinctive, so it's good for them to step back and realize that not everyone is out to hurt them.

Traditions and things passed on from past generations influence them. For instance, if they were raised Catholic but are not practicing as an adult, they may still want to get their children baptized in the Catholic faith. They are connected to the past and rooted in family traditions. Cancer rising individuals can be distrustful and cautious about trusting others. They dislike loudness, aggressiveness, and unkindness. Caring at heart, they show love through physical touch and doing practical things for their loved ones. Sometimes they worry and fret over the safety and happiness of their friends and family. If they have children, they will take parenting very seriously. Providing a nurturing, motherly, supportive environment will be something they focus on. If they are a parent, they enjoy teaching their children how to read, take care of themselves, and express creativity. If they choose not to have their own children, they might want to work with children in some way.

Committed relationships are important to them. They are attracted to people who are caring, kind, committed, successful, and supportive. Having someone to depend on is valuable to them. They need partners who support them, encourage their intuitive feelings and imagination, and help others.

Physically, Cancer risings look soft, open, caring, delicate, and innocent. Some have a round face and rosy cheeks. There is a warmth and openness to the personality that attracts others easily. Their eyes pierce deep into your soul and there is a sense they understand what you are feeling. Hypersensitive at times, they hide inside their shell until they feel better. The environment has a powerful effect on them.

Cancer risings need to harness protection as this helps them avoid getting hurt or taken advantage of. They need family and friends who will cherish them. They like to listen and help family when they need it. It's important that they also make time to nurture themselves.

How to Harness Planets in Cancer

When planets are in Cancer, you will have intuitive abilities, be interested in nurturing others, and focus on taking care of your home and family life.

Sun in Cancer

Individuals with the Sun in Cancer are intuitive and born with a need to nurture others. Caring and sympathetic, they are natural listeners. Calm and patient, they take time to listen to the needs of others. Natural caretakers, they know what other people need and can supply it. Security is important to them, and they thrive best in the home environment. Loyal to those they love, they enjoy supporting family and friends through difficult times.

Born intuitive, they can use their psychic gifts to help others. This individual might dream of the future or just have an innate knowing about what is going to happen. Deeply connected to the cycles of the Moon, their emotions fluctuate like the tides of the ocean. They can experience sadness for seemingly no reason. These emotions will shift and change but they need to allow themselves to experience them. Connecting within and implementing things like meditation, writing, and yoga can be healing. They need to trust their intuition and inner voice. They can find it hard to let go of the past and are quite nostalgic.

They need to feel that they have a family to rely on. Childhood experiences and the relationship with their parents impact every area of their lives. If they didn't have a loving homelife, it can affect them as adults. They need that nurturing and support from family, and if they didn't have it, they will work hard to build it themselves. Being a parent comes naturally and they want to teach and support their children. If they choose not to have children of their own, then their spouse, pets, and friends become like their children.

Entertaining in the home and spending time with a handful of their closest friends brings happiness. Cooking for others and sharing stories inside the home is the perfect weekend night for them. This individual has a talent for making other people feel cared for and understood. They listen, give advice, and comfort those in need. Emotional worry can affect their health. Possessive, controlling, and sometimes needy, they want to be involved in their loved ones' lives. They are connected to childhood memories and old love, which makes it hard for them to let anyone go from their lives. Letting go of the past can be challenging for them. Their first reaction is to feel. The crablike shell they have helps them protect their soft interior. Protecting others comes naturally, but they also need to learn to guard their own hearts.

Withdrawn and brooding at times, they don't easily trust others with their secrets. If hurt, they sulk and get quiet. They can resort to passive-aggressive behavior to show that they are hurt or get their loved one's attention. They don't easily communicate how they are feeling especially when they feel taken for granted. They need love and affection just like all those they help.

Creative and artistic, they like to express themselves and use their imagination. They also can be good at business due to a cautious and conservative approach. They hold on to money, possessions, and people unwaveringly. No matter how much money they have, they rarely feel secure enough. Emotional fears of lack can plague them, which makes it hard for them to take risks. Being direct can be challenging because they can be shy and introverted. Some might act tough, harsh, and unfeeling at first meeting.

Cancer Suns need to connect emotionally with others and share common interests. They shine in the home and family arena. Being useful, feeling needed, and providing for the needs of people they care about are their gifts. People are drawn to their watery, sensitive, open personality. People like to share their problems with them because they have a soothing presence.

Cancer energy feels like a warm bath or cozy cup of tea. It feels like home and a place to feel protected and supported when Cancer is around. Relaxed and calm, they take their time to make decisions. If they can harness nurturing abilities, their relationships will flourish.

Moon in Cancer

Moon in Cancer individuals are family focused and need a comfortable homelife. Traditional and family focused, they want to be married and have children. If they don't have their own children, they might enjoy working with them in some way. They are intuitive and sensitive. The most emotional of the Moon signs, caring Cancer Moons like to feel needed. Taking care of people and nurturing others is their gift. They are connected to the cycles of the Moon. During a full Moon, they might feel irritable, agitated, and experience difficulty sleeping. Some might feel energized, restless, and cry easily. It is important that they watch what the Moon is doing and how it influences their emotions.

Emotional fulfillment comes through assisting others who need help. Many are drawn to the medical or counseling fields where they can be of service. Empathic and psychic, they pick up on the thoughts and feeling of others. They have a crablike shell that can come up if they need to block out unwanted energy. Other people might perceive them as cold and rigid, but they only do this when they feel vulnerable. Once they trust other people, they are very caring and supportive.

The mother figure plays an important part in this individual's life. They can feel responsible for their family and friends. Happiness comes by creating a stable and healthy home environment. Cancer Moons are homebodies who like to withdraw from the real world to rest and recuperate. As a water Moon, they absorb everything around them and need time to heal. Focused on being a partner and a parent, they do whatever they can to meet the needs of those who depend on them.

They will find happiness through taking care of loved ones, especially their parents. They might feel responsible for the care of a parent when they get older either emotionally or financially. The ebb and flow of emotions inspires them to find their own patterns. Schedules are often based on how they feel, and they can change their plans based on feelings. If the homelife is not loving and supportive, they can struggle to find happiness. Emotional worriers, they can obsess and be controlling. They have to learn to trust other people. Committed relationships help them become easygoing. If they can depend on someone else to meet their needs, they feel less restricted.

Emotional fulfillment and happiness come through harnessing intuition. Trusting their own gut instincts helps them make more informed decisions. Depression can impact them, so they need their family and friends to support them. If they feel neglected or hurt, they can push people away. They are good at nurturing other people but often forget that they have needs too. Nurturing themselves more and thinking about what their needs are will help them find greater balance. Being alone can also be challenging for them. They prefer one or two close companions. Spending time near water can be healing. It helps them connect to their inner self. Trusting their instincts will help them make well-informed decisions. If they can harness intuition, they will become more creative and trusting of the world around them.

Mercury in Cancer

Mercury in Cancer individuals have a vivid imagination. Creative thinkers, many enjoy writing and teaching. Diplomatic, they avoid arguments but can sometimes be passive-aggressive when they have had their feelings hurt. They might enjoy working with children in some way. Traditional in their beliefs, their thoughts about childhood and family impact their decisions in adulthood. They spend a lot of time thinking about how they can help other people. Excellent listeners, they nurture others through communication. Artistic and creative, they may enjoy writing poetry and songs. They are the emotional worriers of the zodiac and tend to overthink. Deep thinkers, they can sometimes appear shy and quiet. Introverted and emotional, they spend a lot of time thinking about things that are important to them. Since they are connected to their childhood, they spend a lot of time remembering the past. If they trust people, they will open up and share personal information, but if not, they prefer to keep their thoughts, beliefs, and emotions to themselves. Imaginative, they often live in their mind, visualizing experiences from the past or things they want to happen. They have an excellent memory because it's connected to their emotions. If they can harness their powerful memory, they can excel at school and retain knowledge.

Venus in Cancer

Venus in Cancer individuals are sensitive in love and need predictable relationships. Comfort loving, they need security and emotional commitment. Taking care of people is how they show love. They connect to people's feelings and can sense if someone they care about is upset. Highly intuitive and empathic to the needs of others, sometimes they can be a mother hen and try to watch over their friends and family.

Sometimes moody, if things are not going well in their relationships, they can feel withdrawn and depressed. They are afraid of being hurt and guard their feelings. Getting too attached to people can be a problem if the feelings are not mutual. Sometimes passive-aggressive, they can give the silent treatment when they feel thwarted. They can be nostalgic as well, which can affect current and future relationships. This connection they feel to past friends and lovers can prevent them from accepting new people into their life. People in their life may notice a seeming obsession with past friends and partners, which can breed jealousy while they believe they are simply reminiscing.

These individuals have excellent memories, and they will never forget past betrayal. It will be hard for them to trust again if someone lies or mistreats them. They will disappear into their inner world and shell. Solitary activities like reading, writing, and listening to music help them process their emotions and express their feelings. Loved ones might not know how they are truly feeling because they process things alone.

They are artistic and creative individuals who often have many talents. Sentimental, cuddly, and motherly, they like to take care of the needs of others, especially their partner. Being possessive and jealous can impact their closest relationships. If they feel ignored, they can feel resentful, although they often avoid direct confrontation. They like to spend time one-on-one with the person they love. Quality time alone with their relationship partner or pet is comforting. Other people typically sense when they are upset, even though they try to mask it. Their facial expressions and body language tend to give them away. They are romantic, warm, caring, and affectionate partners. Harnessing trust will help them feel comfortable enough to open up and be more vulnerable.

Mars in Cancer

Mars in Cancer individuals don't like conflict or confrontation with others. The intense energy of Mars is often suppressed or watered down. They can feel a bit insecure in expressing themselves directly. Sometimes passive-aggressive, they become emotional about things after they pretend to be fine. Anger tends to hit them later and not in the moment. When they start ruminating on memories and experiences, the delayed reaction bubbles up to the surface. Their sex drive is connected to their emotional connection with others. Protectors at heart, they want to help other people who are hurting. Oversensitivity can cause issues in relationships with coworkers and authority figures. They can be argumentative and defensive when they don't feel appreciated. One little thing can trigger them to behave erratically or in ways that seem out of character. Brooding can create a sense of isolation and they can replay old pain and exaggerate memories. This individual needs a good routine to follow to create a healthy and happy life.

They need to care to act. If they don't feel strongly about something, then they don't care about it. They enjoy cooking, entertaining in their homes, teaching, reading, and writing. Fearless and caring, they do everything they can to fight for those they love. If they can be more direct and discuss their feelings openly, it will improve all their relationships.

Jupiter in Cancer

Jupiter in Cancer individuals are born with a multitude of artistic abilities and a great imagination. Gifted at helping others, they are committed and concerned about their family. The more they give to others, the better life becomes. Friendly, kind, and caring, they are good at comforting others. Passionate about making money, they enjoy travel and exploring different types of food. They have an expanded intuition and their gut instincts are rarely wrong. They will dedicate their time to supporting causes they care about. Being part of a charitable organization or volunteering can bring happiness. Harnessing positive thinking helps them manifest everything they want.

Saturn in Cancer

Saturn in Cancer individuals can be cautious about sharing their feelings with others. They often repress their needs because of their fear of being vulnerable. Nurturing others and themselves can be challenging. They feel like other people expect them to be the caregiver. Responsible, serious, and mature for their age, they often feel older than they are. Their relationship with their mother can be difficult and sometimes cold. The lack of nurturing from their mother can influence how they feel love. There is soul learning that involves nurturing. These individuals need to learn how to take care of their own needs.

Due to their childhood, they often take on the role of taking care of everyone around them. They can feel tired and unappreciated. Resentment can build up over time and they have to learn to speak up for their own needs. They want someone to nurture them and take care of their needs. There are times they are afraid of being seen as weak. They use their hard shell to protect themselves.

Deeply connected to the past and their childhood, they are sensitive souls. They feel responsible for other people's emotions and put a lot of undue pressure on themselves. Hardworking, dedicated, and devoted, they work hard for financial security and prioritize the needs of their home and family. Harnessing an ability to nurture themselves will help them heal the past and enable them to move forward.

Uranus in Cancer

Uranus in Cancer individuals are interested in making changes to family traditions. Unique family relationships and living situations influence their outlook on what the home should be like. Freedom loving, independent, and rebellious, they stand out from other people in their family. They care about their family but commitment can be challenging. What is known as a normal family life doesn't suit them. They break out of restrictive and old-fashioned stereotypes. Nontraditional beliefs about family can manifest like living with someone as friends or deciding not to have children.

Affectionate and friendly, they like to help others. Creative, imaginative, and forward-thinking, they have excellent solutions to family problems. They are sensitive and empathic, absorbing everything going on around them. Unstable emotions make them restless. If controlled by others, they will want to break free. They would rather be alone or just friends with someone than involved in a deep love affair. Their partner and family need to give them space to be themselves. Harnessing freedom in family and homelife inspires them to grow in new traditions.

Neptune in Cancer

Neptune in Cancer individuals are psychic and extremely imaginative. Compassion is the spiritual gift they use to help others heal. Deeply connected to the past, they have an interest in knowing more about their ancestors. Idealistic, they can struggle to see their homelife clearly. They have a vivid fantasy world that enhances their creativity. Insights come to them through their dreams and caring for other people helps them connect to a spiritual mission. Sensitive, they often lack boundaries, which causes them to grow tired of absorbing everyone's feelings. Intuition and flashes of insight give them answers they need to solve problems. Introspective, they enjoy writing and listening to music. They benefit from meditation, yoga, and being in nature. Solitary activities help them recharge. They are good at taking care of other people but need to prioritize their own needs. If they harness their psychic abilities, they can develop a deeper connection with a higher power.

Pluto in Cancer

Pluto in Cancer individuals are intense and deeply connected to their home. Passionate about taking care of their family members, they work hard to provide both emotionally and financially. Having material possessions and security doesn't always bring happiness. They often search for meaning in life and think about what they truly value. Intimacy, depth, and committed relationships help them grow. They have a magnetism that attracts people in pain. Powerfully intuitive, they are good judges of character. Natural psychologists, they are good at helping people heal and transform. Secretive and moody at times, they withdraw when they feel hurt. There is a strong need to nurture people they care about. They need to learn to trust people to make their own decisions. Protecting people matters to them, but they have to let their loved ones live their own lives. They have hidden creative talents and artistic abilities that they might do in private. Harnessing healing helps them transform old childhood wounds and move on from outdated family traditions that are no longer useful.

Planets in the Fourth House

When planets are in the fourth house, there is a focus on home and family issues. You often have a connection with your ancestors, family traditions, and childhood.

Sun in the Fourth House

These individuals are homebodies and enjoy being able to relax. They need a haven away from the hustle and bustle of the normal world. Being home is where they feel they can truly be themselves and find happiness. They spend a lot of time on chores, home projects, and taking care of their loved ones. A strong foundation and loving home are critical for personal development. Some individuals with this placement never leave the area they were born. Many take care of their parents or assist with their everyday needs when they grow older. Sticking close to their roots is natural for them. Connections to their family prevent them from leaving or exploring on their own. Their lives are often intertwined with their parents, spouse, and children.

Being a caretaker and helping family is where they find purpose. When they are younger, it's hard for them to leave the nest. Some choose to live at home with their parents, specifically the father. They might feel like they need to please their father and struggle to find independence. They often feel responsible for their parent's health and day-to-day care. Running the home makes them feel safe and secure. Kind, warm, and sensitive, they enjoy showing affection and love to those they care about. They can be imaginative, creative, and artistic.

Very intuitive and perceptive, they seem to have a sixth sense about what is going on with people in the family. They pick up on family members' emotions, thoughts, and worries. They can feel anxious and worry about the health of their loved ones. If they can harness energy by establishing a peaceful, calm, and healthy homelife, they thrive.

Moon in the Fourth House

These individuals will find emotional fulfillment through their family. Emotional bonds and family ties are important for overall happiness. Natural caretakers, they make excellent parents. If they don't have children of their own, they often nurture other people's children or pets. Emotionally, they enjoy living or being near water. Water can be very healing for them.

Changing their living situation or redecorating can make them feel refreshed. They need a stable homelife to feel emotionally secure. They may have not had a stable homelife as a child, but when they grow older, they want to find their roots. Feeling settled is essential for their self-esteem to flourish. They possess an intuitive gift and are very sensitive to energy. They often have a close relationship with the mother figure or a karmic relationship that needs to be worked out. Grandparents can play an important role in their lives, especially on their maternal side.

Compassionate, they enjoy helping their family and friends with their problems. Caring, protective, and involved, they provide a listening ear to many people. They want to feel needed by those they love, so they work to make them happy. Many are drawn to service-oriented careers or working with children. Unstable and imaginative, their feelings tend to ebb and flow like waves. Friends and family need to be patient and supportive during their emotional changes. If they can learn to equip their shell at the right times, they can protect themselves from pain.

Mercury in the Fourth House

These individuals have a desire to study and learn about their ancestors and family traditions. Their parents may have encouraged mental pursuits and learning games when they were children. They were encouraged to learn in the safety of their home. Their parents may have been involved in education. Their family poured their love of knowledge into the home and were enthusiastic about discussing different ideas. In adulthood, they will be focused on their homelives. They tend to worry about family, friends, and loved ones. They like to listen to other people's feelings and situations. Socializing in the home with a few close friends helps them express themselves.

Connecting with people through travel is common. There might be opportunities where they move and connect with people from other countries. They use their knowledge to connect with family. They learned a lot from their parents about communication. They enjoy sharing what they learn with those closest to them. They have an active imagination and creative talent. They may love reading because they can experience another life in the comfort of their home. Shy and introverted, they might find it easier to express themselves through writing. They may pursue a career that allows them to work from home. Mental stimulation is needed in the home environment or they can become restless. Because they can be quiet and only tell their thoughts to those closest to them, they need to harness expression. Through sharing their feelings with others, they will feel freer.

Venus in the Fourth House

These individuals want to be surrounded by beautiful things. They may have a desire to decorate and to have inspirational art or décor throughout their home. Happy memories of their childhood home inspire them to create their own peaceful vision. Some might enjoy playing music throughout the home or even have an art studio. Charming and social, they will enjoy throwing parties and inviting friends over. A harmonious homelife is needed for them to feel secure, safe, and supported. They might meet their relationship partner through family and friends. They dislike harshness and prefer a softer and gentler approach to conflict. They realize that peace and harmony are the most valuable things to have in a homelife. If they can harness beauty and focus on making their home elegant and graceful, they will always find it a place of support.

Mars in the Fourth House

These individuals are driven and want to be independent from their parents. In childhood there may have been conflicts in the home, specifically with the father. They can be passionate, aggressive, and assertive in their home environment. They may feel as if it is difficult to relax when home; they always feel there's something they should do. They can have a strong personality that manifests in their home environment. These individuals can enjoy debating with their loved ones. Issues that may seem small to loved ones are important to them because they get a lot of their self-confidence through their family. Outside the home, they may be introverted and shy, but inside their own home they are bold, straightforward, and stubborn. They can have an intense desire to have children. Teaching their children to be independent and self-reliant can be a main goal. Their high expectations and control over their children can cause conflict especially as their children get older. They don't want their family to feel insecure or unable to survive on their own.

Hardworking, driven, impulsive, and energetic, they work hard to own their own home. Being active inside the home is important, and they like to be outside gardening, mowing, and taking care of the needs of the home. Sometimes they might not know how to settle down and compromise. Their strong-willed nature makes loved ones feel like their needs are not valued. They have to harness positive energy, tame their temper, and learn to include their family in decisions.

Jupiter in the Fourth House

These individuals have an optimistic and generous nature. Stability in the home and family will bring good luck and blessings. They need to have a comfortable home where they can explore and express positive energy. They may have had a happy homelife as a child. If there were conflicts in the home, they would make them doubt their own success. Extravagant at times, they like to spend money on decorating the home. A spacious home makes them feel free. They dislike being forced to stay home more than most. Some would enjoy having land and a place outdoors to go spend time doing hobbies. Material success comes through family, sometimes through inheritance. Travel and exploration will help them appreciate their home more when they return to it. Sunny, carefree, and light-hearted, these individuals want to make sure their children and friends are taken care of. Financial debts can pile up if they don't learn to control extravagance. If they can harness moderation, they will always have what they need related to their homelife.

Saturn in the Fourth House

These individuals can be controlling and feel responsible for their family members. Serious and overly responsible, they often take on the role of caring for one of their parents. They might have been emotional support for one or both parents. They may have been expected to babysit their siblings or work at a young age to help pay the bills. They can be dedicated, committed people who want the best for their family. A parent might have been strict, controlling, or unloving. There might be karmic issues surrounding interactions with the father or an absent fatherly presence in the home. They put a lot of effort into being a good parent and being supportive to their family. Committed to family values, they can be traditional with rules and expectations. They need to learn to let go and have more fun with loved ones. Karmically, they feel responsible for those who took care of them in childhood, such as parents and grandparents. Heavy burdens and responsibilities arise later in life when they feel they have to step in to be a caretaker. If they can harness commitment, they will realize that they can achieve a lot more with the support of others.

Uranus in the Fourth House

These individuals need independence and freedom in the homelife. Having a stable homelife might feel stifling to them. In childhood, they may have experienced disruptive issues within the home. A parent could have been unstable in some way—family separations, divorce, or changing homes frequently is common. Freedom loving at heart, they are quite restless and need to be able to roam. Settling down in one home forever will be difficult for them. A born traveler, they want to pick up and go whenever they feel drawn. As a child they were rebellious and questioned authority. Traditions were not always easy to accept and follow. Family traditions could have also been unique in some way, like being raised on a commune or in a New Age religion that was different from their friends. This made them more open-minded and accepting to the differences in others. They questioned rules and authority because in their mind things need to make sense logically. Conflict with parents often came through disputes or breaking family rules. Highly eccentric and intelligent, if things don't make sense to them, they will rebel. They are not natural followers but like to examine and push people to open up their minds. Breaking free from restrictive beliefs, structures, and expectations play out in the family arena. If they can harness curiosity in positive ways, through learning and social connections, they can transform the home environment to help spur growth.

Neptune in the Fourth House

These individuals are born with sensitivity and idealism in all matters related to home and family life. Easily deceived due to a naïve nature, family life was an area where there was a feeling of illusion, deception, secrets, and hidden information. There was a feeling of uneasiness and mystery about family history and relatives. There is a strong emotional and spiritual connection to one's home. This placement can cause suffering and disappointment related to the homelife. Maybe they found out their father was having an affair, or that their mother was secretly struggling with alcohol issues. These secrets are often hidden from them in childhood. It's not until they get older that they are exposed and reality forces the rose-colored glasses off. They begin to see clearly as they grow older and wiser.

Insightful, empathic, and psychic, they sense and feel the emotions of family members. Learning to trust their inner voice is important, as well as listening to their feelings. Sadness can come through unmet needs and expectations from family, especially parents. They might have felt lonely as a child and spent time playing with imaginary friends. Highly imaginative, this gift helped them escape from the stresses of family life. There could have been times they had to take care of one of their parents or boundaries were blurred in the home, which put more pressure and responsibilities on them. Secretive themselves, they don't always share with their loved ones. Deep, spiritual, and artistic, they want their home to be a place to retreat to find purpose. They might want spiritual artwork, crystals, and candles surrounding them. These individuals may have been taken advantage of or had their innocence betrayed by a family member, often someone they trusted to protect them. Easily impressionable, they need to learn the difficult lesson of having boundaries. If they can harness realism with others, they will see that people and situations possess both positive and negative energies. People are human and make mistakes, especially our parents.

Pluto in the Fourth House

These individuals often experience powerful emotional upheavals and changes within the home. Challenges and power struggles can occur with parents. These individuals are intense, deep, and truthful. If the family has hidden issues, they are good at exposing them. When they try to force their parents to be honest about the issues in the home, they can be met with resistance. Not everyone is comfortable with taboo subjects such as death, loss, addiction, and sexuality. They feel comfortable discussing taboo topics in the home, but often find others are unsettled by these conversations. Connecting deeply with others, especially their parents, is important to them. Deep, perceptive, and assertive, this individual will force their will on the family. They won't take no for an answer when discussing family secrets and emotional wounds.

Digging deep and exposing the truth is essential for them. There could have been a loss of a parent, sibling, or someone close to them in the family at a young age. As they grow older, they will be able to heal these wounds and help other people who experienced similar losses. They can dominate and take charge in the home environment. Keeping their homelife private and ensuring only those who are loyal are allowed into their inner sanctum helps them feel safe. Power struggles occur with their own spouses and children as they build their adult homelife. Past issues can influence their lives. Healing and addressing childhood trauma or hurts will help them build a healthier and more stable homelife. Transformation and rebirth are themes that impact the home. Forgiving parents and family members for wrongdoings will release a weight off their shoulders. If they can harness their power, they can overcome any challenges that arise in the homelife.

Planetary Transits through the Fourth House

When planets transit the fourth house you will feel more focused on withdrawing from the stress of the world, taking care of people's needs, and focusing on your home and family.

Transit Sun

The Sun moves through this house for about a month, and it will impact your home and family. This is a happy and uplifting time that can inspire you to connect with loved ones. You may feel inspired to visit your hometown or family members this month. Self-expression is highlighted and you may be spending more time at home. You need to make time for your spouse, children, and parents. There is a desire to retreat and withdraw from the outside world. If you are typically outgoing, you might feel a pull to find solitude. Entertaining in the home and inviting people over might be a way to connect. This is an excellent time to focus on household projects and getting things in order. When you are focused on issues in the home, your energy magnifies. The energy increases your need for affection, comfort, and finding stability with a handful of close friends. Expressing your creative talents inside the home could lead to new projects or home renovations. This is a time to appreciate your family. Harness solitude and make sure to spend time reflecting on what is important to you regarding your family, childhood, and traditions.

Transit Moon

The Moon moves quickly through the houses, around two to three days, and will bring focus to family matters. When the Moon moves through the fourth house, you will feel more rooted and sensitive to everything in your homelife. There is a strong need to withdraw from the outside world and seek safety inside. Old memories will resurface. Unstable emotions can make you feel irritable, but this is an excellent time to clean, cook, organize things in the home. Harness family time to take a break from stress so you can truly reconnect with your loved ones. If you need time alone, allow yourself to take it. There needs to be a focus on self-care and doing things that make you feel rejuvenated. Contact your parents, grandparents, children, or friends and let them know you miss them. Everything you feel is deeply intuitive; trust your gut instincts.

Transit Mercury

Electric and energetic energy impacts your ability to transmit information in the home environment. Mercury is here for about a month. You might feel like connecting verbally with your spouse, children, and parents. This is a time you might bring up emotionally charged topics that you typically avoid. Communication about feelings will be your focus during this transit. Sharing thoughts, feelings, and memories can bring nostalgia. Remember the good times and don't overanalyze negative family experiences. Embrace the positive and share those memories with those you care about. This is a good time to write, journal, and express feelings. There might be a tendency to withdraw and overthink your emotions. Conversation can help you heal family issues or work out difficulties from the past. This is the time to talk and share! Focusing on the past issues of childhood can be both positive and negative. You can't seem to let go of important information or memories. Allow yourself to process these ideas, thoughts, and opinions with close family. Just let them listen and express it. Harness your ability to share messages to heal yourself and reconnect with family members.

Transit Venus

There can be a need to feel more affection from your spouse, children, or parents. Venus is here for a little less than a month. The energy shifts and reveals deep needs for receiving love. It is important to express your loving nature in the home right now. Cuddle with your favorite pet, your children, or cook dinner for your partner. Entertain in the home and throw a party. Invite your family over and make it a pleasant time to connect. You might be able to overcome past issues and work them out. A natural peacemaker, this is the time to nurture not only yourself but everything involving the home. This is a good time to decorate and make your home peaceful and serene. Connect with your parents because they might be struggling and need that extra love and support. Your home is your castle, and you want it to look and feel beautiful and elegant. Venus wants to share, love, nurture, and support your goals for the home. Tap into Venus's calming energy to unwind and relax. Show your family members that you love them. Do something nice for them or buy them a gift. Venus brings peace and compromise in relationships with family. If you can harness the energy of affection, you can feel love and support from those who mean the most to you.

Transit Mars

This energy will intensify conflict and disagreements in the homelife. Mars is here for over a month. Family members might take things personally and lash out at each other. You might feel frustrated easily. It's like raw emotions are sitting on the surface of your heart. You might be irritated with your partner, children, or something going on inside the home. Be careful about taking your anger out on family. Sometimes the source of your frustration has nothing to do with them. Connect within to figure out what is making you feel angry during this transit. Hold back harsh words and try to be more patient in the home. Don't lash out impulsively. Wait and withdraw to think things through before you say them. You will want to make changes in the home right now. This might not be what you typically do, so utilize this energy for success. Avoid power struggles and try to be more patient. Don't react with aggression but take a deep breath and hear everyone out. Harness the powerful energy of action during this transit. Tap into motivation and drive to create the homelife you desire.

Transit Jupiter

Jupiter transiting through the house of home and family will bring emotional growth. Jupiter is here for about a year. You will begin to appreciate your family and loved ones more. Memories from childhood and the past come up to be healed. Deeper needs are examined and it's a time to figure out what brings you joy. There is a heightened awareness of the positive things in life. It's time to count your blessings, especially with family. Allow yourself to tell your family that you are grateful for them. If there is any tension with family members, this is a great time to move on from it. There will be a need to expand the home, roots, and to connect with comfort. You might decide to travel or even move to a faraway place. There is a heightened sense of adventure and need to explore. If you feel cooped up and enclosed, you might want to purchase a larger home that gives you room to explore. Getting outside, fixing the garden, and decorating the home might bring joy. You might feel more giving and want to help family members see the bigger picture. Your generosity can be used during this time to help family members who are struggling. If there have been family problems, this is a good time to solve them. This transit increases your understanding of others and your family situation. Tap into the positive memories of childhood to get the most of this transforming energy.

Transit Saturn

This transit can last for two to three years influencing your home and family life. You will feel more responsible for your loved ones. This energy can come to teach an important lesson about your childhood. The relationship you have with your parents can change and you might feel like you need to take care of them. Old childhood wounds come up and you might want to distance yourself from your family. You can feel restricted and serious about family responsibilities. It might be hard for you to relax and have fun. Remember that Saturn is here to make you wiser. Learning from the past and cherishing positive traditions will help you navigate this transit. Parenting issues might pop up and you can change how you enforce rules and discipline. This is a good time to be introspective about how you were raised and think about what type of parent you want to be. If you don't have children, this transit can help you consider how you can take care of the practical needs of the family. Insecurities surrounding money, stability, and safety can surface, making it hard for you to trust. There is a sense of lack or a feeling that something bad might happen. This energy is forcing you to look within and feel uncomfortable feelings.

You have control of how you react to people, life, and situations. Controlling behaviors can cause conflict with family and friends. If you hold on too tightly to people, they might rebel and try to break free. Focus on your home and build new traditions. Harness family traditions that worked and that can be beneficial to your current and future home. The past is over and it's time to release old energy. Let go and forgive anyone from your childhood, including yourself. No one has a perfect childhood. If a parent was controlling, strict, or unloving, this impacted the way you nurture others. If you need to change how you show love, this is a good time to do it.

Transit Uranus

This transit shakes up your home and family life for the next seven years, causing many unexpected changes. The energy of change influences your roots, traditions, family, and childhood. Something new and unexpected often happens when Uranus transits our home house. The fourth house is where you find comfort and solitude, but this transit can make you feel uncomfortable. There is an unsettling feeling in the home environment, like something is going to happen that you can't quite put your finger on. Routines change and are unstable. New opportunities with work might make you have to move. Moving away from your stable nest can stir up anxiety. If your homelife has been boring, or stagnant, this transit will stir things up to create change. If you are not growing in the home or family, you will struggle to find stability during this time. Remember that this energy is here to help you escape outdated patterns of behavior or family routines. Change brings newness and sometimes we need a new home to help us move toward the future.

If you normally like to control things, this transit disrupts all your plans. It's best to go with the flow and expect the unexpected. Just when you feel things are settled, the energy rises again to make you adjust to something new. During this time, you may experience an empty nest and see your children leave home. There could be changes with your spouse; they might be home more often or change in some way. Sometimes things change with your work and career. Sudden changes of staff, leadership, and coworkers could impact your stability. It is a good time to release old conditioning from your family that no longer serves a purpose. Harness newness and adapt to the changes that come. Release the past and embrace the future with your family.

Transit Neptune

This transit can create a feeling of escaping from the outside world for fourteen years. There are changes in the way you see your family and childhood. Maybe what you were raised to believe, such as religious values, goes through a mystical and spiritual change. There can be feelings of illusion and even idealism with family members. You might only see the good in others and repress any truths you know. You see what you want to see. Don't be fooled by family secrets and lies. Take the rose-colored glasses off and face the truth about your family and homelife. It is time to see things clearly and avoid running away from past family issues. There might be issues from your childhood that are exposed during this transit. A possible secret, or even something you were aware of on a subconscious level but chose to ignore. These things reveal themselves now and can impact your relationships with family members. This energy can also inspire you to create a more spiritual homelife. Nurture your spirituality and belief system so you can connect to what is truly important. You might decide to create a spiritual room in your home where you can meditate, do yoga, and contemplate life.

There is a need to connect more with the meaning of life and what your soul purpose is. You might want to decorate your home with religious art, crystals, or candles to help create a calming and peaceful environment. Be cautious about keeping things hidden; make sure you are not

deceptive with loved ones. Communicate clearly and openly about matters affecting the home environment. Harness being clear in any areas that impact your home. The home should be where you feel supported, safe, and comfortable. This transit can open up blind spots in your memory about childhood, parenting, and relatives.

Transit Pluto

This powerful transit brings growth to your home and family life gradually, as this transit could last for decades. Many changes will happen in your home and with family members. Pluto is associated with cataclysmic change, intensity, death, rebirth, regeneration, and healing. Intense and deep feelings are surfacing now. You can feel like digging deeper and finding secrets from the past. Something private and taboo might be disclosed about a family member or something that happened in childhood. There is a feeling of loss and grief during this transit because there are deep-seated emotions that surface. Things are exposed and slowly everyone who is important to you seems to go through a metamorphosis. You might feel like you are undergoing mini rebirths and evolving as a person. The person you were before is gone and you slowly are embracing the new feelings you are experiencing. The home is where we need to feel comfortable, but there is a sense that something is lurking beneath the surface. You are tired of superficial people and family resentments can demand attention.

There is a feeling that your home environment can change at any moment. You will feel inspired to be more introspective concerning your upbringing and even explore the type of parent you are or want to be. There could be loss in the home, such as death of a parent, moving, changing jobs, or a child moving out to attend college. With loss comes growth. Your financial situation can grow and experience transformational shifts. Power and control issues can impact family relationships. Jealousy, possessiveness, envy, and insecurity can bubble up, making you feel vulnerable. You have to let go of a desire to control your home and family members. There is a sense of calm when you realize that security does not always bring happiness. Like a caterpillar bursting from its cocoon, you are transforming your entire sense of security. Eliminating old childhood fears or wounds will help you heal on a deeper level. If you can harness evolving and allow yourself and family dynamics to change, things will be much easier.

Ways to Harness Cancer Energy

- Listen to your intuition.
- Spend time at home.
- Focus on family responsibilities.
- Reflect on your emotions.
- Take care of other people's needs.
- Be creative and imaginative.
- Spend time near water.

5
LEO

Archetype: Entertainer
Symbol: The Lion
Sun Sign Dates: July 23–August 22
Energy: Lion
Element: Fire, Fixed
Planet: Sun
House: Fifth

I f you have Leo in your birth chart, planets in the fifth house, or are experiencing planetary transits through the fifth house, this chapter will cover information regarding these energies. If you don't, you can still learn about Leo energy and incorporate it into your life. The placement of the Sun in the sign and house will show where you express Leo energy. It is important to look at what house Leo falls on in your birth wheel because this is where you will want to shine in front of others, express your creative and artistic talents, socialize, and have fun. Harnessing Leo energy gives you an ability to have fun, pursue pleasurable hobbies, find happiness, and express your personality to the world.

Leo Energy Words

Courageous, generous, confident, friendly, affectionate, self-centered, artistic, theatrical, musical, creative, childlike, boisterous, fun loving, optimistic, charismatic, charming, flirtatious, dramatic, proud, playful, determined, loyal, regal, grandiose, bossy.

Leo Motto

As a Leo, I want to express myself fully. I enjoy performing onstage or being recognized for my talents. There are times when I need to withdraw after being social to recuperate. I'm friendly, romantic, affectionate, independent, and freedom loving. I don't like to take orders from others and I feel I should be leading the team. I want people to respect, cherish, and appreciate me.

Harnessing Leo Energy

Leo energy is happy, fun, and affectionate. There is a confidence and sense of dignity about it. Life is seen as a battle that they believe they can win. Leo energy is open, friendly, social, respected, and at times self-focused. There is always something to love and a reason to express creativity and self-expression. Developing confidence and overcoming shyness connect us with Leo energy. Developing self-esteem, trusting one's gut instincts, helps us align with this optimistic energy. Leo energy likes to be in charge, recognized, and treated with respect. This energy desires to express affection, generosity, happiness, and pleasure. It's all about having fun and helping us connect to the things in life that bring us joy. Harnessing Leo energy can help us develop greater confidence, self-esteem, and self-expression.

Harness Courage

Leo is the embodiment of lion energy. Lion energy is courageous, confident, and brave. It wants to be seen and noticed. Leos are respected and often leaders who face adversity. They have a sense of humor and like to make others laugh. This energy is bold and has a strong desire to win. Lion energy is affectionate, social, friendly, and fierce! There is nothing that lion energy can't achieve with a little hard work and a positive attitude. Being competitive, brave, affectionate, and disciplined helps lion energy win many battles. People like the lion for its ability to make us feel accepted as part of the pack. This energy helps us fight battles with confidence and an ability to include others in our journey. It inspires and brings out our creativity. It helps express our desires and passion.

Harness Passion

Leo is ruled by the fire element. Fire burns, roars hot, and can easily take over a situation. Fire energy helps Leo inspire itself and other people. Friendly, social, confident, and open, this energy attracts others. Revered, respected, and sometimes entitled, this energy wants to be first. Fire signs are confident, direct, and honest. Passionate, sensitive at heart, hardworking, and achievement focused, they don't give up. Flirtatious, friendly, charming, and creative, this fire energy brings a sense of excitement and fun to many situations.

Harness Listening Skills

Fixed energy is known to be strong-willed and stubborn. Fixed energy wants its own way and very rarely listens to other people. Everything needs to be planned, thought through, and organized to work. They don't like to be the one to start new things; they prefer to do things the way they always have. Change is stressful and difficult for fixed energy. Working slowly, diligently, and with a single-minded focus is their goal. Fixed signs can be very patient, but also restrictive and controlling. They want their own way. They resist any kind of newness or change to their plans. Listening to others is a challenge because they are set in their ways. It's hard for them to take risks. Feeling comfortable and safe takes priority. Inspired by hard work and tedious effort, they are patient to work hard for what they want. They don't expect things to be handed to them.

Typically, they are the ones who finish projects and are the people others rely on in a crisis. Some might see fixed energy as boring, repetitive, and too reliable. If you need someone to always be there and to trust, then fixed energy is what you are looking for. Committed, they go the long haul and don't give up easily. Tell them they can't do something and they will prove you wrong. Calm, stable, dutiful, and understanding, they will try their best to achieve what they want. If they can harness listening skills, their life improves. Fixed energy is focused on what they believe is right, and opening up to other people's ideas is not always easy. Sometimes they prefer to do things the hard way, even if there is a simpler way.

Harness Happiness

Leo is ruled by the Sun. Feel the warmth and protection. The Sun shines its light on us all. Without the Sun, there can be no life. It breathes life into everything here on planet earth. This is similar to how Leos make people feel. They make people feel loved, cherished, and supported. Sun likes to shine, be in the limelight, be seen, be noticed, and be admired. Its energy is felt strongly and hard to miss. Everyone can harness Sun energy by expressing their creativity and friendly nature. Showing others who we are is Sun energy. It can't be hidden or toned down. It's strong, passionate, bright, and confident. Bold, courageous, direct, Sun energy believes in itself.

The Sun lavishes healing and sustenance on us all. Wherever the Sun is in our birth chart will show where we need love, appreciation, respect, and self-expression.

Have Fun

The fifth house in astrology is the house of self-expression. It's where we have fun and find pleasure. Leo and Sun energy are associated with the fifth house. This area of life rules children, parenting, hobbies, and creative pursuits. Being comfortable to express our artistic gifts, love, and happiness are fifth house issues. The fifth house represents all the energy of Leo. Love affairs and where we shine in front of others manifest here. The fifth house inspires us and motivates us to get onstage and be in the limelight. The fifth house is where we focus on children, sports, gambling, and pleasurable activities. It's the area of life where we want to show other people our talents. Fifth house energy gives us confidence, specialness, and a special gift that we are meant to show the world. This house wants us to get noticed and get attention. If we aren't out onstage getting applause, we might be behind the scenes encouraging our own children to pursue these areas.

Leo Rising

When people first meet Leo rising people, they perceive them as attractive, dignified, powerful, and important. There is a charisma and charm that exudes into the environment. People are drawn to them, but they are also intimidated at times. There is an openness to their personality and people naturally like them.

There is a sense of authority they embody, like a king overseeing their castle. Because of this, others might perceive them as overly confident, self-absorbed, and attention seeking. They have a generous, friendly, and affectionate presence that can make other people feel special. It's hard not to like them. They are savvy and good at getting others to do what they want. They like to be respected, cherished, and appreciated. If someone makes them feel special, they are loyal and devoted.

Leo risings enjoy competition and challenge. They don't back down and possess courage. Confident, brave, and self-assured, they have a relaxed and laid-back personality. At first glance, they intimidate, but once they get to know others, they are very caring and generous. They are natural politicians and want to connect with people who have power. Making the right connections socially is a natural talent they possess, and this helps them reach their goals. They care about what other people think and deep down want people to like them.

Leo risings need to harness creativity. Many are born with an artistic talent, such as playing the piano, a beautiful singing voice, or artistic abilities. Talented in many areas of life, Leo risings like to be leaders. Perceived as laid back, fun, happy, optimistic, and giving, they have a lot of acquaintances. When they feel slighted or disrespected, beware of the roaring lion. Their temper can flair out of the blue, which shocks others.

They may prefer to be alone in these moments to lick their wounds. Normally, they are out in public and in a position where people notice them. Even if they like to hide behind the scenes, they can't stay there long. The universe pulls them out in front of other people and they often get recognition at a young age. They are lucky in their endeavors and able to meet the right people at the right time to open doors for them. Sometimes when they are younger things come easily for them. Success, promotions, job opportunities, and even love can fall in their lap. It's when they get older that they might have to work a bit harder to achieve their goals.

They are flirtatious and know how to give people what they want. When they harness creativity, they feel connected to a higher purpose and to other people. Many are natural leaders and flamboyant. Some might want to dress and act a certain way to get attention. Wearing bright colors, jewelry, and dressing in a unique way might suit them.

How to Harness Planets in Leo

When planets are in Leo, you will focus on having fun, experiencing excitement, being creative, pursuing hobbies, and getting recognized for your talents.

Sun in Leo

Sun in Leo individuals enter the room and there is a feeling that the queen or king has arrived. They demand respect and stand out from the crowd. They are confident, courageous, and self-assured. The lion is the king of the jungle and others look up to them for leadership. They can tap into their innate leadership talents to help motivate others. If they learn to harness courage, confidence, generosity, and their social connections, they can achieve great things. Happy, friendly, social, and flirtatious, this individual makes people feel special. Making them feel respected, admired, cherished, and appreciated will win over any Leo.

These individuals desire love and affection. Often great with children, they have the heart of a child. There is an innocence and kindness that emanates from them. Magnetic and charming, their energy is bright, sunny, and larger than life. They like to have fun and make people happy. If something is boring, they will lose interest and search for something better. They are natural entertainers and many have a creative and artistic gift. If something is challenging, they will work hard to master it. Many are strong leaders and some like to give orders. Sometimes self-absorbed, they can be very competitive and want to shine. They need accolades and to be recognized for the work they do. This motivates them to do more.

They like to feel romance and are known for pursuing people they find interesting. Commitment can be difficult at times because they are attracted to the feeling and newness of relationships. Loyal, devoted, and born with an ability to make people feel comfortable, they make loving relationship partners. They like to express themselves through sports and doing something exciting and risky. They work hard but also like to play hard. Bold and direct when they need to be, they will tell people what they really think. They attract followers and people who look up to them. Many are lucky and can manifest their hopes, wishes, and dreams easily.

Social connections and networking with the right people often open doors for them. They have a big heart and need affection. They make fun, loving, and supportive parents. If they don't have children of their own, they might want to work with children in some way. Self-assured and prideful, sometimes they refuse to listen to others. Stubborn and resistant to change, they prefer to be in control of their own lives. Freedom, independence, and having material security help them pursue their goals.

Moon in Leo

Moon in Leo individuals don't necessarily need to be in the spotlight. Emotionally generous, these individuals have a zest for life. Inspired when they are having fun, being able to express their feelings is important. Warm, generous, and affectionate, they like to support loved ones. Sometimes stubborn and strong-willed, they have a big heart. They love the feeling of being in love. This individual is fiercely loyal. They will defend their friends and family. Playful, flirtatious, and energetic, they enjoy making people happy. Social, friendly, and charismatic, they connect with other people easily. People are drawn to their warm, caring, and sunny disposition.

There is a desire to express creativity and pursue hobbies that bring emotional fulfillment. Emotionally, this individual needs to feel loved, cherished, and respected. There is a sense that their emotions matter more than other people's. They have expensive tastes, like nice things, and want to be treated with a certain level of priority. This energy is royal energy, and it wants to be recognized. Dramatic, theatrical abilities might lead them into acting. Children at heart, they enjoy playing with children even if they don't have their own. If they can harness their natural affection and express it to everyone around them, they will feel content. Giving love to others brings love in return. Spontaneous and adventurous, they want to enjoy life to its fullest. If they feel sad or depressed, it doesn't last long; they snap out of a bad mood quickly. Like the warmth of the Sun, they help encourage those who feel lost or defeated.

Mercury in Leo

Mercury in Leo individuals are confident and have an ability to speak and get people to listen. These individuals can believe that they are always right. Communication problems happen when they refuse to listen to others or take their ideas to heart. Sometimes they can seem like they look down on other people's beliefs or ideas. Rigid in what they believe, it's hard for them to change their mind once they decide on a course of action. Idealistic, sometimes they think big but lack the knowledge on how to accomplish something. They don't mean to be manipulative; they just know what they want and believe they know the best way to get it. A bit stubborn at times, they can be overly sensitive to criticism. They want to be respected, especially for what they think and communicate. Some are charismatic with words, excellent orators, and good at convincing people to do what they want. Savvy, political, and socially adept, they know how to communicate to get others to listen. They have a sophisticated way of communicating and know how to pitch their ideas to the right people. They are good storytellers but can also be prone to overexaggerating their own abilities. They need a creative outlet to express their dramatic and creative personality.

Their words can sway others because of their charming way of communicating with people. People believe what they say because they come off with an air of authority. They are great at seeing the big picture but often miss the small details. Persuasive communicators, they can sell their ideas and projects easily. They possess leadership qualities and are good at presenting, teaching, and speaking to large groups of people. Passionate and creative communicators, they need to express themselves. They can be gifted writers and creative thinkers. People admire their warmth, charm, and honest communication style. Harnessing open-mindedness will help them adapt to new information.

Venus in Leo

Venus in Leo individuals are generous and like to be in love. They can believe that their partner is special and they appreciate people who are affectionate, positive, and fun. They don't want love to be a challenge, but need others to respect, appreciate, and cherish them. They want to have fun and a bit of excitement. They need physical affection to feel loved. These individuals are romantic, loyal, and flirtatious but can have a demanding love nature. They need someone who is willing to take risks and be adventurous.

They enjoy dining out at fancy restaurants, giving expensive gifts, and having quality time with the people they love. Bighearted, generous, and friendly, they need social interaction. Flirtatious, they like their freedom and independence. Commitment can be challenging when the fun and excitement wear off. They enjoy the feeling of being in love. If they can harness affection in relationships, it will help them build lasting connections.

Mars in Leo

Mars in Leo individuals can have larger-than-life personalities. Charming, charismatic, and confident, they attract people with their positive energy. They are used to being center stage and getting a lot of attention. People notice them because of their high energy, assertiveness, and ability to connect emotionally with others. They are social and attract a lot of friends and lovers. They want to be recognized and like to be in positions of authority.

At work they are competitive and want to win. They make friends easily with people in power positions who can aid them in their pursuit of career mobility. Success is important to them, and many find it easy to move up the ladder at a young age. Driven to be seen and noticed, they are natural leaders.

Speaking in front of people and masterfully selling or convincing others that their ideas are best comes naturally. People like them, believe in them, and want to be part of their lives. Being in the spotlight can sometimes get in the way of appreciating other people around them. They can be self-absorbed and overly involved in their own goals. Misjudged for being narcissistic, they don't always realize when they are bragging, aggressive, or domineering. When you bring it to their attention, they will appear shocked and even hurt. They will try hard to change these behaviors because deep down they want everyone to like them. If they feel disrespected, the fiery temper of the lion can roar. Passionate, romantic, and generous, they want to show people they care. Stubborn at times, they get focused on achieving their own goals and can forget about the small details. They see the big picture but often don't prepare or lack organizational skills. Relationships with others and finding love are important to them. Committing to one person can be a challenge because they need autonomy. They like to have fun and take risks and maintain their sense of independence. Harnessing the positive energy that surrounds them makes them stand out from the crowd.

Jupiter in Leo

Jupiter in Leo individuals are fun loving and generous. They are social and have a need for adventure. Always on the go, they enjoy travel and exploring new places to eat and socialize. Dramatic, lively, and flirtatious, they are very charming. Travel, higher education, and learning will push them to grow. Learning new things and taking classes help expand their knowledge. They can feel like they know more than others and take a prideful stance about topics they care about. Overly confident, they know they are talented. Flirtatious and friendly, they love to make other people feel good. This individual has a warmth about them that is comforting to others. Their larger-than-life personality brings them many friends, relationship partners, and work connections.

Creative, artistic, and open-minded, they enjoy attention and praise. Many artists have this placement. Acting and theater might come naturally for them, because they desire being onstage in front of others. Love and romance are important and they are blessed with positive relationships. Naturally generous, they want to feel needed, wanted, and cherished in relationships, which helps them be more giving.

Fiercely independent, they dislike feeling controlled or smothered. Sometimes they look for approval and validation from authority figures. They want people to like them and spend a lot of time encouraging friends, coworkers, and loved ones to pursue their goals. They attract abundance and blessings because of their optimistic attitude. Not everyone is going to support them, but they are confident and have high self-esteem. If they learn to harness their creativity, they will attract opportunities and people who will help them.

Saturn in Leo

Saturn in Leo individuals might look and act older than they are. Super responsible, they can feel inhibited and doubt themselves. Self-expression can be challenging and restricted. They sometimes feel insecure and cautious. Their need for approval and acceptance from others might cause them to repress their larger-than-life energies. They are hesitant to be in the limelight or get too much attention. Finding the right partner to love often happens at an older age. They might be shy and wait for others to make the first move. Once in a relationship, they are committed and loyal partners. Being patient and learning from their mistakes, they will become more confident. They feel that everything gets better with age and they attract more opportunities.

Their conservative and restrictive beliefs about having fun, love, and affection will transform as they gain experience. They want to feel relaxed enough to be fun loving and happy but experience a fear of being criticized. These fears can dissipate with taking more risks and learning to be more vulnerable. It's important for them to learn how to express their feelings and creative talents. They have many talents, but they are very hard on themselves and measure themselves up to others they feel are better than them. Some might even downplay their artistic abilities and not believe they are artistic at all. Harnessing youth and remembering that life should be fun will help them build greater self-confidence.

Uranus in Leo

Uranus in Leo individuals are eccentric, nontraditional, and intelligent. They stand out from the crowd and don't want to dress, act, or behave like everyone else. They are unique individuals who want to be noticed and express their individuality. Innovative and always thinking outside the box, they can be seen as rebellious because they question authority. Sometimes they prefer to be the one in charge because they believe their decisions will be inclusive. Traditions from childhood may change drastically, and they can completely change their belief system. They seek opportunities that give them a sense of freedom. Their open-minded approach helps them accept others who seem different than society expects. Strong-willed and at times stubborn, they hold tight to their own beliefs. Unstable and uninhibited, these individuals are bold, confident, and eccentric. These individuals can have a difficult time following rules or listening to authority figures. Imaginative, intuitive, and creative, they have revolutionary ideas that shock others. Sometimes scattered, they can act erratically and want to force change. If they can harness discipline and develop plans for what they want to accomplish, they will be successful.

Neptune in Leo

Neptune in Leo individuals have a strong sense of purpose and an idealistic personality. Imaginative, they enjoy entertaining and can transform into many different characters. Often illusive, they have a subtle way of getting other people's attention. There is a mysterious quality they possess that is intriguing and gets them noticed. Many of them have an artistic sense of style and a compassionate side. They can make excellent writers, musicians, and artists because of their vivid imagination. These individuals are idealistic, naïve, and believe everyone is good. Born with a big heart, they are generous and giving to those who need help. Some might pursue acting and enjoy teaching. They have fun when they are onstage and can express emotions easily.

These individuals are compassionate leaders who guide others to connect to their feelings and encourage others to find meaning in their lives. Romantic and idealistic, they often get hurt in love. Illusion, secrets, and deception can impact their love relationships. It's important for them to be more practical and see people clearly. Trusting their intuition and developing boundaries will help them protect themselves from disappointment. They need a loving partner and spiritual connection because they are deeply emotional, passionate, and affectionate. These individuals can be more introverted and enjoy spending time alone doing creative hobbies. Although they seem social, they need their solitude to rejuvenate their energy. If they can harness listening and trusting their intuition, they will avoid situations and people who can take advantage of their kindness.

Pluto in Leo

Pluto in Leo individuals walk in the room and people take notice because they have a powerful impact on their environment. They have a magnetic and confident energy that attracts people. People either seem to love them or hate them. They can sometimes come on too strong and seem controlling. Dominant, they might be self-absorbed or driven solely on what benefits them. They can alienate people with their obsessive and jealous tendencies. They work hard to achieve positions of power and prestige. Having a high-level position where they can lead others makes them feel successful. They fight for what they want and have the determination to achieve it. They don't give up easily and challenges seem to motivate them to work harder.

They adapt to change well and thrive in crisis situations. Forceful and courageous, they are not afraid of uncomfortable conversations. They are direct, truthful, and intense individuals. They may experience emotional rebirths and physical transformations where how they feel, think, and look completely changes. They can attract others and have a passionate and deep interest in art, music, and love. It's difficult for them to be vulnerable because they are distrustful of other people's motives. Deep down they are caring, generous, and loving people, but their need to protect themselves from betrayal can impact their ability to connect with others. They may act arrogant, overly confident, or forceful in their expression. If they learn to harness a more trusting nature, their relationships will improve.

Planets in the Fifth House

When planets are in the fifth house, you will want to have fun, be playful, pursue your hobbies, and express your creative side.

Sun in the Fifth House

These individuals are born with many artistic gifts and talents. They want to shine and be in the limelight. Their charisma and magnetic energy attract others. People immediately notice them because of their outgoing, happy, and friendly nature. They have a creative personality that portrays itself in the way they speak, dress, and socialize. They excel at many different things and are natural artists. They express themselves through hobbies such as sports, dance, singing, acting, or writing. Being able to shine in front of others will bring them greater self-esteem and confidence. For them to feel happy, they need to be having fun and doing something meaningful. It might take a while before they realize their talent. When they start to put effort into mastering a hobby or skill, they have positive opportunities that seem to fall in their laps. They are noticed and recognized for their confidence in performing in front of others onstage or in front of groups. A good example of this would be a high school student who is in color guard performing center stage at every half-time show. Sometimes their performances have to involve other people. They learn that social networking and other creative people can benefit them. Many actors, musicians, sculptors, writers, and athletes have this placement.

They benefit by having children or working with children in some way. Because the fifth house is about having fun, being playful, they will want to have children in their lives. They are naturally happy, funny, innocent, and playful. If they don't have their own children, they often find happiness being an aunt or uncle or playing, wrestling, and being silly with their friends' kids.

There is a strong bond with the father figure and many fond memories of childhood. Their parents can be supportive and help them explore their creative talents. If the relationship with their father was troubled, it can be difficult for them to develop healthy relationships. Artistic abilities are often inherited from the father or paternal side of the family.

If they feel appreciated and supported in pursuing their talents, it will help them gain confidence and pursue their dreams. Their strength, stamina, and positive energy help them overcome challenges. True romantics, they gain experience through having love affairs. Commitment can be a bit challenging because they like to feel free to pursue love when they feel it. They have a skill for making other people feel happy. If they feel depressed, it doesn't last too long, because of their upbeat nature. They have an ability to move on quickly and have a positive outlook. If they can harness happiness, they can inspire others to focus on the bright side of life.

Moon in the Fifth House

These individuals have an emotional need for self-expression. Attention seeking, flirtatious, and romantic, they enjoy the feeling of being in love. The problem is that emotions fluctuate and change easily. Their relationships can be tumultuous due to expectations of being valued, respected, and appreciated. Being creative, experiencing love, having fun, and pursuing hobbies all bring emotional fulfillment. They can be impulsive and need excitement in love relationships. Sharing their feelings with others and experiencing intimacy helps them find comfort. They have a strong desire to be in love and have fun with others. Children can bring happiness and fun into their lives. If they have their own children, it can awaken their own creative talents and sense of wonder. Sometimes insecure, they need praise and recognition for their creative talents. They are imaginative and should express their emotions by journaling and writing.

Being part of a team can be fulfilling and help them realize the importance of teamwork. They can realize that everything is not always about them but is about pursuing a common goal. They can be natural athletes and enjoy being part of a club or social circle. Their friends are important people in their lives and they need their support. They dislike being alone and prefer going out, socializing, and meeting new people.

Overindulgent at times, they can spend too much money or take unnecessary risks. They are drawn to gambling and anything that gives them an adrenaline rush like skydiving, boxing, or any type of excitement. They enjoy pushing themselves to the limit to see how far they can go. It is important that they learn how to ground their energy and think things through before jumping into risky situations. They should resist making decisions based on emotions alone.

They often inherit creative and artistic abilities from their mother or her side of the family. Emotionally, they need a connection and emotional bond with their mother. They need someone to nurture their creative gifts and talents. If they learn to harness emotional strength, they overcome negative feelings quickly and move on to something more positive.

Mercury in the Fifth House

These individuals are born with an imaginative and creative mind. Playful, talkative, and witty, they like to make people laugh. At times they are self-absorbed and only think about their own ideas, but they are good communicators. Because they are charming and flirtatious, they persuade people to participate in social activities. They excel at writing, teaching, and the performing arts. They might have musical talents and can be theatrical. It's difficult to change their mind because they are strong-willed and set in their ways. Participating in hobbies, sports, and intellectual pursuits helps stimulate their minds. They like to be doing something fun or socializing with people. Writing can help them release pent-up energy, and it's also a great way for them to jot down creative ideas. They might enjoy entertaining others through storytelling. Friendly and social, they make friends easily. Natural teachers, they enjoy teaching children and might want to be a coach. They have an ability to motivate others because of their positive attitude. If they can harness their powerful imagination, they can write books, teach workshops, inspire others to achieve their goals, and increase their creativity.

Venus in the Fifth House

These individuals are playful, romantic, and have big hearts. Peacemakers, they can understand different points of view, which can make them good mediators. They can receive recognition by participating in hobbies and through artistic self-expression. Because of their imaginative and creative mind, they make wonderful writers. It's important for them to express their feelings. They have a calm presence, but often avoid conflict. They are loving, affectionate, and sensual and like to be in relationships. They like to surround themselves with art, beautiful possessions, and a peaceful environment. They can find themselves entangled in multiple love affairs. In love, they are easygoing, supportive, and committed to their partner. They need to be involved in a peaceful and loving relationship to feel happy. They might enjoy working with children in some way. Harnessing their ability to express love will help them find greater balance.

Mars in the Fifth House

These individuals are assertive, bold, and strong-willed. They take on creative projects and want to be in charge. Natural-born leaders, they always fight hard for their own goals. They pursue their goals with passion and are driven to succeed. They directly pursue their love interests and have strong attractions. They can lack patience and be impulsive. If they like someone, they can be straightforward, confident, and aggressive in trying to win them over. They like the thrill of the chase, so if something is hard to get, they work even harder to win.

Highly competitive, they often excel at sports and are known risk-takers. Always energetic, they are quick to react and make decisions based on their gut instinct. These individuals want to be happy and enjoy life. Fun loving and adventurous, they need people and things that excite them. They might want to pursue the lead role in a play or be the lead singer in a band. Their competitive personality can make others feel uncomfortable. They need to be recognized for their talents and feel appreciated for the things they do. Having children might be something they think about, but if they don't have their own children, they can enjoy playing with other people's children. Harnessing confidence helps them realize that they don't always have to be the best at everything.

Jupiter in the Fifth House

These individuals have an abundance of creative talents. They are generous, adaptable, and optimistic in relationships. Affectionate, they want to spend time with people they love. Giving time, attention, and affection to those they care about is important to them. Their artistic talents are often recognized by others. They have good luck in creative pursuits and in any area that involves self-expression. They can find joy through writing, painting, singing, and teaching. Money and financial success can come through taking risks and pursuing hobbies. Some might have a lucky streak and enjoy gambling. They can be overly optimistic about love and relationships. They like adventure and doing something exciting with people they love.

People like them because of their open and honest approach to life. If they like someone, they will let them know it quickly because they are confident and optimistic. They may find it hard to commit in love relationships because they enjoy their freedom and independence. They may experience multiple love affairs throughout their lifetime before they settle down. Born with a need to roam, they need a special person who allows them to explore. They feel connected to others through travel and learning something new.

They are positive people who have faith in their own abilities. When they use the power of positive thinking, they can manifest their goals easily.

Friendly, warm, and flirtatious, they have many interesting friends. These individuals need to be hopeful and focus on positive energy. They often feel restless, so they benefit by having a plan, routine, and way to organize their life. They are interested in spirituality, and reading, writing, and poetry can inspire them. Overindulgence in pleasurable activities such as love, sex, food, or spending can cause problems. If they can harness moderation, they will attract many blessings into their lives.

Saturn in the Fifth House

These individuals are often serious and insecure about expressing their artistic talents. They may lack confidence in their own artistic abilities. Sometimes they allow criticism to stop them from pursuing things they enjoy. It can be difficult for them to have fun, relax, and be spontaneous. They like to feel in control and have a plan. It's challenging for them to take risks because of feeling guilty and being super responsible. Creative and artistic, they have talents but hide them because they don't feel like they are good enough. When they do decide to work hard on a hobby or project, they are dedicated, practical, and diligent workers. They can compare themselves to other talented people. Their pessimism needs to be controlled or it can affect people they care about. Uncomfortable with expressing their feelings, it's hard for them to have relationships. Sometimes they avoid relationships due to feeling restricted or uncomfortable.

They are on a journey of finding out who they truly are. As they grow older, they become more trusting, open, and confident. They deserve relaxation and need to enjoy life, but their need for control can cause anxiety. Letting go can be a major lesson for them. When they stop caring what other people think, barriers are removed that block them from having fun. They like to be behind the scenes due to a fear of failure. The more confident they become with self-expression, the greater happiness they find. Life will begin to feel lighter and easier when they develop self-esteem. Once they love themselves, they will attract love and be able to experience romance.

Uranus in the Fifth House

These individuals are born with a unique way of expressing their individuality. Many like to shock people with their appearance. Confident in who they are, they rarely care if people like them. Fitting in with others doesn't interest them because they are free spirits who accept who they are. At times they can seem unstable, changeable, and even unreliable. They need to feel independent and free to make their own decisions. Expressing their artistic and creative talents help them connect with a greater sense of purpose. Their need to instigate change can make other people feel uncomfortable. They want to grow as individuals and like to learn about nontraditional things.

Their erratic emotions can influence their relationships, making it difficult to commit. Love affairs often are unhealthy or shockingly painful and end abruptly. Attracted to people who are different from them, they don't often have traditional love interests. People perceive them as intelligent, scientific, and detached from deeper emotions. Change invigorates them and they thrive with unpredictability.

Unconventional about their hobbies, their eccentric talents are often recognized as being innovative. If they have children of their own, they will raise them to be open-minded and to think for themselves. They might not plan on being a parent, but being a parent is a role they will take seriously. They will want their children to be educated, to question what they are told, and to learn from experience. Their children can be eccentric and gifted in some way. Their children can be special in some way or born with a special talent or creative mind.

They want to do things their way and don't really care what others think. Disrupting the status quo comes naturally to them because they seek to bring excitement into their own lives. They don't like feeling bored or stuck in mundane responsibilities. They want to feel free to be spontaneous and make their own decisions. Sometimes they find themselves in controversial situations with other people. Highly intelligent, they believe their way of doing things is right. Deep down, they are stubborn and often resist taking other people's advice. There can be difficulties getting along with those in authority, especially if they don't respect them. They need to control a restless desire for change, so they need to harness stability.

Neptune in the Fifth House

These individuals are chameleons and can absorb the thoughts and emotions of other people. Charming, compassionate, and sensitive, they enjoy being in love. They have many talents and are imaginative, creative, and artistic. Deeply spiritual, their emotions inspire them to express themselves. They make amazing writers who can create stories that people feel deeply connected to. They are drawn to acting and theater where they can be on center stage. They can be secretive, illusive, and they like their alone time. They like to connect to others who are also intuitive, mystical, and spiritual. Idealistic in love, they can fall in love easily and be hurt.

Sometimes they attract people who need help, so it's important to develop stronger boundaries and trust their intuition. Unhealthy relationships can teach them lessons about life and love. Writing poetry, journaling, and listening to music can help them heal from heartbreak. They can believe in a soul mate or twin flame and seek to find that special person they believe was meant for them. It's important for them to learn to be more realistic and practical in relationships. If they have children, they will want to teach them to be compassionate and kind. They understand that no one is the perfect parent, but they will do their best to allow their children to explore their creative side. If they can balance idealism and realism in their parenting style, it will help them feel grounded. They want to have fun, which can often involve taking unnecessary risks. Struggles with escapist behaviors such as addiction to gambling, drinking, and love affairs can cause difficulties if not addressed. Secret or hidden love affairs can happen in their lives when they are attracted to someone who is not free. Falling in love with someone they can't be with can cause sadness and confusion. These individuals have lessons with what true love is. They need to surround themselves with compassionate, caring, supportive friends who share similar interests. Feeling connected to other people and being of service bring fulfillment.

They need to take off the rose-colored glasses and stop idealizing people. If they can channel all their emotions into spiritual art and connecting to something meaningful, they can find peace. If they can harness realism in life and in love, they will find happiness.

Pluto in the Fifth House

These individuals have a strong desire to be recognized for their talents. When they walk into a room, other people sense their intense energy. They can be confident, controlling, jealous, deep, and will demand respect from other people. They have a magnetic and attractive quality that draws people into their lives. There is something about how they express themselves that stirs up psychological issues for others. People can feel vulnerable and nervous around them.

These individuals can be secretive, private, and standoffish because they don't always trust others. They prefer to stay behind the scenes and keep their personal lives private. They want to feel deep emotions and dislike trivial conversations. They are passionate about pursuing pleasure and hobbies. They want to connect deeply in love relationships but can become quickly attached. Once they connect with someone, it's difficult for them to walk away. They can become obsessed with people and can have a hard time letting go of love. Once they express their true feelings and open up to someone, their feelings run deep. Frivolous love affairs don't work for them because they are seeking something transformative and long lasting. They would prefer to be alone than stuck in a surface relationship with people who are superficial or noncommittal. They tend to develop relationships with people who are powerful, successful, and financially stable.

They can have secret relationships or keep things private due to a highly sexual and passionate nature. If they find themselves in an abusive relationship, it forces them to end things and release unhealthy behaviors. They grow through relationships and heal from betrayal by learning to forgive others. Sexual chemistry does not always last, and they have a hard time letting go of people they bond with.

There is an intense need to participate in their hobbies and pursue their interests. Using their power in positive ways helps them manifest their goals. If they are a parent, they can be afraid of not being emotionally supportive to their children. There can be a lot of power-control dynamics they will need to address. They will want to talk about taboo topics with their children, such as sex and death. Deep conversationalists, they want to talk and teach people about things that matter to them. They detest small talk or having to spend time being social if it's not productive.

Determined to succeed, they can participate in risky behaviors. They want to feel alive, and getting involved in high-pressure adrenaline-pumping sports or gambling can be dangerous. Racing cars, skydiving, racing motorcycles, or competing in a dangerous sport might seem attractive to them. If they can harness forgiveness, their intimate relationships will improve and they will find greater fulfillment.

Planetary Transits through the Fifth House

When planets transit the fifth house, you will feel inspired to express your creative talents, have some fun, and pursue your hobbies.

Transit Sun

This is a time to focus on having fun and being creative. Serious issues will not matter right now. It's time to pursue your hobbies and do something that makes you happy. If you like to exercise, start walking, running, or taking aerobics classes. If you enjoy playing sports, it's a great time to join a league. Socialize more during this time and invite friends over, go out to eat, or attend a concert. This is a time for you to do things you enjoy. You might feel happier and more confident during this transit. If you are usually shy, you will feel more outgoing and social. Getting attention from people you care about and being recognized in some way helps you feel seen.

You will feel more confident and daring. This could make you want to take more risks. This is a good time to tell people how you feel and be more affectionate. Happiness exists and you feel more positive about everything in your life. Living life to the fullest and having fun will be on the forefront of your mind. Express yourself and make decisions. Harness creativity and pursue that artistic hobby you have always been interested in.

Transit Moon

There is excitement and a desire to express yourself the next few days. You feel inspired and are in a good mood to connect with others. You will want to engage in creative pursuits and just have fun. Get out of the house and be playful, adventurous, and express your feelings. Let go of stress and tune in to your intuition. It can feel like a weight is being lifted off your shoulders as responsibilities lesson during this time. Thinking more about love and romance can make you seek out new relationships. It's a good time to spend quality time with people you love. There can be some ups and downs with emotions right now. If you feel depressed, sad, or lonely, it won't last long.

You are more inspired to snap out of negative emotions because you are focused on being happy. Sometimes laziness and an inability to focus on tasks will delay projects. It is natural to connect with your feelings, but don't obsess on them. Don't force yourself to complete tasks if you don't feel like it. This is a time to follow your emotions and make time to relax. A little bit of self-indulgence can lead to overspending and overeating. This is a good time to harness emotional expression through writing and communicating your feelings.

Transit Mercury

This intellectual energy will increase your thoughts about being social and creative. A friendly and carefree energy will help you release worry. Over-thinking can be overcome at this time by getting out and doing something fun. This is a time to think about what makes you happy. Picking up a new hobby could be exciting and bring happiness into your life. Don't overthink things right now; just go with the flow. Joke around with friends, make people laugh, and let people know what you think. It can be difficult to focus on practical everyday responsibilities. You will be more imaginative and creative right now. Spend time reading your favorite romantic novel or start writing a book. This is a time to pursue new hobbies and interests. If you have children, you will want to share ideas and spend time with them. Harness mental creativity and self-expression.

Transit Venus

During this transit, you may feel more interested in romance. There is a calm and caring energy that inspires you to socialize more with people you care about. If you like art or listening to music, this is a good time to do it. There is an impulse to be more creative and affectionate. You might feel more friendly, flirtatious, and needy and not want to spend time alone. If you can't spend time with loved ones, try to focus on your hobbies, there is a heightened awareness about your wants and needs. You might want to start a new relationship or commit more in a current relationship. Experiencing intimacy and closeness makes you feel happy. You can be more interested in entertainment and want to attend a play, concert, or party. New romantic interests can come into your life or old lovers you have not seen in a while may pop up. Harness romance and express your feelings.

Transit Mars

This transit will give you a burst of energy. You will feel passionate, driven, and highly creative. A bit restless, you will be more assertive in communication. Getting what you want right now comes easily because you are putting effort into it. You will want to have fun and express your creative urges. Happiness can come by playing with children, pursuing hobbies, playing sports, or spending time with someone you love. Love is in the air, and you are much more romantic than usual. Sensuality is highlighted and you will want to show someone that you love them.

Bold and confident, you might pursue a new relationship. With this intense energy affecting you, you will benefit through exercise and being active. Having fun is the key right now, and try not to get upset about things. Focus on things you have been putting off doing, whether that's golfing, going to the beach, dating someone new, spending time with your children, or taking a class. You can get a lot done during this transit if you stay focused. Trust your impulses and gut instinct. Harness this energy of action and bask in the ability to get projects completed.

Transit Jupiter

This transit will expand your creativity and self-expression. You will feel happier and lighter right now. Positivity abounds and everything seems to be going your way. You might feel more connected to your creative side and will want to try something new. A new relationship could start up or you may meet someone very different from you. There can be a focus on learning a new hobby or trying to express your latent talents. You have more self-confidence right now and can attract positive change in love and in relationships. If you have children of your own, the relationship with them will improve.

As a parent, you help encourage your children to explore, seek adventure, and learn about the world. You might feel more optimistic and social and want to invite friends over for a party. Thinking positively and being open-minded can help you manifest what you truly want. Whether that is getting pregnant, getting a book published, or getting recognized for your creative work, something is going to expand and unfold. Harness abundance and allow the positive energy of this transit to transform your love life and relationships.

Transit Saturn

This transit impacts your creativity, self-expression, and love life for about two to three years. You will have to take responsibility for the choices you make. Being recognized for your hard work and achievements will be on the forefront of your mind. You may feel like other people have not been paying attention to your creative talents, or you have felt ignored. You might feel more burdened emotionally and mentally with responsibilities and can't relax. If you have artistic gifts, you could feel like you work harder than others to get recognized. This transit stirs up your fears of failure and insecurities about being good enough at what you do. You need self-expression to connect to what makes you happy. There is a serious tone influencing many areas of your life, but you can also be disciplined to work hard to achieve your goals.

There is a sense of duty related to your family and you are learning to be patient, dedicated, and practical. Things from the past will come up again and will teach you many lessons. It is a good time to implement what you have learned and the wisdom you have accumulated. You may feel you can't act on what you want, or you feel stifled with expressing your feelings. Things might seem hard and you can feel the universe is preventing you from finding love. You might feel like some outside force is blocking you and you don't feel free.

Everything feels restricted and heavy right now. If you are a writer, you might have writer's block, and if you are normally talkative, you might not want to speak. Having fun is the last thing on your mind right now because you feel so serious. Other people might believe you are acting negative, irritable, and depressed. There are heavy emotions bubbling to the surface, but you need to feel them. If you feel responsible for other people, it can cause disappointment. You might feel that you are always there to help others, but no one is there when you need their support.

If you have been looking for emotional stability and someone with maturity, you could meet someone older than you. If you have children, you might feel burdened by their problems and spend a lot of time focused on their needs. You might be wanting to get pregnant but have difficulties doing so. You might also become a new parent during this transit.

Practical responsibilities take priority, making limited time to have fun and relax. Stress can impact your health and ability to have fun right now. There is a lot of pressure you feel about doing the right thing. If you can harness responsibility, you will realize that this transit is teaching you how to be disciplined and wise.

Transit Uranus

This transit brings unexpected changes, surprises, and disruptions. Issues involving children, love, creativity, and how you want to express yourself are transformed. This electric and unstable energy will affect you for the next seven to eight years. This will be a time of tests that will awaken your talents and help you grow. Uranus wants to tear up outdated, stagnant energy and make sure we move forward and grow. You might feel blind-sided by changes in your children's lives or in your personal relationships. Your children might need your support, advice, and financial assistance. If you don't have children, many people get pregnant unexpectedly during this transit. Unplanned life events shake up your ability to pursue your hobbies and creative pursuits. If you are writing a book, there could be delays or unexpected changes. Restless energy keeps you active and you are forced to explore these new experiences. If you have children, they could act out during this time and challenge your authority. Arguments can ensue surrounding issues with self-expression, individuality, and freedom.

Risk-taking activities might interest you, such as gambling, learning to fly a plane, and bungee jumping. If you are typically cautious, this transit will bring you out of your shell. Testing the limits and doing something you never have done before can be attractive. New experiences can help you grow and explore new opportunities. If naturally shy in love, you could feel more bold, assertive, and wild. Exciting new romantic love affairs can happen, which stirs up problems in current committed relationships. You might attract unusual partners or meet people who are eccentric, rebellious, and freedom loving. These people can challenge you to take risks, but make sure not to do anything you might regret. Be sure to think things through before you make a cataclysmic decision that could change your entire life. Be open to small changes and growth opportunities.

You could feel restless, unsettled, and rebellious. Be cautious about acting impulsively, speeding, or arguing with your children. You might cut ties with people or stop doing hobbies that previously brought fulfillment. Harness freedom and adapt to unexpected events.

Transit Neptune

This transit affects your romantic life, children, and hobbies for around fourteen years.

You will feel inspired by love and might feel overly idealistic. Be careful about meeting new people and make sure you take the time to really get to know them before you commit. It can take a minimum of two years to truly know someone or see their flaws. Don't jump into anything based on chemistry and intense emotions. There can be challenges in love because you can see people as you want them to be and not as they truly are. Self-deception and illusion cloud many areas of your life. There can be a betrayal, loss, or emotional hurt during this time.

The positive side of this transit is an increased desire to express your artistic nature. You might also feel more spiritual and seek answers to the meaning of life. Try to see your children clearly and be realistic about how you can help them. They might be struggling with addiction or relationship problems and ask for your support. Supporting people you feel need saving can cause heartache. Trust your intuition and make sure to be realistic in the ways you can assist others. You might feel tired and struggle with energy levels. This is a good time to develop stronger boundaries with people in your life. Harness boundaries and use this time to take care of your own needs and create art, find a spiritual practice, meditate, or learn yoga.

Transit Pluto

This is a long-term transit that causes change and rebirth. Who you were is forever changed by this transit, but the new you will be stronger and more resilient. Profound changes are unleashed in your love life, children's lives, creative pursuits, and hobbies. There is a metamorphosis slowly affecting your life and there is an intense feeling that you can't escape the future. Accept the fact that change is coming and try not to resist it. Outdated and unhealthy things will be removed from your life. You can feel deep emotions and old wounds involving past relationships often resurface. If you have not truly healed or released the past, this transit will force you to make changes.

Anything superficial or trivial will not interest you. Pluto shakes up your inner life and makes you feel uncomfortable emotions. If you are angry about something, you will have to learn to forgive. This is a good time to let go of the past and find what makes you happy. You might be interested in exploring and learning new metaphysical topics like astrology, tarot, energy healing, and psychology.

Many things will change, and the things that used to be fulfilling can now feel empty and dissatisfying. You are on a search for deeper meaning in life and self-expression. Death and rebirth themes change your relationships and impact how you express yourself. This is a good time to let go of outdated beliefs about relationships, hobbies, and artistic talents. There can be lessons with power and control in love relationships and with children. If you have children of your own, many things can change in their lives. You might want to get overly involved in helping them make decisions. They might have gone away to college and you now have empty-nest syndrome. Allow yourself to feel and adapt to the new experiences life brings. They might be struggling with finding their own path. It's a good time to heal issues related to parenting or your expectations of yourself. If you haven't had children yet, you might now get pregnant, or give birth to your first child, or have more children. Harness growth and allow these changes to lead you to new opportunities.

Ways to Harness Leo Energy

- Express yourself.
- Fall in love.
- Socialize and network with others.
- Have fun and be playful.
- Pursue your hobbies.
- Tap into your romantic side.
- Be happy and positive.

6
VIRGO

Archetype: Analyzer
Symbol: The Maiden
Sun Sign Dates: August 23–September 22
Energy: Service
Element: Earth, Mutable
Planet: Mercury
House: Sixth

I f you have Virgo in your birth chart, planets in the sixth house, or are experiencing planetary transits through the sixth house, this chapter will cover information regarding these energies. If you don't, you can still learn about Virgo energy and incorporate it into your life. The placement of the planet Mercury in the sign and house will show where you express Virgo energy. It is important to look at what house Virgo falls on your birth wheel because this is where you will want to serve others, develop a routine, focus on details, and be more efficient. Harnessing Virgo energy gives you an ability to make the world a better place by pointing out things that need to be fixed, being conscientious, being productive, striving for perfection, and taking care of others.

Virgo Energy Words

Efficient, productive, detail focused, obsessive, critical, observant, caring, service oriented, competent, worrisome, intelligent, researcher, conversationalist, sarcastic, hardworking, honest, responsible, committed, conscientious, reliable, meticulous, modest, uptight, reserved, cautious, organized, prepared, communicative, loyal.

Virgo Motto

As a Virgo, I am a perfectionist at heart who loves to improve things. I am honest and tell others when they are wrong. I have a strong sense of self and enjoy learning new things. I can be critical of my own abilities and have high standards for myself. I enjoy working hard and enjoy pursuing opportunities for career success. I like to write and have open conversations with others. I need mental stimulation in my daily life and like to keep busy. I like to complete projects and get things done quickly. I am organized and need a structured routine. I tend to worry and imagine future scenarios.

Harnessing Virgo Energy

Virgo energy is pure, practical, and organized. This energy is stable and committed to getting things done. Virgo energy has tunnel vision and dives into the small details with cutting accuracy. They are perfectionists who work hard to help others. Virgos enjoy solitary activities like reading, journaling, and learning new things. They are studious, reserved, observant, and private. They are efficient workers who get tasks done. Virgos like making to-do lists to organize their thoughts and activities. Many are gifted writers and teachers and they can explain things in an easy-to-understand way. High-strung at times, they often worry and overanalyze things. They ask a lot of questions to understand intricate details.

This energy wants to feel needed and appreciated for the little things they do. Virgo energy is responsible and committed to what they say. They need a routine, plan, and strict schedule to follow. Virgos have a hard time letting things go and releasing control over situations. They want things done a certain way and are great at helping other people get organized. Obsessive thoughts can cause stomach issues and undue stress. Repeating things or replaying them mentally helps them process and feel safe. This energy needs to vent and express itself through writing and speaking. Virgos like to know what to expect from situations and want to feel prepared. Harnessing Virgo energy brings us perfectionism, efficiency, organization, routine, and a desire to help other people.

Harness Communication

Virgo is a mental sign that is prone to overthinking. Their energy is service oriented. Introverted, it often appears cerebral, analytical, detailed, and observant. There is a purity about them that makes them seem delicate and untouchable. This energy is intelligent, witty, sarcastic, and determined to express itself. Natural communicators, this energy moves through speaking and writing. Having a mental connection with other people inspires Virgos. Virgo energy wants to be of service, maintain a routine, and focus on working hard to get tasks completed. Making lists and prioritizing things help them feel grounded. Chronic worrying can cause insomnia and compulsive thinking. Talking about how they feel with friends helps them process their repetitive thoughts. When they focus on helping others, it helps them balance their thoughts and emotions.

Harness Practicality

Virgo is ruled by the earth element. Earth is warm, grounded, solid, and stable. Earth energy helps Virgo find ways to be practical and help serve others in some way. This energy helps Virgos stay committed in relationships and at work. Virgos grow in confidence as they gain experience in the real world. Shy, modest, and humble, they often prefer to live behind the scenes doing routine tasks. Dutifully accomplishing small tasks and projects that no one else wants to do brings them a sense of fulfillment. Their earth energy enables them to work diligently and efficiently to obtain their goals. They are dependable and can always be relied upon to assist others in a crisis. Natural caretakers, they know what people need and have a way of instinctively doing it. Once they form a plan, nothing can get in their way.

We feel the earth beneath our feet, sturdy and protective. To harness earth energy, you must connect to practical matters. Working, cooking, cleaning, taking care of the physical body, and spending time in nature are all ways earth energy expresses itself.

Harness Flexibility

Virgo is associated with mutable energy. Even though they need to have things planned and organized, they also care about helping people. They adapt easily to the needs of others and want to get along. Mutable energy is flexible, adaptable, understanding, and open to change. It's easy to get along with mutable energy because it's understanding and relaxed. This energy wants to let things happen naturally and go with the flow of life. Mutable signs want peace and harmony. They always see every option and can depend on others to help them make firm decisions. Morphing and taking on the energy around them helps them connect with what others are thinking. Highly intuitive, they know what other people need without being told. Tapping into mutable energy transforms rigidity and stubbornness to flexibility and understanding.

Harness Communication

Virgo is ruled by the planet Mercury. This energy is associated with ideas, facts, and details. Mercury is the planet of communication and social connections. It helps us talk and share our thoughts with others. Virgos are known to be shy, private, and modest. It can take them time to open up to other people, but once they feel comfortable, they are expressive and social.

The planet Mercury is associated with spreading information through writing and speaking. This energy thrives on social media where information is shared instantly with the touch of a button. Mercury needs mental stimulation and an intellectual connection.

Encouraging other people to communicate and express themselves with words is how this energy works. Everyone can harness Mercury's energy by learning how to communicate better, share ideas, and think deeply about things. If Mercury feels blocked in communicating, they will grow restless and move on. Harnessing communication inspires them to express what they think and develop deeper connections with others.

Wherever Mercury is in our birth chart will show how we communicate and need to share information. Writing, reading, taking a class, using our hands in some way, doing a podcast, or teaching others something we learned are all ways we can harness Mercury energy. Connecting to people, being adaptable, and opening up in relationships helps this energy transmit out into the world.

Practical Service

The sixth house in astrology is the house of practical service, health, diet, illness, daily routines, and the work environment. Virgo and Mercury energies are associated with the sixth house. This area of life is where we find responsibilities and structure in our daily interactions. Self-improvement, health, problem-solving, diet, hygiene, and coworkers are all sixth house territory.

This is the area of life where we work to be organized and efficient. Completing chores and tasks brings a sense of accomplishment. The sixth house represents what work we want to do and it often involves the medical or counseling field. When planets are here, there may be an interest in helping those who struggle with chronic illness or helping people take care of their bodies. The sign on the sixth house cusp describes what kind of work we do, beliefs about work, and the work environment. It also reveals potential health vulnerabilities and illnesses. For example, if Leo is on the sixth house cusp, there could be issues with the heart, blood pressure, cholesterol, and circulation. The stresses of daily life reside in the sixth house.

When planets fall into this house, there is a focus on giving and being of service. Volunteering at an animal shelter, working with children in some way, or editing a book for a friend are sixth house energies. The sixth house encourages us to connect with small animals and pets. Many people with planets in the sixth prefer spending time with animals instead of people. Animals bring affection, love, and comfort, so many veterinarians have planets here.

This area of life represents day-to-day preventative things we do to take care of our health. Getting regular dental exams, checkups, and vaccines falls in this territory. Routine and basic tasks we accomplish to take care of the physical body is the sixth house. Developing healthy habits like proper sleep, diet, and exercise will help alleviate future problems. The sixth house embodies all the energy of Virgo. Virgos tend to worry about their health; the obsessive sixth house can enhance hypochondriac tendencies. This is also the area of life that shows what type of relationships we will have with our coworkers. The sixth house energy encourages us to serve, plan, prepare, listen to advice, and implement healthy habits that will impact the future. Harnessing wellness is a sixth house mission that improves health, sleep, routine, and energy levels.

Virgo Rising

When people first meet Virgo rising people, they perceive them as elusive, quiet, observant, and restrained. They may have a youthful appearance or look younger than they actually are. They are grounded, practical, realistic, and generous. The energy they express makes people judge them instantly. Sometimes they are seen as cold, distant, or uninterested. The truth is that they are sizing up the environment before they dare to step foot out of their comfort zone. Once Virgo risings feel comfortable, they are talkative, funny, friendly, and helpful. Large crowds overwhelm them, so they prefer smaller groups. They listen to other people's problems and give great advice. They are agreeable, analytical, and detailed focused. Intelligent and perceptive, they can make other people feel like they are examining them. Improving other people's lives and serving others come naturally to them. They seem serious, cold, restricted, and shy when people first meet them. It takes a while for them to let their guard down. They are focused on fixing things because they want to help improve people's lives. Their earthiness makes other people feel safe and supported.

Virgo risings adapt easily to change because they have to, not because they want to. They prefer a stable, peaceful, and quiet environment to work in. High-level thinkers and problem-solvers, they like to learn new things and find answers. Their perfectionistic tendencies make them want to do everything correctly, so they put a lot of pressure on themselves.

Virgo risings have high standards and need to remember that no one is perfect. They glaringly see their own flaws and work hard to improve themselves. Reliable, responsible, and committed, they don't want to do anything that could hurt others. There is a sense of purity and refinement to their personality.

Virgo risings are loyal and committed in relationships. It takes a special person to bring them out of their shell, but they do have a passionate side that very few see. Details stand out to them and they have laserlike vision to find errors. Many are drawn to publishing and make excellent editors. Writing is a way they can express their thoughts and relieve stress. Overthinking often makes it difficult for them to relax and unwind. The energy of criticism helps them strive to make the world a better place. Criticism is not always a negative trait, but Virgo risings will always offer advice to help people improve. They expect feedback to help them improve because they believe that's how they help others.

Virgo risings notice everything. They love routine, order, and cleanliness. They can obsess on certain things and areas of life. For instance, they might want their kitchen to be immaculate before they can relax in their home. They strive to be hardworking and efficient. Laziness irritates them, so they expect others to work fast. Virgo risings push themselves to accomplish tasks in a timely fashion. Dependable and responsible, they are the person at work everyone asks for help. They enjoy being of service and helping get things done.

Virgo risings can experience stomach issues due to worrisome thoughts. The mind is a powerful tool and they benefit when they learn to control it. Changing their perspective and focusing on the positive things helps shift them out of compulsive thinking.

Virgo risings energy is soft, understanding, and caring, which makes them excellent social workers, teachers, doctors, and nurses. They are prone to stomachaches, nausea, and appetite changes. Physically, Virgo risings appear youthful, intelligent, sensitive, and studious. Being alone and having solitude in their daily lives helps them recuperate. Virgo risings need to harness their analyzing ability because this helps them solve problems and feel like they are improving things.

How to Harness Planets in Virgo

When planets are in Virgo, they inspire you to be practical, hardworking, perfectionistic, and service oriented. You might want to develop a routine, get organized, focus on your health, and work hard to complete tasks.

Sun in Virgo

Individuals with the Sun in Virgo are conscientious, intelligent, and practical. High-strung, picky, and hardworking, they like to accomplish things. They are perfectionists who want to do everything right, so they enjoy organizing things. Routine, structure, and organization are important to them. Detail oriented, they notice small errors and are natural editors. People can perceive them as critical, but they just want to make things better. They are shy and cautious when they meet new people. Once they feel comfortable, they enjoy talking and sharing ideas. Overthinking and anxiety can make them feel overwhelmed. Prone to stress and nervous tension, they can get stomach issues such as ulcers. They like to control situations and have to learn to let go and trust the process of life. They dislike change but can be adaptable if they have to be.

Conscientious, they care about doing a good job. Their active mind can cause obsessive-compulsive thoughts. It's hard for them to stop worrying and ruminating. Sometimes they struggle with sleep problems such as insomnia. Mindfulness exercises and meditation can be helpful with restless thoughts.

Their energy is kind, innocent, caring, grounded, and reliable. Highly efficient, they like to get things done right. If something is disorganized, they will start to find solutions and communicate ways to make it flow. These individuals can burn themselves out because they take on too many tasks and have a hard time turning people down. Many can be workaholics because their work is connected to their self-esteem. They work tediously and efficiently even without praise. Helping other people and animals brings happiness and fulfillment. In relationships they are committed, loyal, and supportive. Routine is key, as is being able to participate in their favorite hobbies. They need a physical outlet to release their mental energy. If they learn to harness faith and trust the universe to take care of things, these individuals will feel less pressure. Feeling appreciated for the work they do and being recognized for their talents make Virgos happy. These individuals excel at maintaining order in chaos. They strive to make things better and are focused on diet, health, exercise, and work.

Moon in Virgo

People with the Moon in Virgo are intellectual, responsible, introverted, and at times critical. They like to feel comfortable before they open up to other people, so many prefer their own company. Sometimes emotionally restricted and perfectionistic, they need to learn to love themselves. Highly critical, they can be too hard on themselves. They notice every little detail and nuisance in relationships. Overanalyzing, obsessing, and replaying scenarios can make it difficult for them to relax. Trusting other people takes time but they are extremely loyal. Dedicated to taking care of people they care about, they will do anything to be helpful. Sometimes they take on too much, and that includes other people's problems. Developing strong boundaries will help protect their energy.

Thinking is how they solve problems, but love is hard to rationally explain. They like to know why things happen the way they do and why people feel a certain way. There are times they have to learn to accept that sometimes they won't have all the answers. Truth seekers, they are skeptical of anything that is impractical. Perfectionistic and professional, they excel in their career and work. There are very few people who can keep up with their work ethic and stamina to get tasks done. Serving others in some way and making the world a better place is important to them.

Emotional fulfillment comes through feeling helpful, appreciated, and organized. They feel happy when there is a structure and routine. People are drawn to their down-to-earth approach, communication skills, and caring nature. Emotionally, these individuals need to feel organized, with a sense of control, and an ability to analyze things. Taking care of people who are sick or working with animals brings fulfillment. Many are drawn to nutrition, healing, and counseling. Journaling can help them release stress and anxious feelings. Harnessing self-acceptance will help them realize they don't need to be perfect; they are perfect just the way they are.

Mercury in Virgo

Analytical and intelligent people with Mercury in Virgo are born with an active mind that dives into the details. People depend on them to find the correct answers. They seek knowledge and have a practical approach to communication. They are intelligent and think fast on their feet. Their witty and sarcastic nature makes people laugh. Natural communicators, they express themselves eloquently through writing and speaking. They can teach people how to do things in a practical, methodical, and hands-on way. These individuals enjoy learning things and memorizing details. Subjects such as research, science, technology, social work, teaching, and publishing inspire them. Their minds are always active and they can struggle with sleep problems. They need mental stimulation and enjoy reading, journaling, and taking classes. Difficulties come when they take on too much work, projects, or responsibilities. Balance is key or they can feel overwhelmed. They want to be efficient, appreciated, and productive. If they can harness moderation, it will relieve stress and help them relax.

Venus in Virgo

Individuals with Venus in Virgo have high standards and can be picky in love. They have a checklist for a perfect partner and it's hard for them to find what they are looking for. Their high expectations can limit the relationship pool. They need to learn to give people a chance and not be so critical. Cautious about who they open their hearts to, they have a hard time being vulnerable. They want a partner who shares similar interests. An intellectual and mental connection is needed to stir up their emotions. Sharing common hobbies or interests helps them connect with others. They care more about quality time, communication, and commitment than physical intimacy.

They want to feel special and develop relationships slowly, often starting off as friends. Sometimes perceived as cold, unloving, or critical, they need committed relationships. Their love nature is realistic and practical. Doing small practical things is how they show they care, such as taking out the trash, doing dishes, cooking a favorite meal, or booking a trip. They want peace, harmony, and stability in relationships. Attracting partners who are distinctly different from them can bring them out of their shell. Talking with others helps them overcome shyness. Expectations can lead to disappointment in love. Fretting and worrying about those closest to them can make others feel like they are being critical or don't trust them. The truth is these individuals just want to make things better. Harnessing self-love will help them accept their strengths and weaknesses in relationships.

Mars in Virgo

Mars in Virgo individuals are ambitious and driven to succeed. They multitask and take on a lot of projects. Super focused on work, they need to be careful not to take on too much. They are efficient and productive workers. Mentally strong, they can push through challenges and are blessed with intense willpower. They push emotions aside and focus on making decisions.

Critical of their own abilities, they work hard to perfect things. They are not comfortable with expressing anger and sometimes they need to learn to speak up for themselves. When they suppress their anger, it can manifest as anxiety or stomach issues. If their anger is not controlled, they start complaining and bickering with others.

They might seem confident, but underneath their cool exterior, they can feel nervous. At work, they are responsible and organized. They do more work than most people because of their single-minded dedication. Success and recognition at work motivates them to work harder. Driven to make a difference, they enjoy helping others.

They make excellent teachers and communicate complex topics in a simple way. Sometimes high-strung, excess worry can make them irritable. They can become critical when they get overwhelmed or when they feel they aren't producing things. Harnessing productivity helps them feel motivated to achieve their goals.

Jupiter in Virgo

Individuals with Jupiter in Virgo have a desire to explore the world and accumulate knowledge. Practical and realistic, they appreciate feeling needed. Abundance and good fortune come through working to serve others in some way. They have good luck with achieving their dreams and can be successful pursuing a hobby. Positive thinking helps them manifest what they want. They have an analytical mind and an eye for the details. Open-minded and understanding, they adapt to new beliefs. Gifted with communication, they are friendly and talkative. They love to learn and might have an interest in learning more about philosophy, foreign languages, or travel. Careers in teaching, accounting, writing, medicine, and psychology can be profitable. Talented writers, they might doubt their abilities. They are perfectionists who have standards but they tend to focus on the positive side of life. If they learn to harness positivity, they can manifest what they want easily.

Saturn in Virgo

People with Saturn in Virgo can have a sense of duty, responsibility, and desire for achievement. Responsible, conscientious, and organized, they can work hard to achieve their goals. Success does not always come easy for them. Sometimes they are critical and have high expectations for themselves. Strict, analytical, and shrewd, they can forget to have fun. They can get overwhelmed with small details and trivial issues. It is hard for them to relax and enjoy being in the moment. They are overachievers and do everything to work harder than others. Life challenges and difficulties happen in early life to teach them how to cope with disappointment, loss, and loyalty. Trusting others might be difficult for them due to their personal experiences. They might have had to be their own father or lacked support from their own parents. Super responsible, they might have cared for or had to provide financial support to family members. They want things done their way and find it difficult to make changes.

Innate pessimism makes it hard for them to see the positive sides of situations. There are times they obsess on negative thoughts and have a fear of taking risks. They worry about security and being successful. Negative thinking can impact their health. It's important for them to feel their emotions and not rationalize them away. Feelings matter and they need to work on controlling their thoughts. Success often comes later in life and they can sometimes feel things don't work out easily for them. With the passage of time and hard work, they will eventually receive recognition for their efforts. Harnessing the wisdom gained through personal experience will help them reach their financial and career goals.

Uranus in Virgo

People with Uranus in Virgo are intuitive, innovative, and rational. There is a powerful ability to analyze and use knowledge to inspire change. Humanitarian desires often lead them into career fields where they can be of service. They seek autonomy and don't want anyone standing in their way of getting tasks done. If people try to control how they work, they will rebel. Making their own routine and schedule helps them feel grounded.

They can be more open-minded and accepting of unique and different points of view. Fiercely independent, they have a desire for unique relationships. Eccentric themselves, they appreciate other people who aren't afraid of taking a risk. Unexpected changes happen at work, but this can benefit them. They can care about diet, nutrition, and innovative health treatments. Thinking outside the box and coming up with revolutionary ideas helps inspire those around them. Worrying less about making all the right decisions helps alleviate stress. If they can harness spontaneity, they will receive unexpected opportunities.

Neptune in Virgo

Individuals with Neptune in Virgo can have a strong desire to help others. Having a belief in something greater than themselves helps them find a sense of purpose. Both grounded and idealistic, they can benefit when they find balance. Finding a spiritual connection and belief system helps them feel supported. They can be attracted to meditation, yoga, and alternative healing practices. Some with this placement have psychic abilities and a strong intuition. It's important for them to listen to their inner voice to prevent getting bogged down in negative thinking. Practical at heart, these individuals can also seek ways to escape from mundane responsibilities. There is an imaginative and creative side to their personality. They think about making the world a better place and often escape into their mind.

They can have natural writing abilities, and they can use their detail-oriented mind to create imaginative stories. Even if they worry and obsess over their problems, they have a sensitive side that softens them. They feel other people's problems and want to make them feel better. Developing boundaries helps them avoid getting hurt. Many are blessed with artistic and creative abilities. They could be gifted musicians, writers, painters, and make beautiful things. If they can harness their intuition, they can develop greater trust in their spiritual gifts and the practical world.

Pluto in Virgo

Individuals with Pluto in Virgo are not afraid of having difficult conversations. They don't mind talking about taboo topics like death, sexuality, and power. Studying intense topics and doing research come naturally for them. They have a fascination with psychology and philosophy. They have a penetrating mind that can solve complex problems.

They spend a lot of time analyzing their weaknesses. Ultra focused on personal growth, they experience psychological and emotional rebirths. Unwavering, when they are focused on achieving something, it's hard for them to give up. With single-minded focus, they slowly plan how to reach their goals. They experience transformation in areas involving work and health. These individuals are nostalgic and learn from their past mistakes. Hardworking and perfectionistic, they work hard to achieve their goals. Controlling at times, they like to have a routine and plan for their lives.

Life can surprise them, forcing them to adapt and grow. They are determined and work hard for recognition, so they often find themselves in positions of power. Many find a sense of purpose when they can serve others. They have a gift for helping people transform their lives. If they learn to harness trust, their relationships will improve.

Planets in the Sixth House

When planets are in the sixth house, you will want to focus on health, diet, routine, and practical service.

Sun in the Sixth House

These individuals are organized, meticulous, and intelligent. Service oriented and health conscious, they have a sensitive stomach. Their emotions affect their health and stress can weaken their immune system. They are sensitive to their environment and a stable routine helps them feel prepared. Adjusting to change isn't something they like to do, but if they have to, they will adapt. They thrive when their environment is structured, and this is why they make efficient workers. Getting things done in a timely matter and correctly is important to them.

Being of service and helping people in practical ways inspires them to pursue careers as physicians, veterinarians, nurses, social workers, and in detail-oriented career fields. Giving advice and being productive helps them feel useful. Owning small animals or working with them in some way can bring comfort. They might want to have a therapy dog or get their dog trained to assist people in need.

They can neglect their own problems and lack self-care because they are often focused on the needs of others. Modest and hardworking, they can get burned out if they take on too much. They are dependable workers who are trusted to get things done. Learning to relax can help them recuperate and improve their overall health. Easily stressed, they need to take breaks from work and take time off. They need to balance diet, exercise, sleep, and work routines. In relationships with coworkers, they can have high standards and are perfectionists. They have a gift for bringing order to disorganized environments. They make excellent editors, writers, teachers, and learners.

Mentally active, they can be obsessive and consider every possible outcome. Their obsession with having things a certain way can cause difficulties in their relationships. Critical, they are hardest on themselves. They tend to involve themselves in other's problems because they want to solve them. Exercising and eating right are important to them. These individuals can be hypochondriacs, which can lead to increased stress. Irritable at times, they can verbally lash out at others when they feel out of control. If they can harness relaxation, they can alleviate unnecessary worry and stress.

Moon in the Sixth House

These individuals value comfort, organization, and routine. They need to embrace change and release the need to control. They can relax by incorporating self-care techniques such as breathing exercises, yoga, meditation, and walking. Overthinking can take over their life, which can impact their mental health. Responsible, reliable, and efficient, they can become workaholics. They need to find a balance between work and making time for relaxation. They are perfectionists with high standards for themselves and others. They find emotional fulfillment through completing tasks, which can be unhealthy in excess. Emotions are difficult for them to process because they often overanalyze their feelings. Helping other people and being of service also brings emotional fulfillment. They may change jobs frequently until they feel they are making a difference. Coworkers can be supportive or seen as a hindrance. They can be attracted to the medical profession or interested in careers as dieticians, nurses, radiologists, or social workers.

It's important that they have a practical routine. Diet, exercise, and rest will help them feel better. These individuals are sensitive to their environment, which can affect their health. At an early age they might have many different allergies. Their energy is depleted easily so it's important for them to develop strong boundaries. They believe actions speak louder than words, so doing practical things for others is how they show love. Learning to accept their own flaws and realizing that no one is perfect will help them find greater happiness. Positive thinking exercises will help them balance negative thought patterns. If they harness positive thinking, they will find greater meaning in the work they do and the people they serve.

Mercury in the Sixth House

These individuals have active minds and are prone to overthinking. Intelligent, practical, and efficient, they like to learn. Excellent communication skills help them express themselves through writing and speaking. They have an ability to multitask and work on several projects at once. In their work environment, they are overachieving and dedicated. Their communication skills can open doors for them in their career. They may receive recognition for their skills in writing and speech. They enjoy growing and improving. They are health conscious and may be very mindful of their unhealthy habits. Forever students, they enjoy taking classes and learning new things. They are perfectionists who can put a lot of pressure on themselves and others. Helping those in need can bring a sense of emotional fulfillment.

They have a nervous disposition and seem to always worry about their day-to-day activities. They are always thinking and need to learn how to relax. Mentally restless, their hypercritical thoughts can impact their health. It's important that they focus on implementing positive thinking. Meditation and exercises to quiet their mind can help them. If they can harness mindfulness, it will help open doors for achieving their goals.

Venus in the Sixth House

These individuals want peace and harmony in their work environments. Even though they are worriers, they usually experience good health. When they feel stressed, they can overindulge in eating and drinking. They have a detail-oriented and practical approach to work duties. Pleasant and caring, they like to help people with small tasks. They may meet their partner through work. Imaginative and creative, they inspire others with their ideas. Maintaining a healthy routine is important to them. They need harmony in all areas of their life. Difficulties with coworkers or a toxic work environment can weaken their immune system. They enjoy doing practical things for people they love. Their high standards and tendency to criticize others can make them feel impossible to please. Doing a good job, being liked, and having someone to love are main motivators in their lives. Their cautious nature and shy disposition make it hard for them to show love through physical affection. These individuals are very independent and may not feel like they need someone else to fulfill them. Harnessing self-love will allow them to be open to loving others.

Mars in the Sixth House

These individuals can be assertive and speak their minds. They can be perceived as dominant and overbearing, but deep down they simply care about making things better. Motivated to succeed, they can put a lot of pressure on themselves. Impulsive at times, they control their emotions to focus on the task at hand. They are focused and responsible, putting major focus on completing their tasks. Exercise may help them relieve pent-up stress. They may express their anger through some sort of physical outlet. They have high standards for coworkers and expect others to work as hard as they do. If they are not in charge at their workplace, their coworkers can see their desire to help as a personal attack on their intelligence. They can cause conflict in their workplace because of these tendencies, which can impact their own productivity. They can be competitive at work, always wanting to advance. They work well under pressure because they are used to self-induced pressure. If they can harness tolerance, it will help alleviate stress at work and home.

Jupiter in the Sixth House

These individuals are successful at work. People like them and are attracted to their positive outlook. Coworker relationships are often positive and bring opportunities for advancement. Perfectionists at heart, they put a lot of pressure on themselves to smile, think positive, and help other people. Dependable, loyal, and friendly, they attract good fortune through working. Taking care of people in need comes easily because of their caring and compassionate personality. Having a strong routine helps them maintain good health. They benefit from having a healthy diet and exercise program; they can be prone to overeating. Moderation is the key that helps them find balance. Overall, they are blessed with good health but need to have a consistent routine.

Benefits can come by working in the medical field or by doing work that helps others. The more they take care of people who need them, the more abundance enters their lives. They can be restless, so routine can help them feel more grounded. They enjoy moving around, being active, and traveling. The more organized, efficient, and practical things are, the happier they will feel. Extremely generous, they give a lot of time and energy to tasks that need to be accomplished. Hardworking and successful, they motivate other people to work harder. They need freedom in the work environment and opportunities to travel. If they harness a routine, they will be able to control their restless nature.

Saturn in the Sixth House

These individuals are responsible and dedicated workers. Their workaholic tendencies make it hard for them to make time for family and hobbies. They spend a lot of time worrying and overthinking about work issues. They need a healthy work-life balance to prevent difficulties in their homelife. They can neglect their own feelings, preferring to pursue success. They can be high achievers and can have high expectations for themselves. They take work seriously so it's hard for them to have fun. Making friends with more easygoing personalities might alleviate some of the pressure they put on themselves. Work can become their focus and they can find it hard to adapt to unforeseen changes.

Rigid at times, they can struggle to express their true feelings. Worry and stress can impact their health and immune system. They can be obsessed with feeling in control and like to set rules for themselves and others. Being in a position of authority fulfills them because they like to create an efficient work environment. They expect coworkers to follow their rules and not take advantage of the system. A structured, stable, and peaceful work environment helps them feel balanced. Control issues can impact their day-to-day relationships. Eating right, exercise, and getting enough sleep are important for them to release pent-up frustration. Harnessing relaxation and focusing self-care can positively impact their productivity in the long run.

Uranus in the Sixth House

These individuals can experience many unexpected changes at work. They are highly intelligent and have a good memory. Sometimes they struggle with unique health problems that can be difficult to diagnose. They enjoy having freedom in their work environment and can be bored by repetitive tasks. Attempting to instigate changes at work can cause disruptions with coworkers. These individuals want to grow and do things differently. Their restless nature can make it hard for them to be stuck at a desk. Getting outdoors and traveling for work suits them well. They have a creative way of getting tasks completed but can be disorganized. Solving problems and working in a scientific field will help them utilize their mind. They stand out at work by thinking outside the box and being innovative. Rebellious to authority, they may question the rules and traditions of their workplace. They believe forcing change helps people grow, so they believe they are justified in their actions. Maintaining a consistent daily routine can be challenging for these individuals. They might change their diet and exercise erratically. They want to break free of restrictions and do best if they are given autonomy.

They can unexpectedly be forced to change jobs and leave coworkers. Getting along with people at work can be difficult, especially if they feel they have to conform to other people's routines. They can be seen as unstable and unreliable by more practical colleagues. Being part of a group or leading a team helps them build confidence.

They are eccentric in the workplace and carry superstitions that others cannot understand. Alternative healing and medicine fascinates them, so some might pursue careers as a chiropractor, radiologist, or surgeon. They can break barriers and are drawn to research. If they can harness stability, they can have more focus when completing tasks and build relationships in their career.

Neptune in the Sixth House

These individuals are extremely sensitive to the environment. Empathic, they absorb other people's thoughts and emotions. Allergies and unexplained illnesses are common and can be hard to diagnose. They have an elusive energy and personality that may confuse coworkers. People can perceive them as secretive and withdrawn. They are very sensitive to criticism from those in power. The way people treat them, especially in the workplace, influences their physical health, leaving them feeling depleted. They can expect to be fulfilled from their work, but this can be a struggle.

They can feel disillusioned with their career and may feel like they do not know what they want to do. If there is conflict at work, they may call out sick to avoid the situation. They can feel unsettled with a strict routine and when they are in a traditional work environment. They can be prone to zoning out and not paying enough attention to work matters. Imaginative, creative, and compassionate, they are drawn to careers in medicine, psychology, performing arts, music, and counseling.

Developing boundaries helps them protect themselves and conserve their energy. The more inspired they are, the more tasks they can accomplish. They want their work to be meaningful, so helping others can be important to them. Getting enough sleep is crucial because it impacts how they think and feel. They don't like to be rushed, and when they have deadlines, they may be frozen with stress, seemingly unable to work. If they get overwhelmed by responsibilities, they escape and find solitude. They work best when they have privacy and silence. Their sensitivity to their environment can distract them from focusing and being productive.

There are times when they feel discouraged by their repetitive daily life. Serving others and pursuing work in metaphysical areas such as energy healing, yoga, and astrology can bring happiness. They care about children and animals, and many volunteer in the community.

It is important that they learn how to ground their energy. Creating a sense of stability will help them balance powerful emotions. They get their feelings hurt easily and can be idealistic about day-to-day matters. Their mental health is directly connected to their physical health. If they work hard on implementing a healthy routine in their lives, it helps them conserve their energy. They need to eat right, think positive, and get enough sleep to perform their best. Harnessing boundaries helps protect their kind heart from the negative energy of the outside world.

Pluto in the Sixth House

These individuals can experience growth and transformation through work. They tend to obsess and worry about getting things done. Intense, perceptive, and passionate, they want to have a controlled work environment. A solid routine is important for them to feel settled. In daily life, people are either attracted to them or intimidated by their powerful energy. Passionate workers, they do everything with intensity. They can be controlling in their work environment and like things done their way. Critical and detail focused, they expose things that need fixing. They can be obsessed with their own health and routines. Their need to control situations and people can cause conflict with coworkers. Open and honest, they are quite blunt in how they communicate and will tell others when they are upset about something. Sometimes they can get overly emotional about work issues and relationships.

If they allow change, they can grow and adapt when there is upheaval in their routines. They can experience many changes with their health and the way they view work. Obsessed with their health, they can have strict routines involving diet and exercise. They are the person everyone at work shares their secrets and problems with. Secretive and private, they possess a quiet strength that attracts others. Careers in psychotherapy, research, medicine, business, and politics suit them. Having success at work is important and they need to feel they are helping people improve. Working in a taboo career attracts them as well, so being a mortician or energy healer can be fulfilling. They can be a powerful influence in their work environment and inspire others to work harder to achieve. Productive workers, they have stamina and accomplish things with great intensity. They have a drive to succeed and be in positions of authority. Making money is important to them because it brings security. If they can harness acceptance, it will help them relax and release their need to control their environment.

Planetary Transits through the Sixth House

When planets transit the sixth house, you will want to focus on taking care of your physical body, diet, health, and health routines.

Transit Sun

This is a good time to focus on your diet and routine. You might get motivated to exercise and become actively involved in self-improvement for the next month. Tap into this energy to accomplish work goals, be productive, and get organized. You may be inspired to serve others in some way, so this is a good time to volunteer. Pay attention to your work tasks and relationships with coworkers. Get to know the people you work with by socializing more and sharing creative ideas. You are motivated to make time to declutter and establish a new routine. You might feel a need to have more fun at work. There could be positive vibes right now that bring recognition for the work you have done. You could be publicly recognized for the work you have accomplished.

You will feel more positive, confident, and motivated to get things done. If you are typically worried about things and stress about work responsibilities, you will feel a lot less concerned about the details. There can be a push to focus more on your personal well-being and health. Happiness comes through realizing that you can make time to do things that bring pleasure. If you can't travel for work right now, take some time off and go on a vacation. It is important to make time for your personal life and realize that work is not everything. Harnessing the ability to enjoy life will help bring fun into daily routines.

Transit Moon

This is a time when you will feel more productive. For the next few days, it is hard to separate your emotions from work. If you feel good, your work performance will improve, but if you are feeling down, you could struggle with staying focused. You will be feeling more inspired to help others and focus on their needs. Finishing tasks and paying more attention to little details will help you become more efficient. How you feel is influenced by work and your daily routine. Make sure to get enough sleep and eat healthy foods to increase your energy levels. You may be questioning if your work is emotionally fulfilling; if it isn't, you might want to make changes. Trust your intuition during this time and listen to your heart. You will want to spend time with animals; they can bring comfort and reduce stress.

Relationships with coworkers could change during this time. You may have people wanting to share their problems with you, and this can be tiring. Coworkers might want you to get more involved or commit to projects. You might question whether you're in the right job. There can be a lot of self-doubt, anxiety, and unnecessary worry. There can be anxiety about your health and you may want to schedule medical exams. You could be more vulnerable to stress and feel drained through social activities. It might be challenging to have a stable routine right now. Your diet, sleep, and exercise plans may fluctuate. Listen to your body, pay attention to how you feel, and adjust your daily activities accordingly. Stress can impact your health during this time, so it's important to relax and not get too emotional about things. Don't overreact, pick your battles at work, and don't waste your energy on things you can't control. This is a time to harness structure and get practical about your daily routine.

Transit Mercury

This is a good time to focus on organizing your daily routine. Don't let others distract you with gossip that can get in the way of your productivity. This is a good time to get things done. You will be focused on the details right now and there are a lot of basic tasks that need attention. Things are busier than usual and work issues need attention. You might be asked to put more effort in at work and lead a new project. There is more communication going on in the office. You may be traveling more and maintaining a busy schedule. You might want to make to-do lists, get bills paid, declutter your work area, and get tasks done that you have been putting off.

There can be some anxiety about your health, which will motivate you to schedule physical checkups. Overthinking can impact your ability to come up with solutions. Don't get too bogged down in the details but try to see the larger picture. You might be researching ways to improve your diet, manage work stress, and improve sleep. It's important to feel good to have enough energy to continue working hard and tackling additional responsibilities. Practical matters will weigh on your mind. This is a good time to learn something new; get a certification that will benefit your work and bring future success. This is a good time to think about what type of career you want to pursue. You can be indecisive about what to do at work or how to accomplish tasks. Harness your ability to get organized and make plans you can follow through on.

Transit Venus

During this transit, you will want to focus more on creating a peaceful and harmonious work environment. If your work environment is normally tense and stressful, this will be a good time to confront these issues. It's a good time get more involved in making work a better place. You can help coworkers compromise and act as a mediator where there is conflict. People listen to you right now and appreciate your calming influence. Your focus will be on strengthening relationships with coworkers. Socially, you shine at work right now and can get more attention. It can be difficult to focus on work responsibilities and you might feel lazier than usual. Procrastination can cause delays with getting tasks completed. Socializing too much at work can distract you and impact your productivity. Cooperation and working together for a common goal can be rewarding. You feel friendlier than usual and more focused on having fun. Finding something you love to do will be your focus. New relationships could start through work or through work connections. Your daily routine is not as organized as usual, and you might want to be more creative and imaginative. If you can harness harmony in the work environment, it will increase trust with coworkers and help you remember what you love to do.

Transit Mars

This transit will increase your drive to complete tasks. You will be more focused on work during this time. Everything speeds up and your daily life gets busier. You can feel more irritated when plans don't work out. You will feel a need to take charge at work and will want to motivate coworkers to be more productive. Conflicts and disruptions can arise with coworkers. You want to speak up more and tell people what you really think. Keep yourself busy and use this increased energy to focus on projects, hobbies, and work you want to do. There is a desire to be more active and think about diet, exercise, and your health. You may feel more restless during this time and need more intense physical activity. You feel impatient and are prone to make impulsive decisions. Pursuing your goals and working passionately for what you want will increase during this time. Control your emotional reactions, take a deep breath before acting, and use logic to solve problems. Slow down, be more patient, and pay attention to the details to avoid rash mistakes. Harnessing patience will help you calm your emotions and focus on the responsibilities that need your attention.

Transit Jupiter

This transit brings good luck and positive energy into your work life. You find more joy at work right now. Positive feelings increase when you feel you are being of service. You will feel more generous and have a desire to give more of your time and money to charitable projects. You might feel more appreciative about the work you do, coworkers, and having a daily routine that makes you feel productive. Optimistic about the future, you may feel more grateful for your good health. You might want to focus more on taking care of other people. You often benefit through coworkers and might get recognized for your efforts. Success comes easily during this time as you are more optimistic about practical life. You are a reliable, dedicated, and efficient worker, which helps you have the energy to get tasks completed. There can be a chance at new job opportunities that might increase your income in some way or allow you to travel more. You can find happiness in the simple things in life right now, such as sleeping, eating, and having a workout routine. You can also overindulge in things you enjoy, such as food, drinking, and relaxing. Harness gratitude and enjoy the benefits that come through being of service.

Transit Saturn

This transit impacts your work, routine, and health for the next two to three years. You will have to take responsibility for your practical needs and might feel more pressure during this time. There is a lot of pressure you put on yourself, but you may feel like unseen forces are making things more difficult. You feel that you need to do everything by yourself and that you can't rely on others. The truth is that you might be more cautious about showing weakness or vulnerability. Responsibilities tend to pile up and you can feel burdened at times. Duty can create feelings of guilt as you can hold yourself to a higher standard. Try not to be too critical of yourself during this time and don't worry so much.

You feel more serious, anxious, and critical of yourself and others. Even if you are doing a good job, you focus in on the small details and mistakes. This can make you feel moodier and irritable toward others. You are disciplined and more focused on work, which influences your expectations of coworkers and how they should be completing their work. Focus on your own efforts and resist controlling other people. You have to focus on your own routine, tasks, and work ethic. Hard work comes naturally to you, and you are more committed to succeed. Not everyone can work as diligently as you do. Learn to manage your time, take breaks, and plan for the future.

You are more focused on achievement right now and want to have recognition through work. This often feels blocked, and you struggle to see any positive movement in the work arena. Patience is important and you have to wait for things to change. There are many things that need to be done and you are a natural at getting organized. If there is disorder, you will work hard to fix the problems to make things better.

Stress and anxiety can impact your physical body. You might experience health problems or get sick more often during this transit. Changing your diet and habits will help you manage these issues. Make sure to schedule dental, eye, and medical appointments to check any symptoms you are experiencing. Harnessing structure will help you feel in control of your daily life and reduce stress.

Transit Uranus

This transit will cause unexpected changes with your routine and health for the next seven to eight years. There is an unsettled and disruptive energy influencing your daily life. You might get diagnosed with an illness that influences your productivity and ability to work. There are new things that happen that cause you to question where you work and how you get things done. Daily routines are shaken up and you have to adapt. There can be a desire to change your daily routine; maybe you decide to start a new diet and exercise plan. You could change jobs or get promoted or even fired. There is something outside of your control that is influencing your schedule and day-to-day activities. If you have felt bored and stagnant at work, this energy will force you to try something different. Exploring more innovative ways of doing your job can open up new possibilities. One minute you feel like being productive and the next procrastination sets in, which makes it difficult to focus. If work is limiting, you might want to break free, rebel, and question authority. You need to feel a sense of autonomy and independence in the work environment right now. You might want to question traditional ways of doing things and make drastic changes to your routine, health, and relationships.

Changes in your daily routine can create additional stress. You might feel more restless and unable to depend on a stable paycheck. Your work hours might change, people might quit, or you could get new management. These changes can impact your health. Overthinking and intellectualizing your emotions need to be avoided. You might decide to start working on making money doing an exciting hobby. There can be an interest in unconventional types of work related to the mind-body-spirit connection and different alternative healing modalities such as energy healing, meditation, herbal medicine, and yoga. Harness open-mindedness to pursue nontraditional ways of doing things and focus on taking better care of your health.

Transit Neptune

This transit can affect your health and work for about fourteen years. You can be more susceptible to illness due to a heightened sensitivity to your environment. Worry and stress can weaken your immune system. There can be unexplained or mysterious medical symptoms that doctors are unable to figure out. It's important to get second and third opinions on any diagnosis or treatment plan. There can be difficulty getting an accurate diagnosis because the physical symptoms can be elusive.

You will want to escape from daily responsibilities and having to work. Developing and sticking to a routine will help you feel more grounded. Things feel unsettled and you can feel disillusioned with life right now. It's difficult to figure out what tasks you need to accomplish. You are feeling more imaginative and daydreaming a lot more. It's hard to get anything done because you feel more tired than usual. You might want to find more meaningful work and are drawn to spiritual pursuits helping those less fortunate. Careers in social work and counseling can be beneficial. It's important for you to develop stronger boundaries right now. Harnessing intuition can help give you answers when you feel lost and unsure of what decisions to make.

Transit Pluto

This is a long-term transit that transforms your daily routine and personal habits for the next decade. Your work and health are affected, and you will need to address issues head-on. Deep emotional issues could trigger physical symptoms or force you to address health issues you have been ignoring. Get medical appointments done; you might have to start taking a new medicine or go through a medical procedure. There can be an interest in alternative medical practices, and you will explore ways to heal yourself. This is a good time to get rid of bad habits that might be negatively influencing your health. If you smoke, you might decide to quit, and this can be very difficult. New habits can form easily; just be sure they are healthy habits that will improve your overall well-being. Hidden emotions and anxieties you have repressed can bubble up to the surface. Pluto shakes up your day-to-day activities and forces you to feel new things. It is time to see how your past habits and routines have impacted your health and ability to heal. Learning more about healing and even going to counseling might be beneficial. You need to be able to process intense emotions and open up to change. Controlling situations and struggling to let go of the past can trigger new challenges, and new things like astrology, martial arts, energy healing, and psychological tools will be interesting to explore.

The type of work you do will change, as well as relationships with coworkers. You can put a lot of pressure on yourself and feel burdened. It's okay to ask for help and take time off work if you need it. You are evolving as a person and going through many rebirths. There are feelings of loss and sadness that make you want to work alone. You will feel more private during this time and try to hold on tight to old structures. This might be the time you decide to change jobs and become your own boss. Owning your own business and finding a job that brings deeper meaning into your life can be fulfilling.

Ways to Harness Virgo Energy

- Pay attention to details.
- Help someone in need.
- Write and journal ideas.
- Establish a routine.
- Declutter and get organized.
- Exercise and eat healthy.

7
LIBRA

Archetype: Peacemaker

Symbol: The Scales

Sun Sign Dates: September 23–October 23

Energy: Creative

Element: Air, Cardinal

Planet: Venus

House: Seventh

I f you have Libra in your birth chart, planets in the seventh house, or are experiencing planetary transits through the seventh house, this chapter will cover information regarding these energies. If you don't, you can still learn about Libra energy and incorporate it into your life. The placement of the planet Venus in the sign and house will show where you express Libra energy. It is important to look at what house the sign Libra falls on in your birth wheel because this is where you will want to compromise, negotiate, find peace, find harmony, and nurture relationships. Harnessing Libra energy gives you an ability to express your artistic talents, seek fairness, focus on other people's needs, and develop stronger intimate relationships.

Libra Energy Words

Peaceful, artistic, creative, balanced, intelligent, fair, knowledgeable, loving, harmonious, committed, diplomatic, attractive, flirtatious, beautiful, elegant, charming, indecisive.

Libra Motto

As a Libra, I am a person who likes to be in relationships. I want fairness and believe in justice. Sometimes I neglect my own needs for my partner. Other people's happiness is often more important than my own. I am good at compromise and struggle with conflict. I want peace and harmony in all aspects of life. I prefer being friendly, easygoing, and harmonious. I can be indecisive because I can understand both sides of an argument. I work hard to balance my thoughts and emotions.

Harnessing Libra Energy

The scale of balance is the symbol associated with Libra. This energy symbolizes justice, equality, and fairness. It's no surprise that this energy increases the need to compromise and find harmony and is a calming influence. Libra rules business partnerships, marriage, relationships, love, and thinking about others. Libra is the only sign of the zodiac whose symbol is not a living thing, because the scales are metal. This energy finds out who it truly is through other people, often a relationship partner. It's this deeper meaning that reveals what Libra energy is truly about, which is relationships. It's about focusing on other people's needs and putting other people first. This energy can be peaceful, easygoing, supportive, and creative. Libra energy finds its purpose through connecting and developing relationships.

Libra energy values beauty, companionship, and harmony in all areas of life. Libra energy inspires us to focus on other people's needs and nurture relationships. Adapting to what other people believe comes easily as Libras see the truth in different opinions. The goal of this energy is to keep the peace and not rock the boat. Learning to avoid conflict by making sure to listen and fully understand other people's points of view is Libra's strength. Sometimes seen as noncommittal and indecisive, staying balanced is their focus. Pleasing others and ensuring their happiness is also important, but so is avoiding anger, conflict, and uncomfortable situations. Libra energy often wants comfort at any price and can be dependent on others. It might believe that it needs someone else to take care of them and many dislike being alone. Understanding opposing points of view, mediating disagreements, and fostering compromise are Libra's gifts. Being objective, considerate, and thoughtful about other people's viewpoints helps us connect with Libra energy.

Harness Imagination

Libra is associated with creative energy. They appreciate beautiful things, such as art, jewelry, and clothing. Not only are they intelligent and pursue learning, but they also enjoy expressing their artistic talents. This energy intensifies a passion for music, painting, writing, and theater. Making things better in the world is their gift. They have an ability to compromise, so pleasing others is important to them. They often focus on what others want, even sacrificing their own needs. Sometimes they stay in the middle and refuse to pick either side. They can see the benefits and challenges that exist in all choices. As the scales of balance, they are always weighing both sides. If their energy gets too focused on one thing, it has to adapt and find the middle path. Their creative energy inspires their imagination and helps them express thoughts through writing and communicating ideas. Cultured, this energy finds ways to be gracious, refined, and courteous. This energy can help us focus on maintaining a calm, supportive, and peaceful nature. It intensifies our need to find common ground and loving relationships. This energy challenges us to get more comfortable with conflict and teaches us how to be more objective. Harnessing this energy can help us create beautiful things and become aware of the importance of healthy relationships.

Harness Choices

Libra is ruled by the air element. Air signs are the thinkers of the zodiac. We breathe air and know that it's there but it's hard to see it. Air energy is hard to grasp because it's invisible, detached, and intellectual. At heart, Libras are seekers of knowledge, and this energy blesses them with both mental acuity and a desire to learn. Balancing our thoughts, emotions, and the practical issues of life can be difficult. It requires balance, compromise, and a reasonable approach to emotions. Libras are born to do all these things and often shine when doing them.

Tapping into this energy involves connecting with the mind and the heart. Socializing with others is also important to learn more about the world. Understanding other people's beliefs can help Libras develop more supportive relationships. Having a relationship is important for Libra's survival. At times, they might feel like they can't do things on their own. The need for companionship and friendship helps them find balance. In fact, peaceful, calm, and caring relationships can help them feel emotional fulfillment. Partnering with others in some way, being open-minded, and focusing on compromise can help them connect emotionally. Air signs find answers by thinking things through, which helps them be fair, understanding, and open-minded. They are often calm in a crisis and detach from emotions and rationalize the path that needs to be taken. This energy wants to express itself, although this often happens through other people. An elusive energy, it's mercurial, rational, and sometimes hard to grasp.

To connect to air energy, we need to learn how to analyze our thoughts, beliefs, emotions, and emotional needs.

Leading the Way

As a cardinal sign, Libras want to lead and come up with fresh ideas. Libra is associated with the fall season. Its energy feels similar to when the trees, flowers, and plants begin to change colors. The world begins to slow down and things become calm. Creative and artistic, they inspire others with their ability to get along with others. Cardinal energy motivates and inspires others to try new things. It encourages us to focus on other people and utilize them to get the job done. Starting something new and allowing change opens up unexpected opportunities for success. This energy sometimes gets distracted on the follow-through and expects others to finish the project. It is off to the next new idea and expects other people to do the hands-on practical work. Giving advice, finding solutions, and quickly moving on to the next project suits this energy best. This energy lacks the detail focus and planning skills to initiate the tasks that need to be accomplished. They often leave that challenge for the fixed signs. This energy grows bored with monotony and would rather think of ways to change routines and outcomes. Sameness can inspire them to shake things up and do something different. This energy is invigorating and energizes the entire environment. Tapping into this energy can help us become more creative, confident, and open-minded.

Nurture Partnership

Libra is ruled by the planet Venus. Venus's energy is calm, romantic, fair, peaceful, and social. Because it's attracted to beautiful things, it can appear sensitive, gentle, and harmonious. This energy nurtures love and intensifies a desire to please others. This energy can show how we meet our partner and reveal what type of partner is most compatible for us. It reveals how we show affection and what types of relationship partners we attract and are drawn to. Beauty can manifest in many ways and there is a sense of gracefulness, politeness, and refinement that Venus's energy brings into our lives. It's a peaceful, calm, and pleasant energy that wants to be considerate of others. It avoids harshness and conflict because it wishes to always find a balanced approach. It's hard not to like Venus's energy because of its charm and sociability. Venus strives to avoid conflict by compromising, being noncommittal, and not taking sides. Venus's energy is focused on expressing itself in a balanced way. Focusing on the needs of others comes easily and partnerships can bring a sense of security.

Focus on Others

The seventh house rules marriage and partnership. It represents our spouse and partners we commit to. It can show what type of marriage we might encounter and even reveal our chances of divorce, separation, or remarriage. Not only does the seventh house represent intimate relationships, but it also shows our experience with business partners. This area of the birth chart is also called the descendent or seventh house cusp. The sign that falls on the seventh house cusp can have a considerable impact on partner choices, the types of people we attract and are attracted to, and reveals how we show love in relationships. Experiencing intimacy and finding companionship is crucial to our psychological well-being. Having supportive, caring, and healthy relationships can help us blend our personality with others. Finding support and being able to depend on someone else is an important seventh house lesson. Achieving our goals comes easier sometimes when we team up with others. This area of life shows how we work peacefully with others and how we handle enemies in the personal and business world.

Libra Rising

When you first meet Libra risings, they appear charming, graceful, elegant, and polite. Because they are attractive and friendly, people often like them instantly. This is because they have a way of soothing others and making them feel supported. Libra risings strive for harmony in all areas of life. These individuals possess a peaceful nature and work hard to avoid conflict. Diplomats at heart, being able to get along with others helps them feel calm and balanced. Being alone can be difficult for them. In fact, being in a relationship is often crucial for their sustained happiness. If people are cruel or if they think they are not liked, it can bother them. They can be people pleasers because they want to get along with everyone. They are talented at finding ways to compromise, make peace, and please others. Sacrificing their own needs to focus on other people can cause some challenges. In relationships, neglecting what they want and refusing to speak up for themselves can lead to secret resentment. Sometimes they are labeled as noncommittal or too appeasing because they don't want to offend anyone. Although, they can also be opinionated and have strong beliefs about equality and justice. When they do speak up, it's usually if they see someone being mistreated. They can enjoy fighting for the underdog. Some might possess artistic and creative talents such as music, art, and theater. Intellectual and rational, they often like to study and learn new ways of expressing their artistic side. As an air sign, they enjoy expanding their minds and can be interested in reading, teaching, law, travel, and science.

They seek fairness and believe that everyone's ideas should be respected. Because they are natural mediators, they can debate many different topics. Their behavior can make them appear indecisive, especially when making difficult decisions. They like to weigh the pros and cons of every situation before acting. They can withdraw from others if they feel pressured to choose or decide too quickly. Although, there can be times when certain topics trigger intense emotions. In these moments, they often speak up bluntly, fighting for fairness and equality.

Libra risings are trying to maintain equilibrium, especially regarding their thoughts, feelings, and relationships. To feel comfortable in their environment, they want to conform, blend in, and avoid conflict. Sometimes they can become overly accommodating and give in to others too easily. Having boundaries can help them protect themselves and learn when to advocate for their own needs. It's important to them to experience love, and they can be flirtatious, affectionate, supportive, and dedicated partners. Being alone can be difficult for them because they are social creatures who often find their identity through other people. In friendship, they can be supportive confidants with excellent listening skills. They are known to be persuasive and fair and give supportive advice. There is a graceful energy around them and people are attracted to their charisma. They are tactful when they disagree with someone and charming enough

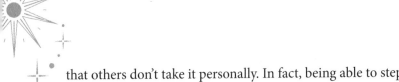

that others don't take it personally. In fact, being able to step back and talk through things peacefully with others can be a talent they possess.

Libra risings can appear easygoing, relaxed, but sometimes get labeled as lazy. It's true that they like to relax and many don't like to feel rushed. Enjoying the finer things in life and pursuing hobbies can bring emotional fulfillment. Detaching can help them when they feel overwhelmed by their emotions and practical responsibilities. If they feel stressed or anxious, they can seek solitude. At other times, they might prefer to be around other people versus overthinking their problems. They are the scales of balance and often shift like a pendulum in terms of what they want. Socializing helps energize them and is a way they get support from people they care about. Having relationships can help them increase their self-esteem and sense of belonging. Partnership is at the heart of their soul learning. Balancing their personal lives and relationships is their primary focus.

Libra risings enjoy making everyone around them happy. Pleasing others comes naturally and sometimes they struggle with focusing on their own needs, which is why they tend to focus on their relationships. In fact, they can be overly focused on making everyone around them feel supported and cared for. People often appreciate their easygoing and supportive nature. Master negotiators, they know what other people want and need. It's easier for them to attain their own personal goals when they learn to speak up and be more self-focused. They also can find that partnership helps them achieve their future goals at a faster rate. If they can harness supportive relationships, they can find emotional fulfillment and a sense of belonging.

How to Harness Planets in Libra

When planets are in Libra, you will be focused on relationships, finding balance, prioritizing the needs of others, and learning more about yourself through compromise.

Sun in Libra

Sun in Libra individuals can find their sense of identity through having relationships. From a young age, they have a strong urge to bond with others. Some of their greatest lessons come from dating and love. They often seek romantic connections and want to experience the feeling of being in love. Being in relationships enables them to build confidence and express their flirtatious side. Dating multiple people does not suit them because they prefer to have committed relationships. Sometimes they can end relationships too quickly and be indecisive about their feelings. A big lesson for these individuals is to learn self-love. Putting themselves first and realizing that their partner can't always be responsible for their happiness can be an eye-opening experience. There are times they can feel overwhelmed in relationships because they put a lot of pressure on themselves and have high expectations. They might also prefer to spend time with friends or with people they are attracted to without getting too serious. Companionship can be more fulfilling than a passionate romance.

They crave social interaction, so forming close bonds can help them feel connected. Having positive relationships in their lives can be beneficial to their self-esteem. Not having healthy relationships might contribute to feelings of loneliness, sadness, and anxiety. Being alone and not having a partner can sometimes be difficult. It's important for them to remember that it's better to be alone than to be in abusive relationships. Gifted mediators, they are great at deescalating conflict in stressful situations. People often turn to them for balanced and impartial advice. Among friends, they are often the one who is in the middle trying to bring peace and harmony between both parties.

Not only are they born with artistic gifts and talents, but they are also intelligent and enjoy learning. They can be modest, shy, and value beauty, love, and fairness. By making other people feel good, they seek harmony, which helps them find greater balance.

They value equality and justice, which can make them peaceful negotiators who get along well with others. On the other hand, they also need to be careful about being too concerned with what other people think. They might avoid conflict and disagreements or conform to keep the peace. Learning to speak up for themselves is challenging at times, especially if it involves an authority figure. They can feel depleted and taken advantage of when they compromise too much. Developing a stronger relationship with themselves is crucial because it helps them get to know what they

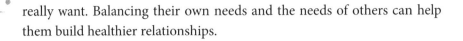

really want. Balancing their own needs and the needs of others can help them build healthier relationships.

Moon in Libra

Moon in Libra individuals can find emotional fulfillment by finding peace and harmony. Their happiness and comfort involve being in relationships with others. Not only having love, but also having friendships is something they cherish. They are masters of giving other people what they want because they are gentle, romantic, peaceful, and understanding. They seem to naturally understand what other people need. Experiencing harmony and maintaining a tranquil environment can inspire their creative side. Many have artistic abilities they express through music, art, and theater. Avid learners, they often enjoy reading and taking classes.

They believe in fairness, justice, and equality. Many are known to speak up and advocate for the rights of others. Because of this desire, they might be interested in law, advocacy, and politics. If things are out of balance, they often seek to restore equilibrium by withdrawing from social interactions. Having a calm, stable, and supportive environment is crucial for them to feel comfortable. Their emotional happiness is dependent on the kinds of relationships they have. It's important that they pick healthy and supportive partners if they enter an intimate relationship. If they get involved with abusive partners, it can have lasting effects on their self-esteem and ability to cope.

Having mental rapport with others is important to them because they enjoy debating topics with people they trust. The element of air influences their emotional nature, making them more likely to intellectualize their emotions than to actually feel them. Strong reactions from others can overwhelm them at times because they are not comfortable with conflict. Seeking harmony in relationships is their priority, which at times can lead to neglecting their own needs. They often have a knack for making other people feel comfortable and supported. Listening to others and giving solid advice can help them feel useful. Sometimes they struggle to understand how they feel or how to verbalize their emotions. They might show how they feel by being affectionate and doing practical things for people they love. They crave loving, intimate relationships and often find emotional fulfillment through having a significant other. Marriage can help them feel safe, stable, and secure. Being alone can make them feel uneasy and uncomfortable. This is why they often marry or live with someone at a young age. In fact, they would much rather spend time with their partner or a specific friend than with large groups of people. Sometimes they can be shy and can become very attached to people they care about. Often other people don't realize how much these individuals truly care about them.

Happiness can come by having someone to depend on, finding balance, and building harmony in relationships. Social butterflies, they prefer being friendly and flirtatious. Sometimes they can get confused about what they really feel because they are natural thinkers. They are constantly trying to balance their emotional nature. Their first instinct is to think things through before they act, and this can make them excellent negotiators. They have an ability to see both sides of emotionally charged issues. Avoiding conflict comes naturally for them.

Speaking up and being assertive can be challenging at times. In fact, they might also feel confused about what they really believe because they can see the truth in many conflicting issues. Staying planted in the middle is important for them to maintain balance. They would rather focus on other people's feelings because they care about supporting others. Following the lead soothes them and can bring comfort. Establishing stability in their lives brings harmony. If they can learn to tap into their emotions, it will help them grow stronger.

Mercury in Libra

Mercury in Libra individuals are intelligent and balanced with an easygoing approach to learning. They enjoy educational pursuits such as reading, writing, and research. They might have an interest in teaching, politics, and law. Discussing topics such as art, beauty, and entertainment can help them expand their mind. They might also like to speak up and fight for justice. Many are excellent communicators because they can understand other people's points of view. Natural mediators and problem-solvers, they balance opposing viewpoints.

People trust them and they can help calm people when they are upset. Communication in relationships is crucial for them to feel supported. They need a partner who can mentally challenge them and help them grow. Intellectual stimulation helps them avoid boredom. Indecisive at times, they can struggle to figure out what they really believe in.

Natural peacemakers, they can give supportive relationship advice. They tend to compromise and help people come together to avoid disagreements. Being fair when communicating with others can make them seem indecisive and unreliable. Sometimes they are indecisive and withdraw from picking a side. They often turn to others for advice. But sometimes they challenge it or decide to do the opposite. Harnessing self-reflection helps them tune in to what they value and believe.

Venus in Libra

Venus in Libra individuals crave being in love and experiencing relationships. They are great at compromise and can be kind, generous, and focused on pleasing others. In relationships, they dislike rudeness, cruelty, and abrasiveness and want to avoid negative people. They are sensitive to the energy of others and prefer to be around positive people. There are times when they seem to attract more combative partners or relationships with colleagues. These experiences challenge them to grow. They thrive when they can experience peaceful and harmonious relationships. They have a desire to treat people fairly, respectfully, and can at times be too accommodating. They see the good in people and expect others to be like them. When they find out the truth that most people aren't as focused on others, it can be disheartening. Sometimes they neglect their own needs and prefer catering to others, especially in intimate relationships. Because of their compromising nature, they can attract more assertive partners who might take them for granted. They might be attracted to dominant people who take charge and do things for them.

Choosing the right relationship partner is crucial for their future happiness. Sharing ideas, feelings, and dreams with their partner helps them connect in a deeper way. They want to be treated with kindness and enjoy romantic gestures. Committed to those they love, it's hard for them to be alone. They prefer spending time socializing, discussing their interests, and being flirtatious. Harnessing healthy relationships can help them increase their self-esteem.

Mars in Libra

Mars in Libra individuals reflect on their emotions before they speak up. Slow to anger, they tend to hide their irritation or unhappiness. They want peace and will do what they have to do to avoid conflict. Charming, peaceful, and accommodating even when they are challenged or upset, it's hard for others to see when they are angry. They can smile and act like they are content, even if they are struggling inside with intense emotions. Controlling their anger can become a constant challenge. Sometimes others can perceive them as passive-aggressive because they seem to conform easily and don't readily speak up. Calm in a crisis, they stay evenly balanced, fair, and weigh all options before they act. They avoid conflict in the external world and often intellectualize their anger. Suppressing negative feelings is sometimes easier for them than feeling them. If they do debate, they will use knowledge to win their arguments. At times, their desire for fairness can irritate others because they want their support. Experts at conflict management, their ability to focus on the needs of others makes them a calming presence in heated situations. They are a peacemaker and want everyone to get along. When they do fight battles, it's usually defending other people and fighting for those who are mistreated. The passionate energy of Mars is toned down with this placement and strives for harmony. If they can harness greater confidence in speaking up in challenging times, they can develop stronger self-confidence.

Jupiter in Libra

Jupiter in Libra individuals are concerned with justice, fairness, and morality. They are generous, persuasive, and diplomatic, which often brings good luck and abundance into their lives. In relationships, they value commitment, friendship, and harmony. Physical and sexual attraction is not as important to them as experiencing a grounded, stable, and supportive union. In fact, many of them have good luck in picking a compatible partner. Many times, their relationships are long lasting, and sometimes their partner is from a different culture, country, or background from them. For example, they might meet someone while working or traveling overseas. Some people with this placement find happiness through travel and might end up living in a different country.

Being social and networking with groups of people who are adventurous, free-spirited, and open-minded can be fulfilling. It's important for them to make time for socializing with people who share similar ideas, beliefs, and philosophies. In fact, discussing religion, philosophy, culture, and history are things they are interested in learning more about. They are on a search for experiencing abundance and expanding their knowledge. They enjoy education and many are avid readers. Some are forever students and take classes throughout their lifetime. They have many different interests and a passionate desire to explore the world.

Natural teachers and speakers, many of them will pursue careers in higher education, psychology, marketing, government, and public relations. Some of them might pursue artistic and creative avenues and have a love of beauty to share with the world. Maintaining harmony in their life and relationships is important because they want to bring peace to the world. They have a strong desire to make the world a better place. Harnessing peace in all areas of life helps them attract positive relationships, opportunities, and success.

Saturn in Libra

Saturn in Libra individuals are naturally patient, practical, and cooperative in relationships. Their intelligence blesses them with a sense of tact and refinement. They seek stability in relationships and take commitment seriously. In fact, they are not the type to just date around. Saturn in Libra individuals can be serious in matters of the heart. At times, they restrict themselves to avoid expressing feelings. Fears of commitment can delay marriage and it's often due to indecisiveness. Trusting others and showing emotional vulnerability can be challenging. Partnership might take a bit more work for these individuals due to a cautious and skeptical nature. Once they do commit, they are steadfast, extremely loyal, and reliable partners. In many areas of life, they can feel super responsible, which is why they put a lot of pressure on themselves.

Focusing on practical matters and new ways they can take care of the needs of others is when they feel more comfortable. Taking care of themselves can be more difficult. It's important to remember to make time for their own needs. This can prevent compassion fatigue, depression, and burnout. It might be beneficial to pursue friendships with those they feel comfortable with first. In general, they need to find a sense of peace and security in their relationships. Business partnership can help them achieve their goals and bring success.

It's important for them to maintain a sense of balance, especially when they feel stress, anxiety, or experience unexpected life changes. Frustration can lead to negativity at times. Thinking more positively can help them snap out of irritable moods. They can try to control things in moderation, but they need to realize some things are out of their control. Harnessing wisdom helps them implement important lessons and apply them in their relationships.

Uranus in Libra

Uranus in Libra in individuals often question tradition and explore alternative ways of interacting in relationships. Eccentric, creative, and individualistic, they have a desire to explore taboo subjects that most people are afraid to acknowledge. Their strong sense of individuality makes them good at honoring other people's unique opinions and beliefs. Even if they don't agree with others, their value of harmony and fairness makes them easy to get along with. But there are times when their need for self-expression can become imbalanced and cause conflict in their relationships. They often want to change societal beliefs about love, justice, and partnerships.

Unconventional in many areas of life, they like to feel free in relationships. Old-fashioned and outdated beliefs about marriage, love, and monogamy are not appealing to them. They want to experience growth in relationships and need to feel challenged. They sometimes push the limits of social convention to see if they can force change. Shocking others, being unique, and innovating can bring many interesting interactions into their lives. They might attract relationship partners who are similar to them or very different from them.

Rebellious about living up to other people's expectations, it's sometimes difficult for them to follow other people's rules. In fact, questioning authority by forcing their opinions on others excites them. Part of them might enjoy making people feel uncomfortable. Because they are freedom loving, their desire for independence can make it hard for them to conform to societal expectations. They want to break out of the mold and chart their own unique path. A strong stubborn streak makes it difficult for them to compromise with others, especially if it's something that impacts their autonomy. It's important for them to harness compromise in relationships and allow other people to have their own unique beliefs.

Neptune in Libra

Neptune in Libra individuals possess an idealistic and spiritual outlook. They strive for inner balance, which enables them to adapt to life's challenges with acceptance and faith. They are born with idealism and a belief that the universe will take care of them. Romantic at heart, they are sensitive souls who believe in true love. They might be on a search for a soul mate. Compassionate, caring, and imaginative, it's important that they see things clearly in relationships. At times they can be very romantic and even sacrifice their needs for their partner. Other times they might withdraw and be afraid of getting hurt.

Balancing their feelings and thoughts will help them find a sense of equilibrium. In the end, this can help them build healthier and stronger relationships. When they feel stressed, they avoid conflict and refuse to socialize with others. Solitude can help them get centered, so they might benefit from activities such as meditation, journaling, energy healing, and grounding.

Guided by their belief in a perfect world of fairness, justice, and love, they often expect that other people are like them. Disappointment and sadness can come through relationships, especially when they did not see things clearly. Their path can become easier when they listen to their intuition and trust their inner voice. Spiritual, artistic, and creative, they often enjoy writing poetry, listening to music, and seeing beauty in the world around them. They are known to sometimes overextend themselves and give a lot of their time and energy to helping others. It's important that they don't neglect their own spiritual goals for their partner. Sometimes they can feel taken advantaged of and even betrayed in relationships. At times they feel people see their kindness as a weakness.

Developing stronger boundaries can help protect them from unhealthy or toxic people. Learning to fill up their own emotional tank first before offering to help others brings wisdom. Harnessing self-love is an important lesson that can help them find greater balance in their lives.

Pluto in Libra

Pluto in Libra individuals can have a strong urge to bond and experience deep intimacy. Developing meaningful relationships that are powerful and transformative is often their priority. Some might obsess about their partner and they are known to be passionate, determined, and loyal. Some might appear jealous or possessive, which could make others feel like they don't trust them. It takes them time to open up and trust someone. They are perceptive and highly intuitive individuals who wait until they get to know someone before they share their inner feelings. Fairness, justice, and equality are things they passionately fight for. They often enjoy fighting for the underdog.

Their partnerships often experience cycles of death, rebirth, and transformation. Pluto brings change and deep-seated fears to the surface. Issues with trust and intimacy are often the greatest lessons. Through their personal experiences, they can learn to heal old wounds that prevent them from fully committing in relationships. All or nothing in love, they find it hard to connect emotionally if there are not intense feelings or physical chemistry. They want to dig deep with a partner and merge spiritually. When they communicate in social settings, they are comfortable discussing taboo topics such as death, sexuality, trauma, grief, and injustice. Harnessing the ability to let go while allowing change in their relationships will help them grow.

Planets in the Seventh House

When planets are in the seventh house, you will be focused on relationships, marriage, partnership, and working with others in cooperative ways.

Sun in the Seventh House

These individuals find their main identity by developing lasting relationships. They value harmony, romance, and partnership more than most people. Socially graceful, they attract many people into their life because of their easygoing nature and calm demeanor. They are not someone who enjoys dating around and they typically value commitment in relationships. Although they are sometimes indecisive about their feelings, they enjoy having a reliable partner. Some are attracted to many different types of people. It's important for them to pick the right partner. This is especially true with marriage because it can impact their overall happiness.

Indecision in relationships can make them seem unreliable at times, but it's because they often doubt their inner voice. They might prefer to be friends with someone first. Sometimes they can confuse people about their intentions because of their flirtatious nature. Their loving, affectionate, and attentive personality makes them easy to get along with. Dating might seem challenging at times. In fact, it can be difficult for them to find the right partner. There are many lessons they have to learn in the area of love. Many can be conflict avoidant, which can make them run away from difficult conversations. If a relationship is unhealthy, they might stay in it due to fears of being alone or of hurting someone's feelings. They can try to maintain the peace at all costs. Sometimes they might neglect their own needs and focus only on their partner's needs. It's important that they find their own sense of identity and self-worth outside of their relationships.

They seek fulfillment through pleasing others and are excellent at compromise. Seeing both sides of an issue in their relationships can help them negotiate solutions. They should be cautious about marrying on impulse. It's recommended that they take the time necessary to really get to know their partner. A good rule of thumb is to realize that it can take about two years to truly know someone. Before that time, they can experience a honeymoon period where they typically see what someone wants them to see. Someone's true personality and bad behaviors often reveal themselves with time.

This placement can show the potential for legal issues, disputes, separation, and even divorce. Legal issues can arise in marriage involving custody matters, finances, and material possessions. This placement can create learning in relationships and bring heavy emotional lessons. These individuals need peaceful and supportive people in their lives to feel happy and balanced. If they feel trapped in a negative relationship, it can sometimes be difficult for them to make changes. Breaking free, letting go, and moving on from unhealthy relationships helps them develop a stronger connection with their own inner needs. It's critical that they find someone who will value and respect them for who they truly are. It's important to learn how to balance fulfilling their own needs with the needs of others.

Moon in the Seventh House

These individuals often find their emotional fulfillment and happiness through relationships. They can experience fluctuations in their relationships and even experience several relationships throughout their life. Their emotional and financial security often comes through their marriage partner. They crave security, commitment, affection, and comfort in relationships. To feel supported and cherished, it's crucial that they maintain healthy relationships. Picking an emotionally supportive partner can be fulfilling for them, but being single can be difficult, and sometimes they rush to marry early in life. They need to be careful about reacting on emotions only in relationships. They should spend time getting to know someone before they make a serious commitment. If they do this, it can prevent unnecessary heartbreak and emotional pain. Having someone to depend on can help them find greater balance. Because their emotional happiness is tied to having a partner, it's important that they select a compatible partner. Trusting someone can help them feel emotionally secure and stable. Being able to rely on someone during stressful times can help them create the sense of security they need. If they don't find a supportive, calm, and peaceful relationship, they can experience separation, breakups, and divorce. There might be times in their life when they have to take care of their partner and provide for their needs. Also, they might need to rely on their partner for financial support. In relationships, they often have karmic learning related to developing their own sense of self-worth and love for themselves. Healthy relationships often come after they have learned to be alone and stand on their own two feet. Harnessing introspection will help them learn to nurture their own emotional needs.

Mercury in the Seventh House

These individuals are blessed with the gift of communication. They are excellent mediators and their negotiation skills help them convince others to listen. A mental connection with a partner is more important to them than physical attraction. Discussing their thoughts, feelings, and emotions with others helps them destress and process their emotions. They need to find an intimate partner who likes to communicate as much as they do. A partner who shares similar interests and hobbies will also help them feel supported. They can become restless and bored in relationships that don't challenge their mind. In fact, they might end a relationship if they feel the communication is stifled or if someone is too quiet. They are intelligent and fair, which enables them to see competing points of view. Conflict is not always a bad thing, so speaking up for themselves might take some practice. They can be social butterflies who enjoy talking with other people about their creative ideas. Listening to other people's problems can make them excellent counselors. Because they are persuasive, they can excel in marketing, sales, and in business partnerships.

Worrying is one of the most challenging lessons they have to learn as well as controlling their anxiety. They tend to overthink and can overanalyze their own emotions. They need to focus on maintaining peace, harmony, and a balance between their thoughts and feelings. If they are dating, they can constantly question their friends and family for advice. If they are in a committed relationship, they can spend a lot of time talking about it with others. They need to step back from their relationships to see things clearly, which will help them solve problems on their own. They are great at giving advice but can feel other people don't truly listen to them. Because of this, they can seem detached during conversations. Harnessing greater balance in communication will help them build stronger relationships.

Venus in the Seventh House

These individuals can be romantic and charming in relationships. Spending time with people they care about helps them find happiness. Peaceful at heart, they seek harmony in love and personal relationships. They are calm, loving, and peaceful partners who need stable and healthy relationships. Getting comfortable with conflict and standing up for themselves can be difficult. They can struggle with being assertive, especially with their marriage partner. They are charming, flirtatious, and often seek to please other people. After all, harmony and fairness are important to them. They often focus on taking care of other people's needs before their own. It's common for them to attract more dominant partners who are more aggressive than them. They benefit from learning to nurture their own needs. Being alone is difficult and they can feel lonely if they aren't in an intimate relationship. Spending time talking, flirting, and getting to know others helps them connect.

People are attracted to their elegance, refined nature, and calming presence. Socially, there are very few people who don't like them. They have a way of winning people to their side in arguments. People perceive them as agreeable and trustworthy. They can benefit from having a business partner. At times they are like chameleons, blending and adapting to get along with people around them. In fact, staying firmly planted in the middle is where they feel most comfortable. If they can harness self-love, they can develop deeper and healthier relationships.

Mars in the Seventh House

These individuals can be passionate, independent, and impulsive in relationships. Rash, assertive, and courageous, they fight for what they want. They enjoy the feeling of new love and the excitement of a challenging relationship. The thrill of the chase can be inspiring for them. In fact, they can pursue love interests passionately and obsessively. They might have a tumultuous and unstable love nature. Sexual chemistry and having physical attraction with a partner are an important prerequisite in their personal relationships. They might be attracted to a powerful, combative, and independent type of partner. Because of this, their partnerships can be filled with arguments, disagreements, and some power struggles. At times they may act impulsively, and this can damage trust in their relationships. They need to be cautious about trying to overpower their partner or instigating arguments. When frustrated, their strong emotions can rise quickly to the surface, which makes it hard for them to hold back. There is a bluntness and directness to their personality. Relationships are often a place where they feel they can express their darker emotions and true nature. There can be several abrupt and intense endings in relationships. Powerful attraction can make it difficult for them to move on from certain people. If there are too many challenges with a partner, it's wise advice that they should move on and find someone new. They might lack patience, especially in love and business. They react quickly and passionately in the moment, and this strength can also help them heal abusive or destructive relationship patterns. Their marriage partner often has a great impact on their success or failure. They benefit if they can avoid power struggles and harness patience in their relationships.

Jupiter in the Seventh House

These individuals are generous and optimistic in relationships. Happy, friendly, and open-minded, they value commitment. They enjoy travel, movement, and being outdoors because they have a strong need to roam and explore. They increase their knowledge about the world through socializing with other people. Fiercely independent, their energy is contagious and they can uplift those in their inner circle. They often gain financially through their marriage partner or business partner. Good luck and fortune often fall in their lap because of their positive outlook and can-do attitude. Having intimacy in their personal relationships helps them connect deeply with others and find happiness. They often have an optimistic outlook about love and they tend to see the good in people. In fact, their personality can make their partner want to grow and be a better person.

A positive and healthy relationship inspires them and helps their overall sense of well-being. Sometimes there can be more than one marriage with this placement. The abundant energy of Jupiter can bring many people into their lives. It could be difficult for them to commit or pick just one partner. It's not uncommon for them to develop a relationship with someone from a different country, culture, or religious background. They value an intelligent, adventurous, and independent partner who allows them a lot of freedom. A jealous or possessive partner will make them want to break free and escape. This position often shows the possibility of more than one marriage partner. It's also not uncommon for these individuals to choose not to marry at all.

Jupiter can bring good luck in business and negotiation. They have an ability to help others compromise, find peace, and meet in the middle. These individuals truly see the good in other people. Because they are extremely giving individuals, they can sometimes feel taken advantage of in their relationships. Abundance follows them easily and their positive mindset attracts what they need in the right moment. Harnessing balance will help them learn the importance of giving and receiving.

Saturn in the Seventh House

These individuals are often serious and responsible in relationships. They can be loyal, devoted, and committed partners once they find someone they trust. Disciplined and responsible, they work hard to make their relationships work. They might struggle with trusting others fully and are cautious about being emotionally vulnerable. A restrictive attitude about love can cause fear and anxiety, which prevents them from getting too involved with anyone. Romance might seem unrealistic because they are practical realists. They want a relationship that is stable, comfortable, and long lasting. On the other hand, sometimes they can marry young and feel it's destined. Karmic relationships from past lifetimes are common with this placement. There is often a debt they have to balance or something they want to learn. Their relationships teach them a lot about themselves and often teach them about responsibility. Outside influences such as parents, in-laws, or children can impact their relationships. There are times when they feel burdened, but it's because they put a lot of pressure on themselves. Super responsible from a young age, they feel pressure to take care of their partner's physical and emotional happiness. They find it easier to do practical things to show their love and it can be difficult for them to be intimate, communicate, or express feelings. Wisdom and practical experience often come with time and patience. As they get older, their relationships get easier. They can be attracted to people who are much older because they value maturity, success, reliability, and financial security.

Some individuals with this placement feel that their ability to find a partner is blocked. There are times when it can feel like the universe is preventing them from meeting the right person or finding love at all. They might marry later in life and often to someone older who can take care of them.

They might decide to remain single and focus on developing business partnerships to obtain success. Sensitive and sometimes self-conscious, they can stay longer than they should in unhappy relationships. They don't like to give up and are determined to succeed at everything they do. It can be difficult for them to break things off especially if children are involved. They will work hard to work things out. Putting time and effort into relationships is a priority, but they also need to learn to let go when it's time. They might feel as if the universe is testing them regarding love and romance. They learn important lessons and become stronger based on their personal experiences. Harnessing the wisdom to release relationships and allow change will help them move forward in life.

Uranus in the Seventh House

These individuals can be eccentric, rebellious, and freedom loving. They do not follow classic traditional beliefs about marriage and partnership. Open-minded, nontraditional, and rebellious when they are in a relationship, they thrive on change. Because of this, they often experience unstable love affairs and relationships. From a young age, they can feel different from their friends in many ways. Questioning rules and traditional values inspires them to chart their own path and beliefs about partnership. Commitment can be challenging for them because they value their ability to roam free, explore new things, and seek adventure. If they feel that people are controlling or trying to possess them, they might end things abruptly without any explanation. Sometimes they can enter relationships on a whim and many times it's based on unstable feelings they experience in the moment. When they change suddenly, it can shock those around them. Uranus in the seventh house can bring unexpected relationship struggles such as divorce, separation, or difficulties maintaining a stable partnership. Many people with this placement might experience divorce or shocking endings to relationships.

Individuals with this placement often prefer to be friends and enjoy nontraditional relationships. Because they are social and friendly, they have a lot of acquaintances. Being part of a group might be more important to them than one-on-one relationships. Things like living together and not adhering to societies traditions suit them best. Being single can help them maintain a sense of autonomy and freedom. Free spirits, they can enjoy socializing and spending time with other free-spirited individuals. They are often attracted to unconventional, unique, intelligent, and creative people. Many become attracted to people who are very different from them in some way, such as people who speak a different language or have a different religious belief system. Due to their high intelligence, it's important that they pick partners who can challenge their beliefs and who are not afraid to discuss uncomfortable topics. They are friendly but can also have a detached approach in love and people might perceive them to be uninterested or even cold. It's true that they detach from their emotions and maintain a practical and rational approach to relationships. One of their strengths is their ability to help others without losing themselves in the process. They have good boundaries and a humanitarian focus on helping the collective. Serving others and helping people in some way helps them grow. Balancing their desire for freedom and companionship can help them avoid boredom. Harnessing autonomy in relationships can help them open their mind to having stable long-term relationships.

Neptune in the Seventh House

These individuals seek meaningful relationships with others. It's important for them to trust their intuition and see people clearly. They can be idealistic and romantic toward people they are attracted to. Extremely sensitive, they can attract relationship partners that need emotional, spiritual, or financial support. Sometimes people take advantage of their kindness, and this can leave them feeling disappointed. Disillusionment can come through relationships and after experiencing heartbreak at an early age. They can suffer from being deceived, and due to a lack of boundaries, it can leave them vulnerable to selfish people. Finding a spiritual, supportive, and compassionate partner can help them connect to a greater sense of belonging. They are attracted to sensitive, artistic, and creative people who can help them tap into their imagination. It's important for them to learn the difference between love and pity in relationships. These individuals can sometimes attract people who struggle with addiction or have unhealed pain. They are compassionate and like to help others feel better. They can see people with rose-colored glasses, and this impacts the type of relationships they get involved in. Entanglements with unhealthy or abusive partners can teach them many lessons about compromise and commitment. One of the greatest things they need to learn is developing stronger boundaries.

Unselfish in love, they sacrifice their own feelings for their partner. They are intuitive and sometimes have psychic experiences that help them. Being fooled by others' words and actions can be prevented when they trust their intuition. Their greatest test is seeing other people clearly and accurately. These individuals can experience hidden secrets, illusion, and deception in personal relationships. Secret love affairs can occur with this placement because they might not feel others will approve of their relationship. Outside influences can impact who they are able to be in a relationship with, such as falling in love with a person who is not free, already married, or in a position of authority. They can keep their love hidden and private from the outside world. At some time in their lives, they might feel victimized by someone they trusted. People they trust may hide important things from them to protect them, and because they are so trusting, they don't always see it. Due to their struggles in relationships, they might seek solitude and search for a connection to a higher power. They might start to seek platonic relationships where sexuality is not as important as similar values. Finding a partner who shares their spiritual beliefs can create happiness. They can learn a lot about themselves and the meaning of life through their relationships. Harnessing clear thinking can help them learn that everyone has positive and negative personality traits.

Pluto in the Seventh House

These individuals crave deep, transformative, and meaningful relationships. They are known to be sexual, mysterious, intense, and passionate in love. Speaking the truth and experiencing sexual intimacy are important to them. Their greatest wound can come from intimate relationships, especially from their marriage partner. Picking a supportive, loyal, reliable, and trustworthy partner can help them reach their goals quickly. If they choose an unstable partner to share their lives with, it could cause difficulties in many areas of their life. The person they marry can be a force of change in their life. If they have been hurt in relationships, they can react by becoming private, secretive, and protective. They like to maintain a sense of control in relationships. They need to be careful about becoming jealous, possessive, and distrusting without reason. Pluto here can ignite extreme emotions, intense feelings, and end relationships abruptly. If these individuals decide to commit to someone, they expect a serious bond to develop. They don't do lukewarm feelings; in fact, it can be all or nothing for them. When they are attracted to someone, they will let them know it energetically or by telling them directly. The darker side of love can manifest in their relationships. In partnerships, they can experience power and control dynamics. Their relationships can go through mini deaths and rebirths, which force them to see their partner and themselves differently. Change is at the forefront of their relationships. One danger of this placement is attracting a partner who can become emotionally, mentally, or physically abusive. It's important to end these relationships quickly and cut ties to protect themselves.

They experience emotional transformations and unexpected endings. There can be more than one marriage with this placement. This can play out in different ways. For example, they might experience the unexpected death of a spouse, separation, divorce, and even abandonment. Growth and wisdom come through marriage, but sometimes this is an area of life that requires healing. It's important to realize that they deserve healthy, supportive, and loving relationships. Because of their loyalty, it's hard for them to give up on someone they love. Ending a relationship or marriage can be difficult, but if they are being mistreated, they often have the strength to do it. Pluto represents healing and enables them to be resilient. In business partnerships, these individuals often are strategic and pick a partner who can benefit them financially. It's important to build trust with others; this is the key to lasting relationships. Appearing strong is important to them and they have a powerful sense of purpose. If they can harness openness in relationships, they can feel greater support by allowing loved ones into their inner world.

Planetary Transits through the Seventh House

When planets transit through the seventh house, you can be more focused on your marriage, relationships, and business partnerships.

Transit Sun

The Sun transiting the seventh house can heighten your interest in relationships. You might start a new relationship or want to spend more time with your significant other. Your relationships might be challenging right now, but you're learning to compromise with others. This transit encourages you to focus on relationships and issues of commitment.

You might feel more inclined to listen to your partner's needs right now, but also want to speak up about what you need in a relationship. Self-discovery emerges during this cycle and can make you want to communicate more with others. There is an emphasis on companionship and in supporting others. Doing things alone can be more difficult because you feel that other people bring comfort. You can be much more friendly, social, and extroverted right now.

This cycle can make you feel more creative. In fact, you might feel inspired to draw, paint, write, and make beautiful jewelry. You can be more focused on your artistic interests and might want to attend concerts, go to the theater, and visit a new art museum. It's a great time to share your interests with your partner.

Anything you do right now that focuses on collaboration and listening to the ideas of others will bring positive energy into your life. Success can come easily when you include other people in your decisions. You might feel more balanced right now and much more focused on cooperation, harmony, and diplomacy. This is a good time to harness appreciation and let other people know how you feel. Harness your relationships with others and be more affectionate with the people you care about.

Transit Moon

During this fast transit, you might feel more protective of yourself and your relationships. You can feel more sensitive and emotionally raw. Empathy for others comes to the surface as you can see how other people's feelings are just as important as your own. Issues with commitment, trust, and security are on the forefront of your mind.

Communication is highlighted right now. There is a greater need to express yourself with those you are closest with. You will want to tell people how you feel about them and can be more sensitive to other people's feelings.

If you're not typically psychic or intuitive, this transit can awaken your inner emotions. Your intuition can increase and you might worry more about what other people think about you. Because you feel more sensitive right now, your emotions can fluctuate. These ups and downs might cause you to want to spend time alone and withdraw from social activities. You might feel sad for no reason, cry more easily, and reminisce about the past. Feelings of loneliness might pop up, but there can also be a sense of peace through withdrawing into yourself.

Happiness comes through finding balance and harmony in relationships. You might realize how much you need other people. Emotions can ebb and flow right now, so it's best to not make any major relationship decisions during this time. Wait and be patient for this energy to shift, then see how you truly feel. There can also be challenges in relationships due to your indecisiveness and desire to avoid conflict. You might have to speak up for yourself or stand your ground. Harnessing emotional connections and listening to other people's advice can help you work through relationship challenges. In fact, you can become more grateful for those who are in your life during this transit.

Transit Mercury

This transit can increase your desire to communicate with your partner. You might feel a bit more indecisive right now and try to balance many different opinions. It's an important time to take other people's needs into account. Communicating with your partner one-on-one will help clear the air and reach compromises everyone can agree on. You may feel like sharing your feelings with your partner even if you typically don't do this. Increased communication and negotiation can help solve many issues. The urge to network is intensified right now and you might want to connect with people you haven't interacted with in a while. If there is conflict in any relationships, you can feel inspired to step in and mediate. You can see both sides of people's arguments right now and might feel more diplomatic right now. Harness cooperation to enhance and bring peace in personal relationships.

Transit Venus

This transit can increase your desire to experience love and romance. The next five weeks heighten a sense of passion, intimacy, and harmony. You can feel more focused on contemplating one-on-one relationships. People might be drawn to you right now and you can feel more friendly. In fact, it's not uncommon to start a new relationship and meet someone who piques your interest.

Your relationships can be a place where you want to seek affection, comfort, and support. Casual relationships can make you feel less comfortable right now because you are looking to deepen connections. Issues about commitment can pop up and be discussed and hashed out.

During this transit you might be able to bring greater harmony to personal relationships that have been struggling. Your ability to mediate and negotiate conflict between others can help build stronger ties. Because of your sense of fairness and desire to make other people feel appreciated, people listen to you.

Marriage proposals aren't uncommon right now. You might finally decide to take that big step. If you're married or committed to someone, it's a good time to show that you care about them. Romantic feelings flourish during this time, so it's a good time to do something special for the person you love. If you aren't in a relationship, you might start thinking about finding a companion. Even if you are a free spirit, this transit might help you realize the positive side of having companionship and people to rely on. It's a positive time to harness feelings and express them to build stronger relationships.

Transit Mars

This transit can bring conflict and challenges in relationships. It might be difficult for the next eight weeks to compromise because of irritability, anger, and frustration with others. There is a restless and impulsive energy affecting you, so it's important to slow down. Powerful emotions can influence how treat your partner and associates.

Be cautious about taking things personally or trying to instigate arguments with loved ones. Rash decisions can lead to conflict, especially if you don't listen to what others are saying. Conflicts can arise when you try to express your own needs. In fact, this is a time in your life when you might start standing up for yourself. If you have not been using your voice to be assertive, people will be caught off guard by your directness.

You might feel like you have enemies, or it can feel like people are more vocal about their dislike about things you have done. You could feel shocked by the reactions of those closest to you. There can be a lot of misunderstandings, so try to be patient and don't react emotionally to other people. Step back and think things through before you respond.

Relationships can be passionate and volatile right now. Sexual desires and passions can increase, which awakens a need for physical intimacy. If differences arise in relationships, just make sure to settle disputes amicably. Listen, reflect, and don't avoid important discussions. Try to communicate clearly and with compassion. It's important to be patient and realize this energy will pass soon. It's a good time to reconcile with previous partners or tell people how you really feel about them. Harnessing direct communication can help you move through this transit.

Transit Jupiter

This transit can last about a year and can bring good luck and abundance in relationships. Maintaining a sense of freedom will still be important and you don't want to feel tied down. But you may have an increased desire and start thinking about dating or meeting someone new. This transit is awakening positive feelings and a desire to meet new people.

If you are already in a committed relationship or marriage, you may want to spend time traveling and exploring new places with your partner. Doing something adventurous with your partner or taking more risks in relationships can help you attract positive outcomes.

You might learn something new about yourself and your partner during this cycle. This is a good time to benefit through marriage or business partnership. There is a lot of happiness and joy that can be tapped into, which can help heal many relationships.

If you aren't in a relationship, there can be a desire to make a relationship more formal by making a commitment. Meeting someone from a different culture, religious background, or belief system can expand your view of the world. Any new relationships formed during this time are generally happy and bring good luck.

Although this is a positive cycle, there are times this transit can bring an ending of a relationship. This typically happens if the relationship has become stale, outdated, and you aren't growing as a couple. If you have been fighting more for freedom and independence within a relationship, this transit can open those desires. But there is also a greater possibility of financial blessings that come through meeting new people. This can happen through new business associates or through your social network.

If there are legal matters you have been battling, like divorce or custody disputes, this is a good time to amicably solve these problems once and for all. Your ability to listen to others, find peace, and negotiate what you want can help you right now. Harnessing a positive outlook can help you magnify the energy of abundance, which in turn will enliven your personal relationships.

Transit Saturn

This transit can bring karmic responsibilities and learning in relationships for the next two to three years. You might feel burdened with responsibilities and feel like you need to take care of your partner. There can be issues with your relationship partner, and they might be experiencing serious issues such as health, work, or financial problems. At times you might feel like you have to fix things for them. Your sense of duty inspires you to stay committed in relationships even if you feel frustrated. You might feel more withdrawn and depressed even if you don't know why. Feeling critical of people you have partnered with and questioning their motives is common during this transit. You can be harder on yourself and have high expectations for your relationship partners. Being more flexible can help ease the burdens and heavy energy you might be experiencing. You are learning the art of compromise, which can assist with smoothing over conflicts. It's a good time to focus on practical issues that are causing problems in your everyday life.

Everything you believe about commitment and compromise can be tested during this cycle. If you aren't in a relationship, this transit can do two things. First, it can bring someone into your life who is a bit older than you, and they might help you grow in some way. Second, it can seem to block you from meeting new people and you may feel more alone. Feeling lonely during this transit can help you recommit, readdress, and evaluate your relationships. This experience will help you become wiser and more aware about what you need in relationships. Saturn is strict and brings a realistic perspective about love and relationships. This is a good time to harness patience and know that things will shift and get easier with time.

Transit Uranus

This transit often triggers unexpected changes, shocking events, and potential endings in relationships. For the next seven years, it can feel like there is an electric and unstable force impacting your relationships. Disruptions and surprises can affect your intimate relationships, marriage, and business partnerships. How you view relationships can be altered and forever changed. It can feel like the universe is forcing you to open your mind, heart, and soul to see things in a new way. If you have refused to grow as a person or in a relationship, this transit brings powerful changes.

Feeling free and independent can help you explore what you really want in a relationship. You might feel more rebellious right now and want to break free from restrictions. If you are currently in a committed relationship, you might want to explore nontraditional ways of interacting. You might date more than one person, and you might prefer living together instead of getting married. You might start dating someone very different from you. You might become attracted to a creative and unique person. If you are not in a relationship, you might start a new unconventional or nontraditional relationship. Any relationship started during this transit can end just as quickly as it got started. If you resist making changes, you can prepare for unexpected things that shake up the foundation of your relationships.

This can be one of the most challenging transits of Uranus because it can sometimes lead to separation, loss, and even divorce for those who are currently in unhappy marriages or partnerships. This is a good time to seek relationship counseling to really get in touch with the energy that's impacting you and your life. Uranus is here to awaken and change you in deep ways. The things you need to release and areas you need to grow will be revealed. If things have grown stagnant or boring in your partnerships, this transit can make you feel like the rug has been pulled out from under your feet. There is a sense of instability, uneasiness, and uncertainty that haunts your relationships right now. Allow yourself to feel uncomfortable emotions and express your needs to your partner.

You can change on a fundamental level, which can be a positive thing. This is a time when you will need to reflect on your wants, needs, and desires in relationships. You can feel more rebellious right now and are more inclined to take risks and act impulsively. Slow down, think things through, and ground your energy to avoid making rash decisions. Harness clear communication and allow yourself to adapt to the changes that come your way. Try not to resist things that need to end and allow new energy to invigorate established relationships. Change can be good, and it can pump new energy into your life.

Transit Neptune

This transit can awaken your desire to experience love and deepen relationships. For the next fourteen years, your view on relationships can dramatically change. If you are in a committed relationship, there can be a desire to develop a greater spiritual connection with your partner. You might want to heal your relationship and start to appreciate the friendship you have with your partner. If you are currently married, you might experience a spiritual awakening that impacts your ideas about love and commitment. It can be hard to see things clearly and there can be a lot of illusion influencing your partnerships. It's important to try to see things as clearly as possible in marriage and business partnerships.

Romanticism and idealism can be increased during this time, which influences your emotional nature. What you need to feel love, romance, and affection can be forever altered. You might start to idealize someone or fall in love with someone new. There can be a chance of developing feelings for someone who is not free to love you because they are in another relationship. In fact, love can lead to disappointment when you begin to realize that people are not who you thought they were. Hidden issues and secrets can resurface, impacting your relationships.

Neptune transiting this area of life can lead to separation, divorce, and misunderstandings. This energy can bring disillusionment in love and business. It's important to communicate very clearly with your partner and make sure they understand what you really want. You might realize things about your partner that you never knew before, or old issues resurface to teach you an important lesson. Listen to your intuition and don't ignore the red flags that are popping up in your relationships.

Spiritual understanding can come during this time, which can help you confront romantic, idealistic, and unrealistic beliefs about how your marriage should be. If your relationship is strong, it can grow stronger, and you might finally accept your partner for who they are. It's a good time to solidify your commitment and expectations.

There should be a cautious approach related to any new business arrangements or contracts. If you meet a new business partner, try to make sure you take the necessary time to truly get to know them and their character. Confusion, betrayal, and deception can arise in business dealings and with business partners. It's important to communicate clearly and be careful about being fooled or taken advantage of. Trust your gut instincts and listen to the advice of others who might be seeing things more clearly. It might be best to not start a new business venture during this time. Wait until this elusive and foggy energy shifts. Harnessing boundaries can help you step back emotionally and be more practical about how you see your relationships.

Transit Pluto

This lengthy transit can impact your relationships for many years, causing deep psychological and transformative change. Power struggles can emerge in your relationships, bringing you face-to-face with parts of yourself you never knew existed. You might feel like something has opened a secret chamber inside of you and all these new feelings are pouring out. Fears can resurface and any past trauma that has not fully been healed can bubble to the surface. You might have to feel uncomfortable feelings again and old wounds resurface in your relationships.

Major changes can influence your personal relationships, forcing old patterns to be released. This transit can especially impact your marriage. You might seek deeper physical and emotional intimacy with your partner. If you have been in a committed relationship, this cycle often brings unforeseen endings through death, separation, or divorce. Your very sense of self experiences a metamorphosis. Emotions change and you might feel like the person you were before is gone. Rebirth is occurring in your relationships, and this forces you to grow. Power and control issues can emerge in your relationships as well. These experiences might force you to come to terms with your own negative behaviors and primal instincts. It's like Pandora's box is open and all the secrets are revealed. You have to face intense truths about yourself, your partner, and your relationships. Take a good look in the mirror and allow yourself to talk to someone you can trust. Seeking counseling and support can be a beneficial tool to help you recover from the changes this power cycle brings. The good news is that Pluto eventually brings healing and helps you start fresh. A whole new way of seeing relationships can manifest, and you may finally overcome your fears of commitment and betrayal and heal. Harness forgiveness and let go of negative emotions that stand in your way of developing healthy partnerships.

Ways to Harness Libra Energy

- Compromise with others.
- Focus on relationships.
- Find greater balance in your life.
- Be peaceful and harmonious.
- Nurture your creative and artistic abilities.
- Fight for justice and fairness.

8
SCORPIO

Archetype: Healer

Symbol: The Scorpion

Sun Sign Dates: October 23–November 21

Energy: Phoenix

Element: Water, Fixed

Planet: Pluto

House: Eighth

If you have Scorpio in your birth chart, planets in the eighth house, or are experiencing planetary transits through the eighth house, this chapter will cover information regarding these energies. If you don't, you can still learn about Scorpio energy and incorporate it into your life. The placement of the planet Pluto in the sign and house will show where you express Scorpio energy. It is important to look at what house the sign Scorpio falls on in your birth wheel because this is where you will experience rebirth, transformation, and healing. Harnessing Scorpio energy gives you intensity, strength, power, resilience, and an ability to overcome adversity.

Scorpio Energy Words

Intense, powerful, deep, strong, secretive, passionate, resilient, sexual, possessive, jealous, truthful, loyal, perceptive, psychic, private, transformative, shrewd, competitive, self-reliant, determined, intuitive.

Scorpio Motto

As a Scorpio, I am private, secretive, and intense. I can feel energy and am perceptive enough to understand what is happening around me. Psychic and deeply emotional, I can see through people's facades. I dislike fakeness and superficial conversations. I like to discuss meaningful topics such as death, sex, spirituality, and healing. I want deep intimacy, commitment, loyalty, and trust in my relationships. I need to connect deeply with others on an emotional level to express physical intimacy.

Harnessing Scorpio Energy

Scorpio energy is intense, deep, secretive, and powerful. When we experience change, rebirth, and transformation, we are being impacted by this energy. To awaken Scorpio energy, we can study taboo topics such as death, sexuality, trauma, and healing. It's important to dig deep and feel strong emotions. Experiencing intimacy and connecting with others can help us tap into this energy. Listening to our intuition and trusting our gut instinct helps us connect with this energy.

Scorpio energy is the epitome of change and gives us the courage to face darker parts of life. Metamorphosis, change, and crisis are things that create spiritual growth. Strength and determination can help us overcome pain, and this energy can naturally adapt to survive. Healing ourselves and others is part of the spiritual journey, and tapping into Scorpio energy can help us do that.

Harness Rebirth

In ancient mythology, the phoenix is associated with death, resurrection, and rebirth. Scorpio energy is similar to the phoenix. This bird sets itself on fire when it feels stagnant or burdened by pain. It evolves and the fire forces it to rise as a new and stronger bird. Phoenix energy is intense and ignites deep emotional changes. This energy is strong, powerful, and transforming. It's immensely powerful and allows us to go through symbolic deaths while knowing that we can be reborn.

Change is a natural part of the universe and there is no other sign that knows this better. Because this energy is brave and courageous, it helps us understand that everything in life must go through cycles. These cycles of change trigger lessons and learning in our lives. Phoenix energy helps us let go of the past, release painful emotions, forgive, and start fresh. It intensifies our need to grow mentally, emotionally, and physically. Scorpio energy challenges us to adapt and shed our old skin. It helps us leave behind outdated energies and move forward into a new way of being.

Harness Feelings

Scorpio is ruled by the element of water. This energy brings a calm and soothing approach that attracts others. Water signs are intuitive and connect with people's energy easily. The ocean is deep, intense, and its waves can be calm or stormy. This is similar to how Scorpios feel because they are deep and at times icy. The water energy helps them go deep within and become introspective. Because they are secretive and private, they often live beneath the surface. It's common for them to observe from a distance, sensing things before they act.

Since Scorpios are a water sign, they are emotional and sensitive. They don't always know how to express their feelings or put them into words. Water energy can connect us with powerful emotions and help us recognize our inner needs. If we can be calm, patient, and understanding, it can help us connect deeper with people in our lives.

Water energy intensifies Scorpio's passionate, psychic, and intense mysterious nature. This energy teaches us the importance of feeling our emotions. It can be difficult to be vulnerable, but acknowledging feelings can make Scorpios stronger.

Making Decisions

Scorpio is a fixed sign, which means it likes to feel in control of things. This energy craves sameness and expects others to be as reliable as they are. Small changes can irritate them and many times this causes resistance. Stubborn at times, fixed energy keeps them firmly planted and determined to get what they want.

Their fixed energy intensifies a powerful stamina and work ethic. This energy wants to see results and is focused on productivity. Scorpios like seeing things getting done and not just talking about them. Scorpio likes to plan and take its time before it makes decisions. Slowly strategizing and plotting all possible outcomes helps Scorpios successfully achieve their goals.

Scorpios like to be in charge and find comfort being in control of situations. Because they are fixed energy, they like things done a certain way— usually their way. Fixed energy doesn't like to take advice or be forced to do something it doesn't want to do. Scorpios are fiercely stubborn, because adapting and accepting help is not always easy for them. They prefer doing things slowly, steadily, and staying firm on what they want. There are times when they will have to adapt or compromise to get what they want. They are strategic and always planning twenty steps ahead and like to feel prepared. Making decisions comes easily for Scorpios because they think things through in detail and are always prepared for any outcome.

Transform Your Life

Scorpio is ruled by the planet Pluto. Pluto energy destroys, creates, and has a powerful impact wherever it is in our birth chart. Imagine how it feels to be ruled by a planet whose energy is associated with nuclear power. It's intense, transformative, and explosive to say the least. This is similar to how Scorpios handle life; they can be passionate, secretive, protective, and determined to get what they want.

Death and rebirth are associated with Pluto. This energy is associated with loss, grief, destruction, and the underworld. It's the dark and taboo things in life that Pluto feels comfortable with. Death is a topic that can be uncomfortable and scary for people to talk about. But for Scorpios, they have a natural understanding of it because they are connected to things that hide beneath the surface.

Because Pluto energy represents healing, transformation, and rebirth in our birth chart, it can show where we have a childhood wound. These emotional issues can bubble to the surface to be addressed and healed as we grow older. This energy helps us start over and change our lives when we need to. It's a deep, secretive, and mysterious energy because it profoundly changes things in our lives. In fact, it is known to expose secrets and brings uncomfortable truths into the light. Just like Scorpios, this energy demands honesty, rawness, and loyalty. It can be an unsettling energy at times, but we can feel the inner changes it awakens.

Pluto has an important part in the process of healing our trauma and it helps us face our fears. We can learn to harness Pluto energy when we need to heal, forgive, and release the past. It's all about facing hard truths and looking honestly within to see the parts that need to be transformed. There is no other energy that can impact us the way Pluto does.

At times, this energy can bring a turbulent force into our lives. We can feel like the rug was pulled out underneath our feet. Unexpected events and shocking truths get exposed wherever Pluto is in our birth chart. It can also show us where we need to be brave, stand up for ourselves, and take back our power. This energy helps us become stronger individuals, and through forgiving others, we can truly transform into phoenixes.

Diving Deep

The eighth house is an area of life that is hidden, mysterious, and transformative. It's been a misunderstood house in astrology and a house that many people are afraid of. When planets are in this house, it's actually a blessing in disguise. The eighth house is where we can tap into our power and strength to develop resilience. The energy of this house helps us be reborn and regenerate ourselves throughout our lives. In fact, this house makes us more resilient and helps us recognize our strengths to survive.

This area of life is related to a plethora of intense topics: death, loss, trauma, other people's resources, inheritance, sexuality, sacrifice, secrets, and healing. The eighth house is where we dive deep to find answers to life's problems. It's where we seek to learn more about mysterious and unexplained things. It's where we connect to death and how we deal with grief. Sometimes we have to sacrifice something for other people or for our own peace.

Everything that most people find difficult to talk about, or things that make us feel uncomfortable, resides in the eighth house. It's the place where we can be transformed, forced to change for the better, and are reborn into an entirely new person. Trusting others, releasing the past, and learning to forgive those who have hurt us is eighth house territory.

Sexuality and intimacy are deeply private areas of our lives. By looking at the eighth house, we can find out more about our basic needs. In fact, the sign that falls on the eighth house cusp is often the type of people we have chemistry with and a strong sexual attraction to. But this does not always mean that those people are healthy for us to commit to in a relationship. A lot of painful learning can come through the eighth house and our experience with intimacy. Regarding sex, planets in the eighth house can create an all-or-nothing energy. There might be a lot of sexual partners and experience in this area or none at all. Learning to be more vulnerable and allowing ourselves to experience intimacy through sexual connection can be a powerful lesson.

The eighth house is where we hide things. It's where we experience secrets, betrayal, fear, darkness, and taboo issues. People with planets here are often born with spiritual abilities. They can have a heightened intuition and healing abilities. They are often found helping people with their problems and listening to people's painful life experiences. This is the area of life where we bond deeply with those around us on a mental, physical, or spiritual level.

Discussing issues that are truthful, real, and transforming is eighth house territory. This is the area of life where we rise from the ashes, dust ourselves off, and feel stronger and more resilient after life has knocked us down.

Scorpio Rising

When people first meet Scorpio rising people, they may appear cold, intense, deep, observant, and mysterious. They walk into the room and people feel their powerful confidence. This is a transformative energy that encourages others to share their secrets with them. These individuals have a calm and magnetizing presence that attracts people. Because of this ability, they can help people in a time of crisis and connect to people's pain. Their natural listening skills and understanding of people often lead them to pursue a career in psychology.

Scorpio risings can be counted on to not sugarcoat issues but address them head-on. Because they are direct, truthful, and insightful, they tell other people what they need to hear. There is an intensity about their personality that makes other people either love them or dislike them instantly. Some people might perceive them as overbearing, controlling, and manipulative.

Physically attractive, they can have a sensual energy and are known to have penetrating eyes that seem to gaze right through people. They want to see other people's true nature and peer into the soul, and if someone is not able to go this deep with them, they won't be interested in getting to know them.

Scorpio risings are powerful, passionate, and intuitive individuals who often have psychic abilities. Powerful leaders, they don't like to listen to what other people tell them because they want to have a sense of autonomy. They are known to listen to their gut instinct and trust their own perceptions over what others tell them. Skeptical at times, they do have intuitive gifts and are able to see people's true motives. They are a good judge of character and instinctively know whom they can trust. Because they are self-protective, they can be overly critical, cautious, and distrusting until they really get to know someone and they prove themselves loyal. They might not feel comfortable being vulnerable because they have been hurt in the past.

Scorpio risings can be serious and pessimistic at times. They protect themselves by trying to see things in a realistic way to avoid disappointment. Honesty is important to them and it takes time to trust people. They may have a dark, brooding, and unfriendly personality until they feel safe with others. Then, their charming, protective, and loyal personality traits shine through.

Scorpio risings tend to be possessive, jealous, and controlling in relationships. They really want to bond with someone on a deeper level. Truthfulness and loyalty from their partner are prerequisites. Their alluring energy attracts people, especially those who are wounded in some way. Sometimes they get entangled with people who want to share all their problems and they can start to feel like a therapist. It's challenging for them to find a partner who is on their emotional level. They really need an equal. The perfect partner is someone who can stand up to them and be as strong as they are. They often feel lonely with most people because there is often an imbalance.

Transformation and *rebirth* are natural words they resonate with. They have been tested so many times in their lives that they are able to release and let go of what is no longer serving them. They are used to the energy of change and their emotional nature is always transforming.

Scorpio risings can be shrewd and calculating in business. They work hard to achieve their goals and want to accumulate financial wealth. Money is a symbol of security for them and enables them to be self-reliant. When they harness their perceptive insight, then can make smart business decisions based on their intuition. Born to succeed, they are driven, determined, and productive workers who want to rise to the top.

Scorpio risings go through transformation and rebirth throughout their lives. They can change emotionally, mentally, and physically. There might be times when they experience loss at a young age, such as losing a parent or friend. These experiences with death and dying can change them forever. In fact, they often realize that life is fragile and they want to understand their spiritual purpose. This is why many of them are interested in death, ghosts, psychic abilities, astrology, mediumship, and alternative healing.

Releasing old grudges and forgiving others will help them feel lighter. When they trust the insights they receive, it helps them make better decisions and protect themselves from being hurt. Trusting their intuition is the key to success.

How to Harness Planets in Scorpio

When planets are in Scorpio, you can possess emotional intensity, strength, determination, and an ability to dig deeper into life's mysteries.

Sun in Scorpio

Sun in Scorpio individuals are powerful, strong, and resilient. They are like phoenixes who never stop rising from the ashes, because they keep being reborn over and over again. Life experiences such as loss, tragedy, and betrayal might knock them down. Although, they have the stamina to eventually get back up. They dust themselves off and learn from the past. They have an ability to tap into their inner strength and become forever transformed. Transformation and rebirth are energies they experience every single day.

Digging deep and having difficult conversations suits them best. They are calculating and business minded, which enables them to succeed at an early age. Traditional careers suit them because they like to make money and have material success. But there is a deep need inside of them to help people heal. Because of this, they might pursue a career as a psychologist, detective, or energy healer.

Deeply private individuals, they don't readily share anything about themselves with anyone until they totally trust someone. Once there is trust, they are devoted, loyal, and dedicated partners. They prefer to hide behind the scenes and observe others. Often secretive and quiet, they dislike small talk or superficial topics. In fact, they have a gift for exposing and finding out people's secrets. When they are in relationships, they can be secretive and don't readily share what they are feeling. But they have a way of getting other people to tell them all their secrets.

Success is important to them, so they will work hard to achieve their goals. Positions of power are a natural fit for them because they like to be in control and have the ability to make real change. But sometimes they prefer to work behind the scenes and are very driven and productive workers. They are set in their ways and want things done a certain way. Calculating and shrewd, they attract powerful people who can help them reach their business goals. Their need for secrecy and privacy can negatively impact their relationships with coworkers and associates because they make people feel uncomfortable or like they can't trust them.

Fiercely self-reliant, they would rather do something themselves than ask for help. They can be perceived as a lone wolf who likes to be by themselves. Learning to be more vulnerable and trusting can help them let their walls down. It's important that they learn to allow others to assist them as this will help them build long-lasting friendships and partnerships. If they can harness trust, it can help them gain strength to overcome all obstacles by allowing others to be part of their journey.

Moon in Scorpio

Moon in Scorpio individuals have one of the most emotionally deep, secretive, and powerful Moon signs. At their core, they are powerful and feel everything deeply. Life experiences can force them to go through emotional deaths and rebirths. It's like their feelings are transforming and morphing daily. How they feel about people and things can go through many changes. Because they are intuitive and highly perceptive, they figure out how other people are feeling and what their true motives are. They are one of the strongest Moon signs because of their ability to protect themselves.

Naturally distrusting, they don't like to be vulnerable and are good at self-protection. They have a knack for exposing hidden secrets, and taboo things are often revealed to them because their energy has a way of uncovering the truth. Their psychic abilities bless them with intuition and empathy, which is why they are not easily fooled. Many times, they can recognize when someone is trying to manipulate them. They have a laser-focused bullshit odometer that notices anything fake or deceptive.

There is a harshness about their personality that is always on guard, especially if they feel threatened. If someone hurts them, they give the silent treatment and cut all emotional ties. One of their greatest strengths is their ability to release unhealthy people and things from their lives.

Due to their private nature, they don't readily show approval, affection, or love. Public displays can make them feel uncomfortable. But once they trust someone, they can be extremely loyal and supportive. Experiencing intimacy is important for their emotional fulfillment. They know how to get what they want and are passionate about fighting for it. Even if they have to be alone for a while, they prefer that to being in an emotionally unfulfilling relationship.

People like to share their problems and worries with them because they are good listeners. They possess a magnetic, mysterious, and intense energy that draws others to them. Their penetrating eyes make people feel like they are peering deep into their souls. Their ability to make people feel healed and uncomfortable is equally intense.

They are natural psychologists, who can give wise advice to those who open up to them. In fact, people often come up to them on the street or in the grocery store and pour out their deepest pain. Scorpio Moons realize at a young age that there is something different about their energy. They questioned why people shared such heavy personal things so readily with them. Because of their personal experiences, nothing shocks them; they have a natural understanding of the darker side of life, which includes taboos such as sex, death, trauma, and betrayal.

Emotionally, it can be hard for them to let go of the past or forgive people who have hurt them. The saying "I forgive, but I never forget" was probably coined by a Scorpio Moon. Their passions and desires can run high, and their feelings can go from one extreme to the other. They tend to see things in an all-or-nothing mentality. For instance, one minute they might love someone deeply, and the next they feel like they hate them. Their mood is mysterious and dark at times, which can lead to depression and pessimism. Their emotions simmer beneath the surface and often feel like a boiling pot. People can sense their power and intensity because their body language reveals how they feel.

In relationships, if someone betrays them, they can hold a grudge and cut people off emotionally and never speak to them again. When they walk away, others know it must have been serious. They heal themselves through these painful losses and it helps them understand how to help other people. They often become wounded healers and can become a source of wisdom for others. It's important that they learn to harness forgiveness in all areas of their lives. Releasing the past and starting over again will help them grow stronger and more resilient.

Mercury in Scorpio

Mercury in Scorpio individuals need deep communication and want to learn about the mysteries of life. They are deliberate in their communication and don't say things they don't mean. If they talk, it's usually important to listen to what they have to say because it's typically insightful. Telling the truth and being honest is important to them. Others often perceive them as secretive and distrusting.

Their mind is gifted for research and solving problems. They have a communication style that is investigative and digs deep to find answers. Gifted at getting other people to tell them the truth, it can sometimes shock others how readily they start to talk with them. Their penetrating eyes stare right into people's souls and make them feel exposed. At times they can be cynical, pessimistic, and sarcastic when they talk. Known for having a dark sense of humor, they can sometimes make other people feel unsettled.

Mercury in Scorpio individuals can be private and they don't always respond to questions. Communication can be difficult because they aren't the type to engage in small talk. They want to talk about meaningful issues and taboo topics such as sex, death, and dying. They would prefer sitting in silence with people they care about without the expectation of having to talk.

Once they get to know someone and even after they build trust, there is still a part of them that remains cautious about sharing personal information. They prefer to keep important things hidden. In their mind, knowledge is power, and they want to be the one in control. Putting themselves in a vulnerable situation or feeling exposed in social settings can be traumatic for them. If they can harness deeper communication with people who are similar to them, they can feel less lonely.

Venus in Scorpio

Venus in Scorpio individuals are sensitive, alluring, and mysterious. Their feelings are hidden and sometimes buried but can run deep beneath the surface. At times they appear cold or closed off, but this a defense mechanism used to protect themselves from being hurt. If someone is looking for a lighthearted relationship, a Venus in Scorpio person is not going to take things lightly. They expect total dedication and a soul-merging experience.

It can be hard for them to allow someone to get close, so if they open up, that means there is something special that they feel. Once they do trust someone, they are loyal and dedicated partners. Once they connect, it's hard for them to let people go. In fact, they can be possessive and want to spend a lot of time with their partner. They might become demanding and want to control their partner. This behavior won't always be apparent and they won't likely admit to it.

Dedicated lovers, their feelings are never lukewarm. They take their relationships seriously and can get consumed with their partner. If they like someone, they will let them know it. Superficial relationships don't interest them, so it's not common for them to date around. In love relationships, they want a body and soul connection. They expect complete commitment and loyalty from their partner. They have an ability to get others to share all their secrets with them, but they don't normally share their own.

Crisis and conflict in love can bring passion but can also cause a lot of pain. Because they crave intensity in love, they can get involved in unhealthy relationships. They desire intense closeness, but at the same time they can keep people at an arm's distance. This can cause unstable relationships, or their partner does not always understand their complex nature. Disagreements and power struggles are common with this placement. When they feel slighted, they can get icy or respond with an explosive emotional temper. Either way, they will let their partner know when they are upset. Harnessing trust will help them feel supported and make them capable of building healthier relationships with others.

Mars in Scorpio

Mars in Scorpio individuals can be intense, passionate, and competitive. Extremely passionate, they work hard for what they want. Determined, calculated, and dedicated, they can become obsessive about having things done a certain way. It's obvious that they will passionately pursue their goals and won't give up until they get what they want. But they can also be private, secretive, and prefer to work behind the scenes on their own. Challenge can invigorate and encourage them to work even harder.

Power dynamics can influence their relationships because they like to be in control. Conflict and disagreements can wreak havoc in their personal relationships. Powerful desires can lead to jealousy, obsession, and possessiveness in relationships. They can have trouble letting things go and can be unforgiving if people hurt them. Trusting others and maintaining intimate relationships can be challenging for them. It takes a lot of work to ensure their relationships are balanced and healthy.

Magnetic and sensual, they have a strong sexual appetite and need for intimacy. At times they might be impulsive and pick partners who are hard to get. The chase can be thrilling for them and increase their level of attraction to someone. Sexuality fascinates them and they want to have a deep physical connection with their partner.

Confident, bold, and assertive, they like to speak up for what they want. Brave and resilient, they can overcome loss and heal because of their strong warrior spirit. They have a powerful regenerative ability that can help them heal and move on quickly from heartache. They're unafraid of the darker side of life and embrace uncomfortable experiences with tenacity. If they can get comfortable expressing their desires in balanced ways, they can find that deeper connection they are seeking.

Jupiter in Scorpio

Jupiter in Scorpio individuals grow stronger through transformation and embracing change. The heavy energy of Scorpio is lightened by Jupiter's positive influence. Open-minded and understanding, they attract many positive things into their lives. People listen to their advice because they have a way of making people believe they can do anything. Motivating others comes naturally because they have a powerful and magnetic personality that inspires.

Passionate about pursuing knowledge, they can be a bit restless. Travel and learning inspire them and help them seek things that interest them, such as psychology, religion, and spirituality. They might be interested in traveling to foreign lands and want to explore the ancient cities around the world. Researching occult topics helps quench their thirst for adventure.

Abundance seems to show up for them just when they need it most. When they focus intently on their personal goals, relationships, or career, they find many blessings come their way. Wealth can come when they are mentally, emotionally, and physically dedicated to their goals.

Other people's resources and inheritance are common with this placement. In fact, they might be called to take care of the finances of others or their property. Material and financial benefits can often come through their marriage partner, and they might also benefit through business partnership. They might work with the goods of the dead, write obituaries, develop wills, or manage estates.

When times get tough, they can overcome many obstacles with sheer determination. Being grateful for the things they have can help them appreciate their blessings. As long as they focus on positivity, the more challenging parts of life can be easier to get through.

Jupiter placed here can intensify intuition, and they should remember to listen to their instinct. They are deep individuals who want to learn more about the world. Connecting with others, socializing, and being friendly are all ways they can expand their network. They are generous and fiercely loyal to the people they love. If they can tap into their optimistic energy, it can help them attract everything they need.

Saturn in Scorpio

Saturn in Scorpio individuals are introspective and possess emotional depth. However, at times they can feel insecure, which can cause them to bottle up their feelings. Talking to people they trust can help them process what they are feeling.

Practical and calculating, they are disciplined individuals who work hard to achieve their goals. Responsible and serious, they can struggle with having fun or letting things go. Because they are cautious, they resist change and prefer to be in control of their lives. Transformation and change happen throughout their lives.

Serious and responsible, they can become obsessive. They want to understand why things happen. They can feel like they work harder than others and that it takes them longer to reach their goals. With time and patience, they can slowly achieve what they set out to do. But overthinking and focusing on negative outcomes can delay positive outcomes.

Saturn's energy can intensify coldness and a fear of being vulnerable with others. Relationships can be challenging and intimacy with others might take extra work with this placement. Because of a secretive and private nature, they don't always know how to express their emotional side. In fact, it's hard for them to trust others and they dislike appearing weak in any way. But once they commit to someone, they are dedicated partners.

Focusing only on their practical and physical needs can cause them to get out of balance. Sometimes they neglect their own emotional needs in pursuit of money, power, and success. It's beneficial if they can realize that emotions are also an important part of life. Emotions don't make someone weak but can give them strength. They are intuitive and care deeply but have to work on expressing that. Because if they don't learn this lesson, they can often feel lonely. If they can feel more comfortable with their emotions, it will help them connect with others and feel more supported.

Uranus in Scorpio

Uranus in Scorpio individuals are forceful and persistent. Determined to get what they want, they work behind the scenes in secret. They don't readily share their plans with others, but when they do, it can be shocking and transformative. Because they aren't afraid to take risks or rocking the boat, they often succeed by being innovative.

Imaginative, creative, and unconventional, they can have natural intuitive and psychic abilities. Reading situations and people accurately helps them navigate challenges and turn them into opportunities. Friendly when they need to be, they are good at convincing people to join their organization or causes. Usually, they are good judges of character and are quick to notice people's true motives.

Original and nontraditional in many ways, they focus on strategies for the future. They can rebel against the status quo and want to awaken and open people's minds with new ideas. On one hand, they want to be in control, but then unexpectedly they can do things to force change in their environment. Their rebellious nature makes them want to question authority, rules, and social norms.

Freedom and self-reliance are important to them, but they can get attached quickly in relationships. They can be intense, loyal, and affectionate, but they can also change their feelings unexpectedly. Bottom line is that they don't want to feel controlled or trapped in love. They have a complex personality because they can struggle with jealousy, possessiveness, and a desire to control those they care about. They might have eclectic sexual interests and an unconventional approach to intimacy. Their relationships can go through ups and downs. If they can learn to be more stable and balanced through change, it can help them grow into a stronger person.

Neptune in Scorpio

Neptune and Scorpio individuals are sensitive and want to feel deep connections with others. Transformation often comes through love and relationships. If they have a lack of boundaries with others, it can create unhealthy relationship patterns. They want to merge with others and develop intimate connections. But sometimes they get disillusioned by love and relationships. Sometimes they are idealistic and at other times they are distrusting.

Intuitive and perceptive, they can usually see what is really going on in their environment. Sometimes they ignore their gut instinct and don't readily trust their feelings. It's important for them to listen to their own inner voice and those subtle cues when interacting with others. If they do get hurt, they can shut down and isolate themselves. It can take them a long time to trust or be vulnerable once they experience betrayal.

Sharing their feelings helps them bond with others. But they have to be cautious about taking on other people's emotions and problems. These individuals possess a compassionate energy and are highly sensitive to their environment. It's important for them to develop stronger boundaries to protect their sensitive energy. Stress and anxiety can influence their physical

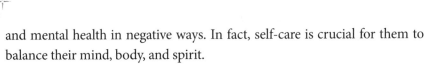

and mental health in negative ways. In fact, self-care is crucial for them to balance their mind, body, and spirit.

Other people often find them difficult to understand because they are mystical, mysterious, and elusive. Sometimes people misjudge them because they can't always see what is really going on with them or they can't figure them out. In relationships, they can seek a soul mate–type relationship. They want to merge and bond physically with their partner. Sexual intimacy can help them connect to higher spiritual realms and open up different levels of awareness for them. But it's crucial that they be careful who they have sex with because they absorb the energy of others, whether that is positive or negative.

Neptune here can bless them with psychic abilities and they often have unexplained spiritual experiences. There might be an interest in life after death. For example, they might wake up in the middle of the night and see a spirit standing at the foot of their bed. During the dream state it's not uncommon for them to experience paranormal encounters.

Because of their natural connection to different states of consciousness, they may benefit through meditation, hypnosis, and learning more about reading the akashic records. They should avoid drugs and alcohol because they can have significant impacts on their mind and emotions. They need to ensure that they dedicate time to nurture and take care of their body, mind, and spirit. They want to find out their soul's purpose and can spend a lot of time researching fascinating topics such as astrology, past lives, crystals, and energy healing.

Pluto in Scorpio

Pluto in Scorpio individuals can experience personal transformation and rebirth through self-analysis. Understanding themselves on a deeper level assists them with understanding others better. They enjoy investigating psychological concepts and learning more about what makes people do the things they do. In fact, they are often attracted to law enforcement and crisis intervention. They can be found binge-watching true crime shows on Netflix and listening to paranormal podcasts. Natural psychologists, they give great advice and understand people's problems.

They have a fascination with sexuality and intimacy. It's often all or nothing in relationships because their feelings are never lukewarm. But there are times when they may appear cold on the surface or disinterested. It's hard for them to trust other people and it takes time for them to open up. Once they do trust someone, they are loyal, devoted, and protective friends. If someone they love needs help, they are reliable and will show up to do whatever needs to be done.

In relationships in general, there can be power, control, and manipulation tactics that need to be overcome. They are complex individuals who desire to dive deep beneath the surface to explore uncomfortable topics most people avoid. They push other people out of their comfort zones to explore the darker side of life. They don't mind talking about death and can make sarcastic jokes just at the right time to shock others. These behaviors are the main reason people either love them or are sometimes afraid of them.

Blessed with stamina, they can work long hours and tap into adrenaline to keep going. Obsessive traits can make them relentless at times. Because they are determined, they like to push themselves to extremes. Determined to succeed, they don't give up easily. In pursuit of their goals, they can be calculated and patient. Just when the time is right, they strike to obtain their heart's desire.

Anything mysterious fascinates them, so they are not afraid of discussing topics such as death, loss, and trauma. Many people are attracted to their strong and powerful presence. People often walk up to them and start oversharing and telling them all about their problems. There is something about their energy that lights up a room and attracts people who have pain. Nothing really shocks them and there are very few things they have not experienced or heard about.

Powerful healers, they often take classes and want to learn more about energy healing fields such as Reiki and healing touch. They understand human nature and have a psychological gift of understanding how to help people with their problems. Because they are intuitive and perceptive, they see right through people and can pinpoint their vulnerabilities. Directly telling people the truth to help them is something they do easily.

These natural abilities lead them to pursue careers in psychology, social work, and medicine.

They are resilient phoenixes and survivors who grow stronger through difficult experiences. Their recuperative abilities help them shed old energies and heal their mind, body, and spirit. Working hard to address their problems takes effort and dedication. Healing their own pain can help them become a healing force in the lives of those around them. It's important for them to harness forgiveness to heal and transform their lives.

Planets in the Eighth House

When planets are in the eighth house, you are interested in death, sex, healing, transformation, rebirth, and metaphysical subjects.

Sun in the Eighth House

These individuals are deep, secretive, and private about their personal lives. Magnetic and mysterious, their presence attracts many people because they have a special way of listening. Natural counselors, people feel comfortable around them and often share their painful experiences. They have a way of diving into taboo topics and are comfortable talking about sexuality, death, loss, and trauma.

Losing someone at a young age, such as a parent or friend, is common. This can change how they see the world. Benefits often come through the father or his side of the family. There is often some type of inheritance, which could be money, property, land, or even a psychic ability.

Sacrifice is often a theme in their lives. They can feel like they have to give up something they care about for the greater good. Letting go and releasing something important to them can help them attract new things into their lives. But sometimes other people can also make sacrifices to help them in some way. Financial and monetary possessions often come through other people or their partner.

Born with natural psychic abilities and a strong intuition, they see through people and understand their true motives. They can bring hidden things to the surface, exposing other people's secrets. Because they are psychic, they can feel other people's energy easily and feel everything that is happening in the environment. Many of them have spiritual gifts, such as seeing ghosts, dreaming about the future, or having gut feelings that turn out to be right. They can sometimes feel different from other people. It can be difficult to relate to people who don't share similar interests and experiences. From a young age they can have unexplained paranormal experiences, which is why they are interested in studying mysterious topics such as astrology, numerology, and tarot.

Their desire for power can make them try to control situations and people. Personal relationships can be challenging for them because they want to connect deeply with others. But at the same time, they might fear completely trusting anyone. They can experience intense energies of greed, jealousy, anger, and possessiveness. Emotional extremes can impact their ability to experience true intimacy. They can experience intense sexual desires, or not feel anything at all. They are only attracted to certain people and need physical chemistry to want to be physical with anyone. It's all or nothing in relationships. In fact, their experience with betrayal can prevent them from fully opening up. Sometimes they can feel lonely and prefer to isolate from other people.

Intense and passionate, they have an aura that draws people into their life. They thrive in crisis situations and seem to know what to do, and say, to get other people to remain calm. Many can be drawn to high-stakes careers like firefighting, detective work, and even suicide hotlines. Helping people with their problems is something they feel inspired to do. The goal is to use their spiritual gifts to help others.

They are reborn throughout their lives like the phoenix. They often feel like they are dying, rising up, and transforming every day. These individuals are known as wounded healers who experience a lot of change that triggers personality shifts. Change is a constant theme in their lives that forces them to adapt and become more resilient.

Part of that mission is diving deep and helping other people heal, which is part of their spiritual journey. Harnessing their intuition can help them make better decisions and find the right path in life.

Moon in the Eighth House

These individuals are highly sensitive and have an intense emotional nature. Hiding their true emotions and feelings from others happens because they worry about not being understood. They have a desire to protect themselves at all costs and don't easily trust other people. Emotionally, they can experience extreme feelings, such as love-hate, anger-sadness, and trust-distrust.

Understanding death on a core level is a gift of the eighth house. Early in life, they might have worried about dying or losing someone close to them. When they were a child, they often had an inner awareness about real-life issues. In fact, they might have had anxiety about losing their parents, pets, and friends. They might lay in bed at night thinking about death.

They might have lost their mother at a young age through unexpected death. Or the relationship with their mother could have been intense and taught them a lot about trust. They can inherit property, money, or a spiritual gift from their mother or the maternal side of the family.

Many see spirits, angels, and ghosts as a child because they are connected to the other side. Because they are born with a vivid imagination and psychic abilities, they can use them to help others. It's not uncommon for them to feel people's energy and sense what other people are thinking and feeling. They are born with a complex emotional nature and this is why they feel very different from others. They can feel lonely even when surrounded by friends and family. They can feel like they are from a different world. They don't readily trust others and struggle with having intimate relationships.

Attracting people with emotional pain is common with this placement. It's good if they can remember that it's not their responsibility to take on other people's karma.

Absorbing everything in the environment can cause health problems, anxiety, and depression. Their energy vibrates at a higher level, so it's important for them to learn how to protect themselves energetically. At times, picking up other people's feelings can cause tremendous emotional pain and sadness. A technique that might help is visualizing a ball of yellow light surrounding and protecting them, especially when they are in large groups. This will create a boundary and barrier around their energy field.

Powerful healers often have this placement and are drawn to careers that delve deeply into other people's lives. They enjoy bringing the unconscious to conscious awareness. In fact, they can excel in careers in hypnotherapy, psychiatry, counseling, energy healing, psychology, medicine, research, detective work, hospice, and any business field.

Their emotional fulfillment can come through helping people in some way. From a young age, people are drawn to them and share their problems. Other people are not always aware of their motivations, subconscious thoughts, or body language, but they notice the subtle cues. They can benefit from meditation and relaxation exercises. Also, journaling their thoughts, feelings, and perceptions can bring comfort.

Sometimes they feel people are always hurting or taking advantage of them. At some time in their lives, they can feel victimized by others sexually, mentally, and emotionally. There is a wound that involves trust and intimacy. Feeling betrayed by those they trusted is a spiritual lesson that can make them stronger. It is important to realize these experiences are part of the eighth house journey. Even if they suffer and hit rock bottom, they will eventually rise like a phoenix out of the ashes. They are survivors who recuperate and transform. In fact, they can heal themselves on a deep level by allowing themselves to process intense emotions.

Benefits can come from other people's sacrifices or the sacrifices they make for others. Their financial success and material comfort almost always come from someone else, such as parents, grandparents, or their marriage partner. Other people's money and resources can impact their lives in positive and negative ways.

Sexual intimacy can bring many lessons into their lives. They want to connect to others through sex and deep emotional interactions. Their emotional happiness is dependent on being able to connect deeply with people. If they can't connect deeply, they can feel lonely. It's important for them to realize that their feelings of loneliness can lessen once they begin to see their oneness with everything. Through healing others, they heal themselves. Wounded healers, they have healing hands and can benefit from studying Reiki and other healing touch modalities. Emotionally resilient, they transform their lives through forgiveness and letting go of the past. If they tap into their emotional strength, they heal from tragedy, betrayal, and disappointment.

Mercury in the Eighth House

These individuals are deep thinkers who hide their thoughts from others. They can seem mysterious, private, and secretive. It can be difficult for them to trust others because they are private individuals. Naturally introverted and quiet, they don't readily share what they really think with others. Sometimes their thoughts are so deep they might not even know how to express them with words. There is a need for conversation that's deep and meaningful.

People can't hide things from them and often tell them the truth. Sensing what is going on beneath the surface, they verbalize the words other people need to hear. Their gift of verbal expression touches others on a deep emotional level.

Born with a vivid imagination, they can often read other people's thoughts. They sense if someone likes them or not, or if they are being deceitful. They enjoy probing other people's minds and trying to figure out if others are telling them the truth. Mental games and exercises strengthen their mind. They need deep mental connections to lead to greater emotional connections.

Transformational thinkers, they excel by diving deep into complex subjects and solving problems. Topics like astrology, tarot, healing, and numerology interest them. Understanding how things work on a deeper level brings opportunities for success. Their mind is like a sponge absorbing everything going on in the environment, so this can lead to confusion, irritability, and depression. They pick up on other people's thoughts easily and it's hard for them to differentiate between their own thoughts.

Psychically gifted, they might have the ability to read minds, although they may not even realize it. Gifted with listening to others, they help others who want to discuss their secrets and past hurts. They can make an excellent psychologist or counselor who can help others heal their problems. Talking about important life matters such as sex, death, and spirituality is important to them. Because they are perceptive and intuitive, they dislike superficiality and fakeness.

In relationships, they can be secretive. Even if they like someone, they may never tell them directly. They prefer other people telling them they like them first because they are afraid of being vulnerable.

Conflict can happen when they don't verbalize what they are feeling. Writing down their intense thoughts in a journal would be beneficial because it can be a great stress reliever. If they have a trusted friend or confidant, it's good for them to express their pent-up emotions. Deep communication with like-minded people can be comforting and help them feel less lonely.

Mental stimulation can come through reading detective books, mystery novels, and metaphysical books. It is important to discuss spiritual topics with people who challenge them to broaden their minds. These individuals want to dive deep in communication and can't handle superficial conversations. Small talk is almost unbearable for them. In fact, they'd much rather be alone than surrounded by conversations that don't have meaning. Harnessing deep communication can help them feel connected to other people and build trusting relationships.

Venus in the Eighth House

These individuals have a secretive and private love nature. Their love nature is deep, possessive, and intense. So, when they fall in love, they don't take it lightly. Intimacy and trust are crucial for them to feel comfortable with a partner. But they can struggle with trusting others and being vulnerable. Being vulnerable makes them fear being betrayed.

In relationships, they can benefit through their marriage partner and tend to marry someone of a higher financial status. Before they can become sexually active with a partner, they like to wait until they fully trust them. In actuality, it's hard for them to ever fully trust anyone with their heart. Before sharing intimate feelings, they need to know how others feel. They have a powerful love nature and are known for being jealous, possessive, and controlling. It's often all or nothing in love and relationships, because they expect a high level of commitment and loyalty from their partners. If hurt, they can become unforgiving, vengeful, and angry.

They are attracted to intense and passionate individuals who challenge them. They require a high level of depth in their relationships. If they don't have an intense connection, they are known to cut ties. Because they are not casual in love, they can feel like most relationships are superficial and empty. Sexual chemistry, commitment, loyalty, and trust are things they need in a relationship. Marrying someone solely based on their financial status won't be enough; they need more than just security. But they are attracted to people who have money, wealth, and power.

Connecting to other people's pain can bring them partners who are unstable, unhealthy, or unreliable. They may learn this lesson the hard way and feel victimized or taken advantage of. Sacrificing their own feelings for their partner or avoiding red flags in relationships can bring heartache. When they become intimate with a partner, they develop a strong attachment that's difficult to break. Emotional depth in their relationships is needed for them to find peace and happiness. They need to learn how to trust others more, which can help them build lasting relationships.

Mars in the Eighth House

These individuals have a passionate and strong sexual nature. People are drawn to their mysterious personality and like to share their problems. Bonding with someone on a physical level connects them to others on an emotional level. Deep and intense relationships that are full of passion excite them. As a partner, they can become jealous, angry, and obsessive. Sometimes they are drawn to passionate, risky, intense, and unhealthy relationship partners. There can be a lot of conflict and drama in their personal relationships.

Driven and competitive, they enjoy pushing people to the breaking point and can be reckless in their dealings with others. Self-centered at times, they focus on having their deep desires met. Temper flare-ups and emotional outbursts can occur when they don't feel like they are getting what they want. They like to live on the edge and pursue adrenaline-rushing activities such as racing, skydiving, and bungee jumping. But these reckless behaviors can lead to accidents and injuries.

When they feel hurt, they can become private, secretive, and even reclusive. They have a fiery temper that seeps out when they have repressed their feelings for too long. It's good for them to exercise regularly and have a physical outlet for their intense energy. They need time alone to process their complex emotional nature.

Researching and delving into topics that require investigative skills suit their personality. Intuitive, insightful, perceptive, they have a knack for digging up secrets.

Working behind the scenes as police officers, detectives, or psychologists is a common career path. They might be drawn to crisis intervention and stepping in during traumatic situations. They are good at reacting in the moment and taking charge of difficult situations. Brave and courageous, they are not afraid to risk their own safety for other people.

There can be conflict and disputes concerning other people's resources and their partner's money. At some time in their lives, they could experience conflict with family members over inheritances, land, wills, and other material resources. There can be challenges with the marriage partner or arguments about financial planning and spending money.

If they do not feel deeply connected with others, they can become bored and restless. With practice and patience, they can become a powerful force of change in the lives of others. Harnessing change in their own lives helps them grow and become more resilient.

Jupiter in the Eighth House

These individuals are blessed with abundance, generosity, and an ability to see the positive in difficult situations. Even if they experience difficult times and challenges, they have the strength to overcome adversity. It's like a guardian angel is looking over them and at times they could feel like their life was saved. Jupiter is all about abundance and expansion. It often protects them from the harsher realities of the eighth house.

Financial resources are often tied to their partner or come through other people in some way. Other people's money can impact them in positive ways. For instance, they could inherit money, land, or possessions from a grandparent. Whatever form it takes, many blessings and opportunities come from those closest to them.

They have good luck in whatever they set out to achieve. They are destined to benefit from other people's generosity. People might sacrifice to provide for their financial stability. Or they may feel that they have to sacrifice something for those they care about. The more they give, the more they receive.

Helping other people can bring them happiness. Because of their healing presence, they can attract a lot of friends. Networking and socializing with people who are interested in the same things they are can bring joy.

When they let go of old energy, memories, and hurt, they grow stronger. Giving up unhealthy behaviors, or releasing negativity, often helps them manifest what they really want. When they truly release the past and forgive others, the universe blesses them with more. Their greatest dreams and wishes will start to come true when they tap into their positive energy.

They can be born with psychic abilities and might experience clairvoyant dreams, intuitive knowing, or sense other people's energy. Natural healers, many are attracted to alternative medicine and natural ways to heal the body. The more they share their insights, the more they grow spiritually. Guardian angels, spirit guides, and deceased loved ones are always watching over them. Harnessing optimism can help them overcome difficult times and move forward with hope for a better future.

Saturn in the Eighth House

These individuals are secretive, serious, and repressive. They should avoid repressing their emotions and allow themselves to be more expressive. Determined and productive, they can work hard to achieve their goals. Sometimes they resist change and they work hard to avoid it. But life is full of loss and unknown situations, which they often learn at an early age. They had to grow up fast and often feel responsible for taking care of others. Death and loss can cause them to experience changes on a deep level. Being self-reliant was something they learned the hard way. Perceptive and realistic, they're afraid of trusting their intuition. In fact, they are too practical at times and doubt their mystical experiences.

Communicating with others can be challenging due to their private, shy, and introverted nature. They struggle with small talk and prefer deep conversations with others. In relationships, they can be committed, dependable, and loyal partners. Repressing emotions and sexual urges can lead to health problems. They may fear sexual intimacy and have rigid attitudes about relationships. It's not uncommon for them to marry someone older or someone of a higher financial status.

Sometimes they dwell on heavy emotions and have trouble having fun. Self-conscious and conscientious, they can worry about things they don't have control over. Worrying just leads to anxious feelings and prevents them from enjoying the moment. Super responsible, they don't like taking risks and resist any type of change. They prefer stability and comfort, but life often forces them out of their comfort zone at an early age.

Karmic lessons force them to transform and they experience many rebirths that change them on a deep level. Feeling responsible for other people's actions, it's difficult for them to understand why people do the things they do. They have high expectations for themselves and others. They need to find hobbies and ways to express their feelings and learn to relax.

People can perceive them as cold or unloving because they put up a wall to protect themselves. Taking care of others' practical needs is easier for them than displaying affection. Restricting themselves too much can impact their ability to experience happiness. Sharing anything personal can make them feel uncomfortable. Learning to trust others will help them not feel so alone. They tend to isolate themselves socially and prefer solitude. Reading books about change and growth and preparing for the future can help them adapt.

There can be past-life learning and karmic issues involving other people's resources. If they inherit money, they might find there are roadblocks or problems with accessing it. They need to see life as a gift and not as a burden. If they can harness flexibility, it will help them feel more comfortable to open up emotionally.

Uranus in the Eighth House

These individuals need their freedom and enjoy studying unique spiritual topics.

Restless and easily bored, they like to associate themselves with deep and shocking conversations. The mystical side of life fascinates them and they have an interest in anything unique or different. Experiencing vivid dreams, astral projection, déjà vu, and out-of-body experiences can happen in childhood. Unexpected psychic visions and auditory sounds come into their awareness out of the blue. Writing down their perceptions and visions is important to tap into their spiritual gifts.

Embracing change while feeling free enough to make their own decisions is fulfilling. They experience transformation throughout their lives. Uranus energy is electric, unexpected, and unsettling. At times they can feel like their entire personality is constantly being reborn.

Standing out and being free to express their true identity helps them maintain a sense of autonomy. They might experience unique attractions to people or question their sexual identity in some way. But because they don't like labels, they can rebel against traditional sex roles. They always test the boundaries of how far they can push their innovative mind.

Death and dying is often on the forefront of their mind. From a young age they might have experienced unexpected loss. They might have had a family member, friend, or loved one die. Traumatic situations can impact their life and awaken their fascination with the mystical side of life. They can become interested in learning more about angels, spirit guides, ghosts, and different religious beliefs.

Financial benefits can come through their marriage partner or immediate family. Other people play a big role in their material and financial success. Things like inheriting money or property can drastically change their life. Change is constant in their lives and embracing it will help them find greater happiness.

Taking unnecessary risks or rebelling can cause difficulties. They feel like breaking free when they are feeling trapped. Thrill seekers, they might pursue dangerous situations because they like to push the limits. But because they are accident prone, they need to be careful about speeding or doing things without thinking them through.

Freedom loving at heart, it's important that they feel they have control over their own lives and that they make their own decisions. Settling down and focusing on future goals can prevent many unforeseen misfortunes.

Neptune in the Eighth House

These individuals have a heightened sensitivity to their environment. It's like they are from a different world, which makes them feel different from other people. There is something mysterious about their energy, and this attracts others. They can be deeply spiritual and have natural psychic abilities. They often believe in a higher power and seek a connection with something greater than themselves, which brings them the strength to overcome suffering.

They are natural empaths and take on the energies in their environment. Compassionate, they can feel other people's pain and have psychic abilities. Because of their personal experiences, they might be afraid of opening up to supernatural forces. It's important for them to understand more about the soul and what happens after death. In fact, they have a natural understanding of death, ghosts, and spirits. It can be difficult for them to watch scary movies because they are highly suggestible. Born with a strong imagination, they are visual and often have visions and unexplained mystical experiences. They can have powerful dreams that give them glimpses of the future. Writing down their dreams is important as they can use them as a guide in their waking lives.

Abandonment issues can make it difficult for them to fully trust others. If they didn't have a healthy home and family life, this can impact their ability to connect intimately with a partner. Because they trusted others too easily when they were younger, they often got hurt. In fact, when they are older, because of their past experience, they are distrustful of people's motives. There are times they can feel like a victim and feel sorry for themselves. They can feel wounded or betrayed by someone they trusted. Having a spiritual path and belief system can bring greater comfort.

Escaping from the world through drugs and alcohol might be a way they cope with negative feelings. This can be dangerous for them because of their emotional sensitivity. Finding more positive outlets to deal with their uncomfortable emotions, such as meditation, journaling, listening to music, and spending time near water, might be helpful.

Many of them feel lonely and prefer spending time by themselves. This happens because they may feel like no one understands or supports them. These feelings can increase their need to withdraw from the world and find solitude. It's not uncommon for them to experience sadness, anxiety, and depression.

Sexuality is a subject that fascinates them but can also cause heartache. Because of their idealistic feelings about love and romance, they trust people too easily. Disappointment often comes through intimate relationships. In fact, they can feel taken advantage of by someone they trusted. They need to be practical and take time to really get to know people. Seeking a soul mate, or meeting someone who is spiritual, might meet their high standards. It's just very important that they try to see people clearly before trusting.

In relationships, they can attract people who are unhealthy, addictive, and even emotionally abusive. Their compassionate and kind nature makes them an easy target because they often feel sorry for others. Although they crave intimacy, they might prefer having platonic relationships where they sacrifice their sexual urges. They need to make sure they find the right relationship partner who is reliable, dependable, and can give them the same level of affection they deserve. In fact, it's critical that they pick their sexual partners carefully.

Due to their highly sensitive nature, they should be cautious about sharing their body with others because they can take on people's negative emotions and energies. Once they are intimate with someone, it can also be difficult for them to end that relationship.

Deception and misunderstandings can arise concerning other people's resources. There could be suffering involving inheritance and confusion about estate planning. Misunderstandings occur due to secrets, hidden things, and miscommunication.

Learning to see things realistically and practically can be their greatest test. Harnessing stronger boundaries with others will help prevent unnecessary hurt and disappointment.

Pluto in the Eighth House

These individuals are intense and possess a powerful energy. There is an air of secrecy about them that attracts others. Born with a powerful intuition and perceptiveness, they often can see through people and situations, drawing out the truth. They can have a healing energy that is soothing, intense, and transformative. In fact, they are often interested in healing and pursue careers in medicine, psychiatry, Reiki, acupuncture, and massage therapy.

Their magnetic energy attracts people like moths to a flame, even if they don't understand why. At times, people might seem afraid of them, either loving them or disliking them instantly. This can cause hurt feelings and misunderstandings when they are younger. But as they get older, their awareness shifts and they begin to harness their powerful energy to help others heal. Great in crisis situations, they have an ability to remain calm and help people process trauma and their intense experiences. Because they are excellent listeners, some might be drawn to psychology and other counseling fields.

It's not uncommon for them to be in a grocery store shopping and have someone come up to them to share that their father just died. People will feel vulnerable around them and like everything they have repressed is being called out of hiding. There is something special about their energy that radiates into the environment like an antenna. They are often able to help people with their problems because they are understanding and have an ability to bring out people's secrets. They help others face all the darker, hidden parts of their personality.

Born with a highly sexual nature, they have a strong desire for passion, romance, and intimacy. There are times when their relationships are ruled by extreme emotions that can impact their love life. Jealousy, possessiveness, and obsession can cause difficulties with trusting others. Regarding sex, it's usually all or nothing with them. They can either have a lot of sexual experiences or very few at all. In fact, it's more important to them to have a deep connection than being physically intimate.

Trusting others can be difficult and a barrier to obtaining true intimacy. Because they understand human behavior, they are good judges of character. It's hard to fool them because they are naturally cautious about believing anything that anyone says. Actions speak louder than words and they watch people's actions.

From a young age, they might have had an innate awareness of their own mortality. They can be fascinated with death and the afterlife. Losing someone at a young age could have awakened painful truths that sparked their interest in learning more about the meaning of life. Pluto often brings a wound in the birth chart, and for these individuals, their wound is an innate knowledge of the fragility of life. As they get older, healing this wound can happen by becoming more spiritual. It is important for them to understand what happens to the body after death and the process of soul evolution. It's important that they can spend time studying near-death experiences, metaphysics, occultism, astrology, and any field that helps them better understand their soul's purpose. Their own understanding about the laws of the universe can help them overcome challenges as they become a transformative healer.

Planetary Transits through the Eighth House

When planets transit the eighth house, you can experience uncomfortable emotions, intense experiences, and losses that change you on a core level.

Transit Sun

The Sun transiting the eighth house often brings transformation and deep psychological changes into your life. This is a good time for leaving things behind that are not satisfying or helping you grow. Searching for something more fulfilling might be on the forefront of your mind. This transit makes you want to withdraw within and reflect deeply on the life you have lived so far. You might feel more emotional, depressed, lonely, and private during this transit. Extreme emotions can flow during this time, and you might feel more secretive and distrustful.

Relationships might be more difficult, which brings up uncomfortable feelings about trust, intimacy, and fears of loss. This powerful energy can help you heal and transform your life. In fact, it's a good time to make changes and start fresh.

Issues from the past can resurface, bringing up old wounds. The power of the Sun can help you find positive ways to think about heavy emotions. Because of this, it's a good time to heal the past once and for all. Your personality can undergo extensive rebirths that can be life changing. There is no doubt that after this transit, you will feel differently about things and a bit lighter. If you harness the energy of transformation, it will help you grow stronger and become more resilient.

Transit Moon

During this quick transit, you might have hidden emotions resurface. You crave deep connections right now and resist anything that is superficial. It is difficult to hide what you are feeling, because emotions can hit you out of the blue and be more powerful. You might feel a need to be more secretive, private, and spend more time alone. There is a need for solitude and reflection, so journaling feelings can help you process them. Your emotions are ebbing and flowing right now, so be cautious about getting caught up in negative feelings. You might feel more sensitive, vulnerable, and lonely. In fact, you may cry more easily than usual and have a hard time concealing things.

In relationships, if you're typically not a jealous person, you may feel more distrusting and possessive. Intense feelings of jealousy, passion, and anger bubble up during this transit. If there are things you have been repressing, this transit will awaken them. The past often comes back to be addressed, processed, and felt. It's a good time to acknowledge your feelings and let them go. If you can harness releasing old emotions, you can gain greater emotional fulfillment.

Transit Mercury

This transit can intensify your need for deep, intense, and powerful communication. There are difficulties thinking about things logically and you are more emotional than usual. There are serious issues that are on your mind right now. In fact, it's not uncommon for old hurts or betrayals to resurface. It can be more difficult for you to communicate and you might need more privacy. Talking about the memories and feelings that are coming up can help you process them with someone you trust. But you can feel more sensitive to others and more secretive. Anything you try to communicate during this time will be based on deep feelings, which can be challenging to express. Intense thoughts and beliefs push you to dig deeper below the surface of what people actually mean.

Actions speak louder than words right now, and you can be distrustful of what people promise. You might feel more irritable and sensitive with others, which can cause more bickering and arguments.

If you're typically social, you'll want to avoid superficial conversations during this transit. You could be craving discussions that are more real and serious. Your thoughts can be transformed during this time, which brings greater self-awareness. Harnessing deep thinking can help you connect with what you truly believe in.

Transit Venus

This transit can impact your desire to connect with others and express your love. It's hard for you to hide what you feel, especially right now. For the next five weeks, you might feel more intense and obsessed with finding love. You want to connect deeply and crave affection. Sexual intimacy and intense feelings are on the forefront of your mind. There can be an increase in sexual desires and a need for developing deeper partnerships. In fact, you might start to express feelings and intense desires that you have never felt before. If you are currently in a relationship with someone, you will change how you express yourself. Although you might typically be peaceful, this energy can awaken darker emotions and feelings of possessiveness and jealousy.

Relationships can change right now, and romance can be more challenging. Your vulnerable areas are feeling raw and your deeper needs are being exposed. There is a good chance you can attract intense, mysterious, and powerful people into your life.

Be cautious about getting overly involved in unpleasant emotions such as jealousy, revenge, and anger. These feelings will need to be felt and processed to get to the root cause. It's a good time to balance your emotions and avoid conflict with others. You need relationships that touch your soul and help you feel alive. This transit helps you get in touch with your sexual needs and desires.

Transit Mars

This transit often brings powerful, passionate, intense, and sexual needs to the surface. You will experience powerful energy right now that you can utilize to achieve your goals. The next eight weeks can be challenging because your emotions can be overpowering. If you have been feeling deprived, you might start to feel angry or resentful about a lack of intimacy in your relationships. There can be more conflict, but it can inspire you to act on deeper impulses that you typically hide. Just be careful not to do something reckless that you might regret later.

Feeling a lack of control can cause frustration, irritability, and anger. Power struggles can occur in relationships because of your intensified emotions. Tension is in the air, and you might feel like you are walking on eggshells with others or they can feel this way about you. In fact, it's like the small things you do inspire others to act out against you or battle with you. Try to remain calm, be patient, and think things through before you react.

Transformation and healing can come by addressing deep-seated issues you have repressed or kept hidden. You can spot fake people right away and may cut ties with family, friends, and lovers. Superficial people and life situations will rouse irritability, aggression, and a desire to lash out.

Relationship disputes with your spouse and significant others can be challenging. There can be more arguments with business partners and issues surrounding other people's money. Harnessing realness can help you make changes and give you the strength to overcome any problems.

Transit Jupiter

For the next year, you can feel deeply emotional and more focused on accumulating shared resources. This transit opens you up emotionally and inspires you to be more generous with others. Encouraging and motivating others can help you achieve your own goals.

Good luck and abundance can come through relationship partners, business associates, and family. There can be changes in how you feel about money and security. If you are typically frugal, you might want to spend more money and enjoy life. You can benefit from other people's money in some way and be more interested in psychological transformation.

You might be interested in searching for spiritual answers and finding the meaning of life. You may feel more comfortable discussing taboo topics such as death, loss, and sexuality and try to uncover secrets. Learning something new, taking a class, and reading emotionally impactful books can bring fulfillment. You might have a sense of adventure and traveling can help you connect deeply with the world. It can also be a positive time to open up and be more intimate with others.

This uplifting energy can impact how you connect to people you care about. You seem to be more focused on intimacy, sexuality, and helping people with their problems.

Diving deep with people you care about helps you connect with them.

If things from the past or uncomfortable emotions come up, you address them with a fresh outlook. Healing the past can be a blessing of this transit and it's like you are finally ready to let things go and move forward. This optimistic energy can help you focus on starting over and allowing positive changes into your life. This is a great time for spiritual growth, even if things are stripped away or transformed. Releasing the past can make room for good things to enter your life.

Because the eighth house is related to other people's resources, there can be opportunities for financial gain. Money might come through inheritance, taxes, or unexpected ways. It's important to harness positive energy to accumulate and enjoy the blessings of this transit.

Transit Saturn

This transit can bring painful and transformative experiences for the next two to three years.

During this time, you can feel tested and experience heavy burdens. Things just seem harder than usual and there are a lot of emotions resurfacing. It's not uncommon to feel responsible for other people right now. Because you are reliable and dependable, other people might rely on you and need your help.

Emotional choices that you made earlier in life will need to be reevaluated. Karma is being balanced and things you have done need to be sorted out. If you have been hurt in the past, those traumatic memories will come up now and force change in your life. It's time to dig deep, feel uncomfortable emotions, and learn from your mistakes. Someone from the past could reappear in your life to challenge your livelihood, relationships, and future goals.

Intimate relationships are tested to the limit, and you may have to let go of someone you love. This is also a good time to forgive someone who has hurt you in the past. If you try to control things too much, it can be more difficult to adjust to the energies of this transit. It will make things easier if you focus on allowing others to make their own decisions and do everything to take care of their needs.

If you are in a committed relationship, you might choose financial security over love, passion, and intimacy. It might be uncomfortable for you to be vulnerable or trust others fully. In fact, you might choose to be alone and focus on building material security instead of developing lasting connections. There can be learning lessons with commitment, and you can realize what true loyalty means in a relationship.

It's time to balance the scales and make things right. Either way, this can be a painful process and you can experience feelings of sadness. Endings can bring up grief, loss, and loneliness, which might cause you to withdraw and become more introverted. It is a good time to talk with a counselor if you are struggling to express your emotions. Although you feel you don't need anyone else to rely on, it can be helpful to get out of your comfort zone and talk to other people.

This is a powerful transit that can help you transform any negative personality traits or patterns that are getting in the way of you finding happiness. If you struggle with control issues, there can be more power struggles in all areas of your life. In fact, you can be forced to face any issues head-on. For instance, if you struggle with addictive behaviors, this is a good time to get disciplined and overcome them.

If there have been things that were hidden from you or you were hiding things, they often get revealed. Undergoing change and dealing with issues related to sexuality, death, shared finances, and resources can bring wisdom. Karmic debts have to be repaid, and this transit makes sure they are. Spiritual growth can come through pain, sacrifice, and loss. It's important to harness wisdom, because it can help you understand the transformative changes you have experienced.

Transit Uranus

This transit can ignite unexpected change, shocking events, and possible loss. For the next seven years it's like the universe picks you up and turns you upside down. Anything outdated, stagnant, and old is forced to change. It can be hard to comprehend the powerful changes that are moving into your life at lightning speed. There can be uncomfortable feelings hanging over you. Change is on the way, and you can feel it on a core level.

During this transit, you could lose someone through death and this can be unexpected. Death can also be symbolic and involve changes that can impact your identity and beliefs.

Any outdated and unsupportive energies will need to be released. If you resist change, the universe has a way of stripping things you care about away and blindsiding you in the process. But you need to remember that this is all happening for your greater good.

If you are living a stagnant life and refusing to grow, this transit will shake things up and it can be electrifying. It might take time to figure out what is happening to your life. At times, it can feel like an unseen force is testing you to see just how much you can handle. The best way to overcome this transit is to accept this new energy and allow change into your life.

Feel free to explore new emotions, thoughts, and beliefs that you never knew existed within. In the end, you have to release some material things and let go of old ways of doing things. You will be forced to face darker parts of your personality. Issues with regarding sexuality and intimacy can be triggers. In fact, it's not uncommon for repressed feelings to come up.

If you are in a committed relationship, the relationship with your partner or spouse can be forever changed. You can struggle to repress or hide anything and can feel quite rebellious. Unconventional feelings and ideas bubble up and can influence how you behave in your relationship. You might want to break free from boring routines and traditional ways of interacting. This house rules sex and you might become more open-minded about exploring and experimenting with your partner.

Exciting and unstable people can enter your life to wake up your inner spirit. Just be careful about changing your life too drastically during this time, because this energy is not stable and you can feel different when it's over. Be careful about getting involved with unstable people or pursuing secret love affairs because any relationship developed during this transit has the potential to end abruptly, tragically, and unexpectedly.

This transit can cause tremendous emotional pain that can affect your physical health, if not handled appropriately. Once this transit is over, you will look back and realize that you are a completely different person than you were before. It's important to harness opportunities for growth and to not hold on to past ways of being in relationships.

Transit Neptune

This transit can last up to fourteen years and can test issues involving boundaries. Illusion and mystery can impact the way you see the world. This is a good time to address your tendency of being too idealistic and seeing everything with rose-colored glasses.

There is a heightened sensitivity to your environment and you might pick up on other people's energy. In fact, you can experience increased psychic experiences, compassion, dreams, and a desire to bond on a deeper level with a significant other.

Sexual relationships might seem confusing and you daydream about spiritual and platonic love. You might feel disillusioned and confused about intimacy and struggle to connect with people in your life. If your relationships are too mundane, you might move on to find someone who shares your spiritual interests.

During this time, you might sacrifice yourself for people you love. Be cautious about giving too much to others and never getting anything in return. It's crucial to develop stronger boundaries during this transit. In fact, boundaries can help you protect yourself from being taken advantage of emotionally, sexually, or financially.

Your intuition is strong right now, so trust your gut instincts about people. There is a heightened sense of compassion and emotional sensitivity that makes you want to help other people with their problems. It's a good time to learn to say no to people who have been using you. Focus on your own needs and give yourself the love that you readily give to others. Be extra careful about being too trusting and ignoring red flags in relationships. You can be easily fooled and people might try to deceive you during this cycle. Pay attention to the energies you feel when you are around people. Stop giving all your love, energy, and attention to others who use you or leave you feeling exhausted.

It's important for you to be more realistic and practical with your finances. Financial matters can seem confusing, and you or your partner might struggle with money issues. This might be a good time to seek counseling and discuss any secrets you have with someone you can trust. Harnessing boundaries will ensure you protect yourself from unnecessary hurt and can help you balance your need to help others.

Transit Pluto

This intense and life-changing transit impacts your life for decades. Loss, grief, and healing are key issues that resurface. You could think about death a lot more and worry about losing people you love. The unexpected death of someone close to you can transform your life. There might be a time during this cycle when you have to grieve, organize a funeral, and handle the material resources of a deceased loved one. Inheritances are common during this transit and there can be increased wealth or emotional benefits. Your bank account and finances can be impacted by unexpected events. There could also be financial and emotional debts to pay. For instance, maybe your partner's father didn't have a will and you had to hire a lawyer to ensure they don't lose their land. Or you had to pay for the funeral of a loved one.

Repressed emotions and unhealed trauma related to sexuality and loss will have to be felt. It can feel like Pandora's box is being forced open and all those deep, dark, intense secrets and hidden parts of yourself are being exposed. You can't hide from the secrets that are bubbling up. Facing the shadow part of your personality during this transit can make you feel vulnerable, but in the end, it makes you more resilient.

In relationships, you might experience intense love affairs or it's possible to get involved with people who mirror the darker side of your personality. It's hard to let go of people you connect with right now. In fact, you can become fascinated and obsessed with someone new. Your desire to control people because of jealousy can cause dramatic conflicts with others.

During this transit, you may feel victimized or find yourself victimizing others in some way. Power and control issues can impact intimate relationships. In many cases, divorce and the ending of a love relationship is common when Pluto moves into the eighth house.

Anything that is not healed will need to be dealt with and you can feel like you are going through many rebirths. Healing unpleasant past experiences, emotions, and even addictive behaviors can help you transform. Understanding your power and addressing issues with exerting power in your life are put to the test. It's a time to harness change, so it's important to let the past die and embrace the new you.

Ways to Harness Scorpio Energy

- Let go and release the past.
- Embrace change and new experiences.
- Explore deeper emotions.
- Experience intimacy.
- Trust your intuition.
- Learn self-protection.
- Heal yourself and others.

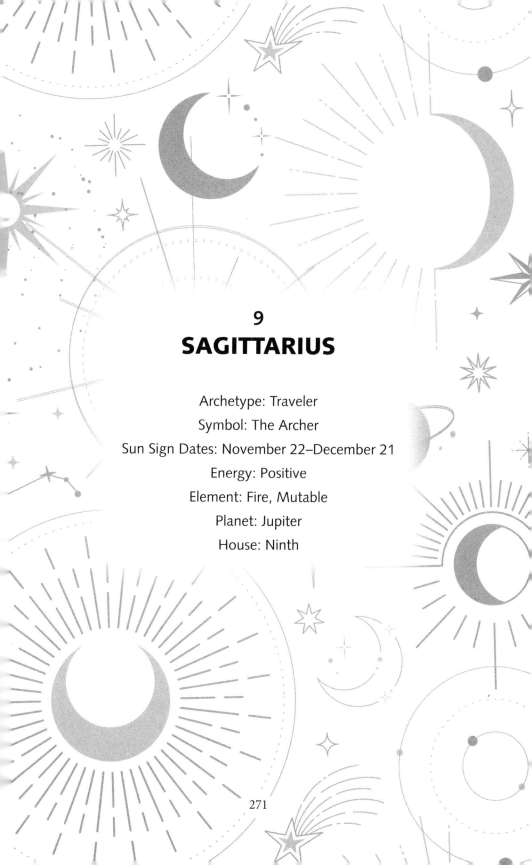

9
SAGITTARIUS

Archetype: Traveler

Symbol: The Archer

Sun Sign Dates: November 22–December 21

Energy: Positive

Element: Fire, Mutable

Planet: Jupiter

House: Ninth

I f you have Sagittarius in your birth chart, planets placed in the ninth house, or are experiencing planetary transits through the ninth house, this chapter will cover information regarding these energies. If you don't, you can still learn about Sagittarius energy and incorporate it into your life. The placement of the planet Jupiter in the sign and house will show where you express Sagittarius energy. It is important to look at what house the sign Sagittarius falls on in your birth wheel because this is where you will be able to harness optimism, be more adventurous, travel to distant lands, and recognize a need for freedom and independence. Harnessing Sagittarius energy gives you hope, increased faith, and a more positive outlook.

Sagittarius Energy Words

Truthful, independent, positive, optimistic, hopeful, cheerful, zealous, restless, expansive, adventurous, jovial, freedom loving, knowledgeable, trusting, generous, outspoken, honest, intelligent.

Sagittarius Motto

As a Sagittarius, I want to be able to do what I want to do at a moment's notice. I need to feel free to explore new things. I seek adventure and enjoy being outdoors. I can feel restless at times, so I enjoy moving around and keeping busy. I try to see the positive side of situations and don't want negativity to prevent me from reaching my goals. I love to travel and experience different countries and cultures. I am on a quest for knowledge and love to learn.

Harnessing Sagittarius Energy

Sagittarians have a positive energy that is bright, friendly, and spontaneous. This energy is adventurous and likes to explore new things. In fact, this energy ignites a passion to learn many different topics. Their ability to always see the bright side of life helps them not stay depressed for very long.

Sagittarius energy oozes optimism and is known to be painfully honest. They are not going to sugarcoat things. Speaking the truth is something they do because they care about helping people grow. There is always a new place for them to travel to, learn about, and explore. Believing in something bigger than themselves helps them realize they have a greater purpose. Being hopeful is the essence of Sagittarius energy. It's truly a strength to be able to see the bright side of life even during challenging times. In fact, they can tap into this positivity when times become difficult. This friendly energy helps us transform negativity and believe in the good energy that surrounds us. Developing a new outlook, being grateful, thinking positive, and having faith are ways we can harness this energy.

Harness Optimism

Sagittarius is open-minded and friendly. They always look for something new and exciting to learn. They are focused on positive things and dislike negativity. They have a positive energy, which strives to eliminate negativity and rigid thinking. It's difficult for them to stay depressed for very long. They are able to overcome challenging emotions because of their ability to move forward.

Sagittarius embodies an open-minded energy that seeks to understand others. Its purpose is to make things better and help people see the bright side of life. Being friendly and making people happy is their natural gift. Intensely freedom loving, this energy creates a need for independence and a belief that they can do things on their own. Positive energy is open to new things because it's broad and expansive.

Many Sagittarians trust the universe, are hopeful, and believe in something greater than themselves. This energy encourages them to see the silver lining when life brings challenges. Trusting the universe's plan and developing faith are ways we can connect with this energy.

Bold and Direct

Sagittarius is ruled by the element of fire. Fire burns, roars hot, and can easily take over a situation. Fire energy helps Sagittarius have the energy to be on the go, move around, and explore new places. Honesty and direct-ness of the fire energy inspires Sagittarians to tell people how they feel. They have an amazing ability to do this in a kind, caring way where people can be open to feedback. Restless at times, they can find it hard to settle down and relax. Being outdoors suits this fire sign best and they like to be physically active. Sagittarians are self-starters and need a lot of autonomy. They enjoy the adventure of traveling and taking risks. Because they are passionate, freedom loving, open-minded, and confident, they often go after what they want. Full of energy, fire energy brings generosity, warmth, and inspiration to those around. People are attracted to their optimism and their ability to radiate friendliness.

Future Focused

Mutable energy is known for adapting and morphing to the environment. This energy helps us be less rigid and inspires us to grow. Sagittarians are constantly looking for ways to get along with others and be open-minded. This energy likes to move, travel, and seek adventure. Changing plans on short notice is easy for them because they go with the flow. Social connec-tions mean more to them than being right. They care about other people but will stand up for what they believe in. Even though they are known to be opinionated, they are willing to compromise. Having the ability to move, travel, and explore can be fulfilling for Sagittarians.

Generous Energy

Sagittarius is ruled by the planet Jupiter. Expansion, abundance, and growth swoop in, making it easy for them to manifest their goals. Generous, happy, and kind, this energy inspires us to be more giving. Open-minded and philosophical, this energy helps bring opportunities and good luck. This energy helps Sagittarians seek movement, freedom, and knowledge. Jupiter expands everything it touches and can lead to overindulgence in the good things in life, such as eating, drinking, and spending money.

This energy is happy and can help us believe in destiny and gives us a sense of purpose. Everyone can harness Jupiter energy by taking positive action, making time to travel, and exploring the world. Telling the truth and doing it in a kind way to help people grow comes naturally for Sagittarians.

Jupiter brings an enormous amount of good luck and generosity. Wherever Jupiter is placed in our birth chart shows where we might want to expand our knowledge, explore new ideas, travel abroad, and find a greater sense of freedom. This energy is all about adventure, open-mindedness, movement, being outdoors, and connecting with people who are different than us.

Seek Opportunities for Growth

The ninth house in astrology is associated with faraway lands, travel, foreigners, higher learning, philosophy, and religion. An intellectual pull to explore and adopt new perspectives comes from this area of life. There is a strong sense of freedom and independence that comes from having planets in this house. This is the area of life where we explore the world through travel, study, and accumulating knowledge. Long-distance travel to exotic and foreign countries is highlighted. In fact, planets here can show opportunities for traveling to and living in a different country at some time in life. There is an interest in relationship partners who might be from a different culture, ethnicity, or religious background. Attraction can come by opening the mind to new partners who are different from us and help us broaden our minds. Commitment is challenging at times when planets are in this house. It's because there can be a wanderlust that creates a restlessness and desire to be self-reliant. Speaking different languages and having a passion for learning about different religions are all ninth house issues.

There is a positive energy that influences this area of life, highlighting optimism, faith, and hope in something better. An abundance of wisdom can come through dedicated study and educational pursuits. There is an abundant energy associated with this house and it's difficult to say anything negative about this area of life.

In fact, it brings feelings of generosity and good luck into our lives. Seeking adventure through travel and a restless desire to keep moving inspire growth. The ninth house's energy inspires us to seek higher knowledge and connect with people from all over the world.

Sagittarius Rising

When people first meet Sagittarius risings, they perceive them as friendly, talkative, and confident. They might appear to always be on the move and constantly darting back and forth. They have a restless, distracted, and changeable energy. They have a positive and optimistic kind of energy that inspires people around them. Many of them have an ability to bring out the best in people because of their fun-loving and jovial personality.

Sagittarius risings can be generous, freedom loving, and independent. Because they are adventurous personalities, their energy can help others want to take more risks and try to learn new things. They can persuade people to believe in themselves and they often shower others with a positivity that is hard to turn away from. Helping other people be open-minded and willing to grow out of their comfort zones brings them joy.

Maintaining a sense of autonomy is important to them. They like the feeling of freedom and they don't want to feel trapped in relationships. Many prefer being single and not committing to only one person. They have a strong sense of self and they don't want to answer to anyone. Picking up and going on a trip on a whim without having to worry about upsetting someone is appealing to them. It's often why they remain single into later life. If they do marry, it needs to be with someone who is intelligent and just as freedom loving as they are.

Relationships can bring a sense of burden, responsibility, and duty. Sagittarius risings would rather just be friends and keep things platonic than to feel like they can't act in the moment. Sometimes impulsive and rash, it's hard to slow down once they make up their mind to do something, or when they get the urge to go somewhere. Whether that is driving around in a convertible with the top down and the wind blowing through their hair, or boarding a plane for Paris on a whim, they need to be able to go.

Even though they are kind, they are also brutally honest and call people out for their bad behavior. They understand others on a deeper level, are insightful, and are very perceptive. In fact, they are genuinely concerned with helping other people grow and be more open-minded. They like to experience joy and are searching for positive ways to express their adventurous nature. If something feels unpleasant, they are often the first person who will speak up about it. It's important to them to feel comfortable in their environment and they are not afraid to change things up. Passionate about learning and exploring philosophical ideas, they are trailblazers in fields such as teaching, publishing, media, marketing, counseling, and any field where they can help others, travel, and connect to people.

How to Harness Planets in Sagittarius

When planets are in Sagittarius, you will want to be free to explore, travel, learn, and seek adventure.

Sun in Sagittarius

Sun in Sagittarius individuals enjoy their freedom. Being able to come and go as they please is important to them. Freedom of movement is crucial for their overall happiness. They dislike being cooped up and stuck in one place for too long. Restless at times, they like to be exploring the environment around them. Socializing with others lightens their mood and fulfills their intellectual needs.

Often opinionated, they are outspoken and confident in their ability to tell others what they really think. Being truthful is important and it's something they value in others. They are seeking a higher purpose and sense of direction. Asking questions is a way they learn more about the world.

Their generosity and kindness enable them to get along with many different types of people. They enjoy supporting others but are also good at attracting what they need. Abundance comes easily because of their positive can-do attitude. Wealth and career opportunities can sometimes fall in their laps. The more trusting and optimistic they are, the more positive energy they attract.

Nothing stops them once they make up their mind to do something. Extremely naïve and hopeful at times, they don't allow negativity to alter their set path. They believe the best about people, situations, and life in general. Faith and hope are strong in their souls, which enables them to overcome challenges with ease. If they do feel depressed, negative, or sad, they can often snap out of it quickly. They truly are individuals who can see the glass is half full versus half empty. Their positivity can be contagious and uplifting to people who are struggling. Helping people on their path brings them a sense of emotional fulfillment and happiness.

Social butterflies, they make friends easily and often with people who are very different from them. They show they care by laughing, joking around, flirting, and teasing others. Their positive energy makes them fun to be around and is the main reason people are attracted to them. Idealistic at times, they often have a spiritual faith that helps them survive life's challenges. Typically easygoing, they do have a powerful need to speak up if something bothers them and they can react impulsively at times. Escaping to a faraway land or ancient city or traveling across town in their car helps them quell their inner restlessness. If they can tap into the energy of manifestation, they can attract everything they need.

Moon in Sagittarius

Moon in Sagittarius individuals can feel emotionally restless. It can be hard for them to sit still for long periods of time because they enjoy moving around. Keeping physically active helps them expunge their high-intensity energy. Being outdoors in nature can also help them feel calmer and find peace. They might enjoy hiking and fishing and activities they can do alone.

They have a happy-go-lucky outlook on life. Bubbly, approachable, and gregarious people are drawn into their circle. In fact, they are one of the most optimistic and friendly Moon signs. Because they are open-minded and accept others, they can stand up for other people. Natural advocates, speaking up for what they believe in and telling the truth can be fulfilling. They feel their best when they feel free to come and go as they please. Fiercely independent, they need to feel self-reliant and enjoy doing things on their own without any help. Adventurous, high spirited, and boisterous, they don't tolerate negativity. If people are toxic or jealous, they will cut them off and move on quickly.

This is a positive place for the Moon and intensifies emotional happiness. These individuals can snap out of negative emotions quickly. Their optimism helps them overcome sadness and depression. Because they are adaptable to change, they can face difficult situations with a positive outlook. They can find emotional fulfillment through exploring the world, meeting new people, and learning new things.

Boredom can make it hard for them to have a solid routine. Because they are so adaptable, they like to go with the flow. Being rushed will irritate them, and they don't appreciate deadlines or ultimatums. Change helps them move forward and taking risks or facing the unknown invigorates them. They have a can-do attitude about everything and a modest confidence that inspires others.

Easygoing at heart, they can be rebellious if they feel someone is taking advantage of them. Their kindness and generosity are contagious. They can inspire others with their positive outlook on life and not even realize it. They need variety, newness, and change in their lives. Happiness often comes through travel and doing something adventurous, such as skydiving, flying a plane, or bungee jumping.

At times their restless and spontaneous nature can lead them to be emotionally impulsive. They want to listen to their gut instinct and can make decisions in the moment. Because of their intelligence and active mind, it's hard for them to relax. If they can harness slowing down, they can find emotional stability.

Mercury in Sagittarius

Mercury in Sagittarius individuals communicate in an optimistic and big way. They are talkative, friendly, and enjoy socializing with new people. They have friends from many different backgrounds. Mental stimulation is important and they need to communicate with others. They are known for their direct and blunt approach. Sugarcoating the truth doesn't work for them, but they do have a charming way of giving negative feedback to others in a kind way.

Being able to multitask is a talent that can help them accomplish great things. They juggle many projects and have the stamina to ensure they all get accomplished in a timely manner. Energetic and lively, they can help get people moving and focused on a common goal. Inspirational speakers, they can inspire others to do great things. Because of their verbal abilities, they can make excellent teachers. They have a way of explaining high-level information in an understandable and basic way.

Discussing unique and philosophical ideas inspires their mind. They might enjoy debating their opinions and beliefs with others. Mentally restless and changeable, it can be hard for them to stay focused. Classroom learning can be challenging for them because of their difficulties sitting still and staying focused. In fact, they do best learning on their own time and in an open environment. Because they enjoy learning about so many different things, it's hard to pick just one. Plus, they get bored easily and need to feel connected to something to dedicate time to reading about it. They can be forever students and like to study on their own, because traditional education doesn't always work out for them. It's important when they are exploring knowledge that is meaningful to them in some way.

Focusing on the big picture is what interests them most. They can feel stifled and trapped when they have to think about the small details. Because their mind is expansive and adaptable to all kinds of information, they can think quick on their feet. They have an interest in traveling overseas to foreign countries, learning different languages, and accumulating knowledge.

Their optimistic way of thinking through problems helps them focus on the end goal. They don't get swayed by naysayers or roadblocks. Because they are positive thinkers, they manifest their dreams easily. The power of their mind can connect them to the law of attraction. Their ability to focus on the positive side of life and abundance is something they were born with. Many with this placement can help inspire others through the most challenging situations by sharing personal stories and talking about ways they can find hope. They can be natural counselors and motivate others with their words. Exploring new information can help them expand their beliefs about the world.

Venus in Sagittarius

Venus in Sagittarius individuals often develop relationships with people who are from a different culture or religious background. Love can sometimes be challenging because they crave their freedom and independence. It's not easy for them to commit in relationships because they are free-spirited and self-reliant. There is also a sense of wanderlust that keeps them searching for something better on the horizon.

Their bold and independent spirit doesn't like to be told what to do. They resist being tied down in relationships. Because they are spontaneous, flirtatious, and easygoing, they attract fun-loving partners. In love, they can be restless and inspire their partner to try new, daring, and exciting things. It's important that they can be adventurous with their partner and learn new things together. If not, boredom can set in and they might move on quickly. Although they are notorious for trying to keep lovers as friends.

When they are in relationships, it can get confusing because they can be both open-minded and judgmental depending on the subject. Bickering with their partner and debating facts are ways they connect mentally. Typically lighthearted and easygoing, relationships that don't put too much pressure on them are the ones they are most comfortable with. The less pressure the better if someone wants to keep them engaged.

Exchanging ideas is an important part of their relationships; also, being able to be straightforward about their feelings. If things get challenging or become too much work, they might feel like running away. It's important for them to control their restlessness and fears of commitment. One thing that can be important is having someone who challenges them to grow mentally and emotionally. If they can commit to relationships while maintaining a sense of autonomy, they can find greater balance in love.

Mars in Sagittarius

Mars in Sagittarius individuals have a passionate drive for adventure and travel. They can be prone to taking risks and being a bit impulsive. They can lack patience and dislike waiting around for something to happen. Acting in the moment and moving around helps them express their highly active energy. They thrive when they have something new to learn, somewhere to go, and new people to socialize with.

Playful and fun loving, they can be optimistic and generous with others. On the other hand, they can also be more serious and enjoy arguing with others about what they believe in. They are confident, blunt, and honest about how they feel. Sometimes when they get angry, they can lash out verbally and wander off to do something by themselves.

In relationships, they need a lot of freedom to roam. They can feel passionate about finding someone to love, but when things get too serious, it's often difficult for them to commit. They don't want to feel controlled by their partner. In fact, any possessiveness, jealousy, or questioning about where they were or who they were with can send them running for the hills. Having a relationship with someone who trusts them, supports their sense of autonomy, and doesn't try to possess them could last.

Passionate at times, they need a little competition in their lives. Because of their restless energy, they might excel at sports, especially outdoor competition. Being physically active can help them balance their emotions. Finding positive ways to express their anger will also help them feel better. Sometimes they feel guilty for losing their temper or venting in the moment. Also, distancing themselves from others can help them get perspective and calm their intense emotions. Deep down, they like to be happy and positive. Restless spirits, they have a desire for freedom above all else.

Jupiter in Sagittarius

Jupiter in Sagittarius individuals are adventurous and optimistic. Free-spirited, they can be generous, happy-go-lucky, and positive. Enthusiasm is magnified with this placement, and they get very excited about meeting new people and doing new things. Financial success often comes easily because of their generous nature. They accumulate a lot of money and material possessions.

Attracting things so easily can sometimes make them feel lazy. They might procrastinate and have difficulties getting motivated. Overindulgence might need to be curbed and they should be cautious about overspending. In fact, because they enjoy all the finer things in life, they can do things in excess, like eating and drinking, which can lead to weight gain. Good luck and good fortune bless them because of their positive attitude.

The world is a place to explore and expand their horizons. Their love of travel and adventure can lead them to visit foreign countries and historic sites. They might have an interest in learning different languages. When they are on their travels, they want to do something adventurous and might enjoy hiking, skiing, and competitive sports.

Having their freedom and independence is something that means a lot to them. Feeling trusted to be themselves and feeling a sense of autonomy bring happiness. Because of their jovial energy, they can help others feel better by inspiring them to think positively. They enjoy studying a variety of topics that are meaningful and quench their thirst for knowledge. Their sense of wanderlust is high and it's like they're on a never-ending search for something they can't quite explain. An inner restlessness pushes them forward and they adapt to change easily. If they can express their generosity, they can attract greater wealth and fortune into their own lives.

Saturn in Sagittarius

Saturn in Sagittarius individuals can sometimes feel like their success is delayed. They might feel like they have to work harder than others to achieve their goals. Lessons with patience and discipline can help them grow wiser with experience. Time is the key for their dreams to come true. Traditional beliefs and religion can be an important part of their lives. Open-minded at times, they still prefer a more reliable approach to the world. They have a philosophical way of looking at life and can balance practicality with their idealism.

In relationships, they might be afraid of commitment or losing their sense of autonomy. They might restrict their generous and optimistic feelings because they have been hurt in the past. Determined and disciplined, they work hard to find focus on learning to be more optimistic. Because they are practical, they can see the world in a much more realistic way and this tones down the typical Sagittarius optimism.

Saturn here can create a negative outlook and skeptical approach to life. Sometimes they can feel they aren't intelligent enough to pursue higher education. Or they might believe they don't have enough money to travel overseas and explore the world. Adventure and exploration can sometimes feel blocked and they don't always know how to get what they want. Their self-esteem can be impacted by their inability to loosen up and go with the flow. Criticalness can prevent them from manifesting positive experiences. In fact, they can have high standards for themselves and others. Balancing a need for structure with their desire for adventure can be in constant flux.

If they can harness a more positive outlook and balance it with their realistic approach, it can make it easier to achieve their goals.

Uranus in Sagittarius

Uranus in Sagittarius individuals can be rebellious, risk taking, and freedom loving. They are fiercely independent, unconventional, and have a growth mindset. In fact, they can resist anything that is too structured, controlled, or organized. They prefer to have the freedom to explore on their own and make decisions in the moment. Acting on their impulses can benefit them, but it can also lead to reckless behavior. It's important that they stop and think things through before they do something they might regret.

Unique and eccentric, they have very different beliefs and ideas about relationships. Financial success can come through luck or in unexpected ways. Opportunities often fall in their lap and can manifest through travel and their social networks. In fact, socializing and networking with interesting people can bring good luck and blessings into their lives.

Movement is important to them because they can feel restless and enjoy the ability to break free from restriction. They can wither if they feel trapped and controlled by people or situations. Free-spirited and opinionated, they want to live their lives the way they want to. Conforming to society's expectations or having traditional relationships does not make sense to them. They are known for questioning the status quo and won't do something just because they are told to.

Imaginative and innovative, they have an ability to see the future. They are intelligent and have amazing ideas of making the world a better place. Helping people on a large scale is important to them. They might join groups or organizations where there is a common sense of purpose to research and find solutions to social problems. Unexpected insights and intuition can be a gift they can use in their lives. They might dream things before they happen. Their psychic abilities can manifest through their dreams, visions, imagination, and in unexpected ways. It's important for them to be open to the messages they receive even if they don't make sense logically.

Neptune in Sagittarius

Neptune in Sagittarius individuals can be spiritual and open-minded. Sometimes they can feel lost, confused, or question their belief system. How they were raised can impact their religious and philosophical views. They might have a desire to learn and study different philosophies about the world. It's like they are on a journey to seek answers to life's most mysterious problems.

There is a magical and mystical energy that they bring into relationships. Because of their compassionate and kind nature, people are drawn to them. They find it easy to understand other people's feelings. They also can put themselves in other people's shoes and understand why they might act and believe a certain way. In fact, they are very empathic and forgiving of others. It's important that they develop stronger boundaries and that they listen to their intuition.

Social chameleons, they adapt to people easily and find ways to connect with others. They can tap into what someone needs and sense what is important to people. Finding a way to help people can bring them a sense of purpose. Because they are idealistic about the world, they often dream of a place where all people's differences and religions are accepted.

At work and in society, they can be optimistic leaders because they seek to find the strength in others. Because of this ability, they can motivate others to join their causes and even sway other people to open up to new belief systems. Spirituality can be an important part of their life and having a spiritual path can increase a feeling of emotional support and protection.

Pluto in Sagittarius

Pluto in Sagittarius individuals can be open-minded with a thirst for knowledge. They are born with a strong belief system and intense desire to understand why people believe the way they do. They value personal freedom and enjoy socializing with people. In fact, they prefer intense conversations and taboo topics such as death, sexuality, and religion.

They can be passionate about diversity, equity, and inclusion and want to ensure that other people are being treated fairly. Accepting different perspectives comes easily for them because they are willing to change and transform. Opening up other people's minds can become an obsession and they want to dig deep when they explore the world. There is a confidence and intensity about their personalities that attracts many people.

They often have a passionate desire for seeking the meaning of life. Deep and mystical, they might enjoy traveling to faraway exotic lands. Exploring different cultures and religions can help them find the deeper answers they are searching for.

Dedicated and passionate, they have an inner desire for growth. They are strong and possess an adventurous spirit that isn't afraid of shedding old and outdated patterns. Their optimism and ability to speak the truth about issues that need solving help them overcome challenges.

Deeply held philosophies about the world can help them preserve a sense of principles when they act. There is an inner strength that helps them overcome loss, heartache, and betrayal. Their understanding of human nature on a core level helps them keep people at arm's length. They don't fully trust anyone because they know what people are capable of.

Valuing other points of view comes easily for them, but they can continue to stand strong in their own truths. They can get bored easily with superficial conversations and seek out people who can challenge them.

Growth is important to them because they don't want to feel stagnant. Exploring different lifestyles and nontraditional relationships can help them find the independence they desire.

Planets in the Ninth House

When planets are in the ninth house, you will be focused on learning new things, traveling, adventure, and exploration.

Sun in the Ninth House

These individuals strive to learn more about the universe and the meaning of life. They often are born into a certain traditional religion and are raised to believe a certain way.

They are seekers of knowledge who can sometimes uphold strong conservative beliefs about the world. Whichever faith they were brought up to believe in as a child can become a focal point for them in their adult years.

In fact, they might find it challenging to sway from that belief system even if it doesn't make sense to them. It's not uncommon for their faith to be tested. As they get older, they often question their entire religious belief system. It's not uncommon for them to rebel against restrictive beliefs to pursue nontraditional ideas.

Life seems to try to open their minds, and this energy can force them to reexamine their beliefs about God, the afterlife, morality, and their place in this world. Through their personal spiritual experiences, their life can be transformed. They can become zealous and enthusiastic about talking about what interests them.

Many are attracted to different philosophies, cultures, and cuisines. Finding their purpose in this world is important to them. This is often done through learning and studying a wide range of topics. Higher education is a way for them to expand and broaden their minds. There might be a fascination with different languages, and they might have an ability to speak a different language. Also, they might have been raised in a bilingual home.

Forever students, they often spend their lives doing things that broaden their mind and life experience. They shine when they are expanding their knowledge. Even if the traditional college route was not taken, they can find joy through taking classes, reading, and studying topics that inspire them.

Freedom of movement is critical for their sense of happiness, and they need an environment that is not restrictive. Oftentimes, they might have experienced a change in their home environment and moved around a lot. For instance, they might have grown up in a military family and uprooted to start over in a new country. Or they might be interested in joining the military where they have to travel, and this gives them the opportunity to live all over the world. These experiences can help them adapt to change easily and be more accepting of people's differences. They can benefit through traveling far away from where they were born. Some might be raised in a different country or immigrate to a different country with their family. They can have a restless desire to travel the world and explore new foods, beliefs, and ways of living.

One major area they are interested in is foreign travel. Exploring the world and different cultures and countries expands their experience. They grow as individuals when they become more open-minded and accepting of different ways of doing things. These individuals can be drawn to foreigners and those who are very different from them. They might be attracted to people who speak a different language, dress differently, and have different religious beliefs. Accepting different religious beliefs helps them become more understanding of people who were raised differently from them.

Their energy is optimistic and contagious, which helps them overcome difficult situations. They have an ability to tap into their inborn faith and hope for a better future. If they feel trapped, maintaining a sense of independence can help them find joy.

Faith helps sustain them in times of crisis and they see that everything happens for a reason. The experiences they have can shape their belief system, but deep in their soul they always keep a sense of wonder and hope that things will work out. They can tap into a positive attitude to manifest their dreams.

Moon in the Ninth House

These individuals find emotional fulfillment through travel and obtaining knowledge. Sometimes they long for faraway lands when they are feeling unhappy. Emotionally restless, they need movement and to feel free to explore. Exploring new places, meeting new people, and expanding their mind helps them find comfort. Participating in hobbies, learning different languages, reading, and taking classes can help them accumulate knowledge.

Their optimistic nature can help them overcome challenges with ease. Their positivity can be intoxicating and inspires others to see the bright side of life. Fiercely independent, many want to remain single because having committed relationships can be challenging. Maintaining a sense of autonomy is key to their emotional happiness. Of course they can have relationships, but they need a partner who is not jealous, controlling, or possessive. To feel emotionally satisfied, they don't want to feel withheld for any reason. In fact, they might be a little afraid of commitment or losing their ability to change if they want to.

Born with natural teaching abilities, they enjoy pursuing higher education. Even if they don't go to college, many are forever students. Taking classes in subjects that interest them throughout their lives is an opportunity for them to meet people and connect.

Emotionally, they need to feel they are contributing to making the world a better place. Many have a spiritual or religious belief system that helps them remain strong during challenging times. They might have been raised differently than others in some way. For example, maybe one of their parents spoke a different language in the home and they might be bilingual.

Living in a foreign country or traveling to historic sites is something that could bring happiness. Opportunities for travel through education, business, or work are common with this placement. Because of their desire for movement, it's important that they make time for family vacations and doing things outdoors. Making time in their schedule to explore new places and relax is important for their emotional well-being.

When they grow older, they might drastically change their belief system to something completely different than how they were raised. Or they can maintain the stability of the traditions they were taught. Their personal experience with religion fluctuates between having faith and then questioning what they believe. To them, life is a journey that can help them change their outlook and figure out the meaning of life.

Seeking a connection to a higher power can help them believe and hope for a better future. They care about being a good person and helping others can give them a sense of purpose. Their optimism can help them motivate others to believe in themselves. If they can get comfortable being where they are, in the present moment, it can help them find happiness in everyday life.

Mercury in the Ninth House

These individuals are intelligent and enjoy exploring the world. Traveling expands their connection with the past and tames their sense of adventure. They are interested in learning meaningful subjects like philosophy, religion, linguistics, and world history. Forever students, they enjoy exploring the world and expanding their knowledge. Mentally restless, they need to discuss and talk about many different topics and ideas with others.

Socializing and networking with like-minded people can bring them good luck and opportunities. Inspiring communicators, they have a natural ability to make people feel at ease. Their friendliness and positivity can motivate others to want to learn and step outside their comfort zone.

Many are avid readers and enjoy learning things on their own. Because they are highly intelligent, they might get bored easily. They need mental stimulation to stay engaged in learning, but they might even have a photographic memory. When they were younger, a structured school environment could have been challenging. It's not uncommon for them to rebel against traditional education and decide to pursue their own unique path.

Sharing knowledge and opinions with others can be fulfilling. They have strong opinions, and they want to debate many different topics. A mental connection in relationships is important for them to feel heard. Surrounding themselves with educated people who can debate multiple topics helps them expand their minds. In fact, they like to play the devil's advocate sometimes and have heated discussions. Communicating with others can bring a sense of connection and inspire their active mind. Talking with people comes naturally, and because of their love of information, they can be natural teachers.

When they travel, they often have a passion for immersing themselves in the culture. It's not uncommon for them to be able to speak multiple languages or have an interest in learning a new language to use on their travels.

They are open-minded and enjoy hearing about what other people's values and religious beliefs are. Some might have an unshakable faith in a higher power. Talking about spirituality can inspire them to search deeper and explore the meaning of life.

Venus in the Ninth House

These individuals can have a love of learning, travel, and education. They can find peace and harmony through traveling and exploring the world. They have a wanderlust for faraway places and a desire for adventure.

Meeting a multitude of different people helps them appreciate people's differences. They might have a strong desire to learn and speak a different language. Studying art, history, religion, and different cultures interests them. They often enjoy eating at ethnic restaurants and trying many different types of food. Wearing clothing from different countries, different styles, and even perfumes is interesting to them.

Foreign travel can bring happiness and open up their creativity. They might like to travel to different countries to visit churches, art museums, and explore the beautiful architecture. They often attract people from a different religious, ethnic, or cultural background. Good luck and happiness can come through long-distance communication through social media, telephone, and even handwritten letters. For instance, they might travel to Italy and meet someone from Turkey, and then fall in love at first sight. Or they might do a study abroad program in college and meet international students from India and make forever friends. They might have better luck finding love when they open up their minds to the possibility of finding someone who was raised very differently from them.

In relationships, there can be challenges with commitment. They can be restless in love and enjoy their freedom and independence. Marriage might be delayed because of a desire to remain single or they often marry later in life. Many with this placement struggle to meet relationship partners they are attracted to. Often this happens because they are looking for people in their immediate environment. Once they realize that their good luck comes through meeting people who are not from where they were raised, this can bring new opportunities in love. If they can harness open-mindedness in love and partnerships, the universe will send them the perfect partner.

Mars in the Ninth House

These individuals crave travel, movement, and adventure. They have a thirst for adventure and can be avid travelers. Exploring the world and learning about many different cultures, religions, and languages fascinate them. They are born teachers and have a passionate way of sharing information that helps people grasp challenging subjects. Because they are interested in many different topics, they can cycle through one interest and quickly move on to the next new passion. In fact, they know a little bit about everything! They are intellectual sponges who absorb information easily. They are ambitious about accumulating knowledge about religion, philosophy, spirituality, and travel.

They can become intense and passionate about what they believe in. When they are younger, they can have strong opinions and can even be labeled as a zealot because of their beliefs. Extremely passionate about what they feel, they can easily sway others to their side with sheer enthusiasm. Their energy attracts others into their life who share similar beliefs and those who have a desire for adventure.

However, how they were raised and what they were taught to believe can sometimes lead to conflict with others. But mostly it leads to a conflict within themselves. Many question their own religious philosophies and the purpose of life. Profound changes can influence them emotionally, which often leads to a complete breaking away of the traditional teachings of their childhood. They often do this to seek their own answers and find their own path.

Personal experiences can change them on a core level and shape the way they look at the world. They want to understand why people believe the things they do. They might become interested in New Age topics like astrology, numerology, and healing.

It's not uncommon for them to struggle spiritually and even feel guilty because of their varied beliefs. This helps them learn to be more accepting and open-minded of different religious practices.

An inborn faith, hope, and belief in a higher power are the gifts of this placement. No matter which spiritual path they take, inwardly, they believe that there is a purpose for their life. They aren't someone who loses faith easily, and they can have a deep connection to a higher power.

As far as relationships go, they can be physically attracted to someone who is from a different culture, ethnicity, religion, or family background. Sometimes their partner speaks a different language or their immediate family does. It can be difficult for them to meet a partner in their local area or hometown. They have better luck meeting people who are from faraway countries and through their travels.

Also, many with this placement might enjoy being single and maintaining a sense of freedom. Being independent and self-reliant is important to them, but if they want a relationship, they often need to look abroad.

They can have a powerful drive for movement and often have to travel a lot in their lives. For instance, maybe they were born in a military family and lived overseas. They might work for a company that requires a lot of travel or connecting with people from other countries. Adventurous and restless, they truly like to surround themselves with people from many different walks of life. If they harness the value of people's differences, it can help them achieve their personal goals.

Jupiter in the Ninth House

These individuals enjoy learning and making other people feel good. Their generosity and kindness are contagious. Many enjoy helping others and teaching people things about the world. Friendly and optimistic, they can inspire people around them to focus on the positive side of life. They can truly see the glass as half full versus half empty. Jupiter here blesses these individuals with a strong faith and belief in a higher power. Often, they are born with an innate sense of purpose and know they are here for a special mission.

Because of their restlessness, they are always seeking new things. It's like they are on a spiritual quest with their thirst for understanding. They want to know why they are here on this earth and explore many different topics to help make sense of it.

There can be an interest in learning more about religion and philosophy. Some might enjoy traveling and exploring ancient cultures.

Abundance and blessings come through learning, travel, and communication. Studying and mastering different languages can interest them and they might be bilingual or raised speaking a different language.

Broadening the mind through reading and taking classes can connect them with many different types of people. Socializing and networking can help them attract the support they need. If they can become more open-minded, it will bring greater joy into their lives.

Saturn in the Ninth House

These individuals have traditional ideas and strong convictions. Sometimes they can be rigid in their belief system, judgmental, and have trouble opening their mind to different views. If they were raised with conservative beliefs about religion and morality, it can be challenging for them to open their minds.

They might prefer a more practical approach to education and learning. Studying subjects that resonate with their sense of duty and practicality helps them become disciplined students. Many work hard and can study harder than others but still struggle to get the recognition they desire. It can take longer for them to achieve their goals related to higher education. But it's important that they be patient because with time and patient effort they often see the fruits of their labor.

Traveling might be uncomfortable for them, or they might have a fear of flying. These fears can come from a deep-seated need to be in control.

There can be personal experiences that push them to question the meaning of life. The values and beliefs they were taught as a child are often tested. Due to karmic and past-life issues, they might feel restricted or struggle with religion in some way. If they were previously dogmatic or believed in a strict moral code, unexpected things can happen to help them become more understanding of different opinions. They are learning that just because they might not practically understand something, it doesn't mean there is not truth in it.

Releasing outdated information about the world can help them become more open-minded. Overcoming feelings of responsibility regarding traditions can help them feel lighter. It's good to find other supportive friends and groups to share their interests with. If they can learn to relax and be more generous, it can help them achieve their goals. Developing a more optimistic outlook can help them overcome negative emotions such as depression, loneliness, and sadness. Thinking positive and being more open-minded about the world can help lighten their load.

Uranus in the Ninth House

These individuals can be interested in shaking up outdated beliefs. They don't want to be judgmental because they believe that everyone should be allowed to express their true nature. Innovative, scientific, there are times they like to shock people to force them to change. Unconventional subjects are interesting to them, and they can spend a lot of time studying unique topics. Any topic that is foreign, different, alternative, and eccentric inspires their imagination. Because they like to think outside the box, they are often found questioning traditional religion, philosophy, and morality. Many of them can live a shocking lifestyle that their family and friends might not understand. It's important to them to be themselves and have a sense of authenticity.

Deep down they are very individualistic and don't want to follow the crowd. Rebellious and free-spirited, they can grow bored with traditional education. A normal classroom might not suit them because they are strongly forward thinking. When they are learning something, they can question teachers and people in authority. It's evident from a young age that they learn in different ways and can't be put inside a box.

Fiercely independent, they are often nomadic, moving from place to place. Travel is important to them as is accumulating knowledge through their journeys. Travel can be a way for them to expand their social network and broaden their minds. Because they can feel restless, they need unique travel experiences to awaken their desire for learning. It's like they are on a quest for secret knowledge and ways to question society's rules. Thinking outside the box, especially in terms of spirituality, helps them accept many different opinions. They can enjoy studying spiritual and New Age topics like astrology, meditation, and energy healing.

They are friendly and social and have a way of motivating other people to change their mind and release outdated views about the world. Religion and philosophy might have been something they studied to help make sense of why they are here on this earth. Unexpected changes in their life can trigger an awakening for them to question what society has taught them to believe.

Even if they were raised to believe a certain way, they often break away from traditional values and religious beliefs. They might feel like their family and friends don't accept them. This can leave them feeling lonely, but they'd rather be true to themselves than pretend to be someone they are not anymore. Finding their own spiritual path and belief system can bring a greater sense of purpose. In fact, it can lead to meeting other people who share similar interests. Striking out on their own and exploring topics that interest them heal any wounds they have surrounding their faith.

Neptune in the Ninth House

These individuals enjoy studying spirituality and can have an idealistic view of the world. Daydreamers at heart, they have a vivid imagination that expresses itself in creative ways. Learning more about spiritual topics helps them figure out their soul's purpose. There can be disillusionment or even suffering that comes through spirituality. This can be intensified if they experience shame and guilt arising from a strict religious upbringing.

Sometimes they can feel disappointed with traditional education and might have never felt like they fit in. Many of them are born with artistic and creative abilities, but they don't always know how to express them fully. They are truly idealistic and see the good in many different belief systems. Adaptable and open-minded, they listen to and understand other people's problems. Because of their compassionate nature, they can attract people who have problems. They might even decide to study psychology to try to better understand themselves and others.

Because of their fascination with world religions, art, and culture, they like to explore. Taking a spiritual retreat is a great way for them to meet like-minded people to share their dreams with.

Easily influenced by strong zealot types, they can be deceived if they don't think for themselves. Because they tend to see the good in people, they can sometimes get hurt by those who don't have their best intentions at heart. Being emotionally vulnerable is not a bad thing, but it's important to remember to have strong boundaries. They can be influenced by controlling spiritual teachers or sucked into a religious cult due to their trusting nature. It's important that they listen to their gut because it can prevent them from being taken advantage of.

Escaping from the world with a good book or through learning mystical knowledge can be fulfilling. Because they are compassionate and kind, they are more accepting of different beliefs and customs. Travel can be a way for them to connect to a spiritual path. Exploring different religions and visiting ancient sites can help them connect to history. The experiences and people they meet during their journeys can inspire them and act as spiritual mentors along their path. Walking their own path and learning self-acceptance will help them connect more deeply with their soul.

Pluto in the Ninth House

These individuals are intense students and have a competitive drive to learn. Self-motivated, they can push themselves extremely hard in their studies. They want to have a sense of control over knowledge and information. They often have a passion for transforming the beliefs of those around them. Breaking free from the religious dogmas they were taught as a child can help them transform and grow in wisdom. Although, they should be cautious about getting involved in religious cults or with spiritual people who might want to have some type of control over them. Because they are drawn to intense and taboo knowledge, they might pursue special practices and rituals that are outside the mainstream. Highly intuitive and perceptive, they have a powerful need to connect with other people who think like them. They can grow wiser and more accepting of other people's beliefs through direct experience.

It's not uncommon for them to be attracted to secret and hidden knowledge. Passionate about transforming the beliefs of those around them inspires an interest in astrology, death, mysticism, occultism, and healing. Because they are drawn to intense information and rituals, it's important to trust their intuition.

There can be an emotional wound involving religion and a belief in life after death. Studying death and dying can help them make sense of the process of loss and how people need to grieve. The death of a loved one or friend can have a deeply impactful effect on their mind and emotions. The fundamental questions about what the purpose of life is can haunt them, and they can feel like their beliefs are stripped away from them in an instant.

Forever changed, they begin an exploration of new information and try to make sense of the world. Healing comes through becoming more vulnerable and open-minded. They can learn to heal themselves through travel and seeing the world. For instance, they might want to travel to places with historic significance like Egypt. Walking around the ancient pyramids and seeing the Great Sphinx can be inspirational. Traveling Europe and visiting medieval churches and investigating hidden symbols in architecture can also become their passion. The most important thing for them to remember is that they are here to overcome outdated energy and to embrace new ways of being. Throughout their lives they can experience transformation and rebirth of their belief system. Tapping into change can make unexpected things easier to adjust to. In the end, they will become stronger and more resilient because of the life experiences they have had.

Planetary Transits through the Ninth House

When planets transit the ninth house, you can feel an urge to seek adventure, travel, explore the world, learn new things, and network with others.

Transit Sun

This transit can inspire your desire to travel and explore new places. You might feel more restless and have a need to feel free. In fact, this energy can make you rebel from your daily routines. For the next month, you might feel more adventurous and spontaneous.

Travel can be your focus right now. If you normally are a homebody, you can feel a desire to get outdoors and explore new places to shop, eat, and mingle. It is a good time to plan that trip you have been putting off. You can be more motivated to booking a family vacation or your dream vacation. You can have the energy and stamina to keep moving right now, which can help you get a lot more accomplished.

Communicating with others and connecting with new people can open up new opportunities. You might meet people through your work travels or through attending conferences. These connections can help open doors or assist you in achieving your goals.

You might experience a positive change in your mood. There is an optimistic vibe in the air and that can help you focus on socializing and meeting new people. It's a good time to attract good luck and abundance. Focus on what makes you happy and what inspires you to expand your knowledge.

During this cycle, you might become more interested in pursuing spiritual truths and opening your mind to new beliefs. It's also a good time to take a class or get certified in something you have been interested in. Take a class, learn how to meditate, or read new metaphysical books.

Your perspective about the world might change and you might see things in a fresh light. It's hard to focus on responsibilities right now because you feel more distracted. It can be a good time to escape from the stresses of everyday life. Getting outdoors, moving around, or going for a hike in the mountains can help you relax. Try not to sweat the small stuff right now and tap into this optimistic energy.

Transit Moon

This transit can make you feel restless and more positive. For the next few days, you can have a desire to roam and explore new places. Your sense of adventure and your desire for travel return. This positive energy surrounding you can make it easier to get your mind off unpleasant emotions. Allow yourself to tap into this positive energy while it lasts.

You can feel more inspired, and this is a good time to connect within and find comfort through meditation or spending time in nature. You might have a lot more energy right now, so take advantage of this transit's energy. You might feel less serious and more confident to explore the world.

Although you might be pondering the meaning of life, try not to get too emotionally attached to your strong emotions. How you feel about things can shift quickly and change. If you can release negative feelings, it can help you feel more confident about the future. The Moon transiting here can make you feel more appreciative and thankful for the little things. Tap into this energy to help heal and let go of any negative feelings from the past. It's a good time to move forward and never look back.

Transit Mercury

This transit helps you think less about practical matters and more about your ideals. You might feel more philosophical and ponder the meaning of life. This is a good time to figure out what you really believe in and how these beliefs can help you achieve your goals. It's a good time to take a class, read a new book, and communicate with people who inspire you. You might feel adventurous and a bit rebellious concerning deadlines. In fact, you can feel mentally restless and have more trouble concentrating.

Traveling overseas for work or planning a new vacation can help you feel less restless. It's a good time to organize, develop a routine, and focus on practical goals. It might be beneficial to make a list of tasks.

Connecting, socializing, and networking with people can bring new friendships. You might want to get more active in groups or take a class in something you have always been interested in. You might be thinking more about the big picture and have trouble focusing on the small details.

Transit Venus

The energy of this transit can influence your love relationships. Someone very different from you can catch your interest. You might be attracted to a partner who is raised very differently from you or even someone who is from another country. Your interests can change during this time and you can be drawn to exotic places, people, ideas, and restaurants.

Exploring new things and socializing with interesting people can help you overcome boredom. You seem to feel more inspired to enjoy your freedom. If you have been stuck in a monotonous relationship, this is a great time to do something spontaneous with your partner. You can feel more adventurous and rebellious during this time. Just be cautious about starting or ending relationships too abruptly. You might change your mind once this energy shifts.

You can feel more generous and positive about love for the next five weeks. It's a good time to express yourself and people might find you more charming than usual. Your popularity can bring good luck in your business endeavors. It's a good time to harness peace, harmony, and affection in your relationships.

Transit Mars

This transit can inspire assertiveness and a passion to question what you truly believe in. You might feel more enthusiastic than usual and have a lot more energy. There is a new restlessness that has emerged, pushing you to seek adventure. You can be bored with the status quo and want to shake things up. Your energy level is heightened during this time, which can inspire you to travel more.

This is a time when you might pursue hobbies that allow you to compete. Your need for freedom and independence has intensified. It might be hard to sit still and focus on tasks. It can be beneficial to get outdoors and do something physically active to burn off the excess energy.

For the next eight weeks, it can be a good time to share your opinions in bold ways. It won't hurt to speak up and be straightforward about what is important to you. Be more cautious about pushing people's buttons and taking your anger out on others. You can feel a bit feisty and want to challenge others. Be patient and think things through before doing something impulsive. Harnessing confidence during this transit might help you make changes that help you grow.

Transit Jupiter

This transit might inspire you to be more positive and energetic. The next year can increase your optimism, which can help you see things differently. Positivity abounds, and you can feel more optimistic about the future. You may want to explore new ideas and expand your social circle. If you aren't normally adventurous, you could feel like taking more risks. This transit can help you feel more open-minded and accepting of other people's differences. Helping others is a focus right now and you could feel more generous toward others.

You might be interested in going back to school and connecting with people who are different from you in some way. You can feel drawn to people who are from a different culture, country, or religious background. The new people you meet can challenge your belief system and help you grow.

You could feel more restless right now, which causes you to want to break free from constraints. If you are in a relationship, you will need a lot of freedom and more autonomy. Being able to act in the moment to maintain a sense of independence can be important to you right now. Success and good luck often come through business connections and possibly through foreign travel.

You might have the opportunity to travel more or decide to take a vacation to a special place you have always wanted to go to. This is a good time to put intentions out to the universe because you can easily manifest your dreams. The universe can open doors for you, so it's important to take advantage of this positive energy. If you can focus on expanding your ideals and on developing a greater sense of purpose, you can find greater fulfillment. This is a good time to tap into your faith, which can help reduce stress and bring a greater sense of purpose.

Transit Saturn

This transit can help you focus on and assess your belief system. For the next two to three years, you can feel blocked, restricted, and a bit challenged in terms of being able to explore new things. You might be searching for the meaning of life and desire a greater sense of purpose. Because Saturn can test your faith and beliefs, you might struggle with understanding why things are happening. In fact, there can be a complete reassessment of your religious and spiritual beliefs. You might be strategizing and investigating your own religious beliefs. Resistance and skepticism toward certain dogmas can create challenges. It's not uncommon to take your beliefs more seriously or be more cautious about opening your mind.

Sometimes this transit can bring maturity and you might grow wiser through the past experiences you have had. There can be feelings of depression due to struggling to find your new path. It's important to balance responsibilities and try to snap out of negativity.

This is a good time to study abroad and travel to faraway places. You can feel more inclined to write, teach, and network with others who share similar values. It's a good time to harness optimism to make sense of the vast amount of information you are sifting through. Try to let go of negativity, pessimism, or outdated ideas that are preventing you from expanding your mind.

Transit Uranus

This transit can create unexpected changes to your belief system. This transit can impact you for the next seven years. Exploring the world of the mind through accumulating knowledge and long-distance travel is the thing you feel focused on right now. You might feel more rebellious and start thinking outside the box because you don't want to conform. The old way of doing things is shaken up and you are forced to grow, expand, and open your mind. There can be changes that inspire you to go back to college or take classes in interesting topics.

Rebelling against set rules and traditional religious values can help you figure out what you truly believe in. This is a good time to figure out what your soul purpose is and how your old belief system might be holding you back from growth. Uranus forces stagnant energy to transform. Although change is needed, this can be a painful process. You might have a desire to be more unconventional and this can bring interesting people into your life. This transit can awaken your desire to be nontraditional and explore eccentric ideas. The people you meet can trigger an awakening and shake up your life.

There can be opportunities for foreign travel or changes in your travel plans. It can be a difficult time and you might feel unsettled. The energy can feel electrifying and if you are a person who enjoys stability, this transit can be challenging. In fact, after this transit is over, you will feel forever changed on a core level. There is no going back to the old way of doing things or believing in the things you used to. A complete metamorphosis can create new opportunities for growth and make you a stronger person.

Transit Neptune

This transit will influence how you feel about religion, education, travel, and adventure.

For the next fourteen years, you can feel quite lost and experience confusion regarding travel and higher education. There can be a sensitive energy impacting your life, which can make you want to withdraw and spend time alone. You might even feel disillusioned with your religious and spiritual beliefs. These new feelings can lead you to explore new spiritual ideas such as astrology, meditation, and world religions.

During this time, you can become more dedicated to a spiritual path. Finding a deeper connection to a higher power can help you find greater joy. You are more impressionable than usual and feel more compassion for others. This is why helping others can help you find a sense of purpose.

There can be a desire to escape from heavy responsibilities. Solitude can bring peace and comfort. You can benefit through reading, writing, taking classes, and learning something new, which can help you connect with a restless urge for knowledge. Try to harness your intuition to connect to things that help you find answers to the meaning of life.

Transit Pluto

This is a long transit that is the harbinger of deep changes that can affect your philosophy about life. You can feel obsessed and more passionate about accumulating knowledge. You begin to realize that knowledge can bring power. If you have not taken classes or attended college, this transit might awaken this desire within you.

Listen to your intuition right now and trust your perceptions. You are more psychic and intuitive during this time. This energy can bring cataclysmic changes to your life and your view of the world. Anything that is outdated or superficial will need to be wiped away. A fresh start and perspective will help you adapt to this powerful energy.

Intense feelings such as jealousy and revenge can bubble to the surface. Superficial relationships, beliefs, and lifestyles will go through a transformation and stagnant energy will need to be let go of. It's a good time to release anything that might be holding you back or keeping you stuck in the past. Meeting new people, traveling to new places, and learning new things can help you change your way of thinking. Sharing your ideas and socializing with others can inspire you to make big changes.

You might be more passionate and dedicated to pursuing your goals. It's a great time to write a book or share the private side of yourself with others. It's a good time to harness strength and use the wisdom of what you have learned to help you tap into the positive energy of this transit.

Ways to Harness Sagittarius Energy

- Think positively.
- Travel to a foreign country.
- Learn a different language.
- Seek freedom and independence.
- Speak the truth.
- Spend time outdoors in nature.

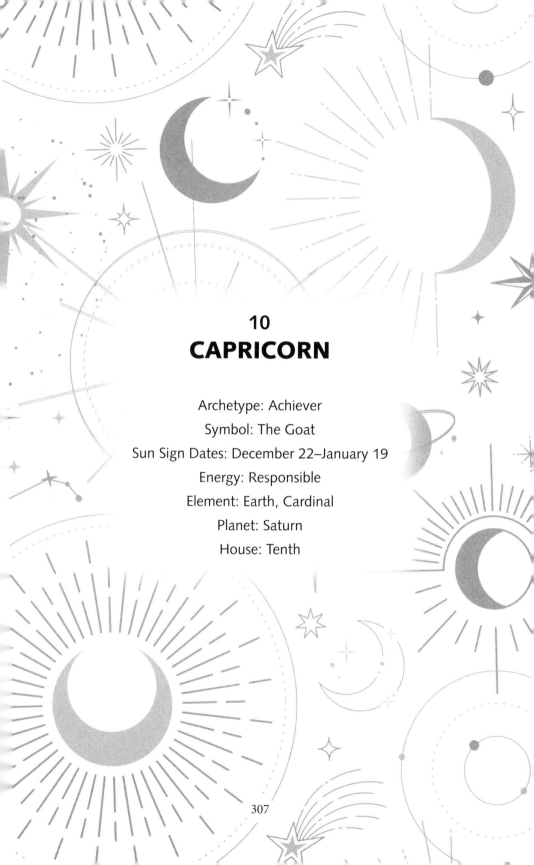

10
CAPRICORN

Archetype: Achiever

Symbol: The Goat

Sun Sign Dates: December 22–January 19

Energy: Responsible

Element: Earth, Cardinal

Planet: Saturn

House: Tenth

I f you have Capricorn in your birth chart, planets placed in the tenth house, or are experiencing planetary transits through the tenth house, this chapter will cover information regarding these energies. If you don't, you can still learn about Capricorn energy and incorporate it into your life. The placement of the planet Saturn in the sign and house will show where you express Capricorn energy. It is important to look at what house the sign Capricorn falls on in your birth wheel because this is where you will be able to harness responsibility, practicality, structure, and a desire to achieve your goals. Harnessing Capricorn energy brings greater success, productivity, work ethic, and a desire to take care of the practical needs of others.

Capricorn Energy Words

Productive, structured, responsible, practical, realistic, fatherly, success-ful, hardworking, authoritarian, critical, controlling, patient, wise, serious, inhibited, restricted, mature.

Capricorn Motto

As a Capricorn, I feel super responsible from a young age. Sometimes people think I am older than I really am. I am serious and like to feel a sense of control. It's difficult for me to show emotion and be vulnerable. I like to work hard and want to be successful. Financial security is import-ant to me because I like nice things and want to provide for my family.

Harnessing Capricorn Energy

Capricorn energy is responsible, cautious, controlled, inhibited, and at times heavy. There is a certain rigidity and coolness that can make them appear uninterested. Their energy is associated with doing things and being pro-ductive. This energy is associated with pursuing a career, success, work, structure, and status.

Topics such as finances, business, politics, commitment, and security are associated with this energy. Practicality and a strong work ethic are the gifts of Capricorn energy. To awaken this energy, Capricorns are ambitious and often seek a career path that can bring them success and fortune. When they strategize, plan, and wait patiently, they achieve their goals. They are responsible and sometimes worry about letting other people down. High expectations can create a sense of burden and they can sometimes feel anxious. Controlling things is a common defense mechanism they utilize when things seem unstable.

Negative thinking can impact them, causing a pessimistic view of the world. It's hard for them to believe positive things will happen because they know that everything in life takes time, effort, and patience to achieve. If things are too good to be true, they will sarcastically let people know. Capricorns don't like to feel vulnerable and many have difficulties showing affection. They prefer to do something practical and helpful for those they love. Learning to be disciplined and hardworking are ways to harness Capricorn energy. This energy can help us realize what type of work is best for us and inspire us to dedicate the time and effort needed to build long-lasting success.

Harness Duty

Capricorn is a responsible sign that is down to earth and realistic. Sometimes they feel like they are holding the weight of the world on their shoulders. Capricorns have a responsible energy that is connected to practical matters such as career, finances, tradition, and commitment. People with Capricorn energy can often act like a father figure who wants to give practical advice on how to survive in the real world. They are old souls and from a young age appear mature, cautious, dependable, and disciplined. This energy makes Capricorns take everything seriously and sometimes they struggle to have fun. Pessimism can impact their ability to acquire abundance and block the energy of success. Trusting the universe and developing a bit of optimism can help them reach their goals faster.

Harness Productivity

Capricorn is ruled by the element of earth. Earth energy is stable, comfortable, reliable, and long lasting. This energy helps Capricorns find practical ways to solve their problems. Committed and dedicated to working hard for what they want, they don't give up. Their career is important to them, and they get a lot done with sheer discipline. Their sense of hard work and efficiency helps them focus on being productive. They typically can get more tasks done than their counterparts. Earth signs like to see the results of their labor. Capricorns are traditional and committed partners. They are cautious about emotions and prefer to prove their love in practical ways. Material and financial success can help them build a sense of stability. Feeling secure is important to them because they like to know what to expect. Change is difficult for them, and they often like to control things to lessen their anxiety. Sometimes they have trouble taking a break from work and relaxing. Earth energy requires time to ground itself and withdraw from the stress of everyday life. It's good for them to spend time in nature hiking in the woods, fishing, hunting, or spending time with family. We can feel the rootedness of the earth and its ability to help us plant ourselves firmly to work hard for the future.

Harness Patience

Capricorn is cardinal energy and wants to be in charge. Capricorns are serious and cautious about making any changes. Patient and dedicated workers, they want to inspire others to work hard. Success comes naturally for them because they are disciplined. Planning things and coming up with practical ways to solve problems make them excellent leaders. Capricorn is one of the most hardworking and responsible signs in astrology. Because they are rigid, they don't waste their time or energy on things that won't bring success. At times they can be inflexible and like to structure. Having a clear set of rules and expectations helps them thrive in work and in life. Just like the mountain goat who climbs up the mountain, it doesn't matter how many times they might fall because they always get back up. As a cardinal sign, Capricorns strategize, plan, and set future goals. They will work their way up that mountain and often it's later in life that they reach the top of the success ladder. Harnessing patience helps them connect with cardinal energy.

Develop Structure

Capricorn is ruled by the planet Saturn. The energy of Saturn is associated with duty, responsibility, karma, work, and burdens. Saturn energy is concerned with making us pay our dues and balance our debts. It helps us realize the seriousness of life and that we must survive through hard work and effort. We can be more pessimistic and harder on ourselves in the area of life Saturn influences. There is a feeling that we can't relax because we have a lot of work to get done. In fact, Saturn makes it difficult to be light-hearted, trusting, and free. This is why many Capricorns are labeled as cold, unfeeling, or strict. The truth is they have a softer side to them, but it takes time for them to feel comfortable.

Developing a plan and creating structure in their lives is what Capricorns do best. Feeling secure and stable is crucial to happiness. Saturn energy can delay things and seems to block certain opportunities. This is because Saturn rules time, patience, and wisdom. Capricorns are long-range planners and have a skill for always looking toward the future. They want to move up the ladder at work, attain a high position where they can be in charge, and make good money. Financial security is important to them not only for what it can bring materially, but for how they can use it to help others. Money equals power and they know it can also make life's burdens a bit easier to bear.

Sometimes this energy makes it difficult for them to truly feel emotions. It's much easier to connect with practical issues like paying bills, getting a job, saving money, and planning for retirement. But we must remember that Capricorn is also called the water goat. Its symbol looks like a goat with the tail of a fish. This shows that they have a deeply emotional nature. They not only live on the land, but also in the sea. When they want to or if someone taps into their caring heart, they can show great compassion. Capricorns are blessed with practicality and intuition that they can use in dark times. They have a sarcastic and dark sense of humor that sometimes shocks others, but they like to make people laugh.

Harnessing the power of Saturn energy can help us achieve our goals through structure and discipline.

Shine at Work

The tenth house in astrology is associated with social status, career, success, work, and the public. In the birth chart, the tenth house cusp is called the midheaven. The sign that falls on the cusp of the tenth house can show what types of career fields someone is interested in. How ambitious someone can be is seen by looking at the tenth house. Planets here can bring prestige and push someone into the public arena. Professional aspirations and career goals are priorities for tenth house people. When planets are in this area of life, someone can be an overachiever and a workaholic. There can be a powerful desire to be successful and achieve a high-level position at whatever cost. This is the area of life where we experience authority figures and learn what power and status are really about. Harnessing tenth house energy can help us be disciplined, determined, and steadfast in our career goals.

Capricorn Rising

Capricorn rising individuals are serious, responsible, disciplined, and cautious. There is an air of maturity that surrounds them. Because they are dependable, practical, and realistic, they recognize the truth about the world. It's hard to fool them because they are careful who they trust. People might misjudge them and think they are boring, rigid, unfriendly, and even cold. They often have a serious look on their face and a no-nonsense vibe. Once in a while someone might get them to soften and see a smile peek through.

When someone has Capricorn rising, it gives a sense of reliability to their personality that helps other people feel supported. This personality trait helps them attract people who are looking for practical advice. Fatherly energy oozes from them, and people who are seeking that type of bond are often attracted to them. Because they are ruled by the earth element and have Saturn energy, Capricorn risings have strong boundaries and protect themselves. They don't want to be overwhelmed by drama or superficial conversations. These individuals want to experience life by working hard, focusing on their goals, and supporting their family and friends. They are attracted to people who are more emotional than they are. Other people can help them come out of their shell of protection and loosen up a bit. Sometimes they might feel down or sad for no reason. Their personality is serious and they tend to worry about a lot of things. Depression can make them withdraw from people and get even more quiet. They don't always have the words to explain how they feel. The rising sign is a mask and Capricorns are good at pretending they are happy when in reality they are struggling with heavy burdens. They don't want to appear vulnerable or overly emotional. In fact, this trait can make it difficult for them to ever ask for help. Doing things on their own and working extra hard suit them best.

How to Harness Planets in Capricorn

When planets are placed in Capricorn, you will focus on career and work. You can also feel more responsible, successful, practical, hardworking, and productive.

Sun in Capricorn

Sun in Capricorn individuals are realistic, practical, and hardworking. From a young age they seem older than they really are. Many feel older and prefer to surround themselves with people who can teach them things about the world. They are often the child at the kitchen table listening to the adults talk about real-life problems instead of playing with the other kids. They aren't afraid of hard work and like to plan for everything. Practicality helps them focus on things that really matter and they don't believe everything they hear.

Born skeptics, they are a bit pessimistic about human nature. They see the reality of the world and how people can use others to rise to fame. Earning their own way and putting in extra effort to achieve their goals can give them a sense of accomplishment. They have a natural understanding of business and what people want. Because they want to be noticed at work, they desire recognition for the tasks they do. Social status and politics in the office interest them and they seem to know the right people to connect with. Capricorns like nice things and usually dress well and like to be professional. Making money and building financial success increase their self-esteem and sense of purpose. They work hard to move up the mountain but sometimes it takes them a little longer to reach the top. They have a sense of duty that inspires them to be resilient and patient. Step by step, they slowly dedicate their life to productivity and efficiency. They respect other people who work hard for what they have. In fact, they often root for the underdog and can make friends with people who are a little rough around the edges. Because they take things seriously, they can find it challenging to let loose and have fun. If they can find colleagues and relationship partners who are the opposite of them, it can bring them out of their shell. They can have a witty and sarcastic sense of humor that makes everyone laugh.

Loners at heart, they are reserved and at times feel numb. They can experience dark moods where they feel irritable, sad, and depressed for no reason. It's hard for their loved ones to see them this way because typically they are strong. A sense of humor is something that can help them snap out of negative emotions. Also, when they feel a sense of purpose and know that other people are relying on them, they work hard to move toward their goals.

Capricorns are loyal and like to follow through on what they promise. *Dependable* is the keyword to the kind of person they are. Commitment is something that means a lot to them. Having a partner they can depend on and trust inspires them to achieve greater success. They like to provide financial security for their loved ones. If they can harness their own practical advice, they can manage challenges that come their way.

Moon in Capricorn

Moon in Capricorn individuals have a strong urge to be productive. Realistic and practical in matters of the heart, they don't trust others easily. It takes some time to win them over and they can be quite skeptical about emotions. Sometimes they restrict their feelings and repress them. They would much rather focus on work and achievement. Doing something practical and using their hands in some way can bring comfort. Making money and being financially stable can bring emotional fulfillment.

They can find happiness by maintaining a sense of stability and feeling safe. Safety comes when they can find a job that helps them financially. Being able to pay their bills and have what they need is the first step for them to open up to new experiences. They might crave recognition for the tasks and accomplishments they have. It's not enough for them to get applause from their family; they really need it from their supervisor.

Workaholic tendencies can leave them emotionally depleted. They don't always take care of their health and stress can have a big impact on their physical body. Expressing their feelings by talking to someone they trust or even a counselor can help them process anxiety and worry. If they can harness positive thinking and more optimism, their emotions can become more balanced.

Mercury in Capricorn

Mercury in Capricorn individuals are calculating, ambitious, and patient. Often, they are shy and reserved. Communication can seem restricted or blocked for them at times. They can struggle with finding the right words to express their feelings. They might be attracted to talkative people who can get them to open up. For them to share what they are thinking with others, they need to trust. Gossip and superficial conversations can annoy them. Because they are achievers, they would rather be thinking and talking about work or their next big project. They are good at handling details and planning for the future. Their mind is focused on their own goals and obtaining success. Rational, practical, and disciplined, they enjoy conversations with reliable people. Mentally, they are slow to decide and like to think things through. They can often be heard asking for more time to decide on important projects. Being rushed can make them feel anxious and irritated. They are objective thinkers and don't do anything without a reason. Pondering success and daydreaming about their goals helps them attract what they want. Because they are dependable and productive, they often rise up the ladder at work and obtain a leadership position. It's important for them to overcome being cautious to communicate and work on toning down giving orders.

People don't always appreciate being told what to do, but there are other ways to inspire people to focus on work. Due to their serious nature, they often think negative thoughts. Their self-esteem can suffer when they are hard on themselves. Thinking positively can help change the way they feel. Their ability to make people laugh unexpectedly helps them gain allies. In social settings, they are often the one making a dry or sarcastic comment.

Venus in Capricorn

Venus in Capricorn individuals are cautious and skeptical about love. They might appear cold and unemotional. Deep down, they care deeply for someone but struggle to show it. They are not known to be the most affectionate partner. They prefer to do practical things for others and are dependable. People can rely on them to be there when needed to offer financial support or a down-to-earth approach to problems. In love, they are faithful, dedicated, committed, and loyal. Marrying someone who is more successful and financially stable brings comfort. If they don't marry someone financially stable, they often work hard to provide security and material comfort to those they care about. They are responsible and usually don't say something unless they mean it. If they do tell someone they love them, to them, that is a serious thing to say. Playing games in relationships is not something they do. In fact, they dislike conflict, drama, and emotional displays. Extremely private about their love lives, they don't like to share details of their relationships with others. They can be jealous, possessive, and insecure in relationships. If they can harness greater trust with their partner, they will also lessen their fears of rejection.

Mars in Capricorn

Maris in Capricorn individuals are quietly powerful and in control. They have a demanding, forceful, and magnetic energy. Blessed with a fierce determination to achieve their goals, there is very little that can stand in their way. Once they make up their mind to do something, they do it. Driven to achieve, they crave success and work hard to rise to the top of their profession.

Strongly self-reliant, they don't like to depend on other people to take care of them. Obstacles are nothing more than stepping stones, in their opinion. Because they are strategic, calculated, and hardworking, there are very few people who can compete with their level of work ethic. They are go-getters who thrive in a high-stakes environment. They can have a passionate and earthy love nature but at other times they may feel cold and uninterested. Attracting a partner who is a lot older than them can teach them about intimacy and love. They are drawn to partners who are successful, serious, responsible, and wiser than them. Tapping into intense emotions can help them overcome any obstacle and become more resilient.

Jupiter in Capricorn

Jupiter in Capricorn individuals are ambitious and hardworking. Through hard work and sheer determination, they gain a high position. They have the willpower to achieve their goals and a disciplined work ethic that will help them reach the top. Success is often achieved gradually, and it can take a bit of time before they see the fruits of their labor manifest. They don't have to worry about success because Jupiter brings good fortune. They can have a natural instinct for business, finance, and real estate. Making money is important to them because of the security it brings. At times they can resist spending money and be frugal. Then there are times when they are lavish spenders and want to go all out. They keep a budget, which enables them to buy expensive items when they need to. If they can harness the power of generosity, they can start to accumulate money, people, and influence, which will help them reach their goals.

Saturn in Capricorn

Saturn in Capricorn individuals are responsible, serious, and disciplined. There are times they feel restricted, especially when emotions are involved. Being vulnerable can make them feel uncomfortable. Sometimes people misjudge them as unfeeling, cold, and disinterested. Self-sufficient and independent, they don't always take advice from others. In reality, they are super responsible and often feel a huge weight on their shoulders. They can be harsh at times because of their ability to focus on reality. Life can be hard, and Saturn teaches them from a young age that they have to work for what they get. These individuals learn from direct experience. Task focused, they are productive and efficient in everything they do. Determined to succeed, they work tirelessly in pursuit of their goals and dreams. Overbearing at times, they can enjoy being in positions of authority. A leadership position often falls in their lap, but not until they put in the hard-earned effort.

At work, there are very few people who take work as seriously as they do. They put a lot of pressure on themselves to do things perfectly and can hold themselves to a higher standard. It's important for them to remember that they are human and can make mistakes. Loneliness stems from difficulties communicating and sharing with others. This is often due to an innate timidity and shyness. Dark thoughts can plague them and they can feel sad about how they perceive the world. They experience dark moods and in these challenging times their sense of humor can save them. Witty, sarcastic, and unexpectedly funny, they lighten up any serious argument or situation with a quick joke. People don't always expect this from them, so it makes them even more funny. If they can develop relationships with dependable, reliable, and faithful friends, it can help them feel more comfortable.

Uranus in Capricorn

Uranus in Capricorn individuals have a strong desire to focus on the future. They want to succeed and achieve their goals. Working for others can be difficult because they don't readily follow orders. Rebellious at heart, they need to make up their own rules. They can follow the rules as long as they make sense and when they are the authority on matters. They expect other people to respect them and they value people's hard work and experience. Their career and work can experience many changes and fluctuations. They may unexpectedly change jobs, move for a new opportunity, or go back to school for an entirely new career path. They like to grow and challenge themselves, and when things get stale, they might want to shake things up. Capricorn likes traditional and Uranus likes nontraditional. There are two distinct personality traits within them that are in battle at times. Balancing these two very distinct needs can take some effort, but with time, they can master them. Fighting for what they want and doing what is right is important to them. They are responsible and hardworking but have a more lighthearted approach. Having fun and making people laugh can make them happy. There are times they can be both rigid and open-minded. They have a complex personality that is good at organization and at times domineering. Feeling free and grounded at the same time is a blessing of this placement.

Neptune in Capricorn

Neptune in Capricorn individuals are disciplined, practical, and committed. They are here to find someone who gives their life purpose. Courageous in their search for success, they work hard to achieve their dreams. This placement can lighten a typically strict personality and help them trust their feelings. Fighting hard for the underdog and for those who are mistreated can make them feel useful. Creative ideas and their imaginative mind can help them create unique goals. Success can come through dance, music, art, and spirituality. They need a job that allows them to be creative and inspire others. Being of service and helping solve complex issues can lead them into career fields such as medicine, science, psychology, and natural resources. Conservation of resources and ensuring ways they can also give to the larger community might be something they are passionate about. Once they dedicate themselves to a purpose, mission, or group project, they work patiently to see it flourish. If they can figure out how to balance realism with idealism in their search for success, they can create beautiful things that bring them material success.

Pluto in Capricorn

Pluto in Capricorn individuals are born with a drive and passionate desire to succeed. They are responsible and have a strong sense of ethics. Tradition and morals are things they take seriously. Although, they don't typically enjoy anyone telling them how to believe or how to act. They attract powerful people into their lives who can assist them in achieving their goals. Having a successful career where they are in a position of authority helps them maintain a sense of stability. They understand power and how it can be used to either benefit or hurt others. Calculating, they can make friends with the right people who can further their future goals. They want to surround themselves with deep, intense, and hardworking people. Friends and lovers need to be committed and devoted to them. Strategic thinkers, they don't put their energy into things that don't bring results. They are productive and patient enough to wait for the right time to make changes. Rebelling against authority and the status quo helps them rebuild the world the way they want it to be. Forgiving others can be challenging but it will help them in their search for prestige, recognition, and financial stability.

Planets in the Tenth House

When planets are placed in the tenth house, you will be focused on work, achievement, recognition, career, and success.

Sun in the Tenth

These individuals are ambitious and disciplined workers. Having a career is important to them and they often shine in the work arena. They work best in a stable, secure, and structured work environment. Their sense of responsibility is strong and they can feel like they have to work harder than everyone else to succeed. It's more likely that success comes in the middle of their life. Because of their traditional values and conservative approach, they need a stable job where they can provide for their family. When others are stressed, they do well under pressure. They appear calm, cool, and collected; no one would realize the amount of pressure they put on themselves. At times they can feel burdened with the responsibilities they take on and anxious about day-to-day life. Change is difficult for them, and they like to feel in control of their environment.

They avoid taking risks and rather have a solid plan and step-by-step instructions. Having a successful career is one of the most important things in their lives. From a young age, they are focused on obtaining the education and skills needed to feel accomplished. Many are concerned with obtaining a high-status position where they can work in the military, government, business, law, politics, and even finance. This placement can bring financial success and leadership opportunities. They like to be in charge and need to be cautious about becoming too dictatorial. In fact, their sense of identity comes through work and gaining respect. Because they are hardworking, they struggle to find time to relax or take a vacation. Their personal relationships can be impacted by their focus on their career. It's important that they learn to prioritize other areas of their lives like health, family, and hobbies. For instance, their family might feel neglected and start to believe that work is more important than they are. Too much focus on work can lead to conflict and disagreements. Their self-esteem is strongly influenced by the type of work they do, and they want to shine in whatever career field they choose. At some time in their career, they can find themselves onstage or having to present in front of large groups of people. Harnessing a good work-life balance is crucial and will prevent them from regretting missing out on special moments with their family and friends.

Moon in the Tenth

These individuals find emotional fulfillment through their work and career. They might crave recognition and are passionate about obtaining success. They are achievers who are disciplined and patient to work toward their goals. Security and comfort often come through their work and being in a position of authority. It's hard for them to work for other people and they like to have autonomy in their career. They can find happiness by owning their own business. It is crucial to their emotional happiness to have a career that supports them financially, emotionally, and materially. They enjoy having material things and making money so they can provide for their family. If their career is unstable, they can become stressed and worry about their future. Emotionally, they can go through many ups and downs at work. If they can trust their intuition, it helps them figure out who they can trust. Controlling projects and other people might happen if they don't feel stable or trust people. Because they can be responsible and serious, it's hard for them to feel comfortable and have fun at work. They're so disciplined and this is why they are efficient and productive workers. Completing mundane tasks and projects brings them a sense of inner satisfaction.

If they don't feel like they are respected or making enough money, they can experience moodiness, irritability, and frustration. Their emotional nature ebbs and flows, which is directly associated with their sense of success. They often throw all their energy and emotions into their career and may struggle to not take work home with them. Overworking can deplete their energy and they need time to recuperate. It's healthy for them to take breaks and get away from work. Their family might feel like work means more to them than family time. It's important that they find ways to balance work and home responsibilities.

When they are advancing and feeling appreciated at work, they will be happy. Sometimes they struggle in relationships and might marry later in life because they are so focused on their career. Life is not just about work, and once they get to where they want with their career goals, it might be too late. Later in life, they may regret giving up certain opportunities for fun and excitement. They can begin to realize that they have achieved financial success but realize that money doesn't always bring contentment. If they can realize the value of family and career, life becomes easier to manage.

Venus in the Tenth

These individuals take relationships and love seriously. People are attracted to their charm, witty sense of humor, and ability to listen. They are not the type to date around and prefer having committed relationships. Because they are driven and hardworking, they put a lot of effort into maintaining relationships. They understand that without effort and discipline, love can wither. They attract people who are similar to them and share traditional values. Successful, hardworking people who take care of themselves are appealing. On the other hand, they can attract people who need to be taken care of in some way and they help bring security to their lives. Older people with more wisdom and life experience can enter their lives and act as mentors. They might fall in love with someone a lot older and it might be uncomfortable for them to pursue these types of relationships. Because they care about what other people think and how they are perceived, they typically don't like public displays of affection. Sometimes they meet people through work or traveling for work. They need a harmonious, peaceful, and supportive work environment to feel comfortable. Relationships with coworkers can be helpful and support them in attaining their career goals. There can be times when they have to be more assertive, direct, and mediate conflict with others. At work, they can be popular, and partnerships can enhance their career potential. Experience teaches them how to get along with difficult people and how to become a better manager. This placement of Venus can bring opportunities to create a sense of refinement, beauty, and peace to the work arena.

Don't neglect your partner or family because of work. It's important to find a healthy balance between work and relationships.

Mars in the Tenth

These individuals are competitive and have an ambitious drive to succeed. Self-reliant and independent, they are passionate about having a career and strive to be recognized for their accomplishments. Their work comes first, and they dedicate a lot of effort and energy into achieving their goals. Hardworking and disciplined, they have stamina and can work long hours. Motivated to get things done, they are productive and efficient workers. However, they tend to take on too much and get frustrated. Their anger can seep out at work and there can be conflict with coworkers and management. They aren't afraid to tell people the truth and call out things in the work environment that a lot of people might be afraid to acknowledge. At times they are aggressive and fight to reach the top.

They are resilient and can overcome crisis by taking charge. In challenging times, they know what to do. They are good at delegating tasks and are natural leaders. They have a confidence and boldness that makes it easy for people to follow them. Earning the respect of others at work can motivate them to work harder and they want to prove themselves. These individuals might be drawn to careers in law, business, politics, military, and government. They make good employees, but they don't always respect their superiors unless they feel they can look up to them. If they feel appreciated and rewarded, they will continue to dedicate their energy and life to their career. They can lack patience and often act on impulse, which can rub other people the wrong way. Some of their coworkers might be afraid to speak up or feel they are too competitive. In fact, they might expect people to work at their pace, and they have to realize that other people can't always do as much as they do. They might get so immersed in work that their personal lives suffer. They can find themselves amid conflict throughout their careers, especially with coworkers. Disagreements, bickering, and jealousy can affect their relationships with colleagues. When Mars is here, there can be a difficult and severed relationship with their father. They might try hard to change their personality so they are not similar to their father. Later in life, they might rekindle their relationship with their father.

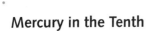

Mercury in the Tenth

These individuals are strategic thinkers and patiently plan for the future. They like to think through every potential situation that might affect their plans. Being prepared and organized helps them maintain a sense of control. They enjoy talking about their career and things they can do to obtain success. Superficial or frivolous discussions don't interest them because they are focused on what is practical and attainable. When they set their mind on a task, they can become obsessed and completely immersed in what they are doing. Being efficient and task oriented makes them an excellent employee who can be relied on to finish what they started. Intellectually stimulating careers help them feel challenged. In fact, they might excel at communication, writing, and teaching. Social connections and networking with colleagues can help them feel supported. They like to brainstorm ideas and learn about other people's opinions.

Jupiter in the Tenth

These individuals benefit through their career or interactions with the public. Travel can be a big part of their job and they are able to socialize with many different types of people. They might find themselves in politics or in government positions where they rise quickly into a high-status position. Regarding work, good luck and fortune seem to come easily for them. They are inspiring to others because of their optimistic and friendly approach to work. Other people respect them and appreciate their positive attitude. Even though they are hardworking, they also know how to take a break, have fun, and relax when they need to. Financial success comes when they are a bit older and as they steadily rise up the corporate ladder. They can receive recognition, awards, and appreciation because of the quality of work they do. They have a generous personality that enjoys helping others in some way. The harder they work, the more they accumulate. Encouraging and inspiring coworkers with their career success is a way they like to give back. They are happiest when they work in a positive and supportive environment.

Saturn in the Tenth

These individuals take career responsibilities seriously. From a young age they were taught about the importance of hard work. They might have had to grow up fast and be mature enough to help work and support their families. Their childhood could have been strict or money might have been scarce. Saturn here often experiences hardship and understands the important of having financial security because they might have gone without it before. Working hard and achieving their goals helps build their self-esteem. Being in a position of authority where they can make the rules is important to them. They are responsible, practical, and disciplined workers who take tasks seriously. At work, they can try to exert a lot of authority over other people. Restricting other people's autonomy might backfire on them. It's better if they focus on their own work ethic and style instead of trying to change others to work like them. They have a stamina at work that most people can't understand. Work is a duty in their mind and a way for them to build success. Strategic and calculating about the future, they are planners who plot every word and action. Ambitious spirits, they don't want anyone to distract them from their future goals. Money and social status help them feel safe and secure. They are most comfortable when they are working and focusing on their career.

Achievement focused, it's hard for them to be lighthearted or have fun at work. Serious workers, they take on a lot of duties and are not always good at delegating to others. There are times they can feel overwhelmed and taken advantage of at work. Because their work ethic is so strong, other people tend to expect them to do all the detailed work. They are great at planning and very organized, which is why they can be productive. There are times when they need to release control and allow other people to help them. One of their most challenging lessons is allowing themselves to be vulnerable and trust others. They can restrict themselves and avoid socializing at work even if coworkers try to include them. If they neglect their relationships, they might have career success but end up feeling lonely. Learning to balance their work commitments with family responsibilities is a constant test. If they can harness a work-life balance, it will help them not focus solely on work.

Uranus in the Tenth

These individuals often experience unexpected changes and upheavals involving career. Dramatic change can bring many ups and downs in the area of work. They might struggle to figure out what they really want to do. Or there can be struggles with finding employment. Sometimes they can change their mind after they get a certain degree and want to pursue an entirely unique career path. They can be restless and crave a sense of freedom in the work environment. It can be difficult for them to work for someone else. Nontraditional about societal rules and social status, they might experience conflict with superiors or those in positions of authority. They are a bit rebellious and might try to instigate issues to spur change in people's beliefs and outdated ways of doing work.

They need excitement at work, and a career that gives them a lot of autonomy suits them best. Careers in science, technology, humanitarian causes, and artistic fields help them utilize their creative mind to solve problems. Self-expression is important to them, as is working with people who help them grow. Social and friendly, they are gifted networkers. They have many acquaintances, and these connections can help them land new job opportunities. Once a job becomes boring, they have an urge to shake things up. If they stay stuck doing something they don't enjoy, it can seem like the universe strips things away. An example might be their company shuts down and lays everyone off. They have to pick up the pieces and start over in their career. Change brings experience and growth into their lives. These unexpected fluctuations in their work make them stronger and help them realize what is truly important to them. They often have a desire to help other people and they can be drawn to volunteer work. Things like joining the peace corps or even the military might cross their mind at some time in their life. Expressing their unique, eccentric, and out-of-the-box thinking can lead them to pursue careers in writing and teaching. If they can see the difficulties in their career as stepping stones that guide them to something more fulfilling than just a paycheck, they can find greater happiness.

Neptune in the Tenth

These individuals are idealistic about their career and work goals. People might think they lack drive and ambition. When they are young, they might feel confused about what type of career is best for them. Because they are drawn to many different subjects, it's hard for them to choose. They can feel disillusioned and lost regarding social status, ambition, and recognition. In fact, they can feel a desire to hide from the public eye and work in private.

Imaginative and idealistic, they don't always realize the amount of effort and hard work required to obtain employment. They can spend hours fantasizing about the perfect job but then not take practical action, such as doing a resume, walking in to introduce themselves, or applying on time. Procrastination can sometimes prevent them from obtaining employment. These are all lessons they will learn, and through experience, they will build greater skills in planning.

Learning to be more practical and realistic about the effort and planning of finding a job will help them in the future. Neptune here can make them talented and blessed with artistic abilities. At some time in their lives, they could be recognized for their creative abilities and they could win awards. Not as ambitious as other people, they can have a more relaxed point of view concerning success. Making money is not going to fulfill them because they need to also feel a sense of purpose in the work they do. Helping others and spirituality are often a big part of their career decisions. They might be interested in psychology, ministry, or social work because they have a knack for helping people with their problems.

Compassionate and kind, they often attract people who need help or healing. Developing stronger boundaries can protect them from taking on the emotional pain of others. When they do have a job, they are often the person their coworkers come to to get advice. It's crucial for their mental health that they have a peaceful and harmonious work environment. Toxic leadership and coworkers can impact their health and happiness. Working alone suits them best, as well as doing something creative, such as performing arts, music, and entertainment. If they can harness boundaries, it will help them build strength and the resilience to pursue work they feel is meaningful.

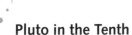

Pluto in the Tenth

These individuals are ambitious in their search for success. They work hard to achieve their goals and they don't let anyone stand in their way. They have a powerful presence and attract others easily. Charming and magnetic, they often find themselves in a position of power and become leaders. They are calculated and they want to succeed no matter the cost. Selecting the right friends and social connections often open doors for them to walk through. Colleagues and coworkers support them because they possess a sense of loyalty that people admire. They have a passionate work ethic, self-control, and often work behind the scenes or in private to obtain their goals. Careers in medicine, psychology, criminal justice, business, and research can nurture their deep desire to solve mysteries. They are intense and do well in a crisis. They are natural at giving orders and delegating what needs to be done. Taking charge and speaking the truth when needed gives them the reputation of being a no-nonsense person. They might believe in the bottom line, which can be project completion or making money. Strict, disciplined, and at times rigid, they don't give up. If they are stuck in a boring job where they aren't moving up or being given opportunities, they cut ties. Because of their sense of loyalty and commitment, they might stay in a job longer than they should.

They can experience many changes in their career, which transforms how they view money, success, and power. Being laid off, fired, or experiencing conflict with authority and coworkers can teach them many lessons. At some time in their lives, they might decide to completely change their career path. If they can harness the ability to let go and move on from the past, they can grow and evolve.

Planetary Transits through the Tenth House

When a planet transits the tenth house, you can be focused on work, career, achievement, recognition, and being productive.

Transit Sun

This transit can inspire you to be more focused on work. For the next month, you might question what career you are in or if you need to find a new job. If you have a job you like, you can be more focused on reaching your goals. You may feel more disciplined, driven, and ambitious right now. This is a good time to focus on long-range plans and what you want in the future. You might feel more sensitive about your reputation and how people perceive you right now. Practical matters take precedence, helping you focus on standing out. You might want to shine and be recognized for your hard work and accomplishments. This is a good time to accomplish your goals and learn to be more disciplined. Through your own effort, you can finally get a promotion, an award, or approval from those in authority.

Transit Moon

This transit doesn't last long but it will certainly stir up emotions about work. You might want to reevaluate whether your goals and emotional fulfillment match. There can be some dissatisfaction with where you are in your career. Your popularity can increase right now, and you can feel more sensitive to other people's thoughts and emotions. Be careful about oversharing or telling people your problems. You may feel more sensitive about your career and what it means to succeed. This month you can work on developing goals and connect with what type of work is meaningful to you. Burnout is common right now due to overworking. It's a good time to take a vacation and get away to recharge your energy. You might feel more responsible than usual and want to get things done. Your productivity can increase and you might get noticed by those in authority. It's a good time to harness confidence in your ability to get tasks accomplished.

Transit Mercury

This transit can influence how you communicate at work. Avoid negativity and don't worry about things you can't control. You can feel overwhelmed with responsibilities and overanalyze things. Try to ground yourself and think practically about what you need to feel good about your career. You might be thinking a lot more about your career and future goals. Right now, communication seems to increase, and you might spend a lot more time on the phone. You could get recognized at work and in the public eye for some of your innovative ideas. You might feel more disciplined and responsible about tasks and feel more productive. This is a great time to plan and strategize for the future. You could be thinking more about promotions and ways to market yourself in your career field. Being social and meeting new people can help you increase your popularity. Someone you meet through travel or communication can assist you in new projects. It's a great time to tap into the energy of multitasking as you get a lot more done during this cycle.

Transit Venus

This transit can be a favorable time to get promoted. You might also receive some type of recognition for the work you do. You appear more charming, friendly, and flirtatious during this cycle. At work, people seem to want to spend more time in your presence, and socializing with others is highlighted. This is a good time to share your creative ideas with others. If you are working on a group project, you might feel inspired, and this can allow you to express your artistic side. If you aren't in a relationship right now, you could meet someone from work or through your career connections. It's a good time to harness sociability and allow other people to get to know you better.

Transit Mars

This transit can create a passionate drive to succeed. You might dedicate more energy to business and career activities. You might feel more ambitious and want to be recognized for your accomplishments. There can be an intensified desire to be noticed and get out in the public eye. You can experience challenges and some conflict with colleagues or those in positions of authority. There could be disagreements about how the company is running things or you might demand that others listen to your opinions. You can be more assertive and speak the truth about work matters. Some people might feel uncomfortable and feel that you are aggressive. You might decide to make changes and look for a new job. Be careful about acting impulsively and forcing changes you might later regret. Slow down, calm down, and think things through before you make important work decisions. If you can harness the increased energy, you can get a lot more tasks completed.

Transit Jupiter

This transit brings a positive and optimistic vibe to your career endeavors. You can receive financial blessings and possibly a raise. Jupiter here brings good fortune in whatever career projects or tasks you need to accomplish. There is an expansive and abundant energy impacting your relationships with colleagues. Career advancement can start to happen for you now. In fact, you might travel more for work and a special business trip might fall into your lap. Reaching out to social connections and utilizing your popularity can bring opportunities. You might be in the limelight now and receive a lot of positive feedback about the work you do. Leaders might start to notice your work and you could win an award or even start a new job. Career goals and plans seem to come naturally for you during this cycle. The more you tap into this positive energy, the more abundance you can experience.

Transit Saturn

This transit can cause challenges in the work arena for the next few years. Saturn can bring both positive and negative influences. It's a good time to focus on career development and taking classes that will benefit your career. You might get a job promotion, but you might have to take on more responsibility. There can be tests and karmic lessons at work in your career. Challenges at work can help you become more self-confident and resilient. You can feel more disciplined and ambitious about reaching your goals. You can feel motivated to complete tasks, get organized, and be productive.

There is a seriousness in the air that puts some pressure on the way you work. It's important to remain patient and strategic. Whether you want a promotion or to switch careers, Saturn will force you to look at these things. You can feel cautious and distrusting right now. Just make sure to see the positive side of situations. Remember that hard times won't last forever because things will change if you don't give up. Dedicate yourself to a structured plan of where you want to go. Take small steps toward your goals and slowly work toward what you want to see happen. You might feel more concerned about the future; this is a good time to ponder what is important. Reassess your goals; build a solid way ahead for yourself.

With time, this transit can bring career success and elevate you into the public eye where you can receive recognition.

Transit Uranus

This transit can bring unexpected and shocking changes to your career. This unsettling energy can influence your career and your home and family for about seven to eight years. You can feel a desire to break free from rules and regulations. There is a chance for you to become restless and quit your job. This typically happens if you have been unhappy and not growing. If you don't quit, you might experience some type of change that impacts your income. New management might shake things up or people you depended on for support might leave.

You can feel unsettled right now at work and struggle to feel comfortable. There seems to be an unexplained energy of change lurking in the air. It might feel like something is going to happen, but you don't know what it will be. In the work arena, you will need more freedom now and might want to shock people. Speaking up about your innovative and creative ideas will inspire you to challenge yourself. The boring routine that was once the norm will be questioned and you could walk away from ways you used to accomplish tasks.

Newness is in the air, and you can feel more alive when you embrace the change. The people in your life, such as parents, supervisors, and authority figures, might experience a lot of unexpected changes. You might find you need to help your parents more or have issues pop up in the home and family. It can be difficult to feel stable right now. Try to tap into the energy and realize that these changes will also help you grow as a person.

Transit Neptune

This transit lasts for many years and can awaken a desire to find meaning in your work. This elusive energy can cause confusion, misinterpretation, and deception. You might not feel like you can see things clearly related to work and your goals. Emotions can run high right now and you can feel more sensitive to criticism.

You might feel that people are keeping secrets and at times you might not truly know what you feel about things. You might not be seeing authority figures clearly or you might idealize people right now. Try to be practical and see situations clearly by taking emotion out. You can feel disillusioned with the work you do. In fact, you might not feel appreciated at all.

Sometimes you might want to change jobs because you want to be making a difference. If your work is not fulfilling and you aren't finding a deeper meaning in what you are working toward, you could leave. There is a strong urge to withdraw from the public eye and you might call out sick more often. You might want to avoid work and your colleagues because you feel a need to spend more time alone. You can feel that people are projecting their problems onto you. It's like you act as a mirror for everyone's pain right now. It's important to develop stronger boundaries and make sure to communicate clearly with others.

Transit Pluto

This long-lasting transit brings deep and gradual changes to your career. Your long-term goals seem significant, and you are more passionate about pursuing them. Competition in the workplace can stir conflict. There is something new about your energy that makes people take notice. Pluto can make you appear more magnetic and powerful. You might have an ability to see through lies and deception. Calling out the truth of what is happening at work can make people feel uncomfortable. Secrets are often revealed during this transit.

Your company can go through a complete restructure or someone in power might retire, leaving everyone fighting for the top position. You might attract negative attention from authority figures or feel they are criticizing your work. Challenges are intended to push you to work harder for success. You are resilient and have a powerful drive to achieve your goals. Jealousy from coworkers might pop up during this cycle. In fact, people might feel threatened by your new sense of strength and charisma.

You seem to have a powerful impact on your work environment and it will either repel or attract people. Avoid power struggles and controlling behavior. Find new ways to destress and implement self-care into your life. It's important to maintain a healthy work-life balance and take necessary breaks when needed. Everything is intense right now and a sense of urgency can transform how you perceive things. Step back and think things through in a practical and nonemotional way to ensure success.

Ways to Harness Capricorn Energy

- Work hard and be productive.
- Get organized and disciplined.
- Be more calculated and write down your goals.
- Develop a financial plan.
- Be patient.
- Balance work and family.

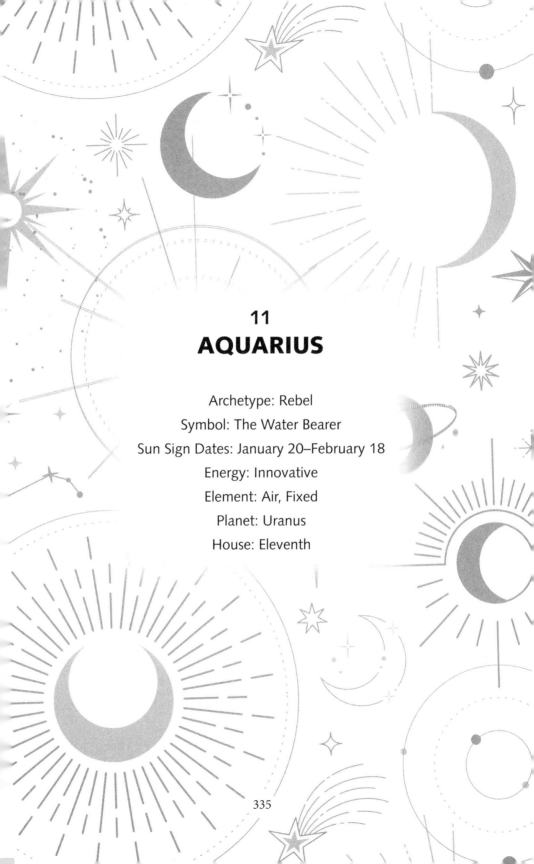

11
AQUARIUS

Archetype: Rebel

Symbol: The Water Bearer

Sun Sign Dates: January 20–February 18

Energy: Innovative

Element: Air, Fixed

Planet: Uranus

House: Eleventh

I f you have Aquarius in your birth chart, planets placed in the eleventh house, or are experiencing planetary transits through the eleventh house, this chapter will cover information regarding these energies. If you don't, you can still learn about Aquarius energy and incorporate it into your life. The placement of the planet Uranus in the sign and house will show where you express Aquarius energy. It is important to look at what house the sign Aquarius falls on in your birth wheel because this is where you will be able to harness individuality, independence, freedom, intelligence, and creativity. Harnessing Aquarius energy gives you inspiration to be innovative, think outside the box for solutions, question authority, be more rebellious, and not be afraid of thinking differently than others.

Aquarius Energy Words

Freedom loving, rebellious, independent, nontraditional, friendly, eccentric, unique, creative, imaginative, intelligent, knowledgeable, open-minded, restless, curious, detached, humanitarian.

Aquarius Motto

As an Aquarius, I like to be free. I am unconventional and unique, which sometimes makes people uncomfortable. I enjoy nontraditional relationships where I can be myself. I sometimes rebel against authority or close-minded beliefs. Changing society and helping people help me feel like I am making a difference. I am social and like to network with many different types of people.

Harnessing Aquarius Energy

Aquarius is a detached and intellectual sign. It can seem unfeeling and even cold at times. But then it can be friendly, accepting, and social. Aquarius energy likes to be different and can refuse to conform. This energy can be difficult to understand because it's social but doesn't get too wrapped up with emotion. This energy is associated with groups, friendship, humanitarian causes, and networking. To understand this energy, we can think about world problems and find out-of-the-box solutions to solve them. Aquarius energy wants to be free, independent, and is sometimes rebellious. It's a liberal energy but fixed in its opinions. To tap into this energy, it's important to question what you were taught to believe. The traditional approach is questioned by Aquarius energy. They want to do things that make sense to them and most times those things question the status quo. This energy can make other people feel uncomfortable because it rebels against authority figures.

Things that are unique, eccentric, and different are the core of Aquarius energy. Spending time trying to cure cancer or join the peace corps to volunteer in a foreign country after college are choices that resonate with this energy.

We can feel this energy when we are embracing the unexpected and exploring shockingly new ideas. This energy is paradoxical because it can be friendly and judgmental if someone questions its beliefs. It can enjoy socializing but is perfectly content being alone. Aquarius energy helps us realize the importance of communicating and using our minds. This energy enjoys helping people but in a detached way where it doesn't get emotionally involved. It shines when giving solutions to problems and making the world a better place. Learning to listen to others can be challenging because of a strong sense of personal freedom and stubbornness. Thinking outside the box, being creative, and being more innovative in our thoughts are ways to harness Aquarius energy.

Explore Solutions

The sign Aquarius is associated with innovative energy. They are solution focused and forward thinking. Traditional ideas bore them, so they are always pushing the limits. Exploring new ways to solve problems inspires their creativity. Strongly independent, they need the freedom to be themselves. A bit eccentric and different from other people, they enjoy shocking others with their unique ideas. The reason Aquarius is innovative is because it doesn't want to do things the traditional way. It questions authority and asks society hard questions. The word it likes to use the most is *why*. It challenges the past and wants to awaken imaginative ways of solving problems. Innovative energy is connected to the higher mind and sees into the future. It can feel intellectual, free, and open-minded. Aquarians often feel they were born into a past time period because they feel like they are ahead of the times. Their ability to see and think about the future is extraordinary as well as their ability to challenge fixed mind-sets. They might feel like space aliens who traveled to a new world that is uncivilized and full of crisis. This energy values thinking, reasoning, and scientific knowledge. Rebelling from authority and tradition makes this energy capable of not caring what other people think about them. This strength helps innovative energy push the limits of belief and embark on creating new and fascinating things.

Innovative energy believes there is a solution to every problem. But this requires doing things very differently. It can be challenging to take risks, but this energy pushes everyone to grow. Activities like reading, playing games, solving puzzles, and exploring the environment are ways to tap into innovative energy.

Think Outside the Box

Aquarius is ruled by the element of air. Similar to the air we breathe, this energy is light and hard to feel. Air energy helps Aquarians focus on networking, communicating, and learning new things. Freedom loving, independent, and open-minded, they want to challenge societal norms and shake up outdated belief systems. Air energy wants things to make logical sense. If things are too emotional or dramatic, they have an ability to help calm others with a rational approach. Solving problems is what air energy does best and they do this through communication. This energy enjoys socializing and meeting interesting people. It doesn't mind making other people feel uncomfortable. Air energy likes to ask a lot of questions and if something doesn't make sense, they will call it out. Learning more about the world by reading, taking classes, and meeting unique people can help us connect to air energy. Air energy flourishes when it's free to adapt to its environment. When we tap into original ideas, we can harness the gifts of air energy.

Stubborn Beliefs

Aquarius is a fixed energy and is deeply rooted in what they believe. They have an assertive independence that asks a lot of questions. If something doesn't make logical sense, they will tear it apart and give various reasons why they are right. Once they make their mind up, it's very difficult to change it. Because they live in their head as an air sign, the fixed energy enhances stubbornness. They are complex individuals and they can appear open-minded, wild, friendly, and outgoing. But once you challenge their belief system, they can also be fiercely dogmatic. It can be shocking to witness the duality of Aquarian energy. They fight for the rights of others and the freedom of belief without restrictions. This is why they are known to question and rebel against authority. But because of the fixed energy in their personality, they can be a blend of traditional and nontraditional. It will take some time to figure out how to communicate with them in a way that doesn't offend them or have them assertively lash out. Aquarians are known to defend their right for freedom and they dislike firm opinions, but it's funny because they often hold strong opinions themselves. Harnessing fair and open communication can help us connect to fixed energy.

Awaken and Grow

Aquarius is ruled by the planet Uranus. This energy is unstable and electrifying and it can inspire our creativity. Uranus is the planet of change and disruption. This energy is associated with the unexpected, rebellion, eccentricity, and revolutionary ideas. Uranus will show where we find our own individuality and uniqueness. It will shake up our lives in areas where we are stagnant. Uranus wants growth and inspires unconventional ideas. It can help us embrace new energy and beliefs we never thought about before. Uranus awakens us to truths we have avoided. This can be a painful process as most of us are creatures of habit and don't enjoy change. The unexpected energy of this planet can shatter our security. Moving forward is the only thing we can do when Uranus ignites an area of our lives. We are forced to adapt to a new world when this energy pulls the rug out from underneath us. Uranus is all about freedom and being able to explore innovative and eccentric ways of doing things. It walks to the beat of a different drum and it lets us know. Uranus rules anything that is nontraditional, such as alternative lifestyles and ways of behaving that push the limits of society. Focus on being more open-minded and freedom loving wherever Uranus is placed in the birth chart.

Network and Connect

The eleventh house in astrology is associated with hopes, wishes, and dreams. This area of life is where we connect with others socially and network. This house governs the groups, organizations, and clubs we choose to belong to. Where we gather with other people who share similar interests is eleventh house territory. Making friends and accumulating acquaintances can help us meet the right people at the right time. In fact, the friends and acquaintances we meet in the eleventh house often can support us in achieving our goals. There is a strong sense of needing to connect with groups of people and feel included. The eleventh house impacts our ability to enjoy being around people and working harmoniously toward a common goal. Humanitarian causes that are focused on larger society issues, such as fighting homelessness, poverty, and child abuse, fall into this realm. The focus of this house is not on finding its own pleasure. The eleventh house inspires us to think positively and believe that we can make changes.

Aquarius Rising

Aquarius rising individuals are intelligent and logical. People might perceive them as distant, aloof, and unemotional. But they can also be kind and humanitarian. Their personality can sometimes confuse people. They act unusual and different from other people and stand out in a crowd. Sometimes how they dress or look is quirky and unique. Nothing shocks Aquarius risings because they believe they know a lot about the world. The thing they enjoy most is shocking others. They can inspire others to think outside the box and ponder unconventional ideas. If possible, they enjoy doing things differently than others. Fitting in is not something they desire to do because they prefer to express a unique and artistic personality.

Highly independent, they enjoy maintaining a sense of autonomy and can often rebel against authority. Following other people's rules can be challenging for them. For them to follow, they need to respect someone.

People can perceive them as nontraditional because they often like to question how things are being done. If something doesn't make sense, they will be the first to point it out. Their logical approach to problems can be creative; they prefer being innovative and come up with shocking ideas.

Aquarius risings are freedom-loving and independent souls. Because they are ruled by the air element and Uranus, they are detached and rational about life. On the other hand, they are friendly and open-minded, which attracts people. They are natural networkers and have many acquaintances. Friendships and being social are a big part of their lives. Making friends with people from many different walks of life helps them open up their active minds. Even though they are open-minded, they have a surprisingly stubborn and strong-willed side to them. It's a bit of a paradox that they can be so open-minded about certain things but then forcefully resistant to change. There is some inflexibility to change their beliefs, which can be surprising to others.

Being part of groups and organizations can bring happiness. Connecting with new acquaintances and making friends with people who can support them help them reach their goals. They enjoy helping others on a larger scale and donate their time to humanitarian causes. Volunteering for causes that can have a powerful impact on society attracts them the most.

How to Harness Planets in Aquarius

When planets are in Aquarius, you can be friendly, nontraditional, rebellious, creative, and focused on being part of groups.

Sun in Aquarius

Sun in Aquarius individuals are unconventional, eccentric, and unique. They don't think or act like people expect them to. They often want to shock people with how they think, look, and dress. Standing out in a crowd can make them feel seen. Having the freedom to be themselves and not conform to the way society wants them to be can make them happy.

Opinionated and intelligent, they shine when they are challenging traditions and rebelling against dogmas. Sometimes they strike their own spiritual path and cut ties with the religion or way they were raised. If they were raised in a strict or conservative environment, they often rebel and change their belief system to be very different from their immediate family. They seek growth and want to expand their minds. Anything that is stagnant in their lives and not encouraging growth is what they seek to reform. Even if they were raised in a traditional way or taught to believe in a specific religion, they will question these values and seek their own answers. Conforming to what was taught just for the sake of it doesn't interest them. In essence, questioning things is what they do best. They are revolutionary leaders and not followers. It's hard for them to follow any organized structure. They want to find their own answers, and this means they can often go on a mental journey and research religion. They might start out a devout Catholic and end up considering themselves agnostic. If they were raised to believe in God, they might like to dive into hedonism or earth religions. Going against the grain and rebelling from rigid belief systems helps them find out who they really are. They can be very fixed in their opinions and it's difficult to get them to change their mind once they make it up.

Moon in Aquarius

Moon in Aquarius individuals can be imaginative, rational, and emotionally balanced. Happiness comes through being free-spirited and having self-reliance. They connect to others without taking on their problems. This quality can help them make a lot of acquaintances, but they might have limited close-knit friendships. Social and energetic, they spend a lot of time getting to know people. Communicating with people about what they believe in can inspire them. They often find emotional fulfillment through connecting to people's minds, and when someone can connect to their mind, it's a rare occurrence. In fact, it will be difficult to let that person go. Typically, in relationships, they like to maintain a sense of freedom and are fiercely independent souls. But if they can find someone who is on their mental level and who shares the same beliefs, they will be forever friends.

Open-minded, they have a need for self-expression. Shocking people and standing out from others can make them happy. Feeling like everyone else can get boring and they like to awaken uncomfortable feelings in others to help them grow. They can feel passionate about ideas, philosophies, and they are often forever students. Well balanced emotionally, they have an ability to remain calm in a crisis. Pursuing their hobbies and associating with large groups of eccentric people can bring emotional fulfillment.

Mercury in Aquarius

Mercury in Aquarius individuals are highly intelligent and clever. They are broad-minded and emotionally detached. Because they are inquisitive, they spend a lot of time thinking about inventing new ways of doing things. In fact, finding solutions to the world's problems, such as a cure for cancer or alien life on other planets, is what they think about. Many are scientifically minded and excel at traditional science and mathematics. They might even dabble with astronomy, astrology, and philosophy. Chances are they will join groups or organizations where they can debate ideas and have intellectual discussions about the future. They are always pushing themselves to think differently than everyone else. In school, they can rebel against traditional learning and prefer to learn things on their own. They can sometimes feel isolated and it's often because they think differently. Highly eccentric, they are unconventional thinkers who have advanced ideas. Making people laugh or catching people off guard and seeing the shock on their faces is mentally inspiring.

Venus in Aquarius

Venus in Aquarius individuals often fall in love with a friend or meet their partners through their acquaintances. They are intellectuals and sometimes detached from emotions. They can find romance confusing as they prefer a logical approach to matters of the heart. They can confuse others at times with their extremes in behavior because they are friendly, helpful, and have a giving nature. It's true they are humanitarians, but they prefer helping people in an impersonal way and they don't typically bring emotions into it. They serve because they feel it's the right thing to do. How they can have relationships and maintain their sense of freedom is often on their mind. While they enjoy spending time socializing, networking, and sharing ideas, things like intimacy can be difficult for them to figure out. Being in a relationship can take a lot of work because they need to feel free to explore their hobbies and interests and enjoy doing things solo. Because of their large circle of friends, they need a relationship partner who trusts them and doesn't get jealous. Naturally popular, they know a lot of people and prefer platonic friendships over sexual relationships. Emotions are not something they feel totally comfortable with, so they prefer to be friends with others.

Mars in Aquarius

Mars in Aquarius individuals have a drive and passion for knowledge. Learning new things is important to them as is being free to explore the world. They are quick-witted and highly intellectual. Thinking things through is important, especially before they act or have to make important decisions. There are two sides to their personality that often conflict with each other. On one hand, they are freedom fighters who are a bit unpredictable. Then at other times, they want to be part of a group and do things with others. Intimate relationships can be challenging for them and their partner. The main problem is that they can have strong desires that are a bit eccentric, unconventional, and quirky. Sexual relationships are more about passion, and because of their strongly rational nature, they can be a bit unstable in terms of wanting to be involved and then detaching themselves from others. Committing to just one person can be challenging. In fact, they might want to remain single and date many different types of people. Interacting with people who are open-minded and understanding of their complex nature can help them maintain relationships if needed. But oftentimes, they prefer being on their own and able to explore the world when they want to.

Jupiter in Aquarius

Jupiter in Aquarius individuals attract many friends and acquaintances. Opportunities and good luck come through their social circle and through networking. They are friendly and enjoy learning new things. Traveling with their friends can bring happiness because they are always on a search for adventure. Restless at times, it's crucial that they have freedom to explore the world. They get bored easily, and this can make it hard for them to stick to a career mainly for financial reasons. Benefits come through mental and intellectual stimulation. Exploring their own belief system by being part of groups and organizations can bring a sense of purpose into their lives. Because of their strong intuitive abilities, they might enjoy discussing spiritual topics with their friends.

Saturn in Aquarius

Saturn in Aquarius individuals have a rational and original mind. They enjoy studying and learning new things. Self-disciplined and responsible, they struggle with keeping up the traditions of the family they were raised in or exploring the nontraditional beliefs they are attracted to. They might have a sense of duty to the traditional side of life, but deep down they are unconventional and eccentric in their beliefs. Issues of control can pop up throughout their lives, and when this happens, they can rebel. Deep down they are free-spirited and crave independence. They learn many important lessons in their younger days. Shrewd and strong-willed, they might try to manipulate people to get what they want. Leadership positions can fall in their lap because of their hard work and ability to be productive. Because of the delayed energy of Saturn, success often occurs at a later age.

Uranus in Aquarius

Uranus in Aquarius individuals often question tradition and explore different spiritual practices. There is nothing they are afraid of exploring and they are natural networkers. Building social networks and joining meaningful groups to search for answers to life's problems is where they shine. They are original thinkers or innovative about how they solve problems. Some might say they are geniuses who walk to the beat of a different drummer. It's hard for them to conform to what society wants them to be. They are always thinking outside the box and trying to come up with new solutions to the world's problems.

Strong-willed and determined, they believe they are right about things. It's almost impossible to change their mind or ideas about things that matter to them. They are complex individuals because they are so open-minded and value freedom of thought. Then at other times, they are rigid and resist change. Being part of a group or organization where they can make a real difference is important to them. Their sense of humor sets them apart from others and they detach themselves from emotional drama. They need connection and making friends with people who share similar philosophies can support them in reaching their goals. Who they know is very important because it's these very people who often bring them good luck and open doors for new opportunities. Unexpected and shocking events might impact their lives, but they have a logical and practical way of handling crisis. When they need support during difficult times, there are always people around who step up to support them.

Neptune in Aquarius

Neptune in Aquarius individuals are visionaries who believe the world can be a better place. Idealistic at heart, they tend to see the good in society and believe people can do better. They work hard to bring their ideals into fruition and want to believe that people can be compassionate. Their kindness and ability to help others are wonderful personality traits they possess.

They are innovative and express themselves in creative ways. Their greatest desire is to break free from the traditional beliefs they were taught. Opening up their own minds and encouraging others to open up theirs is a natural talent they have. They are fascinated by nontraditional and unconventional beliefs. They like to shock people with spiritual talk and are attracted to the mysterious side of life. Talking about religion and philosophy inspires them to learn new things and increases their ability to understand others.

Because they are humanitarians at heart, discovering new solutions, beliefs, and ways to solve complex issues like homelessness, child abuse, and addiction might interest them. Being part of a group or organization that shares similar ideologies can help them feel like they are part of something bigger than themselves. Serving others is important to them and they like to do this on a large scale. Impacting large groups of people, countries, and cultures and creating massive changes to make people's lives better bring a sense of purpose. If they can tap into spirituality and find ways to connect with a higher power, they might find that they can access deep information they normally wouldn't have access to. Solving the world's problems is what they truly want to do, but it takes a group of like-minded people to support them in their dreams of a better future.

Pluto in Aquarius

Pluto in Aquarius individuals are inquisitive and open-minded in their approach to the world. Deeply insightful and self-aware, they often see their flaws and try to change them. They can be distrustful of others and second-guess people's motives. Because they are more attached to the mind than the emotions, they can let things go.

They can be rebellious and want to change everything. It's best if they can slow down and be more patient. It's important that they recognize that stability is a crucial aspect to happiness. Drastic change for a purpose is understandable, but wreaking havoc on their environment or other people for the sake of change is not always the best answer.

These individuals can be inspiring to others, and because they are group focused, they want to share their knowledge. Deep down, they want to make the world a better place. But they believe that the only way to do that is through powerful upheavals and letting go. Because they have experienced loss and drastic changes in their social lives and with friendships, they understand that sometimes they have to let things go. The old patterns and beliefs that need to be transformed happen naturally because of their ability to embrace rebirth.

Planets in the Eleventh House

When planets are placed in the eleventh house, you can be interested in friendship, networking, socializing, groups, and making the world a better place.

Sun in the Eleventh

These individuals are friendly and enjoy being part of a group. Charming and flamboyant at times, they can attract a lot of people into their inner circle. Being social and making friends is crucial for their overall happiness. They are known to have many acquaintances and a handful of deeper friendships. They do know a lot of people but can have more superficial friendships. These individuals see people they meet for the benefits they can potentially bring to their lives. Everyone they want to know is usually in a position of power and can help them reach their goals. Being included in groups and surrounding themselves with like-minded people helps them feel comfortable. Gifted at connecting and bringing people together, they often inspire a variety of different types of people to discuss innovative ideas. Their friends and acquaintances are never boring and many of them are seen as unconventional and eccentric.

It's important for them to feel included in groups. They can shine when they are working in a group with a common goal, trying to solve large-scale world issues. Even though they are detached from emotion and more intellectual about service, they are humanitarians at heart. They have a gift for not getting too emotionally involved in other people's problems. Their detached and unemotional approach often makes other people think they are not interested or cold. They care more about solving problems and standing up for what they believe in. Traditional beliefs can teach them a lot about the world, but they often rebel against society's expectations. Pushing the limit and making people uncomfortable inspires them. Debating their ideas and trying to convince others who are more close-minded is a challenge they enjoy pursuing. Because they are eccentric, they like to shock people with how they think, act, or dress.

They often dream of the future and believe in the impossible. Motivated to manifest what they want, they think about what makes them happy and joyful. These individuals truly can attract their hopes, wishes, and dreams. Success comes through their social connections and from networking with the right people. They have a confidence and positive outlook that makes them believe they can have whatever they want.

Social butterflies at heart, they want to be active in the community. They might volunteer to be a Girl Scout leader for their daughter's club, taking the kids camping every month. Whatever it is they dedicate their time and energy to, it is often successful.

They need to learn to balance their personal life with their social life so loved ones don't feel neglected. Their sense of freedom is very strong, and they don't want to be told what to do. If they are in a relationship, they prefer an open and nontraditional approach. Maintaining their autonomy and independence makes them true free spirits. Friends often become lovers with this placement. Commitment can be challenging for them because of their strong passion to rebel against traditional ideas. On the other hand, they can be paradoxical and have a fixed belief system that values some old ways of thinking. They might not like to admit it, but they can be more conservative than they would like others to know. The eleventh house helps these individuals reach for the stars, and just like Aladdin and the magic lamp, they can ask the universe for what they want. Wishing is the key to success.

Moon in the Eleventh

These individuals value friendship and being part of a group. They can express themselves in unique and creative ways. Many of them attract strange and eccentric people. Emotional fulfillment comes by spending time with friends and meeting new people. Socializing, collaborating with others, and discussing similar interests can bring happiness. Because they are emotionally restless and fiercely independent, they value freedom. Being able to do what they want and not feeling tied down is important to them.

Helping people does interest them, but they often do it in a detached and logical way. Other people might judge them harshly and believe they are calculated, cold, and unfeeling. The truth is they do care about serving others and making the world a better place, they just do it in an unconventional way. They use their mind to solve world problems, and this helps them understand human emotion. To them, emotions can be irrational, and they prefer scientific knowledge or innovative ways to understand human behavior. They are prone to overthinking and trying to analyze their feelings. It can make it hard for them to understand what they really want and need. Feeling their emotions can be uncomfortable because their first response is to try to intellectualize them. Experiencing their emotions fully can help them tap into their creativity. Many with this placement have artistic and creative gifts. They enjoy learning new things and expanding their mind. Social media and YouTube can interest them, as well as being a member of groups where people are open-minded and enjoy sharing unorthodox ideas.

These individuals are emotionally restless and like to be moving around doing things. If they can't physically move, they are exploring the depths of their mind. They are prone to daydreaming and fantasizing about their dreams of the future. Visualizing their goals in detail is a good way to manifest what they want. Networking with others helps them meet the right people and these acquaintances can support their ambitions.

They might be so busy flirting and socializing that they have a ton of acquaintances but lack deeper friendships where they can be vulnerable. At times they might appear superficial or emotionally immature regarding friendship. Their friendships seem to fluctuate throughout their lives. But they are able always to meet new people because of their outgoing personality. If they can get more comfortable with their emotions and share who they really are with others, they can develop more long-lasting friendships.

Mercury in the Eleventh

These individuals enjoy communicating with people who have similar interests. Their friends are an important part of their life even if they only have a few. Surrounding themselves with intellectuals inspires their mind. Because they are mentally restless, they get bored easily with traditional conversation. They like to learn diverse and eccentric topics and can be interested in New Age thought. Conspiracy theories and trying to brainstorm crazy scenarios keep them engaged. Discussing taboo topics that shock others can be fun for them and they like to make people feel uncomfortable.

They are friendly and social, which helps them make a lot of acquaintances through networking. Learning new things is important to them; joining a group can help them express their unique beliefs about the world. It's hard to maintain friendships with people who can't communicate well or keep up with them mentally. Sometimes they can feel lonely if they don't have people in their circle who share their interests.

They have a scientific and unconventional way of thinking about the world. Joining a group and discussing topics such as astrology, numerology, and metaphysics can bring happiness. They are often attracted to ideas and people who stand out. They seek to revolutionize their own mind and other people's minds. Futuristic thinkers, they can see the big picture and grasp complex subjects easily. To them, the universe is vast, and ideas are always changing. They are on a lifelong search for knowledge, and they don't like to be tied down to believe in just one thing.

Venus in the Eleventh

These individuals are freedom loving and need a lot of time on their own. They often develop relationships with people who started out as their friends. In relationships, they are intellectual and logical about love. Social, charming, and friendly, they enjoy networking and mingling with large groups of people. Deep friendships are few because they prefer having many acquaintances and enjoy spending time with many different types of people.

Being tied down to just one person can be challenging for them because they seek autonomy in relationships. Commitment is hard for them because they want to be free to love whomever. They can have a nontraditional approach to love and romance. An unconventional approach suits their needs, but they might not feel the same way if or when their partner wants to do the same. They are often attracted to people from a different culture or background from them. Relationships need to be unique and different. The partners they are attracted to can be witty, zany, and at times rebellious. Anything traditional or status quo bores them and can't hold their interest for very long. They have better luck dating other free spirits who share similar beliefs.

They are destined to have unusual relationships and meet partners in unusual ways. Meeting their partner through a group or club is not uncommon. Other people might view love as a strong emotion and demonstration of passion, but these individuals see it as simple, logical, and unemotional. This can be difficult for more emotional types to accept and is one reason they often find themselves never marrying or remaining single into later life.

Mars in the Eleventh

These individuals are passionate about making friends and networking with others. They have a lot of energy and want to be doing things to pursue their goals. Being part of a group and championing causes where they can motivate others suits them well. Driven to succeed, they often are thinking about the future and how they can manifest what they want. Because they are solution focused, they are planners and like to make a list of their hopes, wishes, and dreams. Competitive spirits, they are able use their social skills to network with people who have the power to help them in many ways.

Independent and fiercely self-reliant, they are fans of the underdog and people who work hard to reach the top. Being friends with successful people is their main priority. They can be aggressive and bold in their pursuit to make new friends and acquaintances. The people who are in their lives are often someone who can benefit them in some way. Sometimes they can be perceived as calculating and manipulative. There can be conflict in friendships and with business associates. Because of their impulsive and restless nature, they can say things they often regret. If they are too forceful with their beliefs and opinions, it can turn other people off. Arguing and quarreling with others can irritate others. People might push them away if they feel they are being combative or self-serving. If they are a member of a group, their impulsive decisions can often upset others. They might get kicked out of a group or cut out altogether. When this happens, they can feel angry and jealous of others who are still part of the group. It helps if they can do some self-reflection and recognize the things they do that impact their relationships with others.

Socially adept, they can be a little superficial regarding friendship. This can often make them feel lonely as they get older because they rarely have a loyal friend they can count on. In fact, they can find themselves surrounded by hundreds of acquaintances, but no one really knows who they are. If they can dedicate some time to making friends whom they can give equally to, they will build trust with others.

If they can find time to give back to others in some way through group efforts, they can reconnect with their desire to help people on a big scale. Motivated to change the world, they can be dedicated in pursuing their hopes, wishes, and dreams of the future. If they can control their impulsive nature and develop greater patience, their friendships and group experiences will improve. If they can learn to value other people's ideas as being as important as their own, they can truly make an impact in social settings.

Jupiter in the Eleventh

These individuals are blessed with a positive magnetism that attracts many friendships. Blessings and good luck tend to come through social networking and their friends. They have an ability to draw wealthy or powerful people into their lives. Their friends can be a great source of knowledge and wisdom. Good things come into their lives when they focus on helping other people. Joining groups and causes that can help humanity in some way appeals to them. The more they serve others and share what they have, the more they receive.

These individuals have a natural expansive energy that brings social success. They just need to be careful not to depend on others too much or take things for granted. Jupiter placed in the eleventh house can make it easier to manifest their hopes, wishes, and dreams. The saying "be careful what you wish for because you just might get it" is important to remember. Because of the abundant energy surrounding them, their thoughts are very powerful. What they visualize and imagine can come to them quite easily. So, it's important that they keep a positive and optimistic outlook on life. They need to dedicate time to write down their goals in detail and understand the purpose of wanting certain things.

These individuals are learning the meaning of true wealth. Financial success tends to come easily for them through their social networking. It's true they can feel luckier than others and it's like the universe is granting all their wishes instantly. But this can change if they don't value what true wealth means. They can learn this lesson through a wise friend who can help show them that money doesn't always bring happiness. Good advice, friendly conversation, and supportive people can be more valuable than material wealth. They can reach for the stars and have tremendous luck. If they can surround themselves with supportive friends who give good advice, they will find that they can succeed at a faster rate.

Saturn in the Eleventh

These individuals can feel limited and uncomfortable in groups. Loners at heart, they don't mind their own company and enjoy their solitude. They can be cautious about opening up and sharing their ideas with others.

When they were younger, they might have been ridiculed or treated badly by a friend group. There are lessons to be learned about nurturing and trusting others. Deep down they are sensitive souls who want to be liked. Because they take friendship seriously, they don't have many acquaintances. They often form a few lasting friendships and are devoted to those people.

Small groups suit them best because they don't like to feel vulnerable. Because they are shy, it takes them time to get to know others and people often perceive them as uninterested. The fact is that they act and appear older than they really are. They had to mature early in life and prefer socializing with adults and people they look up to in some way. They respect people in authority and want to connect with those who are successful.

Superficial conversations and chitchat irritate them because they prefer deeper conversations. Being hurt or humiliated can be a fear that blocks them from forming new friendships. It's risky to allow people to get to know them because they have been hurt before by false friends. In social situations, it's difficult for them to loosen up and they have a hard time having fun. They take friendships more seriously than others and prefer to spend time with people who share similar views. They make practical, reliable, and loyal friends and have high expectations for friendships that are often hard to find. Once they develop a strong bond, it's hard for them to let someone go. Even if someone hurts them, they feel a sense of responsibility to work hard to fix their friendships.

They are disciplined to work hard early in life, which can help them find greater freedom as they get older. Learning to forgive others and get out of their comfort zone in groups will help them connect to more people. If they can believe in positive thinking, their dedicated work ethic can attract all their hopes, wishes, and dreams.

Uranus in the Eleventh

These individuals can enjoy being part of unconventional groups. They enjoy making friends with unique and different people. Most of their friends are eccentric and can be artists, philosophers, politicians, and New

Age thinkers. Their friends and acquaintances can benefit their lives in many ways and encourage them to pursue their goals.

They can experience a lot of growth through friends and networking. If a friendship is not helping them grow, they often try to meet new friends. They enjoy being friends with rebellious, innovative, and open-minded people who question authority. It can be exciting to hang out with people who like to shock people. If a friendship or group is boring, they can cut ties quickly and move on. In fact, they have very few deep friendships because most of their friendships are surface-level relationships. They don't like to show emotion and prefer logical conversations.

They can join groups that force them to question their beliefs and ideas about the world. Joining an organization or group that promotes social change or advocates for humanitarian causes can help them feel a sense of purpose. Innovative thinkers, they are interested in solving problems in a nontraditional way. Anything outdated doesn't interest them because they want to focus on new ways of thinking. They have a diverse group of friends from all walks of life and these people can connect them to the right situations, jobs, and groups that help them reach their goals.

These individuals have a strong desire for freedom and independence within friendship and group activities. Their restlessness can inspire them to rebel and they can find it challenging to commit to their long-term goals. Balancing their need for individuality and conforming to the needs of groups can be challenging. But they have an ability to manifest what they want by focusing on visualizing and imagining the future in detail. Thinking positively and believing in the power of the universe to connect them with the right people at the right time opens doors for them. The more they allow change into their lives and open up to different ideas, the better chances they have at attracting what they need. They want to make contributions to society by helping large groups of people. The friends, acquaintances, and groups they are part of can change throughout their lives. Letting go and moving on from these connections will help them learn what true friendship is about. It is important for them to remember that they meet everyone for a reason.

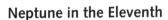

Neptune in the Eleventh

These individuals are idealistic and believe in the good in the world. Dreamers, visionaries, and philosophers, they use their vivid imagination to envision the perfect world. They are artistic and talented but might prefer to use their gifts for the group versus personal recognition. Being involved in charitable causes and helping large groups of people or animals can bring a greater sense of purpose. Compassionate souls, they truly care about the welfare of others and the community. They can be found donating their time volunteering for spiritual causes and human rights groups.

Their lack of boundaries and trusting nature can influence the groups they are part of. They might get drawn into groups where there is deception that they don't realize until it's too late. For example, they might join a group and realize it's a religious cult that is trying to control their life.

They should be cautious whom they make friends with. Illusion and fog can cloud their judgment. The friends they make can become unreliable, mislead them, or leave them feeling taken advantage of. Suffering and disillusionment can come through friends and the associations they make. It is important for them to use greater scrutiny and practical assessment of people before they allow them into their lives. Their trusting and accepting nature can be a strength but at times a weakness that makes them vulnerable to unscrupulous people. Because they are intuitive and blessed with psychic abilities, they can learn to trust their inner voice. Developing stronger boundaries can help them protect themselves from being deceived.

Serving others and making friends with people who share similar spiritual beliefs can help inspire them to help others in deeper ways. Joining a weekly meditation circle or astrology learning circle can help them feel more connected. They need to have friends who share similar spiritual interests because they enjoy discussing mystical subjects.

Pluto in the Eleventh

These individuals can have an intense desire to make long-lasting friends. They expect a level of depth in their friendships and don't take these relationships lightly. Sharing the same interests, being able to talk deeply about what is important, and loyalty are important prerequisites of a friendship. If they can't connect deeply with someone, they won't be interested in committing their energy or time. Because of this, they can experience a lot of changes with their friendships throughout their lives. Sometimes they choose to cut ties with people they have outgrown or can't trust.

Being part of powerful groups, clubs, or organizations that transform people's lives is important to them. These individuals have a strong influence on the people they interact with. Natural leaders, they can influence groups of people and persuade them to participate in projects. At some time in their lives, they can get involved in a powerful friendship, group, or organization, and they might feel like they are being controlled in some way.

When they set their mind on a goal, they are calculated, fierce, and passionate in attaining it. They throw all their energy into meeting the right people who can benefit them in some way. Intense effort is put into achieving their hopes, wishes, and dreams. These individuals are strong and work hard to attain their long-term goals. No matter how difficult things become, they don't allow obstacles to get in their way. They have a single-minded focus on believing that through hard work, dedication, and commitment, they can achieve anything they want. Making a lasting impact on the world and society is something they passionately focus on.

Planetary Transits through the Eleventh House

When planets transit the eleventh house, you can be more interested in making friends, networking, joining groups, and pursuing your goals.

Transit Sun

This transit can inspire you to be more social and make new friends. Being part of a new group or deepening your involvement in an existing group can help you connect with others who share similar interests. During this time, you might feel more focused on your personal goals and want to manifest your dreams. People can invite you to join them for social gatherings and through networking you can meet some influential acquaintances. You're more focused on having fun, talking, and sharing ideas with other like-minded people. You can feel more creative right now and have unconventional ideas about how to reach your goals. There is a restless energy that can influence you right now, but you can use the next month to get out in the community and meet new people. Focus on what you wish for and believe that the universe can help you attain it. Tap into the positive and energic cycle that is influencing your social life and motivating you to do things differently than you have been.

Transit Moon

This transit can influence your mood for the next few days. You can feel more social and have a desire to connect with others. You might want to spend time with your friends and get out and meet new people. Networking and being part of a group can help you meet people who share similar interests. You might feel emotional fulfillment through joining a new club where you connect to people who can assist you in reaching your goals.

You can feel more charming right now and attract a lot of attention. Feeling emotions can be uncomfortable right now and you can want to focus on being more rational and practical about life. There are heightened emotions that can impact your relationships with friends. If there are any issues that have been brewing beneath the surface, this might be the time you finally address them and share your true feelings. People might seem shocked and uncomfortable by your ability to address personal issues right now. It's not typically how you act, but in the end, you are concerned with expressing yourself in the moment.

Transit Mercury

This transit can inspire creative and innovative thinking. If you aren't normally open-minded, you can be more willing to learn new things. You might want to be part of a group where you can discuss topics that interest you and explore your nontraditional ideas. During this cycle you will want to spend time socializing and won't want to be alone. Innovative ideas can come unexpectedly, so it's a good time to keep a journal to write down your new thoughts. If you were raised to believe in a traditional belief system, this transit might open your mind to new ideas. You might start to think more unconventionally and rebel against things you once believed in. Communication with friends increases and it's a good time to join a group with people who share similar interests.

Transit Venus

This transit can increase your desire to make new friends. Forming peaceful and harmonious relationships can happen through current social networks. You can feel more inspired to socialize and meet new people. Going out to eat, joining a yoga class, and doing something fun is important. A friend might introduce you to someone new. Or you might meet someone through group activities. The important thing is that you connect with someone who shares the same interests as you. Sharing your interests one-on-one or with a group of people can bring happiness. You won't want to be alone right now, so you might start dating someone you have been friends with. There is a chance you start to see them in a different light. Your creativity and imaginative side can start to bubble up. It can be a great time to join a new group or start learning something unconventional.

Transit Mars

This transit can motivate you to be part of a group or join a club. The best way to achieve your goals right now is through group activities. Try to allow others to help you and learn to work toward your goals in cooperative ways. You can feel more energetic and have a heightened stamina to get moving. Connecting with others and socializing can quell your restless energy right now.

Because this is a high-energy time for you, it's also a good time to focus on your goals for the future. Ideas seem to flow now, so make sure to write them down so you don't forget them. Stay focused on making changes in the world stage. Your humanitarian drive is strong right now. Even if you typically don't like groups, you might feel like joining a club or organization that shares your beliefs.

You can be quite the zealot right now. Speaking up forcefully for what you believe in can make you want to force others to be more open-minded. You might feel like forcing conversations that make others feel uncomfortable. Just be cautious about trying to dominate others by forcing your opinions on them.

There is an increased drive to see results, but you can be more impulsive and impatient right now. Just be careful not to argue needlessly with others during this cycle because it could just make people want to avoid interacting with you. This is a time in your life when you will need others to help you achieve your goals.

Transit Jupiter

This transit can bring fresh energy and good luck through networking. Your friends can be supportive to you now in figuring out what you really want. Thinking positively during this cycle can assist you in manifesting your long-term goals. This is an excellent time to tap into what your hopes, wishes, and dreams are. You might be asking yourself where you want to be in the future. Daydreaming and imagining where you want to be in the future are good ways to direct positive energy into the world. This will help you attract the right people who can assist you on your journey. You want to be successful and it's good to use your creative mind to visualize in detail what you want.

Even if you normally don't like being part of a group, you might feel different about that now. It's okay to take a risk and join a common cause with other people who believe and hope for a better future. If you can reach out beyond your current circle of friends and meet new people, it can bring greater abundance into your life.

You will want to communicate and discuss your ideas with your friends, and they are able to give you good advice. This is also a good time to attract new friends and acquaintances through networking. Through travel and short trips, you can connect with the right people who might be able to open doors or link you with the right contact. Blessings come to you easily right now and often through your social network.

Transit Saturn

This transit can teach you a lot about what true friendship is. Saturn is the teacher and brings wise lessons into whatever area of life it impacts. For the next few years, you will be forced to take a practical and realistic look at the friendships and associations you have developed. This cycle can feel karmic and destined in many ways. In fact, you might feel like there are things influencing your interaction with others and stirring up issues. You can be forced to grow and let go of outdated ways of interacting with others. If you are part of a group or organization, you might decide to cut ties with it. Any goals, ideas, or relationships that are not helping you grow can be released right now. You might be ready to finally shed old energy and even friends who no longer support you. It's a time to figure out what your higher purpose and future long-term goals are. You might be asking yourself where you want to be in the next ten years, and if the current social circle you have is not encouraging you to get there, it's time to walk away.

Your energy can feel heavy right now and this can affect you physically. There is a chance that you feel more tired and lack motivation lately. There is a heavier energy influencing how you view friendship and what it means to you. This cycle can make you start looking at things in a more practical way. Get organized and start making a list of your goals and of the things that are most important in your life. If you discipline yourself and focus on being patient as you make changes, it will be easier in the long run. Don't beat yourself up for possibly thinking negatively right now. Remember that this transit can change how you view the world, and change can be challenging if we resist it.

This cycle can bring upheaval and unexpected loss. Oftentimes there is some type of ending in a relationship. For instance, you might end a friendship with someone you have known your entire life. When in reality this friendship was not working out for many years, but you might have resisted changing it or doing anything about it. This energy forces issues to the surface to be addressed once and for all. This energy is teaching you the importance of being involved in friendships, groups, and clubs with people who are supportive and can benefit your life in some way.

Saturn can restrict energy and bring delays. You might feel that certain things are blocked right now or you aren't able to join the organizations or causes you want to. Whatever you set your mind to right now needs to be authentic and real. If something is not right for you, this cycle will not allow it to happen. Remember to be patient and know that timing is everything. When the time is right, you will connect with the right friends, groups, and organizations that can assist you genuinely in attaining your long-term goals.

Transit Uranus

This transit can swoop in and cause unexpected and shocking changes. For about seven years there will be a lot of things changing regarding your hopes, wishes, and dreams. The things you thought you wanted to accomplish and your long-range goals will completely change. In reality, you will be experiencing a lot of internal changes, which will impact your surroundings. This can impact the people you spend the most time with. Your friends might even notice that you seem different in some way. They might be the first to tell you that you have changed.

This cycle can make you question your social circle. You might feel like the friendships you currently have are not supportive. If there are friends you feel use you, this is the time to let them know. You might stand up and be more vocal about your needs. This is truly a revolutionary time in your life when you might even shock yourself with how you are feeling. Cutting ties and ending friendships can make you feel lighter. You might walk away from an important group you have spent many years dedicated to. It's like the things that once mattered to you are not as important any longer. You are looking for something new and fresh to dedicate your life to.

The good thing about this transit is that it can bring new ideas and beliefs into your life. You might meet interesting people who share similar interests and establish new friendships. There is also a chance that you can join a new group and get involved in an unconventional project or humanitarian mission. Be cautious about the types of new activities you get involved with and make sure to trust your gut instinct. If something doesn't feel right or is risky, you need to be cautious about throwing all your energy into it. Take it slow and give these new people and groups a chance to prove themselves worthy.

Transit Neptune

This transit can influence your social life for many years. Your imagination and a desire to express your creative side can increase right now. If you are not currently part of a group or community, you might feel inspired to join one. Just be careful about trusting others before you get to know them. There can be some confusion and uncertainty impacting your social connections. Expressing your dreams and hopes for a better future can influence the types of groups you join. If you have been idealistic and only seeing the positive side of your friends and groups, this cycle can wake you up. It's not uncommon to move on from friends and groups. Seeing things clearly is a test right now because Neptune can create deception and illusion. You might start to see people in a clearer way. There is a new awareness awakening in your life. If you have been getting taken advantage of, you will finally realize it during this cycle. There can be some uncertainty about obtaining your future goals, and you can feel more lost in knowing what you want. It's important to trust your intuition because it can protect you from getting involved with the wrong people. You could be learning a lot right now about developing boundaries. You can feel dreamy and find yourself zoning out a lot more than usual. It might be difficult for you to focus or get motivated. It can be difficult to work toward your goals. Achieving what you want can take some work, dedication, and effort. But all the efforts you put into your dreams will end up paying off.

Transit Pluto

This transit can awaken and change the way you view your friends and groups. Your attitude about being part of a larger organization or group can go through drastic change right now. It's a serious time for you and there can be intense power struggles with people you interact with. Your social connections might end. You might decide to walk away from long-term friends because you don't have anything in common with them anymore.

Something might have changed inside slowly and it's still impacting how you feel about people in your life. There can be manipulation and intense conflict with friends and people you socialize with. You might fundamentally disagree about ideas, beliefs, and ways of living. If you are betrayed by someone during this time, it can make you open your eyes to things you did not feel before. Because of the energy impacting your social connections, you might realize what true friendship is or change what you believe about friendship.

This long-term cycle can shift your hopes, wishes, and dreams. The very things you felt were important might be stripped away. You might feel like there has been a death and rebirth experience in many areas of your life. It can be challenging to hold on to the old right now, and anything that is not helping you grow will need to be cut off. Releasing people, things, and beliefs will eventually help you feel lighter and happier. It will take time to adjust to these powerful inner changes, but you will come out of this transit stronger and more resilient.

Ways to Harness Aquarius Energy

- Join a group or club.
- Think outside the box.
- Socialize and network.
- Spend time with friends.
- Develop goals for the future.
- Help others on a larger scale.

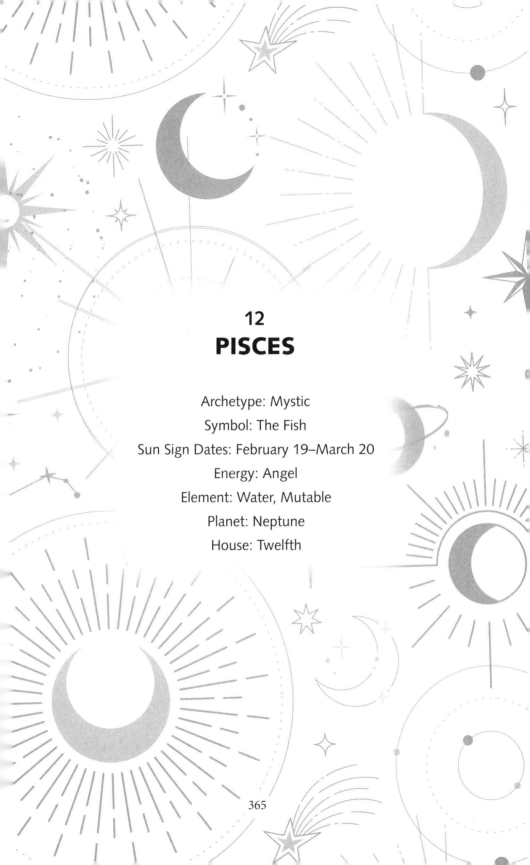

12
PISCES

Archetype: Mystic
Symbol: The Fish
Sun Sign Dates: February 19–March 20
Energy: Angel
Element: Water, Mutable
Planet: Neptune
House: Twelfth

I f you have Pisces in your birth chart, planets placed in the twelfth house, or are experiencing planetary transits through the twelfth house, this chapter will cover information regarding these energies. If you don't, you can still learn about Pisces energy and incorporate it into your life. The placement of the planet Neptune in the sign and house will show where you express Pisces energy. It is important to look at what house the sign Pisces falls on in your birth chart because this is where you could be idealistic, lack boundaries, be interested in spirituality, and have a desire to help others. Harnessing Pisces energy will give you a sense of purpose, a spiritual connection, and an ability to experience compassion.

Pisces Energy Words

Compassionate, imaginative, creative, kind, mystical, spiritual, empathic, intuitive, dreamy, angelic, escapist, secretive, adaptable, idealistic, romantic, artistic.

Pisces Motto

As a Pisces, I am a highly sensitive person and can feel other people's pain. I am compassionate and enjoy helping others who have problems. In love, I can be idealistic and see everything through rose-colored glasses. I believe in a soul mate and want a spiritual connection. I am artistic and enjoy music, theater, dancing, and expressing my creativity. There are times when I like to escape from the world and enjoy my alone time.

Harnessing Pisces Energy

Pisces energy is mystical and spiritual. It feels elusive, angelic, creative, and inspiring. This energy is associated with spirituality, altered states of consciousness, dreams, escapism, and solitude. To awaken this energy, we can study dreams, astrology, yoga, and meditation. Pisces energy creates empathic abilities, intuition, and a strong desire to help others. To tap into this energy, it's important to seek a connection to a higher power or develop some type of spiritual path. Spending time alone, pondering the meaning of life, can help them receive insights that provide answers to their problems. Heightened psychic abilities and imagination are spiritual gifts they are born with. Escaping from the mundane world helps this energy find inner peace.

We can feel this energy when we feel compassionate, kind, and develop a deeper connection with ourselves and others. Trusting the universe and exploring different spiritual philosophies can help us realize that we are souls living in this material world. Pisces energy helps us recognize the needs of others around us. It can also bless us with the ability to nurture others through spiritual service. Learning to listen to our intuition, helping others in need, and utilizing our imagination are ways to harness Pisces energy.

Harness Kindness

Pisces is associated with angel energy. They can feel like angels who fell to earth to learn important lessons. Many can feel like they are aliens, and this is why Pisces energy is similar to angel energy. Angel energy is connected to a higher source and brings an awareness of the soul. This energy can feel dreamy, mystical, and mysterious. Pisceans seem to remember that they have lived somewhere before they came to this earth. Sometimes they feel lonely and isolate themselves from the world. Their compassion, kindness, and ability to feel other people's pain can deplete their energy. Escaping from responsibilities can be a coping mechanism they often use to protect themselves. Learning to have boundaries and greater self-protection helps them recuperate.

Angel energy comforts, listens, and heals everything it touches. It doesn't judge others but accepts people's differences and lends a helping hand to assist those in need. Natural empaths, Pisceans feel everything that is going on in the environment. Angel energy blesses them with psychic, intuitive, and healing abilities.

This energy believes and sees the best in people and doesn't like to focus on negativity. Idealistic, this energy can see the world with rose-colored glasses. Angel energy understands the meaning of spiritual service and the importance of connecting to a higher power. In fact, life becomes easier when we have a sense of purpose and belief that we are here for a reason. Activities like meditation, breathing exercises, prayer, and even spending time alone can help us connect to this sensitive energy.

Harness Feelings

Pisces is ruled by the element of water. Similar to the ocean, water energy is soothing, deep, and emotional. Water energy helps Pisceans feel compassion, kindness, and seek a deeper connection to the world around them. Imaginative, artistic, and creative, they want to express their feelings. Water energy can be affectionate, romantic, and intuitive. It's good at making people feel loved, needed, and supported.

Water energy flourishes when it's taking care of others. Its focus is on helping people and making a difference in this world. Water energy enhances psychic abilities such as clairvoyance, dreams, and visions. Because water energy is calm, it is good at listening to others and nurturing them. Making time for self-reflection and self-care can help us tap into water energy. When we tap into our intuition and creative gifts, we can harness the gifts of water energy.

Adapt to the Environment

Pisces is a mutable sign and easily adapts to change. Often easygoing, this energy doesn't mind changing direction at a moment's notice, like fish swimming in the sea. Morphing to the environment is what mutable signs do best. They can become and pretend to be what other people want them to be. They can easily mimic other people's emotions and body language. Pisces is one of the most sensitive and emotional signs in astrology. Because they are empathic, they perceive things that are hidden and can change to help other people. Mutable energy wants to please others and get along with everyone. When this energy is not grounded, it can feel lost. When it's experiencing stress, this energy wants to rest, escape, and find peace. Chameleon behavior helps Pisceans know what other people need and adapt to the energy of the environment. It trusts the feelings of the moment and believes that everything will work out the way it's meant to. Experiencing peace, harmony, and autonomy is important to mutable signs. Harnessing adaptability will help us connect to mutable energy.

Connect to Spirit

Pisces is ruled by the planet Neptune. Neptune energy is idealistic and encourages us to believe in something greater than ourselves. In Roman mythology, Neptune is the god of fresh water and the sea. Neptune energy is associated with deep feeling and emotions. It helps us learn to be more compassionate, kind, and empathetic. Neptune is associated with spirituality, enlightenment, mysticism, and escapism. This is why we tend to idolize people and situations in the area of life Neptune influences.

Neptune energy is where we often wear rose-colored glasses, seeing only what we want to see and putting other people on pedestals. Because of the heightened sensitivity this energy brings, it can make it difficult for us to protect ourselves. Therefore, developing boundaries is important for Pisceans.

This energy is known to make us absorb the thoughts, feelings, and emotions of other people. Neptune can make us feel more sensitive to other people's pain. Because of Neptune's influence, Pisceans are often prone to feelings of sadness and loneliness. Escaping the world, spending time alone, can help balance out uncomfortable emotions. This energy encourages us to seek the meaning of life and explore our purpose here on this earth.

Sometimes this energy brings secrets into our lives and difficulties seeing reality clearly. There can be deception, lies, and secrets in the area of life that Neptune is placed in the birth chart. Its energy can cloud our vision and we aren't always able to see what is really happening. Neptune can confuse us and bring suffering through loss, heartbreak, or feelings of abandonment.

Sometimes Neptune can make us feel like a victim, taken advantage of, and even like people are out to get us. But on the other hand, its energy can help us connect to higher levels of consciousness through tapping into our intuition, learning to meditate, recording our dreams, and trusting our flashes of insight. It's always a good tip to work on being a little more practical and realistic wherever Neptune is placed in the birth chart.

Escape from the World

The twelfth house in astrology is associated with mystery, illusion, and secrets. It's an area of life that is often misunderstood. This is where we find solitude by escaping from the real world. Diving into our imagination and spending time alone meditating, praying, and pondering the meaning of life is what the twelfth house awakens within us. It's the area of life where we can be spiritual, artistic, and creative. But the most important thing this house teaches us is that we are a soul on this earth with a special purpose. The twelfth house is where we find our oneness with a higher power or seek a spiritual path. It's where we walk between worlds with one foot in the spiritual and one foot in the material. It's a hidden and secretive area of life, and when planets are placed here, people often want to withdraw.

This is the house of compassion, kindness, and spiritual service. The motto of this house is to serve or suffer. Life can get much easier when we focus on taking care of the needs of others. But this should be done in moderation, and we need to remember not to neglect ourselves. The influence of the planet Neptune can make this area of life a lonely place that often leaves us feeling misunderstood.

The twelfth house calls on us to balance spiritual service with practical service. Learning to be in the real world while keeping a connection to spirit is the challenge of the twelfth house. Many people with planets here often have unexplained psychic experiences from a young age. They are born with a highly sensitive personality and often possess empathic abilities. They are interested in learning more about mystical topics such as astrology, dreams, crystals, and tarot cards. Having planets in this house often blesses individuals with spiritual gifts they can use to help others.

Pisces Rising

Pisces rising individuals are sensitive, compassionate, and intuitive. They can develop psychic abilities to benefit people's lives. Sometimes they feel like they are psychic sponges who draw in all the energy that surrounds them. Because of their kind nature and friendly personality, they attract a lot of people. They can appear dreamy, imaginative, and mysterious. They notice things others don't readily see and are very perceptive. But sometimes they are fooled and even taken advantage of due to their trusting nature. When someone is born with Pisces rising, it can make them seem like a chameleon who can transform their personality to adapt to their environment. This personality trait enables them to get along with many different types of people.

Because they are ruled by the water element and the planet Neptune, they are wide open energetically and emotionally. Their lack of boundaries and knowledge of self-protection can affect their physical health and mood. They often absorb the stress, emotions, and chaotic feelings from others and sometimes internalize them. Because of their spiritual abilities, it can be difficult to know what emotions are their own. Even though this is a spiritual gift that can be used to help others, they can sometimes feel depressed and want to withdraw from social settings.

Even if they are struggling, they can put on a happy face when they are around happy people. The rising sign is a mask they show the world, and they are very good at using that mask to survive in the environment they are in. Pisces risings can experience depression, sadness, and anxiety more than others. But they often hide these darker feelings from people close to them and escape to deal with them in private. If they get hurt or wounded by others, they tend to shut down. Sometimes they can feel like a victim and get their feelings hurt very easily. In reality, they just want the pain to go away and they want others to treat them with kindness.

The one thing that can help Pisces risings the most is when they seek a spiritual path or find meaning in their lives. In fact, pursuing a spiritual discipline where they can dedicate their time and energy can bring a deeper sense of connection. Pursuing healthy outlets like Tai Chi, meditation, journaling, and listening to music can bring a sense of fulfilment.

Having a peaceful and calm homelife can help them find ways to heal and recover from the stress of the world. Spending time alone is very healing for them. Being alone in solitude can help comfort them and bring a sense of peace.

Sometimes they can have unique sleep issues such as sleep paralysis, lucid dreams, and insomnia. There are also times when they sleep too little, too much, or sleep can become a way to escape. Developing a healthy sleep routine is crucial and keeping a dream journal by the side of the bed to jot down the symbols and feelings when they awaken can give insights into their day-to-day lives.

In relationships, when they love someone, it's deep and romantic. They tend to be attracted to and experience deep connections with people who are open-minded, spiritual, and creative. People can sense their compassionate energy and be drawn to them like moths to the flame. Because they ooze kindness, they can attract people who need help. This is why it's crucial that they develop boundaries and learn how to tell people no when they need to. There are times when they can feel like a victim in their relationships. Because they give their trust away so easily, they often overshare early in a relationship. They also open their heart too quickly and this can make them vulnerable to being hurt.

Avoiding people and withdrawing happens when they are upset, frustrated, and angry. They can isolate themselves and become reclusive when their relationships are not going well. As far as relationships go, they need to be very careful about who they allow into their inner circle and life. They can attract abusive or unhealthy people. Therefore, it's good to surround themselves with supportive and positive people who can lift them up instead of bringing them down. They need to remember that they don't have to rescue and save everyone. Just like their symbol the fish, they often lack boundaries and are like two fish flapping out in the water without protection. Developing stronger boundaries and listening to their intuition can help them learn greater self-protection. Self-care is a key practice that can help increase their ability to connect within and find balance.

Pisces rising individuals are often extremely imaginative and creative. Expressing their talents and interests can be emotionally fulfilling. As psychic sponges, they are often extremely connected to their fantasy world, daydreaming, zoning out, and imagining things.

Service oriented, they are focused on helping people in some way. Many are drawn to psychology, counseling, nursing, or working with animals. They are known to be spiritual and understanding. They have a desire to feel needed and appreciated. Sadly, they often feel taken for granted in their social relationships. But they can realize later in life that their kindness is a strength and not a weakness. True unconditional love and kindness is a rare thing, but it's one of Pisces rising's greatest strengths.

How to Harness Planets in Pisces

When planets are in Pisces, you will have a desire to connect to a spiritual path, escape from the world, help others, and express your creativity.

Sun in Pisces

Sun in Pisces individuals are idealistic and compassionate. Trusting others too easily can sometimes be a strength and a weakness. Seeing the best in people is something they do readily, but this can also blind them to painful truths. But they get along with many different types of people because of their ability to adapt. Chameleons in social situations, they seem to take on the thoughts and feelings of others. Their magnetic and charming energy can attract many people into their lives. Extremely empathic, they are sensitive to their environment. Because of their highly intuitive nature, they can sense if someone is happy, sad, or angry. Protecting themselves is key and will help them conserve their energy.

Natural counselors, they are good at helping people with their problems. They are compassionate and understanding because they feel other people's pain. Romantic and idealistic, they can glamorize love and search for a soul mate. Sometimes they can experience disappointment and feel disillusioned about love. When the rose-colored glasses come off for the first time, it can be painful for them. Commitment can also be challenging because their feelings are changeable.

But if they have a spiritual and romantic bond with someone, they can be devoted partners. One of the most important things in relationships is that they want to feel needed and that they can help others.

Loneliness can sometimes lead to depression, anxiety, and sadness. Even though they like to withdraw from the world sometimes, they need others to balance them out. They shouldn't be alone for too long and they need supportive friends and spiritual groups to be part of. They have a strong desire to escape from stress and responsibilities. Relaxing and pursuing hobbies with friends helps them tap into their imagination.

They need to be cautious about risk-taking behaviors. Addiction is often associated with Pisces. So, numbing themselves through drugs and alcohol can become an unhealthy way of coping. Anything that helps them not feel their deep emotions can become a crutch. They could abuse alcohol, food, work, sex, and social media, leading to addictive behaviors. But they would benefit more through listening to music, meditation, yoga, and exercise.

Connecting to a higher power and having a spiritual discipline can help them find a sense of purpose. They are often interested in learning about New Age topics like astrology, tarot, crystals, and dreams. Pisceans are dreamy and imaginative, which opens up their artistic and creative abilities. Many are interested in pursuing careers in music, art, and acting. They can even be interested in helping people with their problems, which can lead them to pursue careers in psychology, social work, and counseling. They have a strong desire to express their creativity in whatever type of work they do. If they can't express themselves at work, it's good for them to have hobbies to express this side of their personality. Harnessing their psychic abilities can enable them to help others in deeper ways.

Moon in Pisces

Moon in Pisces individuals are emotional, intuitive, and empathic. They blend into any environment because they are social and adaptable. People are attracted to their mysterious aura and warm presence. They are empathic and can feel other people's pain, which makes them natural healers. Making others feel supported and understood is what they do best.

Imaginative and creative, they often are blessed with artistic talents. They might enjoy singing, playing an instrument, painting, writing, or participating in theater. Creating beauty and harmony makes them feel comfort. Exploring the depths of their mind and expressing their ideas out into the world helps them shine. They often enjoy being behind the scenes and withdraw from the world to pursue their creative interests.

Sometimes they have a knack for exposing secrets. In fact, people often come up to them in the grocery store and share their personal problems and private information. Naturally compassionate, they have a strong desire to help others heal. Because of their ability to offer comfort to people who are hurting, they make excellent therapists, healers, and spiritual advisors. Their ability to put themselves in other people's shoes makes them natural counselors.

Overwhelmed at times by their strong emotions, it's important that they learn to have greater boundaries. It's also important that they learn to balance the spiritual with the practical. They can feel lost at times and want to escape from the world. In fact, they are so connected to their environment that they are easily drained. Because they are extremely intuitive and have natural psychic abilities, they need to learn how to implement self-care strategies. If they take care of their own needs first, they will have the energy to go out and help others. They might have to learn this lesson the hard way, through suffering and physical illness. Eventually they will understand their sensitive nature and how to recuperate their own energy while helping others.

Born with an innate psychic sensitivity, they often have vivid dreams and intuition that is rarely wrong. At some time in their life, they might dream about the future and watch it all play out in the real world. The cycles of the Moon can influence how they feel and what they dream about. Keeping a dream journal can be beneficial. Their emotional fulfillment comes through being of service and doing something that is meaningful and in line with their soul's purpose.

Relationships can be challenging and full of disappointment if they don't pick the right partner. Sometimes they choose to sacrifice their own needs and put other people first. It's important that they learn to see people clearly and avoid idolizing others.

Compassionate and kind, they can find happiness through connecting with other people in a deep way. They can also find emotional fulfillment by connecting to a higher power and pursuing a spiritual path.

Mercury in Pisces

Mercury in Pisces individuals are sympathetic communicators who make others feel comfortable. Sometimes they can be talkative and other times they seem withdrawn. They can fluctuate between being social and at other times withdrawn. They might need more time alone than most people because they enjoy expressing their creative ideas through writing, journaling, or listening to music.

Sometimes they can be secretive and hide their thoughts from others. Communication can be an area where they experience misunderstandings. They need to try to be clear and honest in the way they communicate. Mercury placed here can make it difficult to express their deep emotions through words. It's almost like words don't do their feelings justice. They often feel more comfortable writing down their thoughts and sending an email versus talking in person.

Deception and white lies can destroy relationships, so they have to get comfortable being direct. Speaking the truth can be challenging for them, or standing up for themselves, because they worry about hurting other people's feelings. Harmonious and easy communication suits them best and they feel most at ease with other people who think like they do. In fact, they prefer deep discussions about the meaning of life and spirituality versus practical conversations.

To dedicate the time and energy to study a subject, it needs to be interesting to them because they get bored easily. Highly intuitive, they might zone out and daydream a lot as a child. In childhood they can struggle in school because teachers don't always know how to encourage their creative minds. They have a vivid imagination and are highly influenced by the thoughts of others. They are intuitive communicators who enjoy discussing spiritual topics such as astrology, crystals, and tarot. They can also be talented writers and enjoy reading paranormal fiction. Some might enjoy reading about romance as well because of their idealistic beliefs about love.

They can spend a lot of time in their own mind pondering the problems of the world. Solitude can be an important way to self-care. Getting away from people and having time alone to rest and analyze their own thoughts is crucial for their well-being.

In relationships, they often worry about the problems of people they care about, which can lead to anxious feelings. Their compassionate way of listening and giving advice makes people want to open up to them. They can be natural psychologists who share important nuggets of information with others just when they need to hear it. Tapping into their imagination can help them express their creative talents in different ways.

Venus in Pisces

Venus in Pisces individuals are tenderhearted and idealistic in love. They can be charming and affectionate lovers. People are attracted to their mysterious, alluring, and creative personality. They are compassionate, attractive, and have a subtle way of drawing attention. There is something illusive about their energy. People often feel like they never truly know what they are feeling. In fact, they are known to be secretive, private, and have a hidden love nature.

Unconditional love is something they believe in, but they also enjoy romance in a relationship. Having an affectionate partner who shares their interests is good for them. Although, their idealism can sometimes cloud their judgment and they can attract partners who are unhealthy or even abusive. Because of a romantic view of relationships, they can find themselves drawn to people who have problems. Because of their compassionate nature, people might try to take advantage of their kindness. At times they can be self-sacrificing and put their partner's needs before their own. If their partner has an addiction or bad habit, they might believe they can change them. They need to be careful about having a savior complex where they believe they need to rescue people. When they are in love, they can forgive others too easily and are known to give people too many chances. They want to feel needed and sometimes are attracted to people who they can try to save. Some of these patterns can stem from childhood and it can be helpful to talk with a counselor if they need to.

They might believe in a soul mate and in destiny. In fact, they often are not interested in a partner unless there is an emotional and spiritual bond. Being too trusting in love can cause difficulties and bring heartbreak. There might be times they keep their feelings hidden or develop secret love affairs. They might fall in love with more than one person and struggle to decide who they want to be with. Commitment can be challenging for them unless they feel a strong emotional connection. These experiences help them learn what the meaning of true love is. It can be beneficial when they learn that true love or a soul mate relationship must start within themselves first. They are their own best soul mate. Developing stronger boundaries is one of their greatest tests. Harnessing these boundaries will help them see things clearly in the love department and help them develop healthy coping mechanisms.

Mars in Pisces

Mars in Pisces individuals are not always comfortable being direct. Conflict can be unpleasant for them and they might try to avoid it. They are highly sensitive to criticism but have a hard time standing up for themselves. They can repress their anger and feel guilty when they get upset with others. Sometimes they might believe that it's wrong to feel angry. These feelings are intensified if they didn't learn how to be assertive from their parents. Repressing their anger can lead to health issues such as headaches, weakened immune system, and skin rashes. If they can feel more comfortable with both positive and negative emotions, it can help them incorporate healthy ways of expressing this energy. They are known to go with the flow but can also change their goals due to indecisiveness.

Secretive at times, they can hide their true feelings from others. They need a creative outlet to express their intense feelings instead of bottling them up. Passive-aggressive behaviors can cause conflict in relationships and make it difficult for others to trust them. Their energy levels can fluctuate. One minute they are ready to take on the world and the next day they can feel a desire to withdraw.

The typical fiery passion, rashness, boldness, and confidence of Mars is toned down with this placement. It can be difficult for them to feel driven and make goals for the future. They can give up easily when they feel mistreated or discouraged. To get things done, they need to have an emotional connection or feel a sense of purpose to the task.

Because of their imaginative and intuitive powers, they might have artistic talents. If they enjoy something and it inspires them, it's good if they pursue it. They might be able to make money doing hobbies and expressing their creativity in some way. They might be interested in writing, teaching, painting, and using their hands to make clay items. Whatever it is, they need to express their emotions in a healthy outlet.

Deeply caring lovers, they are romantic and affectionate. Having an intimate relationship can be important to them and they often want to find true love. Because deep down they care about other people and they don't want to hurt others. Their moodiness can make them irritable and sometimes they lash out at others. If they can harness more confidence with their own feelings and find ways to express themselves directly, they will feel more energized.

Jupiter in Pisces

Jupiter in Pisces individuals are generous and friendly. Being extremely concerned with the needs of others can make them sacrifice their own needs to ensure other people are taken care of. They have a gift for seeing the good in others and want to see other people succeed. They would give someone the shirt off their back if it would help them. People feel comfortable around them instantly due to their warm, open, and optimistic nature. They might be a bit shy when you first meet them. But their energy is vibrant and positive, which attracts others.

Spirituality is often an important part of their lives. They can have many interests and a thirst for knowledge. They can often be found studying astrology, mysticism, and world religions because this is where they seek the answers to life's greatest mysteries. They are born with an innate belief in something bigger than themselves. Even if they were not raised to believe a certain way, they often have a strong faith in a higher power and they aren't even sure where it comes from. Finding inner peace and seeking wisdom helps them on their journey.

Adventurous spirits, they might enjoy traveling and exploring new places. Taking a trip to Egypt to see the pyramids or visiting a country where their ancestors were from can quench their thirst for exploration. They like to be on the move and can be restless in their search for adventure.

Jupiter can help protect their energy so they aren't so easily hurt. Sometimes they might feel like a guardian angel is watching over them. Good luck and abundance often come their way because of their happy, positive, and generous attitude. The more they serve others and help people in need, the greater blessings enter their lives. True abundance flourishes for them when they keep an optimistic attitude and realize all they have to be grateful for.

Expressing their artistic and creative talents can help them channel their emotions into making beautiful works of art. Some of them are talented musicians and might enjoy writing songs. If they can harness the power of positive thinking, they will find that they can manifest their deepest desires.

Saturn in Pisces

Saturn in Pisces individuals can be uncomfortable with physical affection or public displays of emotion. In fact, they might resist showing any type of affection with their partner unless they are behind closed doors. They can feel inhibited about expressing their feelings and can restrict their uncomfortable emotions. Emotions like anger, anxiety, and sadness can be difficult for them to feel. The more they ignore their intuition, the stronger their fears become. They can obsess on dark thoughts and pessimistic beliefs because Saturn here makes them see things in a practical way.

Intimacy can also be difficult for them. In private, they are more likely to show their sensitive side once they trust someone. Being vulnerable emotionally or showing weakness is something that can make them uncomfortable. They don't always allow themselves to experience human emotions. They are known for controlling, repressing, and avoiding talking about their emotions. These traits can prevent them from making deeper friendships. But once they trust someone, they are quite loyal and dedicated. Once they allow someone into their inner circle, they open up more fully and share their true feelings.

They have a need to appear strong, serious, and in control, which can lead to repressing their feelings. Their friends and family might perceive them as harsh and unloving at times. But in reality, this behavior is often because of deep-rooted fears of being hurt. If they suffered in the past, it could take them a while to heal. Forgiving others can help them open their hearts to new people.

Super responsible, they often look and act older than they actually are. Saturn here can also make them feel like it's their duty to take care of the needs of their family or help with providing financial support. Because they take life seriously, it can be difficult for them to trust their intuition. Deep down they can have psychic gifts that can help them reach their goals. But they have to learn how to trust them. If they can find a spiritual path and purpose, it helps them soften. They can be disciplined and dedicated in mastering a spiritual path. Having a routine and structure in their lives can help them feel comfortable. For instance, they might do yoga every morning, eat the same breakfast every day, and meditate every night before bed. Having a spiritual routine can help them connect within and get in touch with their feelings.

Isolation can sometimes lead to depression and negativity. Because of their behavior, people might stop sharing personal things with them, and this can leave them feeling lonely. A pessimistic attitude can limit their ability to attain their goals and connect with others. If they can harness a more positive attitude, they can start to see how they can attract positive outcomes.

Uranus in Pisces

Uranus in Pisces individuals often question tradition and explore different spiritual practices. From a young age, they might question the religious beliefs they were raised with. Searching for something that makes sense to them can take some time. Exploring religion, philosophy, and scientific theories can help them find greater meaning in their lives. They want to study things that are unique and different. They might rebel against their entire belief system and create changes that can make other people uncomfortable. They don't really care if people accept them or not because they are free-spirited and authentic individuals.

They grow wiser and develop faith through direct experience. They can have unexpected flashes of intuitive knowing and glimpses of the future. Information seems to come to them from a higher source and they can receive spiritual downloads. Dreaming about the future and receiving symbolic information at night is a spiritual gift they can embrace. They would benefit from keeping a dream journal next to their bed at night.

Creative and imaginative, they need to socialize and pursue hobbies that inspire them because they get bored easily. They can possess artistic and creative talents and enjoy writing, painting, drawing, and playing music. Innovation and open-mindedness help them tap into higher creative talents and they can express their talents through being part of a group or organization.

They have a unique way of expressing what they feel and are highly intelligent. Freedom and independence are things they value because they want to be allowed to believe what they want to. They don't like to be forced to conform or embrace traditional beliefs. They might rebel against societal norms and belief systems. Finding their own truth and seeking their soul's purpose can help them find the meaning of life. They enjoy learning about unconventional and eccentric ideas. If they can tap into their imagination, they can come up with some revolutionizing ideas and ways of helping others.

Neptune in Pisces

Neptune in Pisces individuals are mystical and compassionate souls. They have a genuinely kind and giving nature and it's difficult for them to hurt anyone. Because of their sensitivity, they like to help others and are drawn to the helping professions. Sometimes they can get lost in a sea of emotions and they are not sure if what they are feeling is truly coming from them or the outside world. Their sensitivity to the environment can make them psychic sponges who take on everyone's negative emotions. This ability can leave them feeling sad and emotionally drained. Because they lack boundaries between themselves and others, it's crucial for them to learn to protect their energy. They can benefit greatly through grounding exercises and connecting with their physical body. Things like yoga, Tai Chi, and meditation can be helpful.

Artists at heart, they are creative and talented. They are born with artistic abilities and a spiritual desire to connect through creativity. Making beautiful art, music, and poetry might interest them. Using their imagination to invent new things that inspire others can bring a sense of fulfillment.

When they are in love, they often put people on a pedestal, and they can believe they are perfect. They should be cautious about attracting people who want to take advantage of their kindness or even try to manipulate them. Their idealism can get them involved with partners who are unhealthy or even abusive. Disillusionment and heartache can occur when someone lies, deceives, or is unfaithful to them. When they eventually find out the truth and realize the person is not who they thought they were, it can be devastating.

Detaching from their physical body and dissociating from it can be a survival mechanism they use to survive. When they are in large groups, they might feel like they are outside of their body looking in on everything. This can be a way they protect themselves from feeling things so deeply. Escaping from the world and finding solitude can bring greater peace. But it's important that they escape through healthy ways and avoid drugs, alcohol, or anything that numbs their emotions. Addiction can be a real issue with this placement and can manifest in many different ways. Anything they do to avoid their feelings or numb their pain can be a coping mechanism. There are other positive things they can do, such as meditation, listening to music, writing, getting out in nature, and spending time near water. All these things can be soothing to their soul and help them find balance.

Their ability to connect to a higher power can help them tap into different levels of consciousness. Some of them might be easily hypnotized or interested in hypnosis to find out more about their past lives. They can leave their body or astral project without even trying. Many with this placement dream every night and experience lucidity, which means they seem to wake up within the dream state and are aware they are dreaming. Keeping a dream journal will help them connect the energy of their dream symbols and use these messages to guide their lives.

Pluto in Pisces

Pluto in Pisces individuals transform and grow through a connection to the universe. They are passionate and extremely perceptive, which helps them uncover hidden truths. Their intuition is strong, and they often know things before they happen. Profound changes and intense life experiences impact them on a core level. Like phoenixes, they are forever changed, reborn, and rise from the ashes with the ability to overcome the betrayal and heartache they experience. They often heal through rebirth, letting go, and releasing the past. Because they are compassionate and kind, they might find it easier to forgive others.

Intense and powerful individuals, they often are private and work hard to protect themselves from being hurt. They don't readily trust others and can be skeptical about other people's motives. They understand human suffering and can see through others easily to their very core. It's difficult to fool them because they are empathic and feel people's energy.

Because of their supportive nature, they can make a positive impact on other people's lives. Born with an ability to listen intently, they truly care about helping others heal. People with pain or those who have suffered often walk up to them and share all their dark secrets. They can wonder what it is about them that makes everyone unload all their baggage and tell them very personal information. Complete strangers often walk up to them in the grocery store and overshare. These experiences often lead them to be interested in psychology and counseling.

Having time to withdraw from people and be alone helps them find peace. Their own wounds can be healed through self-reflection and spending time alone. Once they heal, they assist others who are on a similar spiritual journey.

In relationships, they can get attached easily when there is an emotional connection. They might also find that the universe removes people they love from their lives without notice. These changes can feel like destined events that transpire to test their ability to let go. Grief and loss are things they resonate with and understand on a core level. They might be interested in career fields such as psychiatry, social work, energy healing, and alternative medicine.

Learning to balance their spiritual and material needs helps them grow stronger. This lifetime, they may feel a desire to connect to a higher power or start searching for answers to life's mysteries. Many realize that they are a soul who is here for a greater purpose. They can look back and realize that all the painful experiences they went through made them more resilient. If they ground their energy, it can help them connect deeper to everyday life and practical responsibilities.

Planets in the Twelfth House

When planets are placed in the twelfth house, you can be interested in spirituality, connecting to a higher power, spending time alone, and helping others in some way.

Sun in the Twelfth

These individuals are private and enjoy spending time alone. They value their inner world and can like escaping from the stresses of everyday life. A peaceful and harmonious environment helps them feel safe. They enjoy solitude and quiet time to ponder their deep thoughts. Compassionate and tenderhearted, they need a soothing environment to survive. They can be extremely sensitive to negativity and feel other people's pain. They are interested in things that are spiritual, secretive, imaginative, and mystical.

Sometimes they attract people who have problems and they enjoy helping people feel better. This placement is often associated with service and suffering. The more they help others, the easier their life becomes. They can be attracted to the helping professions such as social work, psychology, nursing, and childcare.

Compassionate, sensitive, and psychic, they are born with spiritual abilities. Their psychic abilities and empathy can truly help them understand the needs of others. They can feel other people's pain easily and they try hard to help others feel better. Due to their spiritual nature, they often attract the downtrodden and outcasts of society.

They can prefer working behind the scenes in seclusion and are very private. Because of their interest in staying hidden, they might pursue a life of seclusion, such as becoming a priest, nun, rabbi, or monk. Or they might be drawn to some undercover work as a criminal profiler, psychic medium, or fantasy writer.

Their emotional nature fluctuates, and they can sometimes experience depression, sadness, and anxiety. They can struggle when they are in large groups and find themselves feeling very different from others. It's like they fell to earth and realize they are not from here. They often have the realization from a young age that they are not a physical body, but a soul. They prefer small groups and one-on-one interaction. They can experience depersonalization when they are at concerts, at the mall, or around large groups of people. Their lack of boundaries makes them connect to everything and at times they can feel a sense of oneness to all life. Their everyday life can seem like a dream, like it's almost unreal, and this makes them question their reality. They are interested in spiritual truths and want to understand themselves and others better.

They have a desire to escape from the world and have time alone to figure out the meaning of life. Having a spiritual path or mission helps them build a sense of purpose. They have an innate awareness that they are here for a special purpose. A good path for them would be when they decide to pursue spirituality, meditation, and dedicate their lives to serving others in some way.

A more difficult path could be when they try to escape through alcohol and drugs. They are very susceptible to many forms of addiction, which could become love, work, social media, food, and sex. They should be cautious about using any type of substance that might alter the mind and affect their body. These things can become a crutch that is used to numb themselves from the pain they feel.

"Serve or suffer" should be their motto. Benefits come when they focus on being more spiritual and serving those who are less fortunate. Their lives will become much easier when they understand that they are not a victim but a survivor. Everything that happens to them is for a reason, and helps them become stronger and more resilient. They can help a lot of people by using their natural spiritual gifts and by tapping into their intuition, imagination, and dreams.

Many people with this placement might experience an absent or missing father figure. Their father might have not been a strong presence in their lives. They might have died at an early age, traveled a lot for work, or their parents might have divorced, leaving the relationship forever changed. If their father was in the home, they might have felt there was an emotional detachment and that their father was emotionally unavailable. Maybe their father worked long hours, traveled away from home often, or abandoned the family in some way. However this plays out, there can be a wound that needs to be healed this lifetime. There can also be addiction issues such as alcoholism that impacted the family and the father's life. Sometimes they try to overcome this pain by trying to find a father figure in their relationships.

These individuals can feel extremely responsible from a young age, and they often seek to learn spiritual knowledge to help them understand why the world is the way it is. There might be issues with authority figures and a lack of boundaries that makes it easy to be hurt. These individuals benefit when they focus on having a spiritual path and seeking the meaning of life. Developing a spiritual connection to the universe will help them overcome any feelings of loneliness and separateness they experience. If they can harness their extraordinary psychic abilities, they can help others in deeper ways.

Moon in the Twelfth

These individuals are deeply emotional and spiritual. Their intuition and ability to read what people are feeling are gifts. Kind and compassionate, they care about helping people and making the world a better place. They can appear secretive, private, and mysterious. Their emotional nature is often kept hidden from others. Still waters run deep, and they love deeply.

They can have artistic talents that they keep secret because of fears that they are not as good as other people. Expressing their creative side helps them find happiness and brings fun into their lives. Listening to soothing music and having beautiful art around them can bring comfort. They might like writing, drawing, painting, or singing. Pursuing their creative hobbies can bring emotional fulfillment.

The environment impacts their mood and it's important that they learn to protect themselves. They often struggle with maintaining strong boundaries. They can see the good in others and often ignore red flags. Idealistic, they often view others with rose-colored glasses. Seeing people more clearly can help them develop practical connections. They can learn how to express their intricate emotions through writing, journaling, and recording their dreams. Solitude brings comfort and helps them find emotional fulfillment. They need to have time to withdraw from the hustle and bustle of the world.

They have a delicate emotional nature and they often struggle with the emotional ups and downs of life. There are times they can experience depression and sadness. The cycles of the Moon can influence their feelings. Watching these cycles can become a tool that might help them overcome and understand their complex feelings. They do not necessarily need medication to treat these subdued feelings. But they would benefit by talking about their feelings, writing them down, and processing them with a counselor. Sometimes they are not sure if it is their own pain they are feeling or the pain of others. Because they are empaths, they are sensitive to other people's thoughts and emotions. They can absorb these energies.

Escapism is a key issue of the twelfth house. Because the Moon is here, they may like to run away, hide, and escape from the world. Practical and mundane routines can be boring to them and stress has a negative impact on their health. It's important that they balance stress and anxiety so it doesn't start to negatively impact their lives.

Even though they like to escape from responsibilities, deep down they know that the world needs what they have to give. They are born with spiritual gifts and genuinely care about helping people. They are drawn to the helping professions and often enjoy working with children and animals. Things like astrology, energy work, Reiki, crystal healing, and alternative medicine are things that can be used as tools in their work. Service oriented, they focus a lot of their emotional energy on the needs of others. They just need to remember to spend enough time focusing on their own needs and making time for self-care.

The relationship they had with their mother might have been complex. When the Moon is placed here, there is often a karmic experience of having to take care of their mother because she was not able to care for herself. In fact, they can feel responsible for their mother's happiness. There might be a role reversal in this relationship where they feel like they are the parent to their mother. Their mother could have been sick or struggled with addiction. They perceived their mother as emotionally vulnerable, mentally unstable, and because of this they felt like they had to ensure her needs were met. The bond with their mother can be sometimes unhealthy and enmeshed. This type of upbringing might have caused an emotional wound. If they had to take care of their mother, they might have not had their own emotional needs met. As adults, they might have fears of being vulnerable. At times they can struggle with allowing others to nurture them. They can feel extremely loyal to their mother regardless of the situation they experienced as a child. There are also times they might benefit from their mother and may inherit spiritual gifts or psychic abilities from the maternal side of the family. The relationship with their mother can teach them what is important in life. As they get older, they can heal this relationship and learn how it can make them self-reliant.

Venus in the Twelfth

These individuals are idealistic and sacrificing in relationships. Venus here is deep, understanding, and mystical, which enhances their desire to find a spiritual partner or soul mate. Private and secretive, they can hide their romantic feelings from others and even from themselves. Sometimes their emotions are too powerful to express in words. So, they express their feelings through music, art, and being creative.

Their greatest learning comes through the area of love and relationships. They are private and tend to keep their intimate feelings hidden, sometimes never fully expressing them. Many people with this placement might experience clandestine or secret love affairs. This happens because their expression of love is often private, mysterious, and almost otherworldly. Because they can experience hidden feelings or a secret love affair at some time in their lives they don't judge others. Sometimes the feelings are acted upon and other times they are not. They may not be unfaithful to their partner, but they may fall prey to emotional affairs.

Sometimes they attract a deceptive partner who lies to them or has a secret relationship they don't know about. This can be extremely difficult once they find out the truth, but with time they can eventually heal. It is important that they look within and be honest about their emotions. Romantic at heart, they might fall in love with someone they can't have because they aren't free to be with them. For instance, maybe the person is married or in a position of authority. Forbidden love is often associated with this placement. Sometimes they keep their emotions secret because they aren't sure the other person feels the same way about them. It's hard for them to see things clearly when they are in love.

On the journey of finding the meaning of true love, they have to learn from personal experience. Lessons in love are transforming and push them toward their true purpose, which is to learn what unconditional love is. There can be illusion and deception that impacts their intimate relationships. Heartbreak can come when they feel like they can't be with the person they care about. There might be times when they have unrealistic views on love. It's because they are seeking a higher level of love that is hard to find in the material world. Most people are not able to love unconditionally like them.

The positive energy of this placement enhances artistic and creative talents. They can feel protected by what seems like a guardian angel who watches over them. When they are at their lowest point and are ready to give up hope, the universe seems to answer their prayers. They can have a deep love of spiritual topics and a desire to bond with a higher power.

This placement creates a compassionate and caring love nature and a desire to help those who are struggling. They can fall prey to codependent relationships. Feeling taken advantage of can happen when they fall in love with someone who needs rescuing. They are spiritual seekers and have a giving heart. They often serve as mirrors for others and people project their problems onto them. They can sometimes feel like they have secret enemies and people who want to hurt them. The truth is that they are just getting projected upon because of their empathic and compassionate personality. Developing boundaries and protecting themselves will alleviate these experiences.

Their extreme idealism can shift, and they can become more cautious and practical through direct experience. They are often selfless in relationships and need to be careful not to neglect their own needs. Loving themselves and becoming their own soul mate can help them find balance in relationships. If they can learn to utilize this energy in healthy ways, they can prevent certain situations from happening in the first place. Developing greater self-awareness and boundaries will help them thrive in relationships.

Mars in the Twelfth

These individuals have a passionate desire to escape from the harshness of the world. Their passionate side is often kept secret or hidden. They can be dedicated to finding a spiritual connection and have a strong desire for solitude. Spending time alone is good for them. Withdrawing from the world can be a way they survive and recuperate their energy. Sometimes their energy gets depleted quickly, especially depending on who they are spending time with. Other people's thoughts and emotions impact them greatly. Due to their heightened compassion and empathic abilities, they tend to take on other people's problems without trying.

They often feel an overwhelming sense of purpose and drive to find inner peace. Because they are goal oriented, they can focus all their energy on finding the meaning of life. Reading and researching spiritual and paranormal topics can become an obsession. They can become obsessed with finding answers to the mysteries of life.

Their passion is often hidden, repressed, or restricted in some way. They can repress their emotions and have trouble expressing their feelings. Sometimes they might pursue their passions in secret and live a very private life. Internalizing their intense feelings helps them feel in control. In fact, it's challenging for them to share anything personal until they trust someone completely. There are times they can feel like their own actions are influenced by a force outside themselves.

Anger is a powerful emotion and they might not feel they should express it. They can serve as a mirror for others and angry people can project their feelings onto them. It's important to recognize that what they hide often gets exposed through other people. They should try to meditate every day to relieve their pent-up energy.

These individuals have a strong desire to serve others and help those who are struggling. They can be found fighting for the underdog, especially those who have been abused, abandoned, and neglected. Rescuing people and being a martyr can get them entangled in unhealthy relationships. Having strong boundaries can be useful so they don't start taking on other people's problems. Crisis intervention is their forte and they have an innate ability of knowing what to do in the moment.

Behind the scenes is often where they do their best work. Their emotions are powerful and they can have a complex emotional nature. They might find it easier to communicate their feelings through writing or being creative.

They can get involved with alcohol or other self-destructive behaviors. Avoiding conflict and ignoring their problems will only make things worse. They need to face their problems head-on and not blame others for everything that happens to them. They like to escape from their pain and can find it hard to face the realities of daily life. Prone to depression, it's often caused by finding it difficult to stand up for themselves or express unpleasant feelings. They can overcome their loneliness by spending time with people they trust. It's good if they can make time to pursue hobbies that bring a sense of fulfillment. Doing something they love can help them get their energy flowing. It might benefit them to talk to a counselor about their problems because this creates a healthy outlet for their intense feelings.

Impulsivity can lead to risky behavior and accidents. They need to be careful and pay special attention when driving, using knives, or operating machinery. They can be more vulnerable to cuts, burns, and might have to have surgery at some time in their lives.

They might have had a challenging relationship with their father. When they were younger, their father might have suffered from some type of addiction such as alcoholism. It's also common that they might have felt their father was not there for them emotionally or physically. They may experience an absent or missing father through death, divorce, or abandonment.

The experiences they have can make them seek love and acceptance from others. Turning that energy toward finding a spiritual connection to a higher power can help them learn to love and support themselves. It's important that they don't allow their father's problems to become their own.

The blessing of this placement is the gift of an intense passion to study spirituality and search for the meaning of life. They will benefit by learning to express themselves freely and to trust that others will appreciate their honesty. They can use their voice and words to express what they really think and feel. Embracing challenges will help them grow stronger and more resilient. They can feel happier when they take back their own power and stand up for themselves. If they can harness being firm and more assertive, it will help them communicate openly with others.

Mercury in the Twelfth

These individuals are deep thinkers who often enjoy solitude. It might seem like they hide their thoughts from others. Their thoughts seem to be affected by some outer force that makes them seem out of reach. They may not always express themselves because of shyness and find it difficult to put words to their emotions. There are times when they appear detached and zoned out. Highly imaginative, they like to escape into their mind and fantasize about a perfect world.

Sometimes shy, they might find it difficult to let others into their inner world. They have a private and secretive nature after all and don't like to talk about superficial things. Highly creative, they can have a very perceptive mind. Their first impressions are often accurate because they are highly intuitive. Because of their reflective mind, they are someone who can be highly suggestible and be hypnotized easily.

Practical learning can be challenging for them because they get bored easily. They enjoy learning more about topics that are interesting, creative, imaginative, and spiritual. Reading science fiction, romance, and alien abduction stories suits them best. They might also daydream and want to escape into their mind when they are feeling overwhelmed. Practical responsibilities don't interest them at all because they are on a search for exploring the meaning of life.

They need time alone to recover from their daily life. If they work, they can feel exhausted after being around people all day. A peaceful, quiet environment where they can find solitude helps them process their thoughts and emotions. It is important that they have enough time to be alone to pursue their hobbies. Mental stimulation can come through reading, writing, and journaling. Meditation, contemplation, and listening to music can also bring great comfort and help them still their active mind.

These individuals may be able to read other people's minds and experience psychic communication such as telepathy. Sometimes they might remember their past lives and access information when they sleep and dream. They may have flashes of intuition and they would benefit from writing down their insights. Writing can be a great healing tool that helps them process their thoughts and emotions. They should keep a journal and a pen with them at all times. It's often easier for them to write down their thoughts versus communicating them verbally. They might be born with a spiritual gift such as automatic writing. If they can harness solitude, they can quiet and still their mind, which in turn can reduce worrisome thoughts.

Jupiter in the Twelfth

These individuals are generous and have a great desire to serve others. They exude kindness and compassion, which attracts people to them.

They can be born with intuitive gifts that can be used to help others. Jupiter placed here can act like a guardian angel, often shielding them from the more difficult energies of the twelfth house.

Sometimes it might feel like they are protected from deception, betrayal, and heartbreak. If they do experience it, they may heal and overcome these experiences quickly. One reason for this is that they have an optimistic and positive outlook on life. They tend to look for the good in people and in the world. Benefits can come by doing anything spiritual such as meditation, yoga, traveling to ancient civilizations, and learning more about the religions of the world.

They are often blessed with psychic gifts and they can have visions, memories, and dreams that predict the future. They should keep a journal next to their bed at night while they sleep. It can be beneficial for them to write their dreams down every night when they remember them. They may be interested in purchasing a dream book so they can analyze the meaning of their dream symbols.

They seem to be luckier than most people who have twelfth house planets. Sometimes planets in the twelfth can make individuals feel lonely, isolated, and sad, but those feelings are often lessened by this placement. Jupiter placed here increases optimism, hope, and faith in a higher power. They might seek solitude through escaping the practical world. Ancient knowledge intrigues them and they can dedicate their life to metaphysical studies.

Even if they weren't raised in a religious family, they often have an insatiable interest in learning about different beliefs. Their adventurous spirit gives them a sense of purpose that inspires them to serve others in a deeper way. At times they might feel pulled to travel to a faraway land and might even end up living in a foreign country.

Abundance and good luck come through being of service to others. The more they help others in some way, the more blessings they receive. They can have a positive outlook on life and are inspiring to others. Natural teachers, they have an ability to explain things to others in a simple way. Accumulating spiritual knowledge and studying a variety of topics, such as astrology, crystals, tarot, and world religions, can be fulfilling.

They may grow up in a family that is very different from them, or they don't understand their spiritual interests. Even if they don't share similar beliefs with their family, they can often find that support in other ways. In the end, joining a group or organization where everyone shares the same beliefs can bring comfort. They can benefit by making friends with people who have similar interests and philosophies about life.

Balancing a desire to be social with their need for alone time can be a lifelong lesson. They can feel more sensitive in large groups and feel more comfortable in smaller groups. Because of their empathic nature, they often take on the energy of those around them. Other people are drawn to their contagious positivity and enjoy sharing their problems with them. If they can develop stronger boundaries, it can help them protect their energy.

Material and financial blessings often come through spiritual pursuits. They can realize that true happiness does not come from the outer world or through owning material possessions. If they can harness a connection to a spiritual discipline or practice, they can find inner happiness.

Saturn in the Twelfth

These individuals can be skeptical and cautious about spirituality. Fearful about losing control, they might repress their natural psychic abilities or doubt themselves. Because they are more practical and realistic about life, they can be afraid to trust their intuition. Feeling overwhelmed about things they can't see prevents them from opening fully to the mystical side of the twelfth house.

Struggling with feelings of depression, sadness, and anxiety is common with this placement. Life seems hard at times and the weight of daily responsibilities keeps them moving forward. They have a strong sense of duty that can help them be disciplined to work and serve others in practical ways.

Being vulnerable and expressing their emotions can be challenging for them. They can work hard to cover up their feelings and try to overcome them. Because they are serious and responsible, they can often be hard on themselves. It's normal to feel sad and lonely sometimes; after all, they need to remember that they are human. Feelings of guilt can plague them at times and they struggle to figure out where their guilt comes from.

Karma from the past can be influencing their present life. Saturn creates a need to balance debts from previous actions. There can be relationship karma and could be a past lifetime where they were persecuted for their spiritual belief system. These past-life patterns and fears create a block and make them resist searching for a connection to a higher power. Even if they have an interest in New Age topics such as astrology, they might be too afraid to study them.

Secretive at times, they often keep their goals and success hidden from others. Even though they have compassionate feelings, they might work hard to keep them under control. Repressing their feelings can lead to escapist behaviors and some might struggle with addiction. If they do start drinking, smoking, or doing other drugs, they have a strong willpower to overcome addiction.

Self-reliant, they avoid being dependent on others. Being respected is important to them and helps their self-esteem. Social situations can be difficult because they are shy and private. Even though they do not like relying on others for support, they don't mind helping others with their problems. Because of their reliable personality, many people depend on them for advice and support. They can benefit by embracing the spiritual side of life more and acknowledging their intuitive abilities. If they can harness a more positive outlook, it can help them achieve their goals faster.

Uranus in the Twelfth

These individuals want to break free from restrictive beliefs. Unconventional souls, they are drawn to mysterious and controversial ideas. They have an eccentric and unique personality that can often shock others. Because they like to help people be more open-minded, it's easy for them to discuss uncomfortable topics. They don't mind pushing people's buttons and shocking others with their interesting beliefs. They enjoy inspiring people to expand their traditional belief systems and to become more accepting of diverse opinions. New Age topics fascinate them and nontraditional beliefs inspire them to push others out of their comfort zone. Seeking new experiences and maintaining a sense of freedom helps them tame their restless nature.

These individuals enjoy being alone because they need freedom. Reclusive at times, they enjoy being social but also enjoy their own company. They are adventurous spirits who enjoy pursuing activities that help expand their mind. Unexpected psychic flashes and visions can hit them quickly. Often out of the blue, they can have a strong sense of knowing and seeing into the future. Highly intelligent and innovative, they can have both a rational and emotional approach to life.

Spirituality is important to them and they can enjoy studying astrology and tarot. They are creative and gain insight through visions, dreams, and listening to their strong gut instinct. Seeking a connection with a higher power can help give them a sense of purpose.

Sometimes they might live an entirely different lifestyle no one knows about. They have a unique view of relationships and can find it difficult to commit to just one person. They might prefer to be single. Secretive and private, they tend to hide their true feelings from those they care about. A bit rebellious at times, they need to be careful about trying to escape from responsibilities.

Passionate and loyal, they enjoy making friends with people who share similar interests. Because of their rebellious nature, they can ignite changes around them and shake things up when they feel bored. Deep down there is a fire inside them that inspires them to grow. Their beliefs about spirituality and the meaning of life might go through constant change.

They can have intuitive and psychic abilities that may be used to serve others or open people's minds in some way. They can sometimes see things before they happen and might have the gift of clairvoyance because they are highly imaginative and visual. It's important for them to trust their feelings and perceptions about the future.

Writing is a way they can express their creative and imaginative ideas. Being of service in some way and helping large groups of people can be an important part of their soul mission. The more they help others who are suffering, the more spiritual they become. If they can harness change, they can transform and expand their awareness of the spiritual world.

Neptune in the Twelfth

These individuals are spiritual, highly intuitive, and creative. They are naturally compassionate and empathic, which makes it easy for them to pick up on what others are thinking and feeling. The environment they are in can impact their emotions greatly, so it's important that they have a calm and harmonious homelife. They feel better when they have a structured and organized daily routine.

They can live in a fantasy world and illusion can cloud their judgment. Developing boundaries can help them learn self-protection and keep their emotions balanced. Escaping from stress and practical responsibilities helps them recharge. But they need to get motivated to complete tasks and overcome procrastination. They need solitude more than other people and want to find inner tranquility. Experiencing peace and harmony in the world is important to them.

Because they are sensitive, compassionate, and open-minded souls, they can be natural psychologists. They have a healing presence that attracts others and makes them feel safe. People can also perceive them as illusive, mysterious, mystical, and dreamy. It's like their energy is from another world. They can be private and there is a secretiveness about them that can be alluring.

They are born with psychic abilities but might feel confused about how to use them. Naïve, innocent, and idealistic, they often believe that everyone is caring and trustworthy. Sometimes their trusting nature can cause them to be hurt. They prefer to see other people as loving, kind, and compassionate. When they realize that there are negative things in this world, they can feel overwhelmed and disheartened. Negative things impact them greatly so it's important that they surround themselves with positive things.

Artistic and creative, they can be avid readers who enjoy writing. Expressing their creative ideas on paper helps them feel better emotionally. Spirituality can be a big part of their lives and they can experience vivid dreams, hallucinations, and unexplained psychic experiences. They have an interest in learning New Age topics like astrology, tarot, and crystals.

Listening to their inner voice can help protect them from danger. Sometimes they isolate themselves and withdraw from responsibilities.

When they get stressed, being alone helps them find peace and serenity. Spending time relaxing, listening to music, meditating, or being near water can be healing. It's good for them to have a break from work and find time to relax.

Developing a deeper bond with a higher power helps them transform their pain. They have an enhanced ability to feel connected to angels, spirit guides, and even deceased loved ones. They are interested in exploring hidden realms such as life after death and spirit visitation. They can have many mystical experiences but often keep them secret or hidden in some way. They can enhance their psychic abilities through meditation, prayer, journaling, and grounding exercises. Their lives are happiest when they feel a sense of mission and purpose in this world.

Pluto in the Twelfth

These individuals are secretive and hide their intense emotions from others. They can have a very secretive personality and like working behind the scenes. Their privacy is extremely important to them. Often seen as loners, they prefer doing things by themselves and don't always like asking for help.

Magnetic personalities, their intense energy often attracts certain people who need healing. They can radiate power and have a strong presence when they walk into the room. When they look at people in the eyes, it's like they are looking right through them. People often want to share their problems with them. Their energy attracts or repels others; it feels like people either really like them or don't like them at all. Some people might even feel uncomfortable around them and project their negative emotions onto them. They can sometimes feel blamed for things they didn't do; they don't understand why some people seem to avoid them.

Due to trust issues, they often keep a protective shell around themselves and refuse to allow people into their inner circle. Being vulnerable and opening up to others can be a big challenge in their relationships. Once they commit to someone, they are dedicated and loyal partners. They can develop deeper intimacy with people who share a similar interest in spirituality. Diving deep, seeking answers to life's mysteries, and talking about taboo topics help them feel connected. Transformation and rebirth experiences impact them throughout their lives. They can feel like they are constantly undergoing a metamorphosis and shedding their old personality.

Sometimes they are attracted to positions of power where they can give orders but don't have to be in the limelight. They prefer working behind the scenes and influencing the outcome of situations in private. Highly perceptive, they can read people well. This ability helps them in business dealings and relationships because they seem to know what people's true motives are. Some people might underestimate them and take their kindness as weakness. Because their intentions are often hidden, people can have a difficult time figuring them out. Very few people get close enough to them to know the deeper side of their personality.

In love, they can get involved in secret relationships or with people who need healing. They can have an intense and passionate emotional nature. When they feel a strong attraction to someone, they can experience obsession, jealousy, and possessiveness, which can cause chaos. Their deep feelings, connection, and commitment to someone can make it hard for them to let go of someone they care about. They can become attached to others and often develop unhealthy relationships.

Sexuality and intimacy can be ways they transform emotions and connect to a higher power. Denying and giving up pleasure can be a way they test their willpower. For instance, they might become celibate and deny their intense sexual desires. Endings in relationships can be a major lesson in learning to let go. There can be some type of loss in their lives that changes their philosophy and inspires them to seek the meaning of life. Losing something or someone they care about can be challenging, but it can also awaken and transform their lives.

These individuals are born with psychic abilities and a deeper understanding about issues like death, grief, trauma, and healing. They are interested in spending time alone in solitude and many can benefit through meditation, yoga, and breathing exercises. They like to push the limits and enjoy feeling the adrenaline rush of intense emotional experiences. But they can also get involved with risk-taking behaviors to feel alive.

Addiction can impact their life or the lives of those they care about. They tend to bottle things up and repress uncomfortable feelings. They can have a powerful desire to escape from the world to find solitude. Escapism helps them recover and regenerate their energy.

It's important to make sure they learn how to express their anger in healthy ways, because if not, they could become physically sick. Sometimes they can suffer from strange symptoms that can be hard to diagnose or the symptoms can be difficult for doctors to figure out. When they do get sick or struggle with health problems, it is usually a big wakeup call and spurs them back on the right path.

Connecting within and healing their childhood wounds can help them become more resilient. They are powerful healers who can transform the lives of others because of their own experience in overcoming hardship. Sometimes they had to become their own parent and might have grown up too fast. Losing a loved one at a young age can be something that changes their outlook on life. They might have to learn how to parent and depend on themselves for survival. Seeking a spiritual connection can help them connect to the universe and explore deeper truths.

Planetary Transits through the Twelfth House

When planets transit the twelfth house, you can become interested in spirituality, connecting to a higher power, spending time alone, helping others, and being creative.

Transit Sun

This transit will impact your energy levels. You might feel like hiding behind the scenes and want to avoid social activities. Escaping from the world can help you focus on yourself and your own needs. This is a good time to pursue hobbies and things that bring you pleasure. It can be beneficial to spend time alone and enjoy solitude to get in touch with your deeper feelings. You might feel a strong need for peace, harmony, and escape from the world.

Do something kind for someone else and help someone in need. Being of service and attracting people with problems can happen more frequently right now. You may feel increasingly sensitive to people's energy and more emotional than usual. Issues hidden in your subconscious mind can bubble up and need to be released. This is a good time to let go of old baggage and release the things you need to get rid of. It's a good time to turn within and meditate.

You can benefit by spending time journaling, reading, and being near water. You might feel inspired to express your artistic and creative talents. You can feel more creative right now and tap into this imaginative energy to explore new spiritual truths.

During this time, you might feel drained energetically. You may feel more tired than usual, not sleeping well. If you are typically social, you might want to withdraw and be by yourself. You can feel more introspective and want more time to reflect on what is important. Spending time alone can help you recharge so you can go back out into the world and pursue your goals. You can feel more compassionate during this cycle and should listen to your intuition. That gut instinct can give you the answers you have been seeking. Harness your intuition right now and allow yourself to connect with others in meaningful ways.

Transit Moon

During this fast transit, your compassion and sensitive side can intensify. Emotions are felt in deeper ways right now. When the Moon is transiting the twelfth house, everything feels intensified. If you normally enjoy telling people how you feel, it can feel strange because you might feel more secretive than usual. You have a greater need for privacy and a stronger urge to withdraw from the practical world.

You may feel a low energy level and experience feelings of depression, guilt, loneliness, and discontent. These feelings will pass, but remember to focus on the positive things in your life during this time. Make time for self-care activities because learning more about boundaries can be a major lesson right now. This is a good time to relax, spend time by yourself, and take a break from the world. If you have been burdened by day-to-day responsibilities, you might need a break to focus on what makes you happy. Staying home, cuddling with your favorite pet, watching old movies, and cooking your favorite food can rejuvenate your energy.

Spiritual desires are intense right now and you might feel a strong urge to connect to a higher power. Dreams can be more vivid during this time, so it's important to write them down so you can analyze their messages. Listen to your intuition and gut instinct about things. You can receive answers to problems you have been battling with. Do something artistic or creative during this time like singing, writing, drawing, and painting.

Transit Mercury

This transit can bring issues with communicating clearly. You might want to keep information secret and not readily share things with others. Communication can feel confusing right now. You might have difficulties grasping your thoughts because your mind can feel cloudy and disorganized. If you are normally very talkative, this transit can feel uncomfortable. Your words can seem blocked, and you might just not feel like talking at all. You won't want to chat about superficial things and might want to spend time alone.

You will be thinking more about what is important in your life. Your mind is focused on deeper spiritual truths. You might start a new hobby and want to learn new things like astrology. It's not uncommon to feel more cautious about who and what you want to share. There could be deception, rumors, lies, or feelings of betrayal based on information you share. There can be greater miscommunication and people might perceive things differently than you intended.

Make sure you can really trust someone with any private information before sharing it with others. During this time, you are seeking answers to past issues and problems. You can begin to reexamine the past and analyze things that happened. You need privacy right now and time to research things, meditate, and contemplate life. Uncomfortable feelings arise because of fears of being misunderstood. You are more inclined to listen and feel like you are in deep thought. You might find it hard to find the right words to justify your feelings. Spending time meditating can help you clear your mind and gain perspective.

Find new ways to release stress and alleviate worries about the future and try to live in the moment. Journaling and writing down your feelings can help you process your thoughts. Getting them down on paper might be helpful. Tap into the imaginative energy that is influencing your mind during this cycle.

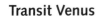

Transit Venus

This transit can awaken your hidden feelings and ignite romantic feelings. You might start thinking about an old flame and reminisce about the romantic adventures you used to have. There is a tendency to be more secretive about how you feel. You may be disillusioned about love and with your relationships. Past experiences might come up for you to learn more about what your needs are. This is a good time to figure out what you want in a relationship.

You might feel lonely, but at the same time you want to withdraw from others and be alone. Negative emotions can be intensified and you can experience frustration expressing your romantic feelings. If you meet anyone new during this cycle, you are more likely to feel shy and keep your feelings to yourself. You might be afraid of being hurt and things you thought were healed can bubble up to the surface to be processed.

This can also be a positive time in your life that brings happiness to many of your personal relationships. Current relationships might deepen or be impacted by your desire to be affectionate. You might prefer to spend time alone with your partner. If you are not in a relationship, you might start a secret relationship or feel a strong karmic attraction to someone who needs your help.

Secret love affairs and hidden relationships can test your ability to commit. Be careful about getting involved with unhealthy people who tend to take more than they give. You can feel more artistic and creative. You can create beautiful art and express yourself in imaginative ways. Listening to music and doing a creative hobby can get your mind off unpleasant feelings. Tap into what things bring you pleasure and joy. Do something new that brings you peace and happiness. This cycle can bring a focus to your spiritual path and deep connections. It's a good time to work on releasing relationships and emotions that are no longer helping you grow.

Transit Mars

This transit can awaken any hidden anger, resentment, or hurt you have been feeling. For the next eight weeks, you might feel like your passion, drive, and energy levels are dampened. You might feel more irritable and agitated, which can ignite your frustration. Anger can be kept secret, hidden, and you might find it difficult to express yourself right now. Even if you want to stand up for yourself, you might feel uneasy speaking up for your own needs. This cycle seems to turn the energy inward, and this makes you feel more passive.

You can feel more tired than usual and lack the energy to pursue your goals. Other people often drain your energy right now so you should try to spend time alone. Make time to journal and express these intense emotions in a healthy way. Exercise might be difficult right now, but it can be helpful to take walks, hikes, and even do yoga, which can help you feel better physically.

You might want to withdraw, retreat, and spend time alone reflecting on your goals. Aggressive people might push your buttons and you might not address things in the moment like you typically do. Avoid people who upset you and try to be more patient. You might feel blocked and not able to express yourself like usual, but this energy will pass. Your imagination is strong now with flashes of insight, inspiration, and even psychic dreams that are trying to give you messages.

This is a good time to conserve your energy and avoid overworking. Withdraw from stressful situations and recharge your energy. If you can take some leave from work and find time to relax, you will feel much better. Once this transit is over, you will be ready to conquer all your goals and obstacles.

Transit Jupiter

This year you could feel more generous and giving toward others. Optimistic energy surrounds you right now. Therefore, it's a good time to tap into the spiritual laws of the universe. Manifesting what you want can come easily now if you focus on positive thinking. There are ways to attract abundance, and tuning in to the New Moon cycles to manifest your intentions can be beneficial. You might start to study new spiritual topics during this cycle.

Eliminating negativity and anything that holds you back is important during this cycle. When Jupiter transits the twelfth house, this fun-loving energy can help you give up bad habits. You might finally be ready to let go of things you have struggled to forgive. This is a good time to heal yourself and forgive others once and for all. You are ready for a fresh start and feel excited for the future.

If you have wanted to travel and visit a faraway place, this might be the time to do it. You might want to be more adventurous and explore the world. Visiting places you have never been, such as churches, hiking trails, and even restaurants, can quench your restless search for newness. You can tap into this friendly energy and connect with people who believe in the same things you do. You may become more interested in spirituality and mystical subjects.

Jupiter enhances feelings of generosity and you might desire to help others more than usual. Serving others and helping alleviate people's suffering can be on the forefront of your mind. You might begin to feel grateful for the good things in your own life. You might want to give back to society in some way. You might like to volunteer and work with children and animals. There can be additional money that you might decide to donate to an important charity. The energy of giving and receiving brings forth many positive opportunities for your spiritual growth.

Help is given during this transit just when you seem to need it. It can feel like you are being protected from everything negative right now. There can feel like there is a guardian angel watching over you, ensuring your success. Tap into this energy of positivity and abundance, because it will help you connect to what brings greater meaning into your life.

Transit Saturn

This transit will last for about three years and can bring karmic lessons back into your life. Things from the past often come up for review for you to heal. Don't resist these uncomfortable situations as it can make them more painful. It seems like the past is coming back to haunt you, which can force you to feel unpleasant emotions. You can feel more restricted, blocked, and even trapped during this time. The energy is heavier than usual and you don't feel as lighthearted as you typically do. Don't resist these feelings but try to be patient with yourself.

Saturn can bring a sense of heavy burdens and a more serious outlook. You might feel more cautious and restricted from expressing yourself. If you are typically easygoing, confident, and friendly, you might notice that you feel more pessimistic, withdrawn, and guarded.

Allow yourself to face the darker parts of your personality. It's a good time to overcome your desire to control things that you don't understand. The biggest challenge right now can be the serious emotions that keep rising up within. If you typically trust your intuition and psychic abilities, this transit can make you doubt yourself. Your faith and spiritual path might be tested as you adapt to this new energy. You might also get disciplined, dedicated, and start putting a lot of work into your spiritual routine. You might try to meditate, do yoga, and exercise more often, which can help you release pent-up emotions.

You might be more focused on diet and exercise. Starting a new routine and planning your meals can help you lose weight. If you have a bad habit that you have wanted to break, now is a good time to do it. This is a time to change, which can help you get disciplined about overcoming negative habits. For example, if you have been drinking alcohol to cope with stress, it can start to become a way of escaping from feeling your emotions. Saturn's energy can help you snap out of this and start working hard to find a healthier coping mechanism. Because Saturn is a teacher, it makes us wiser through direct experience and hard work.

Secrets from the past may confuse you and make you doubt the future. It can be a good time to talk to someone about what you are going through. Saturn is here to teach you something deeper about yourself. Karmic lessons and debts might need to be paid back during this transit. The universe wants balance, and it can help you forgive and move forward once and for all. This is a good time for introspection, and if you have been wanting to go to counseling, this is an excellent time to schedule an appointment. Once this cycle is over, you will feel a weight lifted off your shoulders.

Transit Uranus

This transit can revolutionize and shake up your spiritual beliefs for the next seven years. You might start to question what you were taught to believe by your family and society. If you were raised in a strict religious household or with more conservative morals, you might start to question these things. You might rebel and seek a more nontraditional and unconventional approach to spirituality.

Anything that is traditional will be questioned and you can go through a major transformation of your identity. There can be inspirational flashes of insight and a heightened creativity. You might get more interested in New Age topics like astrology, tarot, alien abduction, and near-death experiences. These new interests can shock those who know you well. Trust yourself and don't be afraid to be different.

This cycle can often bring unexpected and shocking changes that are meant to help you grow as an individual. If you have felt stuck, stagnant, and unhappy, you can feel pushed to change and explore new unconventional ideas. The changes that happen to you during this cycle can completely turn your life upside down. These experiences ignite a new path for you and might lead you to seek answers to the meaning of life.

Psychic abilities can be awakened for the first time and you might learn that you have a spiritual gift to share with the world. Listen to your intuition, because those unexpected feelings can be great clues to help you on your journey.

Hidden things bubble to the surface during this cycle. Secrets could be revealed and parts of yourself that were kept hidden or unconscious will be brought to the light. You might admit something to yourself and others that you have repressed. It's like something deep inside is awakened and you are changed on a core level.

Emotional healing is possible after releasing and letting go of outdated beliefs that were causing your life to be stagnant. People can be surprised and shocked by how you act and the things you do. You might change your entire personality during this cycle. You can look back and realize all the outdated things you left behind. You might feel a little lighter than you did before.

Freedom is an important lesson of this transit and you will need time to pursue things that help you gain independence. Things are often stripped away during this time, leaving you feeling unsettled. Lift yourself up and shake it off. Remember that everything happens for a reason and for your continued growth. You can feel like a completely different person after this transit, which can be refreshing.

Transit Neptune

This is a deeply spiritual transit that lasts for up to fourteen years. You can feel very detached from the practical world and may find yourself zoning out more. Things seem hazy, disorganized, and unclear. You might doubt your soul purpose and feel more confused about the future. There is a lot of illusion and fog surrounding you and the environment. When Neptune transits the twelfth house, you might feel more emotional than usual. Tenderhearted, you might take things more personally. Because you feel more sensitive, you can be easily hurt by others. It's important to develop stronger boundaries because it can help you protect yourself during this cycle.

Empathic abilities can be awakened slowly, and you can start absorbing other people's pain. You can feel extremely emotional and sensitive to other people's energy, thoughts, and emotions during this transit. You might find yourself crying a lot more easily right now. For instance, a certain song, smell, or memory can stir up deep emotions. Your compassion is ignited and you have a desire to help those who are suffering.

Memories from the past can come back to haunt you, such as feelings of abandonment. Be kind to yourself and give yourself time to withdraw and process your feelings. If you are normally social, you might crave your alone time and want to explore solitary activities. Your intuition is running high, and all kinds of insights might happen to give you messages about your relationships and future. Write down your dreams when you wake up as they can be spiritual messages from your soul.

Spiritual awakenings and transformative experiences can occur during this cycle. You might start to search for God or connect to a higher power or devote yourself to a new spiritual discipline. Things like meditation can help you calm your mind and center your emotions. If you can spend time near water, it can also be soothing to your soul. Make time to relax and try to go with the flow. Try not to be so hard on yourself and just be in the present moment.

Trusting others too easily during this transit can cause disappointment. Idealism can be intensified, which might make you see things with rose-colored glasses during this time. If you are not seeing a situation or person clearly, eventually the hidden truth will be exposed. Try to be practical and realistic about what people are promising. In fact, it's good to try to be a bit more suspicious and discerning of others' motives. Pay attention to your gut instinct about people and situations because it is rarely wrong.

Tap into the artistic and creative energies in your environment. Spend some time near water, writing, journaling, and breathing in fresh air. You can feel tired and keep getting sick more often than usual due to being more vulnerable to stressful situations. Allow yourself to relax and withdraw from the hustle and bustle of practical life. Develop a self-care plan with supportive activities that can help you get in touch with your soul mission.

Transit Pluto

This transit can last for decades and can awaken deep emotions, fears, and hidden things in the unconscious mind. You might feel more angry, irritable, anxious, and unsettled during this cycle. It can be a good time to seek counseling and take care of your emotional needs. Seeing a therapist to process the intense emotions that are affecting you can be beneficial. Transformation of your entire personality, thoughts, and relationships can occur during this transit. When Pluto is transiting the twelfth house, things from the past come to conscious awareness and need healing. Any unhealed childhood trauma, wounds, relationships issues, and family problems will need to be worked through.

There are times you can feel like part of yourself is dying. It's like you are shedding new skin and the old parts of yourself are gone forever. It can be an uncomfortable emotional process of rebirth because you are experiencing deep changes. The person you were before this transit doesn't exist anymore.

The challenges you have experienced throughout these years have made you grow stronger and more resilient. There is nothing you can't overcome now as this was probably one of the most difficult times of your life so far. You might have experienced a dark knight of the soul and you had to face your own shadow. Embracing the new person you have become will help you move forward with a powerful confidence and ability to heal others on your new journey.

Ways to Harness Pisces Energy

- Help someone in need.
- Connect to a higher power.
- Be compassionate and kind.
- Develop a self-care plan.
- Make time for solitary activities.
- Utilize a dream journal.

CONCLUSION

Astrology is a map of the soul. It's a spiritual blueprint that can help you understand yourself and others on a deeper level. I truly believe that astrology can help you heal, transform, and become more resilient. When you harness the power of astrological energy, you can develop new tools to use in your everyday life.

All twelve zodiac signs have unique energies that can be tapped to help you grow. For example, if you lack a certain element in your birth chart, you can read about the astrological signs that are ruled by that specific element. If you lack the water element in your birth chart, you might struggle with expressing your feelings and showing affection. If you can read about the water signs Cancer, Scorpio, and Pisces, you can gain a greater understanding of this energy and begin to incorporate it into your life. This can help you create greater balance in your personality and in your relationships with others.

It's never too late to start learning astrology. With a little practice and time, you can learn how to feel astrological energies. I have been studying astrology since I was a teenager, and I am still constantly amazed by how accurate astrology is. Even now, I am still learning new things about astrology.

It's important to remember that you don't have to be an expert to use astrology as a tool for self-awareness. Knowing the basics is the most important thing you can do. If you are interested in making astrology a serious hobby, you can continue to deepen your learning.

I hope you can start to feel the energy and healing power that astrology can bring into your life. Don't be afraid to take a basic astrology class, schedule a psychological astrology consultation, or practice analyzing charts for fun with family and friends. The world needs more people who understand astrology and who can spread the truth of its accuracy. Astrology works and it's becoming more popular every day. My hope is that someday astrology is taught in schools and becomes a normal part of our everyday learning.

To Write to the Author

If you wish to contact the author or would like more information about this book, please write to the author in care of Llewellyn Worldwide Ltd. and we will forward your request. Both the author and the publisher appreciate hearing from you and learning of your enjoyment of this book and how it has helped you. Llewellyn Worldwide Ltd. cannot guarantee that every letter written to the author can be answered, but all will be forwarded. Please write to:

Carmen Turner-Schott
℅ Llewellyn Worldwide
2143 Wooddale Drive
Woodbury, MN 55125-2989

Please enclose a self-addressed stamped envelope for reply,
or $1.00 to cover costs. If outside the U.S.A., enclose
an international postal reply coupon.

Many of Llewellyn's authors have websites with additional
information and resources. For more information,
please visit our website at http://www.llewellyn.com.